19th July 2006

To Dad,

A very happy birthday! I do
hope this lovely book brings back
some memories of our wonderful
trips away together.
Feel like another tour??!

love from the Lown
Richard.

the
CENTURIONS
of golf

Mike Berners Price

This book is dedicated to the early English golfers who helped the Scots turn golf into a game enjoyed throughout the world.... and to Lindsay, Sarah and Michelle for their great support and enthusiasm

ISBN 0-9549172-2-7

First published in Great Britain in 2006 by Radial Sports Publishing Ltd
Kaim End, Hudnall Common, Little Gaddesden, Hertfordshire, HP4 1QJ
www.radialsportspublishing.com

Cover: *Overlooking the 17th green at Hunstanton with the clubhouse in the distance (Photograph by Bob Laughton)*

The Author

Mike Berners Price retired from the Partnership of a major firm of Chartered Accountants in 2003 and has spent the past three years combining his interests in golf, history, photography and wildlife to produce the Centurions of golf.

He is a member of Royal Ashdown Forest, which features in the Centurions, and also Tandridge Golf Club where he has been Chairman of the Golf Committee. Mike is an enthusiastic supporter of CAGS, the Chartered Accountants' Golfing Society which is itself over 100 years old, and he is also a member of the Old Whitgiftian Golfing Society which is well-known for its participation in the annual Halford Hewitt competition at Deal.

Mike has played golf on four continents, including Africa, where he enjoyed a number of the well-known Kenyan courses. His handicap hovers around 10.

CONTENTS

Above: *Panoramic view of the undulating links land at West Lancashire with the sea in the far background*

FOREWORD

SIR MICHAEL BONALLACK

Until 1983, when my wife and I moved to Scotland, practically all my golf had been played in England, apart from the occasions when competitive events took me out of the country. Since then, I seldom play many of the fine English courses which I so enjoyed in my younger days and many of which, I am sorry to say, I have almost forgotten.

It is therefore a pleasure for me to provide the Foreword for Mike Berners Price's very well researched book 'The Centurions of Golf', which brings back so many happy memories.

My early golfing days were spent on the courses of Essex, where I was born and where we lived in a house directly opposite that of the son of the great JH Taylor who not only won The Open Championship five times, but was also the founding father of the Professional Golfers' Association. In addition, he used his considerable golfing skill and experience in designing many golf courses, a number of which appear in this book.

One thing which most of these courses have in common is that they were designed by architects who made use of the natural features of the land, rather than having to move thousands of cubic metres of earth to conform to a pre-determined layout, which tends to be the modern way of thinking.

This may well be due to the fact that in the last few years, it has become increasingly difficult to obtain planning permission on land which is ideal for golf, such as links or heathland, and means that architects have to make the best possible use of what is available to them. Invariably this means creating the necessary features which make a course interesting to play. However, I would suggest that the older courses usually offer a much wider choice of shot selection, with the 'pitch and run' being used far more than is now the case.

It is for this reason that these historic courses will stand the test of time and continue to provide an enjoyable challenge for generations of golfers to come.

I hope that those who are familiar with these historic courses will, like me, enjoy reading about them and reminding themselves what fun they are to play. Equally, I hope that those who read about some of them for the first time will feel sufficiently inspired to find out what they have been missing.

April 2006

Left: Sir Michael F Bonallack OBE

Above: *View across the fifth green at West Lancashire with the well-bunkered par-3 sixth green in the background*

ACKNOWLEDGEMENTS

I have enjoyed great support from a wide variety of people during my two years of research. Fellow members of both Royal Ashdown Forest and Tandridge golf clubs have shown tremendous interest throughout the process. Ashdown is featured in the book but Harry Colt's gem at Tandridge was not built until 1924 and must wait for a later volume!

First and foremost I would like to thank every golf club Secretary from the courses featured in the book. Without exception they have been extremely friendly and helpful and all the clubs were kind enough to allow me to take photographs both in the clubhouse and out on the course. In particular, I welcome their generosity in allowing me to use the old black and white photographs of the early days which express better than words how conditions have changed in the last 100 years. For the more modern photographs and paintings I have acknowledged this kind co-operation in the text alongside each caption.

At many clubs I was also well received and entertained by club historians, archivists and current and former Captains. With this in mind, it is very difficult and almost invidious to highlight some people by name. Nevertheless, I should start by thanking Robert Smith. His golf knowledge, editorial skills and general enthusiasm for the project have been immense. I also owe a

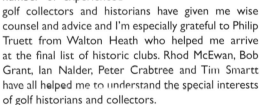

debt of gratitude to Dick Glynne-Jones, a former teacher at my old school, Whitgift, for his helpful guidance.

I am grateful to Donald Steel for suggesting that I should include stories of the Old Manchester Golf Club and of the early days at Crookham. A number of experienced golf collectors and historians have given me wise counsel and advice and I'm especially grateful to Philip Truett from Walton Heath who helped me arrive at the final list of historic clubs. Rhod McEwan, Bob Grant, Ian Nalder, Peter Crabtree and Tim Smartt have all helped me to understand the special interests of golf historians and collectors.

I have been very fortunate to play the vast majority of the courses featured in the book and I've enjoyed marvellous company. At Ganton and Alwoodley I was a guest in the members' midweek competitions and I would especially like to thank Richard Mossman, Murray Todd, Nick Leefe and Michael Carr from those two great Yorkshire clubs. Keith Jacobs and Doug Hayworth enabled me to enter the midweek 'greedy' at Goring & Streetly. Fellow Whitgiftian and Halford Hewitt stalwart, Gordon Garment, showed me the delights of Royal Lytham both on and off the course and I was lucky enough to be entertained by Tony Mason, another Whitgiftian 'Hewitt' man, in a gale at Burnham & Berrow. I owe special thanks to Tony for

Left: *As well as winning two Open Championships, Harold Hilton was the first player to win the British and American amateur titles in the same year*

Below: *Aside from Bobby Jones, John Ball, Junior is believed by many to have been the greatest ever amateur golfer*

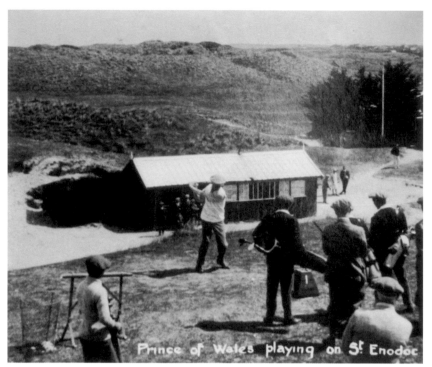

And the marvellous list continues. Sands Johnson and Janet Towse took turns to show me the delights of Formby, Brian Evens and Alan Jackson were my kind hosts at Royal St George's, John Coleman guided me through the archives and around the course at Rye and Bob Fletcher juggled his busy diary to play some holes with me at Sutton Coldfield. I'm indebted to Malcolm Dennes for entertaining me at Porters Park and to Jimmy Scade for the game and lovely lunch at Wildernesse. Vernon Cubbon and Tony Crane helped me to enjoy the old Ryder Cup links at Southport & Ainsdale.

As mentioned earlier, every Secretary was extremely helpful, but it would be remiss of me not to pass especial thanks to Roger Marrett at New Zealand, John Hall at Moortown and Richard Latham at Woodhall Spa. Richard introduced me to my good friends at Radial Sports Publishing, Doug Adams, Stuart Whaley and John Skeet.

I'd like to give a warm 'thank you' to Sir Michael Bonallack for agreeing to write the foreword. Sir Michael was recently identified as one of the greatest players in the history of the amateur game and it was noticeable how strongly his name featured amongst the winners of open competitions run by many of the courses included amongst the Centurions.

Finally, I'd like to thank my parents, John and Wendy for reading the draft and giving me valuable suggestions and to my wife, Lindsay for her support and for accompanying me to the two extremes of England, Mullion in Cornwall and Bamburgh Castle in Northumberland.

helping to find my glasses which had blown at least 20 yards into thick rough!

My welcome was warm in all parts of the country and at clubs great and small. Joe Pinnington and Peter Fraser from Royal Liverpool at Hoylake could not have been more helpful. Barry Coyne across the Mersey at West Lancashire gave me advanced access to the club's new history display and Brian Bowness at Newbury & Crookham helped me to locate some of the old course at Crookham, which is now buried deep in woodland, and then entertained me on the successor course at Newbury. My old work colleague and Oxford Blue, John Clennett, entertained me at Worplesdon, fellow CAGS member, Peter Sachiari, was my excellent host at Woking and my friend from Tandridge, Duncan Ferguson, gave me a day to remember at Brancaster. Former Club Secretary, Malcolm Whybrow, was my kind host along the coast at Hunstanton.

INTRODUCTION

The great golf writer Bernard Darwin recently received a posthumous induction into the World Golf Hall of Fame. His works, including 'The Golf Courses of the British Isles', published in 1910, described in fascinating detail the events and features of a century ago. Since then, many writers have updated the stories in periodicals and golf magazines, and the oldest courses north of the Border were featured in 'The Scottish Golf Book' written by Malcolm Campbell. Less attention has been paid to the oldest English courses and the return of The Open Championship to Royal Liverpool's historic links at Hoylake in 2006, after a gap of nearly 40 years, provided an excellent opportunity to update the English stories after a century of activity.

The first challenge was to decide which courses to include. For example, Walton Heath has a fascinating history but is only about the 450th oldest club in England! Other long-established clubs have relocated in modern times and lost the traditions which went with their original grounds. Others still have survived but been unable to lengthen their layouts to keep pace with modern technology and are now not such a challenge. Many prestigious clubs have disappeared including the Royal Isle of Wight at Bembridge and Royal Cornwall on Bodmin Moor, whilst 30 Mancunians still play for the Old Manchester cups although their club lost its last course to compulsory purchase by the local council in the 1960s. 'Centurions of Golf' addresses the conundrum by including the very oldest surviving courses and then concentrating on the clubs which have had the greatest influence over the spread of the game in England. Thus, Royal Blackheath has

Above: James Braid, JH Taylor, Ted Ray and Harry Vardon at Chorlton-Cum-Hardy in 1916 playing in aid of the Red Cross (Courtesy of Royal Jersey Golf Club)

been included although the club moved from its original 7-hole course on the heath to its present location in Eltham in 1923.

Another early decision was to concentrate on the people and events which helped the game to take root so successfully in England. Without this expansion south of the Border, it is possible that the game might have stayed as a minority interest, practised by experts in the Scottish homeland and in expatriate pockets overseas. Most of the earliest English clubs were founded by Scots, but it is intriguing to note the part played by the expansion of the railways and, perhaps less well-known, by the Church. In the late 19th Century, the Bishop of London was known to be a great advocate of this new and healthy outdoor

activity. Many clubs found that the involvement of the local clergyman encouraged the 'great and the good' to join as well. Stories of Sabbath-breaking abound although Tom Williamson, the long-serving Methodist Professional at Notts Golf Club, stuck to the promise given to his mother on her death bed never to play golf on a Sunday.

It is impossible to underestimate the boost given to the game by the involvement of Establishment, literary and sporting figures including Prime Ministers Balfour, Lloyd George and Churchill, the Aga Khan, Arthur Conan Doyle and WG Grace. However, whilst most early English clubs were quite exclusive, this was not the case everywhere. The treasurer of Furness relieved the ship-working members of one old penny (1d) every Saturday before they played on the links, whilst at Alnmouth, the earliest golfing photographs are dominated by working men from the town. Gog Magog was built as a retreat for the resident graduate dons at Cambridge University.

Before the invention of heavy machinery for felling trees and mowing fairways, many of the early courses were laid out over coastal dunes and inland heaths, as well as common land where the grass was mown by sheep, rabbits and cattle. Golfers suffered frequent conflicts with farmers and the general public and many clubs were forced to move onto private land. However, the beautiful course at Royal Ashdown Forest thrives with the support of the Forest Conservators, players from London Scottish on Wimbledon Common are still required to wear red clothing to warn nannies with prams of their approach, whilst Minchinhampton has built two new courses on farmland during the 1970s but had the foresight to retain the old course on the common where some golfers use orange balls which are more visible amongst the daisies and dandelions. Livestock still graze on Royal North Devon's links at Westward Ho! as well as at Sutton Coldfield and the New Forest courses at Bramshaw and Lyndhurst.

The Great Triumvirate of professional golfers, Harry Vardon, JH Taylor and James Braid, must have played exhibition matches over the majority of the early courses. Braid was the Professional at Walton Heath for more than 40 years, Vardon moved from Jersey to leave his mark at both Ganton and South Herts, whilst JH Taylor moved from Westward Ho! via Royal Winchester and Royal Wimbledon to Royal Mid-Surrey. Many argue that there was really a Great Quadrivium including Alex Herd who started out with the Huddersfield Golf Club at Fixby Hall. A multitude of top Professionals has graced the six English hosts of The Open at St George's, Lytham, Birkdale, Hoylake, Prince's and Deal, whilst Ryder Cup history was also written at Moortown, Southport & Ainsdale, Ganton and Lindrick. West Cornwall produced one of the game's greatest players, Jim Barnes, but he appears in most golf records as an American.

Lady golfers have played a major role in English golfing history. Cecil Leitch reigned supreme at Silloth, Joyce Wethered was a legend at Worplesdon, and Pam Barton from Royal Mid-Surrey might have eclipsed them all but died tragically during the Second World War. The amateurs have also left their mark. Hoylake nurtured two of the best, Harold Hilton and John Ball, whilst Laddie Lucas travelled widely from his home club at Prince's and Horace Hutchinson appears in the early records at several clubs.

Many English clubs owe their survival and success to a small number of individuals, but none can match the story at Sheringham where Henry Craske served as the Club's Secretary for a period of 70 years. Littlehampton would have collapsed without the personal involvement of the Duke of Norfolk, whilst Harrogate acknowledges a Leeds Industrialist, Charles Crabtree, as 'Captain, President and Saviour'. Other clubs have retrenched to survive. Southwold abandoned nine holes following the Great Storm which struck the East Coast in 1953, whilst Brighton & Hove has survived with nine holes following a series of enforced land sales and with the support of the great commentator, Henry Longhurst. Royal Worlington's reputation as a top course with just nine holes owes much to its connection with the Oxford & Cambridge Golfing Society which was one of the strongest early influences in the English game. The Society held their annual matches at several of the top courses including Rye, Woking and Burnham & Berrow, whilst the Oxford University teams golfing at Southfield in the 1920s played an annual match against teams of Ryder Cup strength.

A number of the clubs still share their courses with thriving and independent artisan organisations whilst others have long-since amalgamated the two elements. The Village Play artisans section at Hoylake was founded in 1894 following a fishing disaster to provide onshore work for traumatised seamen, whilst the Cantalupe Club from Forest Row used to field up to 24 golfers playing off scratch in their annual match against Royal Ashdown including Abe Mitchell, Alf Padgham and the Seymour Brothers.

Sadly, clubhouse fires have destroyed a great deal of English golfing history. As well as the recent fire at Royal Mid-Surrey, disaster has also struck at Coventry, Formby, Littlehampton, Royal Winchester and Aldeburgh.

Most courses have had to change considerably since they were first laid out in order to cope with improvements to the ball and with club technology. Mullion abandoned its first hole within six months as golfers were unable to drive up to the plateau fairway from the valley below, whilst the two courses at Yarmouth and Caister kept expanding away from their burgeoning townships on the East Coast until their boundaries met and they decided to amalgamate into one club. Royal Ascot Golf Club has relocated 400 yards down the road to a new layout as the racecourse grandstand redevelopment has moved the finishing straight onto the old holes. The two World Wars had a huge effect on most of the coastal courses which suffered from a variety of defence barricades and military training exercises including tank manoeuvres and aerial bombing, but most clubs managed to keep a rudimentary game going during the worst of times. Saunton and Prince's were totally devastated but both recovered to become top tournament venues.

Amusing and strange stories abound including 'the Hippo that went to War' at Formby, the 'Hitler' tree at Hesketh, 'Supper for One' at the Old Manchester Club and Sir Arthur Conan Doyle's legacy at various clubs including Hankley Common, Hindhead, Crowborough Beacon and New Zealand. Golfing stories are legion, but it is difficult to forget RJ Taylor's three holes-in-one on consecutive days at the sixteenth during a competition at Hunstanton in 1974, or 76-year-old Mary Ann Seighart's two holes-in-one during the same Stableford round at Aldeburgh in 2003. Peter Richard Parkinson broke the British record for the longest hole-in-one when he aced the 378 yard par-4 seventh hole at West Lancashire in 1972.

Golf courses are a haven for wildlife and I will remember the little owl calling by the third tee at Coventry, the barn owl which ghosted across the fairway in broad daylight at Southwold, 20 red kites circling over the clubhouse at Huntercombe, and the flocks of geese flying noisily over the wild course at Goswick. It would be impossible and unfair to select a favourite historic English course, but some things will last a long time in the memory including the quality of the greens at Birkdale, the views of the two different castles from the fourteenth green at Bamburgh, the old church buried in the dunes next to Mullion and the par-4 'call down hole' on the same course, the church in the middle of the course at St Enodoc where Sir John Betjeman is buried, the freshwater spring beside the lake at Notts 'Hollinwell', and the River Wharfe at Ilkley which seems to have a magnetic effect on golf balls! Perhaps the most encouraging sight of all was the large number of juniors practising in the late dusk at Royal Jersey. Harry Vardon would have been a proud man. This history is the culmination of a two-year, 20,000-mile journey and I hope I have been able to convey some of the interest and enjoyment gained whilst visiting and playing England's golfing heritage.

Above: A bronze cast of Vardon's hands, featuring his famous overlapping grip, is on display in the South Herts clubhouse. The grip also features as the Club's emblem

Below: James Braid practising during one of his early visits to Southwold. The clubhouse is still recognisable today

FOUNDERS AND INFLUENCERS

For more than 200 years, Blackheath was the only venue for golf in England. Eventually, Scottish influence also helped the game to take root around Manchester and at Westward Ho! in North Devon (below) and on Wimbledon Common close to London. Harry Vardon's emergence from Royal Jersey also had a profound influence on the development of the game South of the Border.

Royal Blackheath 1608

Old Manchester 1818

Royal North Devon.......... 1864

London Scottish /
Royal Wimbledon 1864

Royal Jersey 1878

ROYAL BLACKHEATH

Royal Blackheath is the oldest English golf club and is situated a mere 20 minutes by train from Central London. The Club and its members have also played a key role in the successful development of several other historic clubs in England as detailed elsewhere in this book. The clubhouse contains a museum of golf memorabilia which provides details of both its own history and that of the game 'South of the Border'.

A round of the Club's original course consisted of three circuits of a 5-hole course on Blackheath Common and this was extended to seven holes, and hence a 21-hole round, in 1843. The main London Road threaded through the heart of the old course and by 1923 traffic had grown to such an extent that the course had become untenable. Royal Blackheath therefore effected an amalgamation with the neighbouring Eltham Golf Club and commenced play on the present course.

The Club claims to have been instituted in 1608 by Scottish golfers who came south following the accession of King James I. Unfortunately, all the records were destroyed by fire at the end of the 18th Century so this date is likely to remain a matter of some conjecture.

The clubhouse holds a famous mezzotint engraving of 'The Blackheath Golfer - William Innes, 1719-1796'. Innes was Captain of the Club in 1728 and he commissioned Lemeul Francis Abbott, RA to paint his portrait in oils, showing him wearing his full uniform, including red jacket and tails. His caddie, a seaman pensioner from the nearby Naval Hospital at Greenwich also features in the picture which

portrays the old course. The original oil painting was also destroyed by fire in unusual circumstances. It had become the possession of Innes' grandson, a general in the Indian Army, and was lost when his house was attacked by mutinous Bengali soldiers at Lucknow, in Uttar Pradesh, in May 1857. The oldest item in the museum is a silver club which was presented in 1766 to the Honourable Company of Golfers at Blackheath, and another early club on

Above: *The clubhouse was built on land leased from King Charles II to Sir John Shaw and was completed in 1664*

display is the putter belonging to Henry Callender and dated 1807.

The early years of the Club were involved with Freemasonry and the first non-mason was not admitted until 1789. From then, the masons-only society was continued by a group of diehard members as the Knuckle Club which set out to play and socialise during the Winter months. This group established the Knuckle Club Medal which was first competed for in 1792. It is now believed to be the oldest golfing medal in the world to have been played for continuously. The Knuckle Club changed its name to the Blackheath Winter Golf Club before this society-within-a-club was eventually dissolved with the medal itself being presented to the parent Club and renamed as the Spring Medal.

The Club also believes that it hosts the oldest open golf championship to have been run continuously. The Boys' Medal was first played for in 1847 and is still open to any boy under 17 years of age.

Early Blackheath members enjoyed boisterous entertainment. As a hint of the past, the museum contains a small ram's horn for snuff which was presented to the Club in 1831 by its chaplain, the Rev. Taylor. The description goes on to explain that the Reverend felt obliged to resign from the Club in 1833 due to offensive songs being sung!

The influence of the Scots continues to feature throughout the 19th Century. The museum contains references to the Blackheath Curling Club dated 1856, and the strength of the game of golf at Blackheath can be surmised from the Club's success in winning The Prize of the Great Golf Tournament which was played for at St Andrews in July 1857 and featured most of the great Scottish clubs. The prize, a claret jug, bears a striking resemblance to the jug now competed for annually at the Open Championship.

The clubhouse at Royal Blackheath is striking. The museum contains the original document from March 1662 which leased the land to Sir John Shaw from King Charles II, and the building was erected by Hugh May for Sir John and was completed in 1664. An unusual feature, noticeable on arrival, is the parking space allocated to the Field Marshal. This office is reserved for the oldest surviving former Captain of the Club, and the clubhouse displays a fine painting of Colonel Kennard who was Captain in 1875 and became Field Marshal in 1894.

The Club received permission to use its Royal prefix in 1901 and the royal connections have continued more recently. The Duke of York became a life member in 1992 and the Club's Patron in 1996.

Like many older clubs, Blackheath was fortunate to have a Professional who served the Club over an extended period. Wally Thomas was Professional between 1922 and 1966 and the clubhouse displays a card recording his gross 66 shot over the new course in September 1928.

The Ladies' Section of the Club celebrated its own centenary in 1990 and the Club also has a long established Artisans' Section, initially formed to enable local skilled craftsmen to play the course at certain times.

The course is mainly parkland but has several interesting features. The seventeenth is a difficult par-4 with the approach to the green over a wide cross-bunker, whilst the eighteenth, a short par-4, requires all but the longest hitters to lay-up and then hit a wedge over the hedge which protects the green positioned immediately to the rear of the clubhouse.

Above: *View from the rear of the clubhouse over the eighteenth green and showing the hedge which protects the green. The tee shot on the first hole must also be hit over the hedge*

OLD MANCHESTER GOLF CLUB

WITHOUT A COURSE SINCE 1960

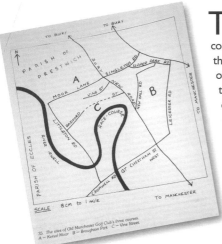

35. The sites of Old Manchester Golf Club's three courses.
A – Kersal Moor   B – Broughton Park   C – Vine Street.

Above: Map of Old Manchester's three different courses (Courtesy of Old Manchester Golf Club)

Inset: The Club's historic crest includes the red rose of Lancashire (Courtesy of Old Manchester Golf Club)

The Club's history is one of resilience tinged with sadness. Despite losing its third and last course in 1960, Old Manchester has limped into the 21st Century thanks to the determination of a small group of latter-day golfers who refuse to let the traditions die. The Club is the second oldest in England after Royal Blackheath and was established in 1818 as Manchester Golf Club by a Scot, William Mitchell, who owned a cotton-spinning mill, and eight of his colleagues including fellow Scot, George Fraser, a cotton merchant and Michael Harbottle, a silk merchant. Fraser became first President and Captain and Harbottle was the first Secretary.

The original course was situated at Kersal Moor in Salford to the west of Manchester on land then owned by the estate of the Clowes Family. The first rules of the Club were drafted in 1821 and were based on those of the Honourable Company of Edinburgh Golfers. In 1842, a significant further rule was introduced: "That in all time coming the medal presented by Mr. Bannerman be competed for by the whole Club in the first week of August each year." The early members established contact with several Scottish clubs. Fraser was a member of Montrose and became an Honorary Member of Bruntsfield Links, Edinburgh, in 1825. Old Manchester adopted the Scottish tradition of weekly play followed by group dining when members were expected to wear the Club uniform of scarlet coats with black collars, silver buttons and an oval badge on the breast pocket with two crossed golf clubs and three balls, the red rose of Lancashire and the Club's motto, 'Far and Sure'.

The first course had five holes and was situated inside the old Manchester racecourse. The ground was very rough and early scores were high. Golf also competed with other activities and it was reported that 100,000 people attended the Whitsuntide race meeting in 1818. 3,000 troops camped on the Moor in 1831 and several thousand people attended a Radical meeting in 1838 and a Chartist demonstration a year later. Cock-fighting, bare-fist boxing and duels were also quite common, and in June 1824, Hugh Pritchard publicly sold his 26-year-old wife for three shillings! In 1829, James Macnamara was hanged for stealing a bale of cloth.

As each putting green and the next tee were situated on the same piece of ground, the Club provided golfers with a wooden measure and an attached length of cord so that players could comply with the various rules including: "balls must be teed within four club lengths from the hole" and "the putting ground extends six lengths from the hole". The Club still possesses a number of these old measures. The Club's first problem with the course occurred in the late 1840s although one of the landowners, Miss Eleanora Atherton, commented that the players were: "very ornamental on the Moor." The minute book of 1850 describes how a competition held in that year was: "the first since the Club was deprived of the south side of the Moor." The position improved in 1869 when the Club acquired rights to play over an adjoining field, at which time the course was increased first to nine and then, soon after, to ten holes.

The Club still plays annually for three of the oldest golf medals in England. Alexander Bannerman first presented a silver medal to the Club in 1837 and it appears that the Bannerman Gold Medal, presented to the Club in 1843, was probably a replacement as it is inscribed: "Presented to Manchester Golf Club by Alexander Bannerman, Esq., 1837". The Atherton Silver Medal was presented to the Club in 1842 and the Shaw Medal was presented by Commissioner of Police, Sir Charles Shaw, in 1843. Sir Charles was a good golfer and won the Bannerman Gold Medal three years in succession from 1840. Malcolm Ross was one of the Club's best known characters. Another Scot, he was Secretary and Treasurer between 1842 and 1868 and again in 1875. In a famous episode in September 1858, Ross was surprised to be the only person to attend the members' regular dinner. Undaunted, he lit one candle to reflect that he was the only member present and then carried on proceedings in the normal way. He wrote up the event in the minute book: "Present: Mr. Ross. In the Chair: Mr. Ross. There was no lack of substantials if a large cod, a saddle of mutton, a goose, two brace of partridge and puddings etc. can be considered enough for one little man...The little man...was alone in his glory and after the third bottle wrote this report...Don't smile at it, gentle stranger, such discrepancies don't occur every day."

It seems that the Club had kept its golfing activities quite small, exclusive and private because Ross was upset to find that golfers from the Club had not been invited to participate in 'The Golf Tournament' organised by The R&A in 1857 and again in 1858. However, by 1869 the Club was on the national golfing map and had held home matches against golfers from the younger clubs at Hoylake and Royal North Devon. Malcolm Ross died in 1880 by which time the Club seemed to be struggling with morale.

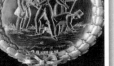

The area around Kersal was becoming more developed, and in October 1882 seven members played in the last medal competition on the Moor. Many of the Club's belongings were sold at auction and nothing was then minuted for a decade until 1891 when a new course of twelve holes was laid out on land leased from Col. SW Clowes at Broughton Park. The opening ceremony was performed by the Rt. Hon. Arthur Balfour who was the MP for Manchester East and Sir William Houldsworth MP, who struck the first ball and was elected as Club Captain for the fourth time. 21 new members were elected to join the seven survivors from the days at Kersal Moor. Sir William played an important role in helping to settle a problem with the new Manchester St Andrews Golf Club which had opened in 1882 and had dropped 'St Andrews' from its name once it appeared that there was no longer a club playing on the Moor. The older Club had decided to print literature headed 'Manchester Golf Club, Established 1818'. A compromise was reached whereby the younger club kept the name Manchester Golf Club and the older one was renamed Old Manchester Golf Club and was allowed to retain all its old medals and records. The Club rejected a merger proposal from North Manchester Golf Club in 1898, and by 1904, the rapid building development at Broughton Park triggered another move, this time to a new 9-hole course situated between Bury New Road and Vine Street.

The Club survived two world wars and although finances were often stretched it was able to celebrate the centenary of Ross's dinner-for-one in 1958 although the helpings were more frugal!

Old Manchester was offered the freehold of the Vine Street course by the Clowes Estate in 1952, but this was not pursued due to the heavy expenditure which would have been required to maintain the river bank and protect the course from damage caused by unruly locals. Instead, in 1958, the land was unexpectedly purchased by Salford Corporation. Local government politics at the time meant that there was no appetite to let the private members' Club continue to use the course after the lease expired in 1960. Old Manchester is indebted to James Johnston and Stanley Carrington for helping it to survive into the 21st Century and for enabling the 30-or-so members of today's Club to continue to play three times a year for the historic medals using the courses at Hazel Grove, Davyhulme Park and a club of the Captain's choice.

Above: James A Johnston 1911-1983 (Courtesy of Old Manchester Golf Club)

Inset: The Bannerman Gold Medal is still played for annually (Courtesy of Old Manchester Golf Club)

ROYAL NORTH DEVON

WESTWARD HO!

Royal North Devon, or RND as it is widely known, is the oldest club in England still playing on its original grounds. The course is situated at Northam Burrows next to Westward Ho! in North Devon and access has been much improved by the updated A361.

Scottish influence was significant in the early days. During the 1850s, General Moncrieff of St Andrews visited his brother-in-law, the Rev. IH Gosset, who lived in Northam. On seeing the Burrows, the General reportedly commented that: "Providence obviously designed this for a golf links." The Burrows had fine natural turf, the sand hills and rushes formed excellent natural hazards, and the sheep, cattle and horses grazing on the common land meant that no machinery was required to cut the grass. The sandy subsoil enabled play in both Winter and Summer and the arrival of the railway to Barnstaple in 1844, and then to Bideford in 1855, was also an important influence in the development of the Club and of the settlement at Westward Ho!

The author, Charles Kingsley, was commissioned by MacMillans to write a romantic novel based on Elizabethan attempts to settle Virginia in 1585-9. Initially he hired rooms at the Old Colonial Buildings in Bideford where tobacco was first thought to have been stored in England. Then, in 1855, he leased North Down Hall from George Molesworth, a retired naval lieutenant, where he completed his famous novel, Westward Ho!

Molesworth used the publicity from the novel, and the new 1854 Companies Act, to help launch the Hotel and Villa Company (Northam Burrows). His vision was to create a resort rivalling Torquay in the south of the county and to provide accommodation for golfers and other holidaymakers. Locals believe that the original project suffered through the lack of a reliable water supply.

A letter written by Dr. George Gosset documents golf played by his father and uncle in 1855 at Northam Burrows: "In those early days, golf at Northam appears to be mainly a Gosset family affair but some of the residents began to take an interest and in 1860 Old Tom Morris came down (from Scotland) and stayed a month at the vicarage and rearranged the course which then began at the Cape Bunker." In 1864, the Rev. J Lymebear convened a meeting to arrange: "for playing the fine Scotch game of Golf at the Burrows of Northam." There was significant opposition from the local Potwallopers (ratepayers) who had concerns about the impact on their grazing rights over the Burrows which was common land and thus open to all. In those early days, flags were frequently destroyed and holes mutilated, but the money earned by the young men acting as caddies for the wealthy golfers enabled

Above: The famous Cape bunker waiting to capture topped drives from the fourth tee

the local villagers to vote in favour of the Club which was officially founded in April 1864 as the North Devon and West of England Golf Club.

The initial Committee of the Club was the whole Lifeboat Committee, with the Rev. Gosset being the first Captain. In November that year, Gosset cut the holes and planted the flags for the Club's inaugural medal competition which was won by Colonel Hutchinson with a round of 118. Despite the promising start, the landed-gentry soon retired back to their hunting, shooting and fishing, leaving the game to retired military officers, the clergy, professional businessmen and men of independent means. In 1867, HRH the Prince of Wales consented to the Club becoming the first non-Scottish golf club to use the Royal prefix, and in June 1868, the men promoted the first ladies' golf club in the world with 47 members and 23 associates (themselves!).

One of the initial rules for the ladies was that: "No other club shall on any account be used on the ladies' course besides a wooden putter." Most of the holes on the ladies' course were between 50 and 120 yards in length whilst holes on the main course varied from 150 to 650 yards and men would typically play with between seven and twelve clubs rather than one! By 1900

however, the ladies' game had developed to such an extent that the Golfers Handbook reported: "Miss MA Whigham, Prestwick, in the Semi-Finals of the Ladies' Championship, drove 234 yards at the eighteenth hole (of the main course) playing a Gutta ball."

In the early 1900s, Herbert Fowler made some important alterations to Morris's layout, and in 1912 the Club hosted the famous Amateur Championship featuring the final between John Ball and Abe Mitchell (then still an amateur) which Ball won at the 38th hole. A large, partisan and vocal crowd arrived from the shipyard at Bideford to support Mitchell, the working man, but this only served to strengthen Ball's resolve.

Like most Victorian clubs in England, RND's membership was exclusive. In fact, 'tradesmen' were not finally accepted as members until 1946 after the Second World War had started to break down class barriers. Much earlier, during the 1880s, local caddies had lobbied for a club of their own. As the course was laid out over common land, they were able to invoke the Northam Award of 1716 which had found that all Potwallopers had equal rights of air, exercise, grazing and recreation. The Club, as Lord of the Manor, granted their request, leading to the formation of the Northam Working Men's Club which was founded in 1888 for

200 golfing members living in the ecclesiastical parish of Northam.

One of England's greatest amateur golfers, Horace Hutchinson, learnt his golf at Westward Ho! where he was spurred on by another famous RND amateur, Arthur H Molesworth. Hutchinson was runner-up in the first Amateur Championship held at Hoylake in 1895 and went on to win The Open Championship in both of the following years. He was also a great golf writer and was one of the first to instruct that golf is about a swing and not a hit. He wrote many famous articles for the Badminton Library including a thought-provoking piece on 'Hints for Cricketers who are taking up Golf' in which he noted that: "The cricketer stops his stroke in order to keep the ball along the ground", which was clearly undesirable in the game of golf.

The great Open Champion, JH Taylor, known locally as 'JH', lived in Northam and started out as a caddie at the Club although he moved away when he was eighteen. In his book, 'My Life's Work', he wrote of his time as a caddie at Westward Ho!. "I was to learn that my short sight was a definite handicap. We lost a ball among the thick rushes and that was a disgrace that the Major would not pardon or condone and for this I was fined three pence. As a result of that afternoon's

hard work trudging around the four and a half miles with a bundle of clubs under my arm I earned half the statutory fee of sixpence." Taylor used his time as a caddie wisely and learnt much about the game in the process. The spirit of JH Taylor looms large at the Club and a number of senior members recall that in his later life he would walk around Northam Village with a pitching wedge and was only too happy to impart a few tips. All remembered him as an upright man who never smoked and never drank. Taylor was closely involved with the formation of the Northam Artisans, the national Artisan Golfer's Association and also the Professional Golfers' Association (PGA).

Playing conditions in the early days were very basic and the state of the greens must have been interesting as there were no fixed days for the cutting of holes. When a group of players found one of the holes: "... too far gone in decay to be no longer endurable", they would use a knife to cut a new hole to which they would putt. The site of the hole was indicated by a gull or rook's feather stuck into the ground at its edge. Local rules stipulated that in teeing off for the next hole: "The ball shall be teed not less than three nor more than four club lengths from the hole lately played." Sand for teeing the ball would be drawn out of the hole just completed, and caddies would often have to lie on the ground in order to stretch an arm at full length so as to reach the ball at the bottom of the hole.

One consequence of the strengthening Artisans' golf movement was that the independent businessmen at Royal North Devon, who were mainly Northam Golf Club members, found themselves stuck in the middle between the main Club's upper-class hierarchy and the working-class craftsman artisans. As a result, another golf club was formed at the nearby Pebble Ridge Hotel. The main Club removed the flags from the course on Saturday night so as to observe the Sabbath when no golf should be played. Members of the hotel club then proceeded to play on Sundays and became known as the Sabbath Breakers. They employed a forecaddie, Johnny Vile, who ran ahead of the first match with a stick and handkerchief to mark out each hole. The last person to putt in each group would remain standing with his putter in the hole so that the next group knew where to aim. It was during one of these Sunday medal rounds that the first competition was won with a set of steel-shafted clubs which had been sanctioned in the US but were not yet allowed by The R&A in the UK. By 1928, so many golfers were playing the course that maintenance costs were increasing and it was decided to open the doors to local businessmen, many of them Sabbath Breakers, who then became provisional members of the main Club.

Formal competitions were suspended during the two world wars but golf was still played over the Burrows. JH Taylor remarked in 1944 that: "Among other disadvantages that Westward Ho! suffers from

Left: Early winners of the Silver Medal included George Gosset, AH Molesworth, Horace Hutchinson and Harold Hilton

during these troubles is the fact that the course has been taken over as a practice bombing site of the RAF which utilises it 3-4 days per week!"

Today JH and his predecessors would still recognise much about golf at RND. The present clubhouse was opened in 1883 and has fine views of Lundy Island, some twelve miles offshore. The first two holes lead towards the sea and then a short par-4 is intersected by the track leading to the beach. The par-4 fourth hole contains the famous Cape bunker which crosses almost the entire fairway and collects any topped drives. Holes ten to twelve are known for the rushes which have sharp points and render most stray shots unplayable. The short sixteenth is testing because the green is small and sloping, and although the par-4 eighteenth appears to be an easy finishing hole, the small ditch in front of the green traps many a mishit approach. At the end of the round, the Club has thoughtfully provided a hose to wash away the inevitable natural manure gathered on shoes and trolley wheels!

The clubhouse contains an excellent museum of golfing memorabilia and the Club is very welcoming to people interested in the history of the game.

LONDON SCOTTISH — ROYAL WIMBLEDON

ON WIMBLEDON COMMON

London Scottish Golf Club was founded by members of the London Scottish Rifle Volunteers in November 1864 after a shooting match held on the common by the National Rifle Association. A local newspaper of April 1982 described the Club's discovery of an engraved sign dated 1863 which might have established London Scottish as the oldest club in England still playing over its original grounds, but this was not subsequently proved and so this honour remains with Westward Ho!

The Club's first headquarters and clubhouse were situated at Mrs. Doggett's cottage under the shadow of the windmill which still stands as a prominent landmark on the common. Lord Elcho was inaugural President and AG Mackenzie became the first Captain. In the Club's centenary booklet, Edward Scudamore notes that: "if Lord Elcho entered the clubhouse, I should deem it wise to stand to attention." Elcho, later to become Earl of Weymss and March, was President from 1866-1881, Captain from 1881-1894 and Honorary Captain until his death in 1914. He was born in Edinburgh in 1818 and was educated at Eton and Christ Church, Oxford. His love of golf stretched over a long playing career from the age of 14 through until his 93rd year. He died, aged 96, in his London home and was buried back in Scotland.

The original course at Wimbledon Common was seven holes arranged around the windmill, and these were generally played three times making a 21-hole round. This format continued until 1871 when Tom Dunn, the Club's Professional, was instructed to enlarge the course to 18 holes. Critical acclaim for the extended course was mixed. One correspondent for the Field magazine wrote: "These Links are capable of great improvement; the third hole is much cut up with heavy carts and horses hoofs, and off the course are nasty gorse bushes, also long grass and gorse at other holes." However another contributor, perhaps more used to the challenges of natural golf courses, wrote that the course had: " been lately so improved and extended as to make it one of the finest courses in this country...within six miles from Hyde Park Corner there is a golfing links equal in extent, and superior in number and variety of hazards, to the far-famed links of St Andrews..." Four new holes were constructed in 1901 to replace those removed to make way for a larger public area around the windmill.

In 1864, the Lord of the Manor of Wimbledon, Earl Spencer, tried to seal off the land at Wimbledon Common for his own private use. This move was thwarted by the Wimbledon and Putney Commons Act, passed by Parliament in 1871, under which control of the common was vested in a body of eight Conservators. Around the same time, the Club expanded its membership to include non-military members and the increased numbers required that the clubhouse be moved from Mrs. Doggett's Cottage to the Iron House. This, not by coincidence, was also the Headquarters of the London Scottish Rifle Volunteers, and Lord Elcho had a senior position in both organisations.

Trouble had been brewing for some time between the military and civilian members. Officers in the Corps had automatic rights of membership to the golf Club whilst others had to face a ballot. Subscriptions were

Above: *Red-clad players waiting to drive at a hole situated close to the windmill on the common*

also higher for civilians and further consternation was caused as Corps' members had free use of the lavatory whilst others had to pay 2/6d per year! By 1874, civilian membership had grown to around 250 people paying four guineas annual membership, whilst military membership remained at around fifty, but this latter group comprised the management and the entire Committee, each of whom paid subs of only ten shillings per year.

Elcho was uncompromising in his support for the Corps side of the Club, and the move of the clubhouse had further strengthened his position and resolve. He exercised a right of veto over most Club matters. The issue of the veto caused serious aggravation throughout the 1870s, and in 1880, Lt. Col. Henry Lumsden, who was to succeed Elcho as President, served written notice on the Club of its eviction from its own clubhouse facilities within the Iron House. The Club's Secretary, Henry Lamb, took a leading role in helping the civilians to identify their own suitable premises at the Wimbledon Village end of the common.

The Committee meeting to discuss the separation started in November 1880 and continued in December and again in February 1881! At one stage, the Corps was accused of gerrymandering with the 'faggot votes' of new members, thirteen of whom had joined on the very morning of the reconvened meeting! Most of these new members had never swung a golf club. Eventually it was agreed that separation was inevitable, but the names of the two separate clubs had still to be resolved. The civilians claimed the name The London Scottish Golf Club, but the military wing countered by putting inverted commas around 'London Scottish' in their own name. Henry Lamb was moved to write a letter to The Field complaining about their reference to The Wimbledon Golf Club as no such club existed. In April 1882, a solution was finally reached following the suggestion of an anonymous correspondent, claiming membership of both 'Clubs', that: "confusion might be fitly terminated, perhaps by Wimbledon players gracefully declining a title which no longer expresses their nationality or constitution, and their retention of which serves only to irritate their former friends."

Colonel George Moncrieff, writing in the name of the civilians' London Scottish section, wrote to the Prince of Wales, later Edward VII, humbly requesting that he should continue as Patron of the Club after they changed their name to The Wimbledon Golf Club, and that he should agree to their using the prefix 'Royal'. The Prince referred Henry Lamb to the Home Office with regard to the latter request, and in June 1882 Queen Victoria acceded to the Club's request that the civilians' club should be styled Royal Wimbledon Golf Club. The two separate clubs co-existed playing from their respective clubhouses until 1907 when the Royal Wimbledon Golf Club constructed its own new course on the Warren Farm land adjoining the common.

In 1908, following the move of Royal Wimbledon

to its new course, the Wimbledon Town Golf Club was established by a small group of local residents. In 1919, this club absorbed the South London Golf Club which was a nomadic club playing over various London commons including Clapham, Streatham and Tooting, and the combined club changed its name to the Wimbledon and South London Golf Club. In 1928, there was a further name change to the current Wimbledon Common Golf Club.

Whilst the military and civilian wings of the London Scottish Club were absorbed with internal politics, they had also to deal with the wishes of the Conservators of the common who were duty-bound to protect the common from any form of encroachment. The Club agreed to abandon play from the Iron House, at the Roehampton end of the common, during the 1880s. This followed agreement from the Conservators that they could have a clubhouse near the windmill. The wearing of red coats was introduced in 1892 to warn the general public of impending danger, and 'pillar box' red upper garments are still required today. Both the

London Scottish and Wimbledon Common Clubs have spare red tops to lend to visitors who arrive unprepared.

One interesting example of the need to minimise damage to the common related to the size of the hole. The local rules at London Scottish stipulated that the hole should be only three inches in size, whereas The R&A stipulated four and a quarter inches. It was not until 1884 that the Club decided to adopt most of the St Andrews' rules which may help to explain some of the high scores in the early years on the common. Full adoption of the St Andrews' rules was finally agreed at the April 1898 AGM.

Many local ratepayers campaigned against the game, and the Conservators had an impossible task trying to please all parties. In May 1881, a meeting was held at the Conservator's office in Lincoln's Inn Fields in Central London. Lord Elcho and Colonel Lumsden represented the 'Iron House' Golf Club, Henry Lamb and Colonel Moncrieff represented the civilian wing from the 'Golf Club at Croft's premises' and Sir Edward Pearson and Mr. Murray represented the ratepayers. Having heard all the arguments, the Conservators agreed to set aside for golf eighteen tees (of 240 square feet each), and eighteen golf lawns (greens) which were to be circular in form and 75 feet in diameter. There was a provision that apart from these features, and the spaces intervening in a straight line between the tees and greens, no part of the common should be used for the playing of the game of golf. It was therefore prohibited by law to hook or slice a ball whilst playing at Wimbledon Common!

The April 1872 minutes of the London Scottish Golf Club record the rules of the Wimbledon Ladies' Golf Club although its official designation was The Ladies London Scottish Club. The minutes noted that the London Scottish rules apply:"except as to Subscription, the Committee and Dress." The care of the course and adjudication of disputes was left to the men who would be Honorary Members of the Ladies' Club. In January 1875, the Conservators were told that the Ladies' Club, 'an adjunct of the Men's', had fourteen members and in 1876, the men presented the ladies with an expensive gold trophy set with pearls. The last winner, in 1879,

Above: *Autumn colours on the common. The Conservators require all golfers to wear red tops as a danger signal*

was Henry Lamb's sister, and she was allowed to keep the trophy when the Ladies' Club ceased to function later that year. The Ladies' section was revived in 1891 when the Conservators allowed the construction of a separate 9-hole course measuring 1,420 yards, immediately to the west of the main course. The original ladies' clubhouse was based at the Thatched Cottage which is still standing and is identified on the current London Scottish Golf Club scorecard.

In the early days, the newly reformed Ladies' Club was said to be almost unbeatable. Issette Pearson was runner-up in the first two Ladies' British Open Amateur Championships and was founder of the Ladies' Golf Union. Lena Thomson won the British Open in 1898. She was celebrated in rhyme by one of the contemporary journalists:

The famous Lena, have you seen her
Deadly short approaches?
When these you see, you will agree
This golfer Tom Dunn coaches.

The ladies' course was taken over to make an Army camp in 1915 and the ladies now play on the newer Royal Wimbledon course.

Caddies were an integral part of the early days of golf on Wimbledon Common. In February 1871, Tom Dunn was told to organise the staff of caddies, and in 1872 the Club tried to reduce the cost of caddying by employing boys from the local National School next to the course. By 1874, the School complained that an average of 36 boys were missing lessons and it was even suggested that, on one occasion, the Club had despatched a cab to pick up the boys just as they were arriving at school. Complaints continued and the Club responded by setting up a Boys' Friendly Society into which their wages were paid. The School Board Attendance Committee warned the Club that they were liable to a fine of £2 for employing boys, and the Boys' Friendly Society was eventually wound up with the Club reverting to the employment of adult male caddies. Organisation of the adult caddies was clearly an onerous task. In October 1892, the Professional was authorised to employ a superintendent of caddies but the post holder soon resigned, and in April 1894, the Secretary was then instructed to apply to the Police Office in Wimbledon for a suitable man to take his place!

Tom Dunn acted as Professional between 1870 and 1881, at which time he moved back to North Berwick in Scotland. In October 1877, Dunn challenged the

Above: 1871 photo of members outside the old Iron House. W Porteous, Captain in 1872-74, is second from the left, AG MacKenzie has a white brim to his hat and is standing next to the man with a large black beard leaning against the flag pole, and RH Usher, Captain in 1870-72 is sitting to the right of the flag pole

Inset: Lt. Gen. Sir James Hope Grant was a prominent early member. This picture was taken in 1867 before the days of golf bags

former Open Champion, Old Tom Morris (by then aged 66) to a 36-hole match. Morris was returning from the Autumn meeting at Westward Ho!. In the course of the match, the two Professionals lost shots in bushes, bracken, rushes, water and whins (the local name for furze), illustrating the difficulty of the course at that time. The match was eventually won by Dunn who went round in 91 and 89. Morris scored 94 and 93. Whilst at the Club, Tom Dunn employed his younger brother, Young Willie Dunn as an apprentice. Young Willie learnt his golf on the common and later went on to win the first unofficial US Open, a matchplay event, at St Andrews, New York, in 1894.

JH Taylor was also employed briefly as the Club Professional between 1896 and 1899, having won the Open Championship in 1894 and 1895 and narrowly lost the 1896 Open in a 36-hole play-off to Harry Vardon. It was not a successful appointment. Playing conditions from the Conservators on the common restricted golf to three days per week and Taylor's interests were focused more on tournament play than on looking after the course, another of the requirements at the time. Following his move to Mid-Surrey in 1899, Taylor's form returned and he won the 1900 Open at St Andrews.

Whilst the Wimbledon Ladies achieved national celebrity, the common also helped develop the skills of several famous golfing men. In particular, Harry Colt, the renowned golf course architect, learnt his golf at Wimbledon and he helped to redesign Royal Wimbledon's new course in 1924. Another famous member, Dr. Laidlaw Purves was a very proficient amateur golfer, winning his last trophy at the age of 71 playing off a three handicap. However, he is best remembered for his role, along with Harry Lamb and other Wimbledon members in founding and designing the Royal St George's course at Sandwich.

The common is still a difficult place to play golf although the course is short by today's standards. The fairways are quite ill-defined amongst the woodland and joggers and dog-walkers are everywhere and seem impervious to shouts of 'Fore!' The Club's history is ever-present through the names of the holes around the course including Elcho (the first hole naturally!), Long Butt (the third hole named after the rifle connection), Caesar's Well and Caesar's Camp (the ninth and tenth reflecting the old Roman presence on the common), Hope Grant (the thirteenth) remembering another of the Club's former illustrious military members, and Windmill (the eighteenth) leading back to the London Scottish clubhouse in the shadow of the windmill.

Golfers looking for a contrast should play both the Common and the Royal Wimbledon courses in the same day. The course on the common is rudimentary but does give a feel of the conditions in the early days, whilst the neighbouring Royal course enjoys manicured conditions and feels a long way from nearby London.

ROYAL JERSEY

HOME OF HARRY VARDON

Jersey has been the home of some of the greatest ever golfers. Six-times Open Champion, Harry Vardon, grew up next to the Royal Jersey course, and Ted Ray, who won both the British and US Opens, was also a local boy. More recently, Tony Jacklin, another winner of both titles, has made his home on the island.

The Club is situated on the eastern side of the island on Grouville Common. The course enjoys sweeping views across the Royal Bay of Grouville to Mont Orgueil Castle which was built in the 13th Century by order of King John of England, who was also the Duke of Normandy, to counter the threat from King Philippe Augustus who had invaded Normandy and thus had possession of the nearby French Coast.

Gorse was planted during the 17th Century to help hide defending soldiers, and this vegetation features prominently at several holes on today's course. The Common was used to graze domestic animals and the grass was also kept short by rabbits. Wind-blown sand from Grouville Bay meant that natural bunkers were found at various points on the Common and they also helped the development of natural hazards on the earliest course.

Before golf arrived in Jersey, Grouville Common was the venue for horse racing, with the first meeting

being held in June 1839. Racing and golf co-existed for a time before the former moved to the west of the island in the early 1900s. During the 19th Century, the area was made rich by the export of oysters from Grouville Bay and in the 1800s more than 2,000 people were employed in the industry with boats arriving from all over the South of England. In 1873, the Jersey Eastern Railway was opened to link the relatively isolated east coast to the capital of St. Helier, and a station was built at Gorey Village, close to the Common, which facilitated the eventual formation of the first golf Club.

Following Napoleon's defeat at Waterloo, Jersey began to attract many former Army and Naval officers as an attractive and relatively inexpensive retirement destination. Unlike the domestic islanders, the incomers had time on their hands and as golf began to spread fast on the mainland, the first steps were taken to establish the game in Jersey. The Club at Grouville Bay was established in 1878 by eight promoters, led by FW Brewster. Other founders included the Rev. WB Holland who was a local teacher, J Craigie who was born in Aberdeen, and J Boeille, another teacher and the only Jersey-born member. Brewster was a relative newcomer to the island and may have been an early member at Royal Wimbledon. Certainly, he had the

Inset: large statue of Harry Vardon, unveiled by Tony Jacklin in 2001, marks the entrance to the Royal Jersey Golf Club

required skills as he won the Club Challenge Cup in Autumn 1879 playing off scratch.

Brewster's likely connection with Wimbledon is supported by the arrival in Jersey of two stalwarts from the London club. Dr. Laidlaw Purves won the Club's Spring 1879 Challenge Cup, and by the time the course at Sandwich had opened in 1887, Purves had become a resident of Jersey. Henry Lamb and his brother David both became non-resident members of the Club in 1879, and Lamb won the Clutton Cup for the best scratch score in Spring 1883. Royal North Devon members also provided early support. AH Molesworth became a non-resident member in March 1882 and won the Clutton Cup that Spring, whilst Horace Hutchinson featured as a winner of the same cup in 1895.

The 1871 Jersey census records the Vardon family living at Amitie Lodge near Gorey Village. Mr. Philip Vardon was a 45-year-old farm labourer and his wife, Elizabeth, had five sons at the time including Harry who was aged just eleven months. The Vardons lived

on the edge of the Common and Harry was later to write of how golf first arrived on the Common: "On one Sabbath Day, a small party of strange gentlemen selected to make their appearance on the Common land. They brought with them instruments with which to survey and mark out places for tees and greens. The story that preparations were being made to play a game called golf was soon spread around the village." In the first few years, some of the holes were cut on the landward side of the railway but these were soon discontinued and the course has since remained on its present grounds.

Young Vardon and his brothers and friends watched the early golfers with interest and Harry later wrote of how they managed to fashion toy clubs out of oak and thorn wood and built their own 4-hole course with 50-yard holes on the adjoining Common. Their first ball was a toy marble but gradually they started to find lost balls on the main course whilst caddying, and helpful members gave them old and damaged clubs with which they learnt to hone their own game. Later, the boys covered the wooden club heads with tin, and it is easy to imagine how the children soon became adept at the new game which was still a novel pastime for the adults on the Common.

With fortunate foresight, the Club's Committee organised various golf competitions for caddies and generally supported the boys. Tom Butel won £1 as the winner of the first caddie competition in October 1889 with a gross score of 88 playing off scratch and Tom Vardon won 7/6d for his third place score of 89, also off scratch. An early Club Captain, Major R Spofforth, employed Harry Vardon as a gardener when he was aged 17 and on one occasion was said to be so impressed with Harry's golf that he told him to: "never give up the sport. It may prove useful to you in the future."

In 1888, many of the caddies were founding members of the Jersey Eastern Golf Club and they were allowed to play over the Royal course after 4pm and on Sundays before being integrated into the Royal Jersey Club in 1983. Between 1890 and the 1920s, the course produced so many first-class golfers that they became known as The Jersey School.

Harry's older brother Tom had several high finishes in the Open and was the Professional at Royal St George's, Sandwich, between 1902 and 1909. Ted Ray was the first Ryder Cup Captain in 1927, whilst five members of the Gaudin family played regularly in The Open and Thomas Renouf came fifth in both 1909 and 1913. Other well-respected members of the 'School' included Thomas and Fredrick Butel, and the Boomer Brothers who won many titles on the Continent.

The best known golfing member of the Club itself was probably the Hon. Michael Scott who won two Australian Open and Amateur titles and became famous as the oldest winner of the British Amateur Championship when he won the title at Hoylake in 1933 at the age of 55. More recently, Tommy Horton has continued the local golfing tradition, leaving school as soon as possible to pursue a successful golfing career which included winning the South African and British Masters titles, plus Ryder Cup selections and five consecutive years at the top of the PGA European Seniors' Order of Merit table. The Club's best lady golfer has been Carol Le Feuvre (Mrs. Gibbs) who represented Great Britain and Ireland in the Curtis Cup. She learnt some useful tips whilst caddying for male members and no doubt her first competitive score of 51 net, playing off a 29 handicap, attracted some attention in the clubhouse!

The golf course has been used for several other purposes since it was laid out. In the early days, huge piles of Vraic (seaweed) were stacked on the Common for subsequent transport inland and a local rule had to be introduced to allow a free drop for a ball lying within two club lengths of a stack. Much more seriously, the course was turned into a minefield by the Germans during their invasion in the Second World War. A few people continued to play golf over the nine holes which were not covered by mines and barbed wire, and the 1943 Club records showed there were still 120 members although nearly half were marked as non-playing.

Although the Jersey Eastern railway line had been closed before the War, the Germans decided to reopen the line and build additional tracks across the course itself in order to transport sand from the beach to nearby cement works. They also constructed embankments and gun emplacements which are still visible today. The full 18-hole course was reopened in 1947 and the Club's fortunes have since recovered. In 1978, a crowd of more than 1,000 watched Tommy Horton and Tony Jacklin defeat the Scottish challenge provided by Brian Barnes and Bernard Gallacher 4&3 to mark the Club's centenary, and in July 1984,

Main: View from near the clubhouse looking down the first fairway, with Fort Henry on the left. Second World War German gun emplacements can be seen to the right of the fairway

Above: Ladies putting on the old fourth green, today's first, around 1900 with Mont Orgueil in the background

Jack Nicklaus and Hale Irwin played an exhibition match against Brian Barnes and Tommy Horton in aid of the Harry Vardon Trust which had been established to support young Jersey golfers. Barnes and Horton won the match 2&1, but Nicklaus won the best challenge of the day when he won a bet on behalf of the Trust by driving the par-4 eighteenth green which measured 312 yards at the time. The Trust benefited further when Nicklaus won a further challenge from Irwin by sinking the putt for an eagle.

On today's course, the par-5 first hole is played parallel with the beach in a northerly direction and, wind permitting, gives long hitters an early birdie opportunity as the green can be reached in two shots. The short second hole was said to be one of Vardon's favourites, and the long, 554-yards par-5 third hole leads out towards the northern extremity of the course. A bunker to the left of the fifth fairway is still known as Hornby's after Gerard Hornby, an excellent late-19th Century golfer who played off plus-5. The Club's records chronicle months of correspondence and special meetings concerning a dispute over the number of shots which the player

was believed to have taken at the hole. Several witnesses believed that Hornby had taken an extra shot in the bunker. Reputations were at stake, compromises were rejected, and Hornby eventually resigned from the Club in high dudgeon.

The seventh hole is one of the toughest and requires a long and accurate drive in order to reach the elevated green in two shots. It is followed by the relatively new short eighth hole which was formally opened by Jack Nicklaus and others in 1984. The tenth is an attractive hole played inland from the beach, and the twelfth is one of the most demanding with its narrow fairway and a large mound in front of the green which throws off any shots hit too softly.

The thirteenth requires a partially blind drive over gorse despite the elevated tee, and both the fourteenth and fifteenth are rated as difficult by the locals. The fifteenth is a long par-3 requiring a well-struck long iron or wood to a green well-protected by gorse to the left and at the back. There is less danger to the right of the green, but that area is not visible from the tee. Recent alterations to the seventeenth have toughened the hole whilst players standing on the final tee can try and emulate Jack Nicklaus.

Boys practising on the course at twilight indicate that the legacy left by Vardon, Ray and the other members of The Jersey School, is in good hands.

EARLY EXPANSION

Several clubs played a vital early role in helping to cement the popularity of the game in England. A number of these courses like Alnmouth, Seaton Carew, Yarmouth & Caister and West Lancashire (below) were established by expatriate Scots whilst others, in the South of England, including Crookham, Kingsdown, Bath and Felixstowe Ferry were helped by golfers from Royal North Devon and Royal Blackheath.

Alnmouth Village..............1869

Furness 1872

Crookham.....................1873

West Lancashire..............1873

Seaton Carew 1874

Southfield 1875

Bramshaw-Forest Course 1880

Felixstowe Ferry 1880

Kingsdown....................1880

Bath 1880

Yarmouth & Caister..........1882

ALNMOUTH – ALNMOUTH VILLAGE

Inset: Harry Vardon driving at the second hole in an exhibition match against JH Taylor in September 1905 to celebrate the extension of the course. Many of the buildings in the picture are still standing today

Alnmouth has a special place in English history. The site has been occupied for at least 4,000 years and is reputed to have been the location of the Synod of Twyford where Cuthbert, the Northumbrian Saint, was made Bishop of Lindisfarne in AD 684. In the 1200s, the town was a prosperous grain port, but in 1336, during the Border Wars, the port was destroyed by Scottish invaders. Further tragedy struck in 1348 when the Black Death again reduced the population, but by the 1700s the port had revived to such an extent that a Preventive Officer had to be appointed to reduce the illegal trade in French Brandy.

The growth of the railway in the mid-1800s killed off the town's coastal shipping trade leaving only fishing vessels but it did encourage wealthy businessmen in Newcastle to build houses in the town and subsequently led to the formation of the Alnmouth Golf Club in 1869.

In the early years, the Club held its meetings in the three-storied Georgian 'Schooner Inn'. Captain Arthur Walker founded the Club with twelve others, including Earl Percy MP, Lord Ossulton and Sir Stanley Errington. The original entrance fee was ten shillings plus a similar sum as an annual subscription.

The land at Alnmouth lying between the steep, bracken-covered hill and the sea is gently undulating and is classic golf links country although it lacks the space enjoyed at other seaside courses such as Westward Ho!, and hence is only suitable for nine holes. The course was designed and created by Mungo Park who later became famous in winning the 1874 Open Championship at Musselburgh. Park was the Club's first Professional.

The Club held its first competition in October 1869 with three prizes. Earl Percy, who had been made Club Captain, presented the first prize, the Silver Challenge Medal. Charles Walker, a founder member of the Club and also a member of The R&A presented the Silver Challenge Cross, and the third prize was a set of golf clubs, presented by the Club. The competition consisted of two rounds of the 9-hole course and was won by Captain Walker, the Club's Secretary, with a score of 81. Reverend Medd was the first winner of the Silver Challenge Cross with a score of 119.

The Press did not document the Club's activities during most of the 1870s, reflecting that the game was still a minority interest in England. However, in 1879 the Club organised a tournament including Jamie Andersen, Bob Ferguson (Musselburgh), Tom Morris, Mungo Park, Ben Sayers and Willie Park Junior. Ferguson beat Andersen after a play-off with Mungo Park coming third and Sayers fourth.

Alnmouth played its part in the establishment of the British Amateur Championship. The Royal Liverpool Club at Hoylake introduced the competition in 1885 and Alnmouth, along with 23 other clubs, contributed to support the event until 1919. Many Alnmouth members

in the late 1800s were also members of other new clubs in the area including Tyneside, Whitley Bay, Newbiggin, Rothbury, Warkworth, Berwick-upon-Tweed and City of Newcastle. Alnmouth helped a number of these clubs in their early days and the Whitley Bay handicaps in 1890 were based on 'Alnmouth +2'.

Alnmouth Working Men's Golf Club is first mentioned in 1878 and started through an agreement between the Burgesses of Alnmouth and the villagers which allowed the working men to play golf on the links without contributing to their upkeep. The course was on common land but subject to the overriding interests of the Lord of The Manor, the Duke of Northumberland, who must also have approved this development. The Club's first trophy was the Mitchell Bowl.

George Rochester succeeded Mungo Park as the Club's Professional around 1889/90 and in 1905 the Club arranged for Mungo's nephew, Willie Park, to design and lay out an extra nine holes slightly inland and above the existing links course.

The extension to eighteen holes was opened by the Duke of Northumberland and celebrated by an exhibition match between Harry Vardon and JH Taylor which Taylor won 2-up. In his speech the Duke commented: "I do not think any of us want Alnmouth to become another Scarborough. Rather a moderately-sized watering place where people can come from time to time to enjoy peace and quiet without the racket of a large watering place."

The Alnmouth Ladies' Golf Club was formed in 1907 although early photographs confirm that ladies had been playing on the links before that time. In 1923, Sunday golf was allowed, but only on the upper nine holes away from public gaze. In 1928 storms threatened the course, especially the fourth and fifth holes. Over the years, much money has been spent to prevent further coastal erosion.

The 18-hole links in 1905 measured only 5,059 yards, and as club technology and balls improved and the course became more crowded it was realised that further changes were required to lengthen it. The Duke of Northumberland, who at the time was Captain of the Club, offered a long lease over the adjoining Foxton Hall which was one of the historic residences of the Percy family.

Foxton Hall became the new clubhouse, an additional nine holes were designed on the upper level by Harry Colt, and the new Foxton course was opened in 1931. The original Alnmouth Golf Club was dissolved at this time and the villagers' rights to free golf were reduced back to the original nine holes which were still intact at the lower level, by the sea. In 1936, the Alnmouth Village Golf Club was formed to take over and run the old links as a separate club.

The original links course has lost some of the bunkers over the years and a Punch cartoon published in April 1910 jested that the Secretary of the Club would be open to offers for advertisements on hoardings, in bunkers and about the course. Fortunately, this never came to pass!

The Duke need not have worried about the town becoming too commercialised. Today, the original 9-hole course provides a simple but enjoyable round. The outward four holes are by the sea and holes three and four are particularly challenging for most habitual slicers who will end up on the beach. The sixth has a blind drive up and over a hill onto the upper level, and the seventh tee is elevated and requires a solid drive back down to the lower links. The view from the seventh tee is spectacular, with Coquet Island and its lighthouse being visible in the distance and the village spreading out to the right.

Although the course is quite short at around 3,000 yards there is only one par-3 and it is quite easy to run up a bogey 5 on several of the par-4s, especially if the wind is blowing. The newer Foxton course has an excellent Dormy House and the two courses combined offer an enjoyable golfing experience in beautiful countryside.

Above: View of the third green and fourth tee, nearest the sea, taken from the hills above the old links. The players nearer the camera have played their shots down to the lower level from the elevated seventh tee and are about to play their approaches to the green. The dark rocks in the background are exposed at low tide

FURNESS

ON WALNEY ISLAND

Furness is the sixth oldest club in England and was founded along the west coast of Walney Island by a group of a dozen Scotsmen from Dundee, most of whom worked at the Jute Works in Barrow. The first nine holes were laid out over Biggar Bank, a short distance from today's course, and the founders faced considerable obstacles as there was no bridge across to Walney Island and golfers had to make their own arrangements with the ferrymen. Clearly there was competition for their custom, and the Club minutes of November 1875 documented that players would: "go as often as possible with the old ferryman."

All members were required to pull their weight. The same minutes quote C Macfarlane as proposing that a heavy fine should be imposed on all members: "who do not attend to clear the ground", and J Carr then added that the Captain should call the roll at the ground on Saturday morning and that a vote of censure be taken at the monthly meeting regarding absentees! There was lively debate about the best way of preparing the course. The first Captain, D Laurence, wanted to burn the grass, whilst Macfarlane preferred to cut it. Mr. Carr proposed a compromise that two gallons of petrol should be purchased so that the grass would be burnt if it did not get cut.

Not surprisingly the golfers' methods of clearing the ground were not supported by the local farmers who had started to erect fences to keep out steelworkers who waded across from Barrow to Walney Island at low tide for recreational purposes. In the highly-charged political atmosphere of the times, a Mr. Bishop proposed that the Club should continue to play over the ground at Walney: "until a prosecution be raised" and at a Special Meeting in March 1876, the Club resolved to show its willingness: "to assist in the struggle for the freedom of the Bank, by crossing the Channel and playing over the railings yet once again before the destruction." Once the infamous Biggar Bank Riots became more serious, the local council purchased the land for public recreation and the golfers moved a short distance to their present location, starting a new course over land at Drylands, leased by a farmer, David Steel, who refused to take payment from the members, telling them that they should: "...gang on wi' your game, and say nowt about it."

The Club was essentially a working-class initiative, unlike many other clubs which were founded by wealthy individuals. Annual membership was five shillings, but most members could only afford to pay

a penny per week and the Treasurer was kept busy keeping a record of the instalments which he had to collect from golfers during their visits on Saturdays. Despite its frugal beginnings, the Club grew in stature. Harry Vardon played an exhibition match in 1916 to celebrate the opening of the new clubhouse and George Duncan played at Furness in 1919 in the year before he won the first post-war Open at Deal. However, funds remained tight, greens were only cut at weekends and fairways could only be cut twice a year. This led to a breakaway group founding the Barrow Golf Club in 1921. Soon afterwards, the Municipal Authority added to the competition by opening a prestigious 9-hole public course which was opened by the Prince of Wales, but the Furness Club survived and enjoyed one of its highlights in 1932 when it staged the Northern Open. The Club has always had close connections with the local shipyard, and in the 1920s the course was dominated by a large airship factory. The ill-fated German airship Hindenburg flew low over Walney Island in 1936, as if to demonstrate the superior size of the massive Zeppelin compared with British models.

The course is best visited in Summer as the fairways can be slow to drain after heavy Winter rainfall. The first five holes run in a northerly direction alongside a housing estate built on land previously occupied by the airship factory, and the distant mountains of the Lake District, dominated by Black Combe, make an attractive backdrop. The short par-3 sixth hole turns west towards the Irish Sea, and then the course becomes more attractive and demanding. Depending upon wind direction, the cliffs and beach feature strongly in club selection, bunkers are well placed to prevent players being too cautious with their line, and the undulations of the land are most evident at the tenth hole which features a 100-foot drop between tee and green. Oystercatchers feed regularly along the fairways adding to the natural feeling of the seaward side of the course.

Main: *Players approaching the green at the par-3 sixth hole situated at the far end of the course from the clubhouse. The Irish Sea lies beyond the fence and good views of the Isle of Man can be seen on clear days*

NEWBURY & CROOKHAM

SHAPED BY GREENHAM COMMON

Insets: The Club plays for two of the oldest cups in English golf. Both date back to 1874. The Open Challenge Cup (left) was presented by co-founder Captain Dashwood Fowler, and later became known as the Crookham Challenge Cup and, more recently, the Newbury and Crookham medal. The Crookham Handicap Challenge Cup (right), now known as the Newbury & Crookham Bogey, was presented to the Club by Charles Stephens of Reading

The length of a disused aircraft runway at Greenham Common is all that separates the current course at Newbury from the original layout enjoyed by Crookham golfers back in 1873. If the original course had survived its military confiscation, then it would have shared the honour with London Scottish at Wimbledon as being the oldest inland 18-hole course in England.

A July 1873 edition of The Field reported that: "... the golfing links commence at the farther end of the common from Newbury, near the Thatcham Station of the Reading and Hungerford Branch of the Great Western Railway. At an inn known as 'Travellers Friend' on the eastern extremity of the common, a clubroom has been obtained for the use of members, and near this house is the starting point of the links... The Crookham Golf Club numbers at present about 20 members, including most of the gentry whose seats

are in the immediate locality." The journal went on to describe how the course had natural hazards including frequent clumps of gorse and patches of heather.

The Club was co-founded by a Naval officer, Captain Robert Dashwood Fowler, who developed the idea for the Crookham course from his golfing experiences at Westward Ho! in North

Devon, and the Rev. John Scott Ramsay, who had been a student at St Andrews University from 1859 to 1863 and will have played golf on the famous links. Fowler was born in 1814 and joined the Royal Naval College in 1826, spending much of his time on overseas duty, including four years on the Canton River. He retired in 1846 and by the early 1870s had discovered the golf links at Westward Ho! His scores on that course were modest, but Fowler's golfing contacts proved invaluable in helping to develop the game at Crookham.

Early visitors to the course from Westward Ho! included General Wilson, General Vassal and George Gosset, whilst influential visitors from Blackheath included George Glennie, Colonel Kennard and their Professional, Bob Kirk. On the Blackheath visit, The Field reported that: "there were several carriages on the ground full of ladies, and others walked with the players watching the game with much interest. The day was very fine, and the glorious views of the Hampshire hills, with the beautiful woods of Highclere Castle (Lord Carnarvon's) was rendered still more enjoyable by the exhilarating air of the common." The journal added that unusual advantages to Crookham golfers included the presence of three packs of hounds, the Craven, Vine and South Berks, within easy reach

and that there was also good shooting and fishing available locally.

Crookham received a temporary boost in 1874 when T Manzie of St Andrews was appointed as the Club's Professional. He was a competent player and defeated Bob Kirk 2&1 in an early match, but members soon realised that they could not afford their new Professional and he moved on to Blackheath where he took over from Kirk after the latter's return to Scotland.

Golfers at Newbury still play for two of the oldest cups in English golf away from Blackheath. The Open Cup is a scratch tournament which used to attract good players from all over the country. The cup was to be retained by the first golfer who won the competition three times and the Club was keen to avoid this eventuality. Two players from Royal North Devon, George Gosset and Herbert Burn, had both won the cup twice and Crookham sent for another Westward Ho! golfer, the renowned Horace Hutchinson, who was at university in Oxford, to see whether he could prevent either of these two gentlemen

from winning for the third time. Unfortunately for the Club, the plan backfired because Hutchinson went on to win the cup three times in a row!

Reflecting on the matter in his 1914 book 'Fifty Years of Golf', Hutchinson recalled: "On the way back to Oxford there was the inevitable change at Didcot Junction, and there whom should I see, with golf clubs under his arm, but George Gosset? I greeted him and asked with interest where he was going. 'Well', said he, 'there's a cup to be played for at Crookham, near Newbury, tomorrow. I've won it twice and I'm going down to see if I can win it again, because if I do, I keep it.' 'Oh dear,' I had to reply, 'I'm sorry, but I'm afraid you must have made a mistake in the day. It's today it was played for, and what's more I've won it twice too, and I won it again today, so that it's mine now I'm afraid,' and I opened its case, which I had in my hand, and showed it to him!"

Interest in golf at Crookham waned during 1880 and the Club's other prestigious prize, the Crookham Handicap Challenge Cup, was handed over to Westward Ho! where their members continued to play for the trophy which became known as the Crookham Handicap Cup. Another vicar, the Rev. Herbert Henry Skrine helped restart golf on Crookham Common in 1891. This time, play commenced from The Volunteer Inn (now demolished) which was based nearer the road leading up to the hills from Thatcham Station. The Devon club happily returned the old Handicap

Challenge Cup and Hutchinson generously agreed to return his Open Challenge Cup so that the Club regained both of its original trophies.

During the 1890s, Crookham attracted many new members including almost the entire staff of seven masters from the nearby Horris Hill School which prepared children for Winchester College. Albert Henry Evans founded the school and became the Club's first Captain in 1892. He gained rugby and cricket Blues at Oxford and, taking up golf in 1891, was playing off scratch within three years. The Club grew steadily during the early part of the new century, and ladies were first recorded in competition in 1911 when Crookham Ladies lost 4-1 to Winchester.

Golf was suspended during the 1914-18 war and the Club was slow to re-form in peace time. However, following support from the Lord of the Manor, ASB Tull, and the proprietor of The Volunteer Inn, the Club restarted competitions in October 1920. Shortly afterwards, the new and prestigious Newbury District Golf Club was opened within a mile of Crookham Common by a syndicate headed by Col. JA Fairhurst. The Club at Crookham decided to boost membership by attracting local artisans as full members at a modest annual subscription of half a guinea. The Fairhurst Syndicate contracted golf Professionals James

Sherlock and John H Turner to supervise construction of its new course, and in May 1923, these two played in an exhibition match with James Braid and Ted Ray to celebrate the opening of the new links.

The two courses co-existed side-by-side until 1940 when the MOD requisitioned Greenham and Crookham Commons under emergency powers for use as an airfield. The course at Crookham was lost forever whilst the nearby Newbury course survived as it was built on the side of the hill just below the common. The Syndicate struggled financially and during the quiet war years the Newbury members took the opportunity to take over the running of their Club from the investors in 1943.

Initially it was believed that the requisition of the Crookham course was only a short-term measure and the Newbury District Club therefore gave temporary membership to Crookham members during the war. This turned into a permanent arrangement when it became obvious that Crookham golfers would never be able to return to their old course, at which point the combined Club changed its name to the Newbury and Crookham Golf Club.

The Newbury course was constructed over 120 acres of parkland leased from Lloyd H Baxendale who was Lord of the Manor of Greenham and lived at Greenham Lodge. Today's clubhouse is housed in the buildings previously used as the laundry and stables to the lodge. When Baxendale died in 1938, the course was acquired by his nephew, Captain Guy Baxendale, and the Club continued to lease the course until 1952 when it was finally purchased by the members for approximately £7,000. During the War, play continued over just seven holes. The bottom part of the course was used to graze sheep, and concrete and tarmac aircraft taxiways were built over today's first, fourteenth and fifteenth fairways.

Throughout all the changes, Jack Hughes provided reassuring continuity. He arrived at the yet-to-be-opened Newbury District Golf Club in 1923 as a 15-year-old shop assistant to the first Professional, FS Perkins. Hughes never had a golf lesson, but through observation and practice his game progressed to such an extent that the members petitioned to have him appointed as the Club's Professional in 1931 and he served for 46 years before retiring in 1977. Hughes finally stopped playing golf in 1991 and few people can have played such a central role in the successful development of an individual golf club.

Today's course is relatively short, but the undulating hillside means that several uphill holes play much longer than they measure, whilst sloping lies, dog-legs and woodland also add complexity. Myxomatosis in the 1950s killed most of the rabbit population which led to the growth of trees in previously open areas on the course. For several years after the Second World War, the first fairway was covered with more than an acre of solid concrete left over from the old aircraft runway. The suggestions book at the time included a proposal that the broken concrete should be sprayed green to cut down on the amount of time spent looking for balls!

The third hole is an attractive downhill par-3. Originally, golfers also had to contend with a

stream running in front of the green, but in 1952 the Air Ministry decided that the flow of water off the enlarged runways would wash away the banks of the stream and the water course was piped instead. Ten German Prisoners of War helped the Club to recover the four holes (fourth, fifth, seventh and eighth) at the bottom of the hill which had been used for agriculture during the war. The second nine is longer and contains two tricky par-3s at the fifteenth and seventeenth holes with difficult angles off the tiger tees. The fourteenth and fifteenth were covered in concrete during the war, and subsequent reparations were helped by swapping concrete required for new roads in nearby expanding Newbury with the top soil displaced by the development.

For a long period in the 20th Century the course was next to the heart of Britain's defence operations and many American military personnel won Newbury and Crookham competitions whilst serving at the airbase. 96 cruise missiles were moved to Greenham Common in 1980 and the Peace Campers became a regular feature on news programmes. Fortunately times have changed, fences have been removed around the airbase and golfers can once again enjoy a round without the sinister reminder of the nearby military fortifications.

Inset: Jack Hughes started work at the new Newbury Club in 1923 before the course opened and he spent his whole working life with the Club, much of it as the Professional, before finally retiring in 1977 (Courtesy of Newbury & Crookham Golf Club)

WEST LANCASHIRE

BUFFETED BY MERSEY WINDS

The inaugural meeting of the Club was held in the Seaforth Hotel in June 1873 and was attended by Messrs Kerr, Watson, Duncan, MacKinlay, Roberts, Grieve and Miln. The names demonstrate the key Scottish influence and the new Club adopted the St Andrews rules from the outset.

The first subscription was ten shillings per year and no entrance fee was charged to the first 40 members. Later joiners paid a ten shillings entry fee. The Field magazine in July 1874 wrote: "We are not astonished to see that a new golf club has been started near Liverpool. The success of the Royal Liverpool Golf Club has been so

great, there is every chance of another club being of service to the district...The course consists of nine holes, some of them at present are rather rough, but the general opinion is that a little play will make it a very good green. The Club has been well supported by the members of the Hoylake Club..."

Strictly speaking, the present course does not share any of the original 9-hole layout, but golf has always been played in the vicinity of Hall Road. Over the years, the Club has made a number of land swaps with the Blundell family's estate, moving gradually seaward to the west of the Liverpool to Southport railway line as the nearby town developed and land values increased. The Club still plays over land covered by several leases from the Blundell estate. The original 9-hole course of 1873 was all inland from the railway line. By 1880, the course had grown to eighteen holes on the inland side, and by 1921 the Club had traded land with the estate and moved some of the holes to the seaward side of the railway. This new land was only accessible by railway footbridge which proved a serious impediment to any plans for hosting major championships.

West Lancashire Ladies' Golf Club was formed in 1891 and for some time played over a separate 18-hole ladies' course situated to the seaward side of the railway. Sand encroachment during the Second World War reduced the ladies' links to nine holes and their separate course was finally abandoned during a later reorganisation. The ladies now play off the red tees over the same course as the men, unlike the arrangement at neighbouring Formby which still maintains two separate courses.

The Club is famous for its connection with the British Amateur Championship. West Lancashire was one of 24 clubs contributing to the cost of the original championship trophy, and the first winner in 1885 was Allan Macfie, who was a member of both the West Lancashire and Royal Liverpool golf clubs.

In Harold Hilton, the Club had as its Secretary someone whom Golf Illustrated described in 1901 as: "A past master of the art of golf." It continued: "... what he does not know about the game is not worth knowing. As a golfer there have been few to equal him and fewer still, perhaps none, have excelled him as his record shows." Hilton played as a representative of Royal Liverpool at all his championships, but between 1900 and 1902 he was also the official paid Secretary at West Lancashire. The minutes of April 1901 note that: "...permission was granted to the Secretary (Mr. HH Hilton) to play in the various Club matches which were shortly to take place and also the Amateur and

Open Championships provided that the absence did not interfere with his duties." The minutes from the following meeting noted: "The Captain (JE Pearson) proposed and Mr. Clark seconded a vote of congratulations to the Secretary on his recent success in the Amateur Championship at St Andrews which was carried unanimously." Hilton's Amateur Championship record is unrivalled. Between 1887 and 1927 he entered 33 times, winning on four occasions and being runner-up three times. In 1911, he won the US Amateur Championship in the same year as winning the home tournament at Prestwick. Competing against the Professionals, he won the Open Championship of 1892 at Muirfield and 1897 at nearby Hoylake.

The Club was extremely important during this era and attracted all the top Professionals to various exhibition matches. In July 1901, the Club hosted a 36-hole invitation match which was won by JH Taylor,

with James Braid coming second, Alex Herd third and Harry Vardon fourth. The Club's early Professionals also featured prominently in national competitions. Sandy Herd was Professional in 1891/2 and won the 1902 Open at Hoylake, becoming the first Open Champion to use the new Haskell rubber-cored ball which he hated as being a foreign invention. Arthur Havers was Professional from 1920-1923 and in 1923 won The Open at Troon defeating the holder, Walter Hagen, by one stroke. More recently, West Lancashire has helped the cream rise to the top. In hosting the final qualifier for the 1976 Open at Royal Birkdale, four young Europeans competed; Sandy Lyle, Nick Faldo, Bernard Langer and Ian Woosnam, all of whom went on to win the US Masters. Faldo was in his first year as a Professional and led the qualifiers with 141 (72 + 69).

Peter Richard Parkinson will also remember a round at West Lancashire. He was Assistant Professional at the Club and in 1972 scored the longest hole-in-one in the British Isles at the 378-yard par-4 seventh hole. The November 2002 edition of Golf World described this as: "...one of the most stupendous shots ever hit in golf."

Although by nature a links course, there are some spectacular sights. Huge ships leaving the Mersey Estuary appear to be almost on the course and the weather can turn quickly from sunny calm to thundering gales.

The course is an excellent test of links golf. The fairways are spongy and well-maintained and the greens run true. The first four holes stretch in a northerly direction away from the clubhouse with the following five holes returning; it is therefore unlikely that players will have enjoyed favourable wind conditions for more than half of the first nine holes. The second nine are slightly more inland and sheltered apart from the thirteenth which is often played into the teeth of the wind. The eleventh is the longest hole and out of bounds beckons as the railway is immediately to the right of the fairway. The fourteenth and fifteenth are both dog-legs and are protected by wooded banks from the worst of the weather, and the final three holes are a good and testing mix of long and short holes.

As the Club is proud to claim: "...if you can play well at West Lancashire Golf Club, you can play well anywhere."

SEATON CAREW

22 HOLES AND 4 LAYOUTS

Seaton Carew is an excellent, traditional seaside links with 22 holes offering a choice of four different courses. The old layout was lengthened in the 1920s following a remark by Bernard Darwin in his book 'Golf Courses of Great Britain' that Seaton was: "grand golfing country but there was not quite enough of it." Dr. Alister MacKenzie advised the Club to abandon some of the inland holes and build four replacement holes on the sandy land which had become available on the eastward side.

Four more new holes were constructed in 1974 using compensation awarded during construction of the Ekofisk Oil Pipeline which runs under the course. The Club anticipated that it would lose part of the course to industrial development but planning regulations prevented any construction within proximity of the new nuclear power station and the Club has benefited from the flexibility The original or Old course measures over 6,600 yards, but the Club is able to stretch the Brabazon layout to test the leading players with an inward nine measuring nearly 3,900 yards.

Seaton was started by Dr. McCuaig who arrived in Middlesbrough to practise medicine shortly after winning The R&A's Gold Medals in 1867 and 1869. At the time, there were very few courses in England and none in the district. The doctor identified the sandy dunes known as The Snooks and belonging to Lord Eldon, which stretched away from the village of Seaton Carew towards the River Tees, as a place where he could practise his skills. McCuaig persuaded a few locals to join him and in 1874 they established the Durham & Yorkshire Golf Club which was renamed as Seaton Carew in 1887.

Unfortunately, the doctor died of typhoid fever and congestion of the lungs in 1891, but by then the Club was well established and the momentum was maintained by the first President, Major Matthew Gray, whose family shipping business employed more than 4,000 people. Gray also ran the Seaton Carew Iron Works and

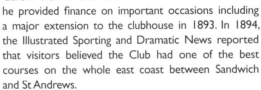

he provided finance on important occasions including a major extension to the clubhouse in 1893. In 1894, the Illustrated Sporting and Dramatic News reported that visitors believed the Club had one of the best courses on the whole east coast between Sandwich and St Andrews.

Gray also died young, in 1896 aged 46, but then the Club had appointed its third key individual, the

Inset: Dr. David McCuaig was the founder and first Captain

Below: The teams from Seaton Carew and Lytham & St Annes assembled for the match between the two top teams in the North of England in September 1895. The Lytham team was strengthened by the inclusion of John Ball Junior (front row, third from right), and Harold Hilton (front row, second from right), who were top Hoylake golfers as well as honorary members at Lytham. The Club's Professional, James Kay, is standing on the left and two of the Club's top players are seated in the front row, R Balfour (second from left) and G Pyman (smoking on right)

Above: The well-bunkered hole named Jimmy Kay after the Club's long-time Professional, with the cranes and chimneys of the Tees Estuary visible in the background

Inset: Club Professional Bert Reveley (left) and Peter Salmon (tall figure to Reveley's left) beat Walter Hagen (under the umbrella and standing next to the Hon. Sec wearing a trilby) and fellow US Professional Joe Kirkwood by one hole during an exhibition match in 1937

Secretary, Charles J. Bunting, whose family have played an important role at Seaton Carew for more than a century. CJ's son, Gilbert, joined the Club in 1900 and played an active role until his death in 1967. As an official of the EGU he achieved the remarkable feat of refereeing six successive Ryder Cup matches. Gilbert's son, Edward, joined Seaton in the late 1940s. He masterminded the centenary celebrations in 1974 and acted as Captain in 1975 and again in 2000.

In 1886, the Club appointed a top Scottish Professional, James Kay, to replace Tom Park. Kay beat JH Taylor, James Braid and reigning Open Champion Jack White in separate matches at Seaton, and in a 72-hole match against his local Teeside rival played across the river at Redcar, Kay beat Chisholm, the Cleveland Professional, 25-up with 24 to play! Kay retired aged 73 in 1927, but within two weeks he had died of septicaemia contracted some five months previously from a splinter in his right thumb acquired whilst chopping old sleepers for the clubhouse fire. The coroner left the matter of compensation to be pursued between Kay's relatives and the Club's insurers.

The Club has a fine tradition of golf matches, tournaments and competitions starting in 1895 with a home match against a team from Lytham & St Annes which had been specially strengthened by the inclusion of John Ball Junior and Harold Hilton from Hoylake.

Edward, Prince of Wales, played at Seaton Carew in 1930, and later in the decade Walter Hagen visited the Club with fellow American Joe Kirkwood during their tour of Europe. Hagen thought that Seaton was not an easy course and commented that: "it provides a good test of golf and is one that I should like to play quite often." 40 years later, Nick Faldo was the joint-leading Professional in a Pro-Am held in 1976, and Peter Baker was joint-winner of the Brabazon Trophy hosted by the Club in 1985.

Seaton is an enjoyable links capable of hosting important championships. As one of the 50 oldest clubs in the world, it also oozes nostalgia.

SOUTHFIELD – OXFORD UNIVERSITY

OXFORD CITY

Golf was played on or close to the current practice area in the 1870s, but a serious fire in 1981 destroyed most of the older records and some of the Club's early history is rather murky. The name Southfield Golf Club is an umbrella term for the company that now administers the course and plays host to three clubs, Oxford University, Oxford City and Oxford Ladies. The 1886 Ordnance Survey map shows a Southfield Farm where today's clubhouse is located which explains the origin of the name.

University golfers played over the neighbouring land at Cowley Marsh in the early 1870s and graduate members of the University created a formal Club there in 1875. Although golf continued on the marsh throughout the 1880s, conditions were frequently poor, and in 1889 the University alumni also played over a 9-hole course at Morrell Park. University golfers held sway in the early years and there was a distinct social stratum of golfers on the marsh, starting with the Graduate members, then Undergraduates followed by Temporary members and finally Supernumerary (i.e. extra) members who were brought in from the local community to help with financing and who were later to become known as Oxford City golfers.

In the 1890s, the University continued to look for better courses and, after Morrell Park, moved first to South Hinksey (west of Cowley) then to Radley (further south), followed by Frilford (south-west of Oxford) before finally moving back to Southfield which at least had the advantage of proximity to the town and to the University itself. Golf on the original nine holes at Cowley Marsh could only be played in the Winter, as in Summer, twelve college cricket grounds with

their related pavilions were in regular use. The course was straightforward and Harry Vardon once played it in 27 shots, 10 under par after nine holes in today's terms! Oxford City golfers stayed at Cowley whilst the University Clubs were wandering, and in 1895, JW (Joe) Gynes, the Oxford City golf handicapper and Magdalen College servant, was appointed Permanent Secretary to the Oxford University Golf Club.

In 1898, the Rev. Georgie Moore of Cowley gave permission for the Cowley course to be extended away from the marsh and to be increased to eighteen holes, provided that a donation was made to Cowley Church School. It is believed that this extension was implemented by James Braid. By 1923, Harry Colt had overseen a further extension to 33 holes, constituting a supplementary or relief Green Course of fifteen holes built to augment the 18-hole Red Course.

Below: The University teams faced formidable opposition. This photograph, dated October 1927, pictures the University players pitted against JH Taylor's team (he is seated 2nd from right in the front row) which included Arthur Havers (front row, 2nd from left), Henry Cotton (back row, 4th from right), Alex Herd (back row 6th from right), Ted Ray (back row, 3rd from left) together with the Whitcombe Brothers

Main: *Players on the green at the uphill par-3 twelfth hole, rated by Henry Longhurst as:"one of the best holes in English golf."*

Inset: *1923 map of the course at the time when there were 33 holes, including the 15-hole Green relief course which has since been lost to development. The fifth hole on the main course (near the Old Oxford and Bucks Light Infantry Barracks) is believed to be the oldest surviving section of the course*

The opening of these Oxford University New Golf Links was celebrated in October 1923 by an exhibition match pitting Cyril Tolley and Roger Wethered against Messrs MacKintosh and Nall-Cain who were respectively Captain and Honorary Secretary of the Oxford University Golf Club. During the 1920s, the University played matches against the cream of the country's top professional golfers and photographs of many of these matches are displayed in the clubhouse.

In the early 1930s, Southfield School was built on part of the relief course and the Club reverted back to eighteen holes with a similar layout to that played today. Today's fifth hole appears to be the only one remaining from Braid's 1898 course. Proof that the Oxford City Club was still the junior club at Southfield after the First War is contained in a June 1918 minute which included a request to the University Golf Club for permission for Oxford City to be allowed to play golf on Sundays. This was granted in June 1919 for play in the afternoons, with full Sunday play being allowed sometime between 1920 and 1930.

During the early 1920s, Oxford City golfers continued as Supernumerary members playing the supplementary Green Course and final equality, achieved around the end of the decade, will have been helped by WR Morris

who became President of the Oxford City Club in 1925, playing off a thirteen handicap. Morris had started with a small cycle repairing business and in 1910 he designed a car which could be produced cheaply. This led to the establishment of Morris Motors Ltd at nearby Cowley. Morris was knighted in 1929, endowed Nuffield College, Oxford in 1937, and became Viscount Nuffield in 1938. He was President of the Oxford City Club for 37 years between 1925 and 1963.

Golfers at Southfield were fortunate to enjoy the services of FH Taylor as Professional for 42 years following Colt's completion of the extended course in 1923. Nationally, Taylor served as Captain of the British PGA and he was able to summon a galaxy of famous professionals to test the University sides. JH Taylor's team of October 1927 included the great man himself along with Henry Cotton, Ted Ray, Charles and Ernest Whitcombe and Arthur Havers, winner of The Open in 1923. George Duncan played in the 1928 fixture.

The strategic importance of the nearby Morris Motors factory during the Second World War meant that rocket guns were deployed on Cowley Marsh and a barrage balloon was sited almost opposite the clubhouse. A local rule surviving through to the 1960s gave a free drop from its base. Land requisitioned for the war effort was finally returned in 1961 when the second hole reverted to being a par-4 rather than a shorter par-3.

At one stage during Lord Nuffield's tenure as President, Oxford City had a theoretical voting majority on the Committee over the University Club. Southfield's 1946 Articles entitled Lord Nuffield to appoint a Director, so that the Board at the time consisted of four Oxford City members, four Oxford University members, and Lord Nuffield's representative who was always from the Oxford City Club. The relevant article was removed in 1969.

Southfield today is a surprisingly green parkland oasis belying the approach through a crowded residential area. Oxford's famous dreaming spires are visible from the fourth tee, and Henry Longhurst, the great TV commentator and former University golfer, described the par-3 twelfth hole as "one of the best holes in English golf."

BRAMSHAW

FOREST COURSE

The Forest Course at Brook in the New Forest was started in 1880 by a retired Royal Navy Lieutenant, Philip Augustus Champion de Crespigny, who lived in Roundhill overlooking the current eighteenth green. In the early days, de Crespigny and a few colleagues, notably Admiral Aitchison and John Jeffries played over a rough 5-hole course. De Crespigny wrote in the 1907 edition of Country Life magazine of how the original: "... so-called greens had hardly known a roller, the course was sousing wet, with no drains, in fact the whole place was as unlike a golf course as it could be."

De Crespigny's private golfing arrangements continued for a decade, but in 1890 he sought permission to build a formal course. Rights over land in the New Forest are complex but permission was granted and gradual improvements, including drainage, were made to the layout which had grown to nine holes at the turn of the century. By the late 1880s, most golfers wanted to play a full round of eighteen different holes, so discussions were held with another 9-hole course at neighbouring Lyndhurst and it was agreed to merge the two clubs, creating the New Forest Golf Club. Entrance fees and first-year subscriptions were set at 10/6d each and players were required to ride a horse or take a pony and trap to cover the five-mile journey if they wished to play a full round of eighteen different holes.

The Club's Gold Medal commenced in 1890 and was played at different courses in alternate months. The first official competition played over the Forest Course was won by de Crespigny who, playing off scratch, scored 174 (47-46-38-43) over four rounds of the 9-hole course. Subsequent medal rounds were shortened to 18-hole competitions. The journey between the two

courses was not ideal, and in Spring 1907 de Crespigny received permission to burn a section of the adjoining furzy waste in order to create a further nine holes on the Forest Course at Brook.

Cricket has been connected with Bramshaw Golf Club from the outset. Bramshaw Cricket Club was established in 1877 on the ground next to the current eighteenth fairway although the local church vestry minutes refer to cricket being played as early as 1859. The two clubs have shared many members and have also had a mutual interest in maintaining playing rights over the Forest common land.

The New Forest itself was established as a royal hunting ground in 1079 by William the Conqueror and local farmers were prevented from fencing land around their properties. As hunting declined over the following centuries, the local population enjoyed various common rights over the Forest and these were finally registered by a Parliamentary Commission in 1858. The six rights

were of pasture (for ponies, donkeys and cattle); estover (the collection of firewood); marl (removing clay to improve agricultural land); turbary (cutting peat for fuel); mast (Autumn grazing for pigs), and the right to graze sheep. Most of the rights are still exercised today by Commoners occupying land and property enjoying these entitlements, and there is no doubt that ponies have been responsible for maintaining the course as it is enjoyed today.

Philip de Crespigny died in 1912 and shortly afterwards it was decided to re-establish separate courses at Brook and Lyndhurst. Roundhill was sold to Major RCH Sloane-Stanley in 1913 and the Major, who was also a Director of both Chelsea and Southampton football clubs, was appointed President and Captain of the Club in that year. After the Great War, the Club considered employing Harry Colt to advise on course improvements. However his original estimate of £750 was rejected as was his revised proposal for piecemeal changes, and the Club decided to limit improvements to the first tee and the eighteenth green. The Club was run frugally during the inter-war years. In October 1932 it was agreed to install an Aladdin lamp in the clubhouse and two small lamps in the dressing rooms, but even

in 1951 it was still necessary to seek donations before electric lights could be installed.

In 1953, a limited company was formed, under the effective control of Sir Oliver Crosthwaite-Eyre and his family, to take over the affairs of the Club and since then it has enjoyed more financial security. A second course, the Manor, was built on the neighbouring private parkland in 1970 and today's clubhouse was built in 1983.

The King's Garn Gutter stream and its tributaries have a major effect on many holes on the Forest Course. The third green lies immediately behind the stream, the fifth green is at the bottom of a steep bank with the stream immediately behind, and the sixth green is also protected by water.

The twelfth is an attractive short hole and the only one with bunkers, whilst the fourteenth known locally as Rustlers' Oak is reputed to be the site of the last criminal to be hung in chains in England. The fallen tree to the left of this fairway is an eerie reminder of those times. Ponies are everywhere on the course and the view back down the final fairway taken from near Roundhill gives a good idea of why Philip de Crespigny devoted so much of his later life to developing the Forest Course.

FELIXSTOWE FERRY

SURVIVING ADVERSITY

F ew clubs can have faced and beaten such adversity. Informal golf was first played at nearby Langer Common and Languard Fort during the 1870s, and the Felixstowe Club can trace its own formal origins back to 1880. Until then, London-based golfers from the Blackheath and London Scottish/Wimbledon Common clubs looking for seaside links had either to travel to Devon or the North of England.

In the Spring of 1880, Lord Elcho, General Lee Hope Grant and the Professional, Tom Dunn, from the London Scottish Club visited Old Felixstowe and laid out a basic course at the east end, towards the passenger ferry linking Felixstowe to Bawdsey across the Deben Estuary. At Whitsun, more Wimbledon golfers tried the new links and on August Bank Holiday a party from London Scottish cut nine holes and played for a Challenge Gold Medal. The winner, GF Muir, presented the medal to Felixstowe Golf Club on its formation in October that year. The trophy was originally known as the Wimbledon Gold Medal, but subsequently became known as the Bawdsey Challenge Gold Medal. The Club's records show that the two great Wimbledon stalwarts, Henry Lamb and Dr. Laidlaw Purves, were also founder members at Felixstowe. In March 1881, Tom Dunn laid out an 18-hole links starting at the 'T' Martello Tower.

Lord Elcho's influence was greatly enhanced by the Club's first Patron, Colonel George Tomline. The Colonel hosted frequent partridge-shooting parties on his estate at Orwell Park which were attended by Elcho. Tomline founded the nearby port of Felixstowe in 1875 and his railway, the Felixstowe

Railway and Pier Company, ran passenger trains from Westerfield, near Ipswich, to Felixstowe.

The Colonel was also responsible for organising the Tomline Wall flood defence which is now owned by the Environment Agency and separates the main Felixstowe course from the new 9-hole Kingsfleet links. As landowner, Tomline authorised the cutting of bunkers, and in 1884, the use of East End House as what is still the clubhouse. Previously, Lord Elcho had used his influence with the War Office to enable the Club to occupy the 'T' Martello tower which still dominates the course.

Above: Player on the tenth green at dusk with the 'T' Martello tower in the background

Inset: The original ladies' clubhouse can just be seen to the right of the Martello tower in this early picture of the links. The building and all of the early ladies' course was lost to the sea during the early 20th Century

The early members were ambitious and in 1883 they appointed Willie Fernie as the Club's Professional. Fernie had been runner-up in the 1882 Open and won the 1883 Open after a play-off against Bob Ferguson, the 1882 Champion. Bernard Darwin, who played at Felixstowe as a boy, wrote in 1946 that: "Willie Fernie...was a beautiful, easy and graceful golfer with an air of almost insolent confidence. I can see him very plainly coming out of his shop by the Martello Tower (a little paradise of pitch and cobblers' wax and divine scents), a white apron around his waist, a shiny-peaked yachting cap sat rakishly on his head, in his hand a half-finished driver which he waggles lovingly and knowingly."

Unfortunately, Dunn's original 18-hole course of 1881 soon became too congested and dangerous. The course was initially reduced to fifteen holes and further reductions followed so that by the outbreak of war in 1914 it had become known as: "the best 9-hole golf green in

Above: Lord Elcho, son of the founder, and FW Wilson watching the Hon. AJ Balfour driving in 1888

Inset: Willie Fernie won the Open Championship in 1883 at Royal Musselburgh whilst attached to Dumfries, and became the Professional at Felixstowe between 1883 and 1887

the world." This course was then almost completely destroyed to make way for a rifle range to train Kitchener's new army of volunteers, and by 1920 the local press described the former course and clubhouse as: "a scene of desolation."

Happily, a number of influential people, mainly locals, determined to rescue matters and James Braid was engaged to reconstruct and expand the course back to eighteen holes. The Club struggled to finance this major reconstruction and matters were made worse by several bouts of serious sea flooding. With the approach of the Second World War, the course was devastated again by defence forces as the land was viewed as being particularly vulnerable to invasion. The links were covered with pill boxes, barbed wire and gun emplacements and troops were billeted in the clubhouse. Fortunately, the course was again reconstructed, this time under the supervision of Henry Cotton, the three-times Open Champion, and Sir Guy Campbell. The official reopening was delayed by heavy flooding in March 1949 and the course was once more completely inundated during the disastrous East Coast floods of 1953.

Sea flooding and coastal erosion continued during the 1960s and many current members recall a short par-3 hole to the east of the Martello Tower. This was totally lost to the sea and a replacement, the fifth, has been added to correct the balance of the course. Flooding struck again in 1979, and in 1987 coastal erosion in the nearby village led to the construction of a further sea defence.

Felixstowe's lady golfers faired even worse. Their original 6-hole course and separate clubhouse were completely lost to the sea. The old wooden clubhouse, occupied in 1894, can just be seen on the seaward side of the Martello Tower in the early picture of the course.

The Club enjoyed the patronage of the Rt. Hon. Arthur Balfour, MP during the late 1880s and he was Captain in 1889. At that time, the town was the height of fashion and the local chemist advertised the Golf Club Bouquet in the local guide book as being:

"...without doubt the sweetest and most delightful perfume extant. Quite the fashion with Felixstowe visitors. Possesses a delicacy of odour which is very fascinating at 2/6d a bottle."

The view from the clubhouse today gives a poignant window on British history. In addition to the East Coast sea erosion and the Martello towers which were built in 1806 as a defence against a possible Napoleonic invasion, the building on the far side of the estuary, Bawdsey Manor, housed Sir Robert Watson-Watt's radar research team. Bawdsey Manor became the first Radar station in 1937 and formed a key part of the Chain Home and Chain Home Low systems which gave warning of potential enemy action, and provided the RAF with vital information during the Battle of Britain. The historic, strategic importance of the golf course at Felixstowe Ferry cannot be overestimated.

The surrounds to the course are also an important wildlife refuge. Hares, water voles, stoats, weasels, field mice, grass snakes, slow worms and common lizards are all found in the area near the Tomline wall.

The course is not particularly long but the onshore winds can be seen in the shape of the trees around the links. The thirteenth and fifteenth holes on the seaward side of the road feature out of bounds intended to steer shots away from people on the sea wall, whilst several holes inland of the road are affected by challenging ditches and other water hazards. The twelfth is particularly unusual, requiring a tee shot over wire netting towards the clubhouse. This barrier is there to protect cars as they come round a blind corner immediately to the right of the tee.

Felixstowe Ferry has recently produced several fine lady players, perhaps helped by shot-making honed in the frequently windy conditions, including England internationals Joanne Hockley and Julie Wade who had a successful record in five Curtis Cup matches between 1988 and 1996.

Main: Putting in the shadows

Inset: Lady members outside their old clubhouse before it was lost to the sea. Men were able to get drinks from the hut but had to observe the notice which advised that: "Gentlemen are asked, instead of applying at the front door, to order their refreshments at the south veranda window where they will find a bell for summoning the attendant"

KINGSDOWN

LEGEND OF THE THREE KINGS

*Above: The Club logo honours
the legend of the three kings*

Kingsdown Golf Club is situated on beautiful and historic downland some five miles east of Bath. Two tumuli, which were excavated in the 1930s, are clearly visible on the fifteenth and sixteenth fairways and archaeologists found broken pottery from the Neanderthal, Bronze and Iron Age periods. Legend tells that three ancient kings have been buried on Kingsdown and that the standing stones on the sixteenth fairway commemorate those leaders. The Club has honoured the legend and incorporated the three crowns into its logo.

Manorial Rights over Kingsdown were enjoyed by the Northey family, and Major Northey was the instigator of the inaugural meeting of the Club which was held in the Swan Inn at Kingsdown in February 1880. Four generations of the family have served as Presidents of the Club.

A contemporary report on the land from John Allan, the Professional at Westward Ho!, concluded that: "I have no hesitation in saying that they are by far the best inland links I have ever seen. The turf is good, there are plenty of hazards and each hole is interesting." It is likely that this first course was of nine holes, played twice for a full round.

The Field magazine reported that the first prize meeting of the Club had been fixed for two days in May 1880: "The first ball will be struck each day at 10.30am and competitors will be allowed to start up to 3pm. There is an excellent train from Paddington at 9am which will enable players to reach the ground by 12 o'clock; but they must be careful to get into the slip carriage for Chippenham and change there for Box Station. There are trains out from Bath at 9.15 and 12." The notice continued: "A dinner will be held in Bath on the evening

of Wednesday, 12th, tickets 6/6d. There is every promise of a successful meeting, several prominent scratch players having noted their intention of being present."

The Open Silver Cup on the first day was won with a gross score of 97 by R Molesworth of Royal North Devon playing off four, and he also won the Club Challenge Tankard on the following day despite his handicap being cut to scratch overnight! Famous golfing members in the early days of the Club included Colonel EH Kennard of The R&A and Royal Blackheath, Horace Hutchinson, WH Fowler who designed Walton Heath, and John Dunn who was also a member at Royal Liverpool.

Early golfers travelled widely and Kingsdown showed flexibility in changing its plans for the 1881 season. The Field reported: "The change from an October to a Summer meeting has been made on the suggestion of a prominent Westward Ho! player and it is hoped that the date will suit those who are going north for the grouse shooting. An additional inducement for them to go via Bath is offered by the Worcestershire Golf Club, who hold their first Open prize meeting on August 9th and 10th."

Although the turf was good, Kingsdown, in pre-automobile days was not a convenient location for Bath residents and towards the end of 1881 the Club opened a second course at the Warren above Bath city centre which is now part of Bath Golf Club. Kingsdown's 1883 AGM approved a name change to The Bath and Kingsdown Golf Club to reflect this two-course arrangement and play at Kingsdown itself became intermittent. However, in November 1890 the Field announced that: "...we learn that the Kingsdown Golf Club has been revived ...Accommodation has been secured at Ford's Farm,

opposite which is the teeing ground for the first hole. Some progress has already been made with the greens, while the rest of the course makes good golf without any assistance from man." Flags would be placed in the holes on Thursdays and Saturdays, but if any player needed flags on other days then they were asked to write to Ford who would make the necessary arrangements for a fee of 6d.

The Club's accounts for 1893/4 show that membership was still very small. There were 29 family subscriptions, 22 singles, seven Honorary Members from Bath Golf Club, one non-resident member and only 3 'strangers play' (green fees in modern terms) all year. The 1896 AGM reaffirmed that the Club should continue to exist and in an early example of marketing, notices were to be placed in the main hotels in Bath inviting visitors to play the links for 2/6d per day or 7/6d for the week. Fairways in the early days were maintained by sheep, goats, cattle, ponies and donkeys, but the Club did spend time and money on the greens and occasionally a horse-drawn roller was used.

The clubhouse in the early 20th Century was situated in the Lower Kingsdown Road immediately below the course. The building still exists as a private dwelling today, although the Club itself moved to its present premises on top of the Downs in 1923. The course was expanded from nine holes to twelve holes in 1925, and in 1931 a further six holes were added, playing over leased land to the south-east of the present course. The leased land was requisitioned for food production during the Second World War and the Club struggled financially when play was resumed over the remaining twelve holes after the war.

Fortunately, matters improved during the 1960s and the course was expanded back to eighteen holes in 1969. This was a major operation, planned by CK Cotton, and actually required fourteen new holes, six new greens and ten new tees in order to fit eighteen holes into the tight confines of the Down. Excellent views of Bath can be seen from the twelfth and thirteenth holes although the surrounding trees to the west of the course now obscure some of the sights enjoyed by the founders back in 1880.

The area is a wildlife haven. Three species of owl patrol the course, roe and muntjac deer are seen regularly, and slow worms and grass snakes are also found. The area is famous for stone quarrying and it is reputed that the mine shaft opposite the Swan Inn in the nearby village stretches underground for one and a half miles. Doubtless, miners and pit ponies have been hard at work under the ground now occupied by the course. The Club's own book celebrating 120 years of golf summarises the position well: "For the club golfer, Kingsdown's course is excellent. It is like a good claret: challenging, but not fearsome; interesting, but not artificial; always presented in near perfect conditions, it has an excellent after-taste no matter what the score!"

Main: *Legend tells that the three standing stones on the sixteenth fairway commemorate three ancient kings*

Inset: *The house in the village named after its former use as Kingsdown's clubhouse*

BATH

SHAM CASTLE

Bath Golf Club shares its earliest history with the club at Kingsdown situated a few miles further east and away from the city centre. It soon became apparent that the Kingsdown course was inconvenient to Bath residents and visitors intending to travel by train, and so local golfers decided to open a separate course on land known as The Warren, on Bath's Hampton Down, situated within a mile from the city centre.

At one time the Down was owned by the philanthropist, Ralph Allen, who arranged for the mining of the soft yellow limestone which is a hallmark of Bath. The stone was moved down the hill via an old railway track and then loaded onto barges and taken into the city via the River Avon and its associated canals. In 1762, Allen arranged for Richard Jones to construct the folly known locally as Sham Castle which stands close to today's clubhouse. The front of the folly, looking towards the city, is beautifully finished and contrasts with the rear which is less ornate in design.

The course at Hampton Down is first mentioned in the minutes of a meeting held in November 1881 at

which a budget of £2 14/- was sanctioned to pay for the cutting of nine holes on The Warren. The following February it was agreed that ES Maskely would look after the Club's interests at Kingsdown whilst Dr. Williams would do the same over the new links on Hampton Down. Unfortunately, plans to hold an Autumn Meeting on the Down had to be postponed as the grass was too long and as a result the tenant farmer agreed that, in future, the golfers would be allowed to mow an acre of grass for greens and make other improvements for an annual consideration of £4.

In March 1883, the Club name was changed from Kingsdown Golf Club to the Bath and Kingsdown Golf Club and this continued until February 1890 when a further alteration was made to Bath Golf Club, reflecting that the Kingsdown course had been resuscitated as a separate organisation.

The ladies of Bath enjoyed their own separate course at Hampton Down which was situated just to the north of the area bounded by the first, second, third and fifth holes of today's course. The very best ladies were also allowed to play on the gentlemen's course provided that they had a handicap of six or better. This strict hurdle was later raised to fourteen but only after most lady golfers had suffered an upwards handicap revision of up to ten shots which actually had the effect of reducing the number of ladies playing on the main course!

In an early act of 'generosity', the minutes of a meeting in March 1902 state that: "It was proposed by Dr. GA Bannatyne and seconded by Major Anderson that leave be given to the Somerset Ladies' County Club to play on the Gentlemen's links on Monday 21st

April for their competition with Hampshire Ladies". In 1905, the men were even more magnanimous and agreed that ladies who were to represent the Club should be allowed to play on the Gentlemen's course for a fortnight prior to the event subject to payment of a green fee of 2/6d per week. They were careful to stipulate that this dispensation was restricted to six ladies who would also have to obtain the appropriate certificate from the Honorary Secretary of the Ladies' Club.

Annual subscriptions for men in 1891 were a guinea and an extra 5 shillings appears to have been charged to all members for the annual cost of cleaning clubs. Apart from the costs of rent and the Greenkeeper's wages, the biggest expense disclosed in the accounts for that year was the £5 14/3d paid to Mary Ruddock for putting out the flags on the course.

The 1893 AGM gave approval for the expansion of the course to eighteen holes and Tom Dunn, who was at the time the Professional at the now defunct club at Tooting Bec near London, was asked to advise on changes to the existing nine holes and on the construction of the new nine which were intended to occupy the whole of the remaining part of the

Hampton Down, excluding the land then occupied by the Volunteer Rifle Range. The rather dangerous proximity of golfers and bullets was a feature on a number of early golf courses!

The Club's early close links with the Royal North Devon club were useful in the appointment of the new Professional, J Hearn Junior, who arrived at Bath from North Devon following the specific recommendation of Westward Ho! member TG Heathiste. The conflicts between the early Professionals' two roles of course maintenance and tuition were well demonstrated by Hearn's contract which stipulated the following terms:

1) Salary of 20 shillings a week;
2) To attend greens (18 holes) with one man to assist;
3) To give professional advice at 1/6d per nine holes and 2/6d for the whole round of 18 holes, but no instruction to be given until 1pm up to which time the greens should have to be usefully looked after.

Hearn left for the United States in 1899 and was replaced by W East who had built a good reputation during his six years at the Abergavenny Golf Club in Monmouthshire, Wales. Harry Vardon and JH Taylor

Main: View from the tee of the short par-3 fourteenth hole played over an old quarry which has been designated as a Site of Special Scientific Interest and contains protected bat caves

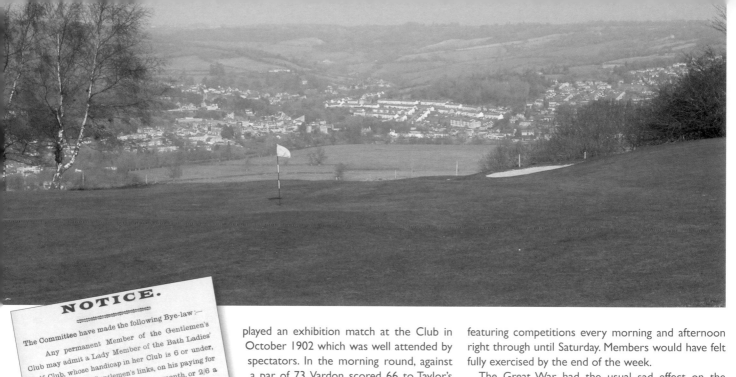

Main: *Winter green at the par-4 fifth with far-reaching views over the outer areas of the city*

Inset: *In November 1892, the men graciously allowed ladies with a handicap of six or better to play over their course. This handicap level was later increased to fourteen, but only after most ladies' handicaps had been raised by ten shots!*

played an exhibition match at the Club in October 1902 which was well attended by spectators. In the morning round, against a par of 73, Vardon scored 66 to Taylor's 74. In the afternoon, both players shot 70. The Club made a profit of £3 12/9d from the match which was held in trust and carried forward to facilitate future exhibition matches.

Taylor must have made a good impression in the exhibition match because in March 1906 he was paid £12 for a two-day visit to make recommendations to lengthen the course and increase the hazards. The changes involved encroaching on the Ladies' course and the main Committee agreed to pay the Ladies' Golf Club £7 10/- compensation for surrendering two of their greens and tees to enable the necessary changes. Not wishing to rest on their laurels, the Committee then contracted with James Braid to advise on further improvements to the course. Braid visited in January 1913 and charged six guineas for advice over improvements at a number of holes. The following year, he played in a 36-hole exhibition match as part of the Club's Spring Meeting with rising star George Duncan, who went on to win The Open in 1920. The Meeting was an impressive and comprehensive event commencing on Tuesday morning with an open handicap event and

featuring competitions every morning and afternoon right through until Saturday. Members would have felt fully exercised by the end of the week.

The Great War had the usual sad effect on the Club's fortunes, but in mitigation, the separate Ladies' and Gentlemen's clubs began to work more closely together and at the January 1917 AGM, a full and permanent amalgamation appeared to have been agreed. This decision was subsequently rescinded with a temporary merger being formalised instead, and the ladies were finally admitted to the Bath Golf Club by unanimous vote at the 1920 AGM.

This new-found spirit of co-operation during the War was not extended wholeheartedly to the Military who had requested permission to train on the links and to use the course for observation purposes. The Committee responded that they were prepared to give access to a small number of soldiers for observation purposes only, provided that they were withdrawn by 10:30 every morning and that all damage was repaired. No horses would be allowed on the playing area and the surface of the course, including all greens and fairways, had to remain undisturbed. It seems that the Military objected to these terms, and in July 1917 the Committee agreed that the Army could use the links up until 2pm for drill although golf would continue in the meantime.

The notice for the 1919 AGM celebrated the keen business acumen of Brigadier General Molesworth who had managed to obtain a mule from the military authorities. The cost of approximately £20 also included a new stall and harness and the notice revealed that nearly half that sum had already been saved in horse hire. Unfortunately, it was also reported that there were no funds available to pay either a Secretary or Professional or to keep the course or clubhouse in a satisfactory state of repair.

In 1921, despite its financial difficulties, the Club managed to raise the finance through a combination of a mortgage and debentures to buy the freehold of the course for £4,000. Some consideration was given to turning the ladies' 9-hole course into a municipal links, but this was not pursued and their old course was abandoned. Traces of the old layout can still be found in the undergrowth around the northern extremities of the present course.

James Braid made another advisory visit to Bath in 1928 when the Club needed help in changing the layout following the purchase of land by Bath City Council to construct a new reservoir on the course. An EGM was held in November of that year when, amongst other items, an appeal was made to members to finance a tractor: "which would obviate the necessity of keeping sheep on the course." The notice continued: "It may be pointed out that sheep on the course, unless cake-fed, have no fertilising value, and that the revenue of £70 per annum, which is received from grazing, is swallowed up by labour employed in cleaning up the course."

Finance remained critical during the 1930s. In 1932, the Secretary agreed to waive £50 of his salary and an Artisans' Section was founded in 1936. Surprisingly, the following year, the Club was able to afford to engage Harry Colt at a cost of £600 to advise on a major revamp of the course including the construction of today's tenth and eleventh holes.

The notice of the EGM to propose the formation of the Artisans' Section noted that His Majesty the King had expressed the desire that, nationally, playing facilities should be made available to the maximum number of people. Perhaps reassuringly however, the notice also added that: "...it is very unlikely that more than a very small proportion of the Artisans would be playing at the same time. It is also unlikely that more than a very few would be able to leave work and be ready to play before 6pm, much less 5:30!" The Artisans continued as a separate section until their eventual amalgamation into the main Club at the end of 1979.

Finance continued to be a worry after the War and in 1965 the Club would have been pleased to accept the £1,000 offered by the BBC to build the tall television aerial by the third tee, although it stands out as a rather modern landmark on an otherwise rural course. It seems that the BBC was dilatory in making payment as a Committee meeting in April the following year noted that the Club was still owed the money.

Much discussion took place in the 1960s over the need for a new clubhouse. The old building was showing its age and the location necessitated a sharp turn up a steep incline from the main road. Ultimately, budgetary constraints and access problems with the alternative site near the new university won the day and the new building was constructed adjacent to the existing premises. The old building is now used as separate changing rooms.

The course has two very tough par-4 holes. The fifth, measuring 466 yards, is played along the edge of the Downs and there are far-reaching views across the outskirts of Bath visible to the left of the fairway. The par-4 thirteenth hole is equally long and leads in turn to the Club's signature hole, a par-3 which requires a tee shot across one of the old stone quarries excavated in Ralph Allen's era.

The course is surrounded by a network of public footpaths which are well-used by walkers and joggers from the nearby university. The course is a regular venue for Somerset County matches and the world famous Bath Spa Hotel is located a very short distance away for golfers planning a special visit.

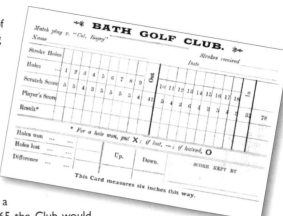

Above: Early card of the course including 'Match play v Colonel Bogey' which measured six inches to enable players to check for possible stymies on the green. The rear of the card explained where strokes were to be taken

GREAT YARMOUTH & CAISTER

DR. BROWN'S TENACITY

Above: *The pub in Salisbury Road recognises that golf used to be played over land nearer to Yarmouth town*

The Club at Great Yarmouth was formed by a tenacious Scot, Dr. Thomas Browne, who worked at the Royal Naval Hospital in the town. He wrote a letter to the Yarmouth Mercury in July 1882 hoping to identify fellow golfers: "There is a piece of common on the North Denes, the property of the Corporation of Yarmouth, which is unusually free of (fishing) nets, on which very fair golfing links might be laid out without expense in the first instance...if gentlemen interested in the subject will kindly call on me and talk it over, I shall be much pleased. I am sure we would soon make a beginning; and were golfing once started, however modestly at first, I think the players would quickly increase in numbers..."

Unfortunately, nobody attended Dr. Browne's meeting but undeterred he later recalled: "I immediately formed myself into a club, a limited liability company with no subscribed capital, elected myself unanimously Honorary Secretary, Treasurer, Committee and finally Captain. Having formed this Club, I received the same afternoon two challenges to play a team match and after consulting with my Committee, Chairman, Treasurer and Secretary, I accepted both of them."!

The doctor chose his early matches wisely as Blackheath, Felixstowe and Cambridge University all helped with the Club's expansion. Browne arranged for patients of his hospital to keep the new 13-hole layout free of furze, and in 1883 the course was expanded to eighteen holes by Tom Dunn, the Professional from North Berwick.

Town expansion caused some of the links to be surrendered and the course was extended north towards the boundary with Caister Borough. The original first and eighteenth holes played from the area of today's Salisbury Road were lost, but the old connections are recognised in the name of the Golfers Arms public house. By 1911, the course bordered Caister Golf Club which had been started in about 1890 and for a short time the Yarmouth and Caister clubs operated as neighbours before, bowing to the inevitable, they merged in 1913 to form the Great Yarmouth and Caister Golf Club.

Harry Colt was asked to design a much longer 18-hole course over the ground used by the two Clubs and the holes abandoned by the process were taken over by Yarmouth Corporation and run for a while as a municipal links.

Dr. Browne was succeeded as Club Captain by WW Poynder, RN in 1883/4 and by Surgeon-Major John Adcock in 1885, but a number of later Captains as well as officers, members and trophies came from Royal Blackheath who gave enthusiastic encouragement to the Club. Horace Hutchinson was Captain in 1890/1. In 1898, members of Great Yarmouth who were not also members of Blackheath sent a gift of £25 to the London club in thanks and recognition of this support. A silver rosewater dish, representing the Great Yarmouth Cup, is still played for annually by Blackheath golfers.

The Yarmouth Ladies' Club was formed in 1884 and had its proudest moment in 1898 when hosting the Ladies' British Open Amateur Championship. The Sketch journal in June reported the tournament in detail: "All the best players were there...Miss Dod (Moreton), Miss Issette Pearson (Wimbledon), Miss Lena Thomson (Wimbledon), Miss Nevile (Worcester) and Miss Barwell (Mrs Bagnall-Oakley; Great Yarmouth)."

The local player did well, reaching the semi-final before being defeated by the eventual winner, Miss Lena Thomson.

The War prevented completion of Colt's revised layout, and by 1919 the Club and the course had serious problems. However, a few stalwarts managed to reinstate the links, incorporating the race track which had been moved from South Dene to North Dene to accommodate the expanding fishing industry. The revised course was completed in 1921 and celebrated by a match between Ted Ray, George Duncan and local players JB Batley and Len Holland. Today's layout is little-changed although major repairs were required after the Second War as tank traps had been laid across the southern end of the course and a Luftwaffe bomb had demolished the eighteenth green and damaged the clubhouse.

At first sight, Yarmouth seems like a slicer's nightmare as the racecourse runs close to the right-hand side of the fourth, sixth, seventh and tenth fairways. However, local rules give detailed guidance and relief in many circumstances. The eleventh hole is the most attractive being played in a valley between sand hills whilst the par-4 eighteenth is the most difficult.

Fog can be a problem at Yarmouth and the Club has a klaxon to summon players back to the clubhouse when conditions become too dangerous.

For more than 70 years, the Club had the second oldest Artisans' Section in England after Royal North Devon. Between 1892 and 1913, and again in the 1930s, the Great Yarmouth Working Men's Golf Club played once a month using the host Club's fairways and greens but making their own teeing grounds which were marked by flags. In the intervening periods, the Artisans played over the municipal links formed in 1913 at the time of the merger. Artisan membership declined after the Second World War and the remaining members were absorbed into the parent Club.

Yarmouth is famous for its association with the term 'Bogey'. In 1890, visitors from Coventry explained their idea for a competition to Dr. Browne who used his contacts with leading players including Horace Hutchinson and John Penn to canvass the idea further. In a Bogey competition, each golfer would play a match

against the course rather than against each other, with the winner being the player who had beaten the course by the most holes. Each hole would be assessed for the score which a scratch golfer would be expected to take.

The format was adopted during the following Winter whilst the Music Hall song with the refrain: "Hush! Hush! Hush! Here Comes the Bogey Man" was popular. During one of the matches, a successful golfer playing with Dr. Browne was described as a 'Regular Bogey Man'. In 1892, Dr. Browne explained the idea to Captain Seeley-Vidal of the United Services Club at Gosport, and as all members of that club had to have a military rank, it was decided that the Bogey Man should be 'introduced' to the Services Club and enjoy the rank of Colonel, which would befit someone of such accurate and reliable skills. Colonel Bogey has been famous ever since and sometime in the 20th Century, Bogey was overtaken by Par with Bogey now reserved for an altogether less reliable performance!

Above: The racecourse runs close to the right-hand side of four fairways in the first ten holes

LONDON SURVIVORS

In the early days, London was surrounded by courses laid out over common land. Famous courses such as Tooting Bec and Streatham were lost to development but others have survived and prospered. The old Royal Observatory is visible from several holes at Royal Mid-Surrey (below).

Redhill & Reigate 1887

Royal Ascot 1887

Royal Epping Forest 1888

Royal Mid-Surrey 1892

REDHILL & REIGATE

ADAPTING TO CHANGE

The Redhill & Reigate course on Earlswood Common in Surrey is short by today's standards and some holes cross each other, but it offers an interesting change and challenge for golfers who are used to reaching for their driver on almost every long hole. Course management and club selection are vital.

For over a century the Club has faced up to and survived a number of threats which have caused other clubs to close or relocate in similar circumstances. The busy A23 runs through the heart of the course, but it is only a factor at the eighth and twelfth greens when the road needs to be negotiated on foot.

Several Open Champions, including Vardon, Braid, JH Taylor, Alf Padgham and Max Faulkner have played at Earlswood, and Brian Barnes has been one of the few to tame the course when, in 1972, he shot 64 whilst playing in an exhibition match with Faulkner, Tommy Horton and the Club's Professional at the time, Geoff Huggett.

As with many early English courses, golf at Earlswood is played over common land and the Club has had to adapt in order to share the space safely with many other users including anglers, footballers, cricketers, dog walkers, bird watchers, horse riders and even boating enthusiasts. In Victorian times, the Earlswood Lakes were a popular day trip destination for Londoners. The Club is the second oldest in Surrey and was founded in 1887 by local man, Charles Hall, and a few of his friends from London who started to play an early form of the game over land on the south-east side of the Common. In the following year, the first formal meeting of the Redhill Golf Club was held in the house of Mr. Greensall Allen, and Charles Hall was appointed as both Honorary Secretary and Honorary Treasurer.

Left: *Golfers playing from the back tee at the tree-lined par-4 fourth hole can try and cater for the dog-leg left by aiming for the church spire which is just visible in the centre of the picture*

The Club's name was changed to the Redhill & Reigate Golf Club in 1889, and in the same year the Conservators of the Common gave conditional permission for the Club to play golf at Earlswood: "...until such time as the Conservators may for any reason deem it necessary to withdraw this permission, which it is understood they are at liberty to do at any time by giving to the Secretary of the Club a fortnight's notice for such purpose." Early relationships with the Conservators were cordial and four of them were made Honorary Members of the Club. In May 1890, the Golf Committee made a bye-law reminding members that they were playing on the Common with the express condition that no danger would be caused to the public. They specified that the word 'fore' was not yet understood by the public and that no authority existed to order people to move: "A courteous request will be found to be an efficacious method of clearing the course."

The Club did, however, face a crisis with the Conservators in 1908. The original members had been largely from the gentry and from the senior professions. In 1906, the Club introduced a restricted category of membership known as 'Burgess' to cater for residents of the Borough who did not quite meet the original 'class' criteria. Burgess members paid a lower subscription but had limited rights to use the course and were barred from the clubhouse. Perhaps unwisely, the Club twice refused full membership to a local Reverend. Hearing of this situation, the Conservators first threatened to revoke their permission to play and then, instead, considered authorising all-comers to play over the course. The position was resolved with a true British compromise. The Club was persuaded to introduce a third category of membership, in effect an Artisans' Section, although these golfers were specifically obliged to give way if they found themselves being followed on

the course by full members. The Conservators handed over responsibility for the course to Reigate Borough Council in 1946.

The Ladies' Section was established in 1896 when Miss DE Hall wrote to the Club to request that ladies of the recently defunct Earlswood Ladies' Golf Club be allowed to play on the main course as it was financially impossible to keep up a separate course of their own. 21 ladies were elected to membership in March 1897.

Redhill & Reigate has had a number of clubhouses including the premises at 28 Common Road which features in an early photograph. In 1912, the Club moved a short distance to occupy premises rented from the London, Brighton and South Coast Railway Company with the added advantage that the Railway agreed to provide a rear gate and path to the station, saving golfers a half mile trek. Eventually the parking problems at the site became impossible to resolve and in 1979 the Club moved to its present location on the opposite side of the Common. The move required a complete renumbering of the holes to ensure that the first and eighteenth were positioned in proximity to the clubhouse.

The Club has also been forced to reorganise the course on a number of occasions as housing development, increased traffic and greater use of the Common by the general public all had an impact. In 1905, and again in 1909 and 1922, James Braid, who was the Professional at nearby Walton Heath, was brought in to advise on changes. In 1923, further alterations were made to accommodate two football pitches, and later modifications included moving holes away from the lakes and from the expanding Woodhatch residential triangle to the south-west of the course for safety reasons.

Trees threaten on both sides at two of the signature holes, the fourth and the tenth. Other testing holes include the long, dog-leg par-4 fifteenth, the uphill eighth hole which plays much longer than the distance shown on the card, and the par-5 finishing hole which is also a dog-leg and has two ditches which cross the fairway requiring intelligent club selection.

Birdwatchers can look out for different species of water birds, including cormorants, on the lake behind the sixth tee. This adds further interest to what is essentially an urban environment.

ROYAL ASCOT

NEW COURSE-2005

The Royal Ascot Golf Club has recently overcome its greatest challenge.

Ascot Heath is world-famous as a horse racing venue and was first developed as a racecourse in 1711 when Queen Anne spotted a natural clearing whilst riding on the edge of nearby Windsor Great Park. She ordered that a course be laid out: "...for horses to gallop at full stretch." The first four-day race meeting was held in 1768 and the Royal race week has been held annually ever since. In recent years the event has become over-crowded and the Ascot Authority determined to make the necessary changes to ensure that the week continued to be viewed as a world-class event. In addition to the complete redevelopment of the grandstand, it was decided to move the straight mile approximately 40 metres northwards and to build an underpass. Traffic on Winkfield Road has now been diverted under the race track so that horses no longer risk injury on the artificial matting and straw which used to cover the old road at that point.

The implications for the Club were that its old clubhouse would have been marooned in the jaws of the underpass and it also stood to lose a further part of its playing area sandwiched inside the racecourse. Fortunately, the Crown owned a nearby farm with an available lease and the Crown, the Ascot Authority and the Club arranged to relocate the whole course a short distance further east. The new layout was opened for play in Autumn 2005.

The Club was founded in 1887 by FJ Patton who was a local lawyer, and Queen Victoria granted the Royal title shortly after bestowing a similar honour on the Royal Ascot Cricket Club in 1883. The cricket club continues

to play on the ground located within the racecourse. Several members of the Royal Family played golf on Ascot Heath including HRH The Prince of Wales who was a Club member and became its Patron around the time of taking the throne as Edward VII in 1901.

The golf course within the race track was famous for its association with five-times Open Champion JH Taylor who designed many of the holes which were still being played more than 100 years after his original work in 1895. Fairway cross-bunkers were a Taylor trademark and an excellent example was found on the old eleventh hole. Before Taylor's work, three separate Clubs played on the Heath. There was a 9-hole men's course, a separate ladies' course, and the St. George's Gymnasium Golf Club, open to local tradesmen as an Artisan's Club.

Joe Longhurst, the Club's Professional in the important early years, helped supervise the construction of

Above: Aerial view of the racecourse, the old grandstand and the old golf course. The cricket ground can be seen in the background below the circular reservoir (Courtesy of Royal Ascot Golf Club)

Taylor's design. Longhurst later designed a golf course at Frankfurt-on-Maine in Germany. His son was christened 'Stymie' which was a joking reference attributed to Longhurst's doctor who remarked that the new offspring would change the amount of time that Joe could devote to the game!

Golf existed for more than a century as the second sport on the Heath, but it certainly benefited from course maintenance and various buildings provided over the years by the senior (i.e. racing) organisation. The new course has been provided by the Ascot Authority, but the Club has had to fund the new clubhouse and it is likely that the two sports will become less entangled now that physical separation has been completed.

Royal Ascot was one of the first golf courses in Berkshire and for a while in the early 1900s it was a top local venue for golfers. However, stiff competition arose from the excellent new courses at nearby Sunningdale, Swinley Forest, Wentworth and The Berkshire so that the Ascot Club, with its old boundary constraints caused by the race track, gradually lost favour.

In 1922, the formal Club ceased to function but Viscount Churchill, the King's representative at Ascot, made the far-sighted decision that the greens should be maintained and a Professional, Walter Ward, was appointed by Colonel Carter, the Clerk of the Racecourse, to look after the interests of local golfers who wished to continue to play golf over the Heath on an informal basis. After the Second World War, the then

Clerk to the Racecourse, Major (later Sir) John Bulteel, agreed to help canvass support for a new golf club and Ascot Heath Golf Club was constituted in 1948. The Club re-established the use of the Royal prefix in 1977 during the Queen's Silver Jubilee when the name reverted to the Royal Ascot Golf Club. Reading between the lines, the Royal Family may have felt a continued association with the game throughout the quiet years as golf was still being played over the same Crown land and it is interesting to note that The R&A referred to the Club under its Royal name throughout the period.

Golfers playing on the new course will enjoy the hazards provided by mature trees. Golf in the centre of the racecourse was necessarily played over flat land and the scenery was made less attractive by the understandable decision by the Ascot Authority to pollard all trees and bushes to a height of only five feet. This gave unlimited visibility to spectators and television viewers following the horses from the grandstand as they ran round the distant side of the circuit. Members in 2003/4 had to show patience and think to the future as, in the short term, the old course was reduced from eighteen holes to nine whilst the Ascot Authority commenced the racecourse redevelopment, some time before the new golf course had been constructed.

Longer-term the outlook looks promising, with a Royal Club playing over a new, more undulating and more attractively wooded site in one of the most prestigious locations in the country.

ROYAL EPPING FOREST

CHINGFORD GOLF COURSE

Chingford golf course occupies land which was previously part of a royal hunting ground, and Queen Elizabeth's hunting lodge, originally built for King Henry VIII in 1543, still survives and is open to the public in nearby Rangers Road. In 1871, the Corporation of the City of London obtained limited powers over some of the local Manors, and under an act of Parliament of 1878, the Corporation became Conservators of Epping Forest in lieu of the Crown. In 1882, the Forest was opened to the public in perpetuity.

The first course was laid out in the Summer of 1888 following an inaugural meeting chaired by EN Buxton, JP and High Sheriff. Major Gordon was appointed Hon. Treasurer and FF McKenzie was the first Honorary Secretary, illustrating the influence of both Scots and the Military in the early history of English golf. The Club was originally to be called Epping Forest Golf Club.

The first course consisted of nine holes and was surveyed and laid out by the Captain of Blackheath, JG Gibson, together with Epping members, McKenzie and FG Waterer, as well as Major Morris and two caddies who were all from the Blackheath club. The Club started ambitiously and Willie Dunn was appointed as the first Professional on wages of £1 per week. Dunn helped increase the layout to eighteen holes and the Club adopted the rules of Felixstowe Golf Club. Gentlemen on the waiting list of Royal Wimbledon were approached to see if they wished to join Epping. Further kudos was gained in October 1888 when HRH The Duke of Connaught became Patron, and shortly afterwards Queen Victoria agreed to the

Club adding its Royal prefix. Together with The R&A, Epping is one of the few Royal clubs playing golf over public links.

Willie Dunn soon decided that his wages were insufficient and resigned to be replaced first by R Tait of Musselburgh and then in quick succession by R Lambert from Woodford Golf Club and then William McEwan from Musselburgh.

The original 18-hole course stretched across Bury Road and up towards the first clubhouse which was located in the Royal Forest Hotel next to the Queen Elizabeth Hunting Lodge. Chingford Plain has always been popular with the public for horse riding, dog walking and other pursuits, and golf has gradually become condensed into the area bordered by Bury

Road to the east and Forest View to the south. Modern equipment has enabled the construction of several holes on the clay soil which was previously too swampy to cater for golf. In February 1894, the Club suggested to the Corporation that golfers should wear scarlet jackets in order to improve public safety, and in the following month the Superintendent of the Forest wrote to the Club confirming his agreement to the suggestion. Golfers today must still wear red tops.

The Club struggled financially during the first few years of the 20th Century, but fortunately CG Roberts, the Honorary Secretary, became Honorary Treasurer. By 1911, matters had improved to such an extent that the Committee felt able to approve unanimously: "...that a presentation of plate to the value of one hundred guineas be made to Mr. Roberts as a token of esteem of the Members." During the presentation ceremony the Captain remarked that without the efforts of Mr. Roberts, it was doubtful whether the Club would still be in existence.

The Club moved to its present clubhouse in 1914, initially as tenants of one of the members and then later as freeholders following the purchase of the building in 1936. Royal Epping enjoyed considerable success during the 1920s and drew interest from the media. A 1928

edition of The Sketch journal featured a large crowd of members who had gathered to watch an exhibition match between Abe Mitchell, George Duncan and two Epping golfers, Philip Wynne and Bert Seymour.

The course today is shared by three golf clubs. In addition to Royal Epping Forest, Chingford Golf Club, founded in 1923, and Chingford Ladies' Golf Club both play over the course which is still owned and administered by the Corporation of London and the Conservators of the Forest. The course does not have numbered tee boxes in order to minimise the visual impact on the course and also ensure that all golfers register at the commencement of their rounds.

The layout is a mixture of wooded forest combined with more open parkland where the course adjoins the developed part of Chingford. The short par-4 sixth hole has an old oak tree just to the left of the green which prevents most long drivers from scoring birdies. The tenth hole is rated as stroke index one and has a drainage ditch in play along the whole length of the fairway. The fourteenth fairway slopes to the left, and in Summer it is difficult to position the ball on the correct part of the fairway so that the second shot is often played with a downhill lie. The par-4 eighteenth is an excellent closing hole requiring a very long second shot to be hit over water to the green which is situated in the corner of the course and next to both the Royal Epping Forest and the Chingford Golf Club buildings.

The public course is good value for money and is worth playing as it hosts one of the world's oldest Royal Clubs whilst at the same time allowing access to golfers of all backgrounds and abilities.

ROYAL MID ~ SURREY
HISTORY SURVIVES THE FIRE

Royal Mid-Surrey Golf Club plays over historic land in Richmond close to the River Thames and has been served by two Professionals who have secured an indelible place in golfing history. JH Taylor worked at the Club for nearly 50 years and was succeeded by Henry Cotton who won his third British Open whilst attached to the Club. In addition, Max Faulkner was employed as Cotton's assistant and won The Open at Royal Portrush in 1951, whilst Cotton's long-term successor, Jimmy Adams, was twice runner-up in The Open and enjoyed an impressive record in the Ryder Cup. Not surprisingly, the quality of these players, combined with its central location, ensured that the Club has enjoyed an enviable reputation. Most of Royal Mid-Surrey's memorabilia was destroyed in a disastrous clubhouse fire in 2001, but the Club has recovered well and now enjoys an impressive new building whilst the corridors are once again hung with photographs of famous faces and tournaments.

King Henry V built a Carthusian monastery, the Charterhouse of Jesus of Bethlehem of Shene, on the land now occupied by the fourteenth and fifteenth holes on the Outer Course. In a prayer before his famous speech prior to Agincourt about "Gentlemen in England now a-bed", Shakespeare records Henry referring to this chantry:"...where the sad and solemn priests still sing for Richard's soul." At one time, Cardinal Wolsey lived in the monastery, and the body of James IV of Scotland once lay amongst building rubble in one of the cells in the Charterhouse. After the monks were expelled during the dissolution of the monasteries in 1539 the building fell into decay. It was eventually removed by King George III, who built in its place the Royal Observatory which stands beside the fourteenth fairway. The aim was to watch the

transit of Venus in 1769, an important aid to finding true north. Indeed, the Richmond Observatory determined 'time' until it was eventually succeeded by the more accurate observatory down the river at Greenwich.

The flat land of Old Deer Park is ideal sporting country. Cricket outgrew Richmond Green in the town centre and moved to the park in 1862, and other sports were encouraged outside the main cricket season. Rugby, soccer, athletics, hockey and archery all became established and a 9-hole golf course was laid out by Tom Dunn from the club at Mitcham, but this only lasted for six weeks before it had to close again for lambing time as the tenant farmer was not prepared to have his sheep bombarded by golf balls.

The Club was officially formed in October 1892 and Golf magazine announced that the Richmond Athletic

Main: *The Pagoda in Kew Gardens is visible from the early holes on the course*

Above: *JH Taylor photographed by George Beldam in 1900 outside his shop with famous England cricketer WG Grace*

Association had decided to form a golf club in Old Deer Park. The farmer refused to co-operate and would not allow bunkers to be dug, but the Crown landlords were more sympathetic and listened to the requests of the Duke of Cambridge who was the first President of the Club and also held the same role at the Richmond Athletics Club. In 1895, the farmer was persuaded to surrender his tenancy to the Club which immediately started digging bunkers over-zealously, causing Golf to comment that: "It is as though someone had taken out a patent and the Club had bought them by the score, and sent a man up in a balloon to drop them at stated intervals." By all accounts, the early Greenkeepers were useless and the Club was persuaded to transfer upkeep of the course to Messrs. Carter, Seed Merchants. However, this tactic was also a failure. Fortunately, Taylor's arrival from Royal Wimbledon in March 1899 was followed in 1903 by the employment of Peter Lees from the Royal Burgess Club in Edinburgh as Head Greenkeeper. Recognising that The Field had described the course as having: "an insufficiency of undulations", and that Bernard Darwin later called it: "...as flat as a pancake", the two men set about making wholesale alterations and more than 100 unemployed men were recruited to construct humps and hollows all around the course. Taylor wrote in Golf Illustrated of how: "The obstacles ...should be the 'borstal system' of a golfer's life, teaching him that the way of the transgressor is hard, but not crushing his spirit."

The improvements were a success and the Club grew rapidly and developed an unparalleled reputation in London. By 1908, the course was becoming too busy causing The Field to comment that such was the increase in motor traffic that Sunningdale, Mid-Surrey and Walton Heath were no longer worth visiting at the weekend except by those who could travel by car before the trains arrived. The 1915 edition of the Golfers Handbook listed the Club's membership at 1,200, including 450 ladies, and concluded that it was the largest for a golf-only club in all Europe. Darwin conjectured that: "Day-in, day-out, there were probably more rounds in Old Deer Park than anywhere but St Andrews."

Taylor's renown caused many famous faces to visit the Club for lessons. The large frame of England cricketer WG Grace was frequently seen on the course, and

shortly after the First World War, the Aga Khan used to have a lesson at 8.30 before travelling up to work in the City. The Japanese Emperor Hirohito also visited Taylor whilst he was in the UK as a student at Oxford University, and Taylor made a special set of clubs for His Celestial Highness from his factory in nearby Sheen. Taylor's clients from show business included Sir Harry Lauder who used to visit Richmond whilst he was working at the London Palladium. Looking back, Taylor attributed his longevity to: "sobriety and contentedness with my environment" which reflects well on the Club where he spent the majority of his working life when not involved in tournaments. Mid-Surrey rewarded Taylor first with honorary and then with life membership.

Taylor also played a significant part in the career of his successor. Writing in his book, 'Golf: My Life's Work', he recalled receiving a letter in 1921 from a gentleman named Cotton in Dulwich who had two enthusiastic golfing sons. Taylor was asked to give his opinion on whether they might succeed as golfing Professionals. He responded: "As they appear to me they are of two distinct types. Leslie is robust and hard-hitting, whereas Henry is more methodical and careful and, I should judge, more inclined to know 'the reason of the cause and the wherefore of the why'...Henry will concentrate and go far."

In addition to Taylor, the Club was able to celebrate the success of its own triumvirate of gifted amateur players. Sidney Fry played off plus-five and was runner-up in the 1902 Amateur championship at Hoylake, Herbert Taylor achieved the same position at Royal St George's in 1908, whilst James Worthington was often a match for these two stalwarts, playing off plus-four. Fry's name crops up throughout much of the Club's history, sometimes because he aired rather forthright views, but he takes the credit for enticing Taylor to join Mid-Surrey which was the single most important development at the Club.

The First World War took its usual toll on the Club and although

The Prince of Wales added further prestige through his captaincy in 1926 and the award of the Royal prefix, membership had dwindled to under 600 by the 1930s. Taking the initiative in 1933, the Club started the Antlers' Open Competition for amateur foursomes medal play, using as a prize a set of antlers presented by the President, Prince Arthur of Connaught. Cyril Gray, who had important influence amongst the Halford Hewitt schools, gave the competition early support and in its first 29 years, 33 Walker Cup players were amongst the winners thus demonstrating the importance attached to the new competition. The Club now also runs an annual open competition for Mothers and Daughters which is played over the slightly shorter Inner Course.

The longer Outer Course is now too short for major championships, but Taylor's influence enabled the Club to host the prestigious Matchplay Championship on seven occasions between 1904 and the 1940s. Taylor won the events in 1904 and 1908 whilst other respected winners at Richmond included Alf Padgham in 1931 and Henry Cotton in 1940, some six years before he moved from Coombe Hill to succeed Taylor as Professional. The first post-war English Amateur Championship was held at the Club in 1946 and won by Ian Patey from Hayling Island, whilst a combined team representing Oxford and Cambridge universities played against the British Ryder Cup squad in a practice match before the latter set off for the US in 1947. Later, Ryder Cup player Peter Townsend enjoyed his visits to Richmond, winning the national Boy's Championship in 1962 and then returning six years later to win the PGA Close Championship in 1968.

The Church has had an important influence on the development of English golf and the Bishop of London, Dr. Winnington Ingram, might have been aware that he was playing over the site of an old monastery when his team of London clerics took on the Winchester Diocese in a match at the Club. The caddies had been warned to be on their best behaviour and all was going well until the fourteenth hole when the Bishop took a huge divot close to the boundary fence. Fearful that he had damaged the course, he called out: "Where did the sod go boy?" and received a rapid response from the caddie: "Over the bloody fence sir, and what's more I knew you wasn't a real Bishop!"

The new clubhouse has allowed Royal Mid-Surrey to offer a fitting tribute, in the shape of a dedicated room, to one of its lady members who might well have become one of the greatest ever female golfers. Pam Barton joined the Club when she was twelve, and by the age of seventeen she had reached three successive British Amateur Championships, winning on the third occasion when it was held at Southport & Ainsdale in 1936. She then travelled to America whilst still a junior member at the Club and won the US Amateur Championship to complete the double for the first time by a British player since Dorothy Campbell in 1909. Barton completed the last 24 holes in the final in one-under-par. She won the British championship again in 1939 at Royal Portrush before joining the Royal Air Force, based at Manston in Kent, where she was tragically killed in an air crash at the age of 26.

The professional record of 64 on the Outer Course was set jointly by Bob Charles and Bernard Gallagher whilst playing in the Eccentric Club Pro-Am in July 1979, but visitors may like to try and beat the amateur record of 62 which was set by a member of the Royal Mid-Surrey Artisans' Club, Pat Cunningham. He actually had a net 63 as he played off plus-one in the medal round in July 1982.

Main: The fine new clubhouse pictured behind the eighteenth green replaced the old building after the disastrous fire

Above: Aga Sultan Sir Mohamed Shah, the Aga Khan, had frequent lessons from JH Taylor (Courtesy of Royal Mid-Surrey)

OPEN CHAMPIONSHIP COURSES

The Open Championship has prospered at Hoylake, Lytham, Sandwich (below) and, more recently, Birkdale.
Deal would also have hosted more than two Open Championships but for severe flooding. Prince's was established
by golfers fleeing the crowded course at Mitcham Common near London.

Royal Liverpool..............1869

Royal Lytham & St Annes .1886

Royal St George's...........1887

Royal Birkdale...............1889

Royal Cinque Ports.........1892

Prince's 1906

ROYAL LIVERPOOL

HOYLAKE

It is difficult to do justice to Hoylake in a book covering a number of courses as the Club itself deserves several volumes. Royal Liverpool is famous for its own triumvirate of amateur golfers, Harold Hilton, John Ball and Jack Graham, and by the turn of the 21st Century, Hoylake had hosted ten Open Championships and eighteen Amateur Open Championships. It also hosted the first home international, England v Scotland, the first Amateur Championship, the first match between teams from Britain and the United States (the precursor to the Walker Cup), and the first English Closed Championship. Perhaps most famously of all, Hoylake was the venue for the 1930 Open Championship in the year that Bobby Jones won his Grand Slam despite scoring an eight on the former par-5 eighth hole.

For a time, it seemed that the modern demands of an Open Championship infrastructure would preclude further returns, but in 1999 the Club purchased ten acres of land formerly occupied by Leas School to help accommodate The Open's tented village, and the positive co-operation of The R&A and the Metropolitan Borough of Wirral allowed the Championship to return to Hoylake in 2006. The opportunity was taken to renumber all the holes, so that the old seventeenth and eighteenth became the new first and second, and the old sixteenth became the final hole. The intimidating old first hole, with its famous out of bounds, became the new third hole.

Hoylake Town developed out of the amalgamation of the three villages of Little Meols, Hoose and Great Meols. In 1835, Samuel Richardson constructed a number of fashionable villas on Stanley Road which runs along the far side of the course opposite today's clubhouse, and

the extension of the Mersey railway from the Docks to Hoylake in 1866 encouraged further development. The Liverpool Hunt Club started racing on the land in 1847 and continued until 1876, and today's out of bounds encompassing the practice area bounded by the former first and sixteenth fairways is part of the inside section of the old racecourse. Hoylake's racing heritage is reflected in the names of the old first and eighteenth holes, Course and Stand, and by the two ornamental pineapples which were once on the paddock gates and are now on the putting green posts.

The 1912 edition of the Illustrated Guide Book of Liverpool, Birkenhead and New Brighton notes that: "The royal and ancient game was played at Hoylake as far back as 1852, when a few Scottish settlers at West Kirby indulged in the pastime over fields on the banks

Above: A view of the clubhouse showing the trench cut into the top of the long mounds known as cops. A ball is out of bounds if it lies in or over the trench

Above: Robert Maxwell teeing off in the inaugural home international golf match between Scotland and England

of the Dee. Some years later, a short course was laid out over the rabbit warrens, but it was not until 1869 that a club was formed."

The Liverpool Golf Club signed its first lease of land in that year with the third Lord Stanley of Alderley. His predecessor, Sir John Stanley, had formed Stanley Road and built the Royal Hotel, now demolished, in 1792 for those taking part in the new fashion of bathing in the sea. Nearby New Brighton was later established as a North Country competitor to the Prince Regent's flourishing seaside town of Brighton in Sussex.

The first course in 1869 consisted of nine holes but was soon extended south in the following year to complete the 18-hole layout. Some of the initial nine holes still feature in today's course. The original first hole now forms part of the renumbered second, the old second is now part of today's third, and the original fourth now relates closely to the present fifth hole. The Royal title of the Club dates back to 1871 which is the year when HRH the Duke of Connaught became President.

Players at modern Open Championships must now warm up at the nearby municipal course and be ferried into the first hole because the existing practice ground is too small for today's long hitters. Nevertheless, the boundaries protecting the existing practice ground will continue to strike fear into players on several holes. The bordering artificial two-foot-high banks are known locally as cops, and local rules prescribe that balls lying in or over the trench

cut into the top of these cops are out of bounds. The cops are particularly prominent on the third hole as they can capture slices from both the first and second shots. Harry Vardon drove his first two shots out of bounds in the 1902 Open, when the hole was played as the first, but still completed his round in 72. Players compensating too far to the left off the tee can instead find themselves out of bounds in front of the clubhouse. The third green is the only hole not protected by greenside bunkers, but the hole is difficult enough without further defences.

Hoylake's independent Artisans' Club, the Village Play, is open to 'fishermen, artisans or tradesmen.' It interacts successfully with the Royal Liverpool Club and celebrated its own centenary in 1994, 100 years after tragedy struck the Hoylake fishing community whilst the fleet was anchored off the nearby North Wales coast. In December, the fleet was caught in a huge storm on the way home to Hoylake. Two boats were lost with all hands on board and 39 men lost their lives. The Village Play Club was formed in the aftermath of this tragedy and provided some onshore diversion for those who no longer wished to fish for a livelihood. The villagers continue to enjoy playing rights and their members help the Club to maintain the course and to act as knowledgeable stewards at major events. Over the years, the Artisans have achieved a number of golfing successes including those inflicted by a Mr. Pulford who between 1897 and 1907 had wins over Vardon, Tait and Hilton.

The Royal Liverpool Club also had a historic influence over the offspring of the Village Play golfers. The Hoose School logbook in June 1895 noted: "… attendance very poor. The employment of boys as caddies by the Golf Club presses heavily on the attendance of the children." Females were not entirely innocent however! In 1896, the log recorded: "…school closed for this week on the occasion of the Ladies' Golf Championship being played at Hoylake." In July 1903, the log reported that: "…nine boys were allowed to caddie for the Grand Duke Michael of Russia." It is interesting to conjecture what the modern golfing map might have looked like had the Russian revolution worked out differently! The Cannes-Mandelieu Golf

Club was founded by the Grand Duke in 1891, and in March 1903, Royal Liverpool sent a strong team out to Cannes, including John Ball, Jack Graham, Harold Hilton and AH Crosfield. Hilton and Crosfield were beaten 4&3 on the first day with Ball and Graham halving their match. The Paris edition of the New York Herald reported that: "....the visitors true form and play are not to be judged by either match, as they were greatly handicapped by the journey, their unfamiliarity with the course and the surroundings and, above all, by the glaring southern light."!

Crosfield described the Cannes Club as the most representative in the world and Lord Eldon, on behalf of the Royal Liverpool Club, proposed the Grand Duke's health, emphasising his dignified urbanity, kindliness and geniality. Fortunately, these results were not indicative of Hilton and Ball's normal standards. In 1911, the former became the first player to capture both the British and American amateur titles in the same year, and he won two British Opens in 1892 and 1897 before winning four British Amateur titles between 1900 and 1913. Ball won the British Amateur title eight times between 1888 and 1912 and the British Open in 1890. Hilton is the only Englishman to have won the American Amateur championship whereas Ball never competed in the US. Aside from Bobby Jones, Ball is believed by many to have been the greatest amateur golfer of all time.

Amateur championships at Hoylake have featured a number of great players at the outset of their careers. The 1975 championship, for example, included Nick Faldo, Sandy Lyle, Nick Price, Mark James, Curtis Strange, Jay Haas and Jerry Pate. Perhaps the strangest event occurred in 1933 when the local referee determined that Cyril Tolley would have to play his ball 'as it lay' where it had rolled under a spectator's mackintosh! Ball won the Amateur Championship three times on his home course. Other notable early winners at Hoylake included Allan Macfie from St Andrews who won the first Championship in 1885 and was stone deaf, Horace Hutchinson who won in 1887, and Freddie Tait whose win in 1898 was shortly followed by his untimely death in the war in South Africa.

Hoylake has also honoured two older winners of the Amateur Championship. Charles Hutchins, a former Captain, won in 1902 aged 53 having taken up the game in his 30s, and the Hon. Michael Scott was champion in 1933 aged 55. His knowledge of links golf learnt at Westward Ho! proved to be extremely valuable. Alex Kyle, a Scot, won the final pre-war Championship in 1939 defeating Tony Duncan 2&1 and their first round of the final was completed in under two and a half hours which shows how golf has changed over the years.

Amy Pascoe from Wimbledon won the first Ladies' British Open Championship to be staged at Hoylake when she defeated Lena Thomson in the 1896 final in front of a crowd of 3,000. Her task was made slightly easier as Lady Margaret Scott had retired after her three consecutive victories in 1893-5, and the prospective favourite, Lottie Dod, did not enter the competition. Three of the four semi-finalists were from the club at Wimbledon. Almost a century passed before the Club hosted its next Ladies' Open Championship when 18-year-old Helen Dobson defeated Elaine Farquharson 6&5 in the final. Dobson repeated Vardon's fate at the old first hole, driving her first two shots out of bounds in her first two qualifying rounds, and she managed to enter the last thirty two placings by a single stroke.

Above: The Hon. Michael Scott won the 1933 Amateur Championship at Hoylake, aged 55. His sister, Lady Margaret Scott, had previously won the first three British Ladies' Open Amateur Championships

Below: Players leaving the renumbered thirteenth green on the par-3 Alps hole. The sand dunes protect the green which is partly shielded from the wind and the flag demonstrates the direction of the prevailing weather

Above: Bobby Jones receiving the Claret Jug in 1930 from Club Captain JGB Beazley during his unique Grand Slam year. Jones subsequently retired from competitive golf at the age of 28

Of the Open Championships staged here, Hilton's win on his own course in 1897 may have been one of the most emotional. The order of play was random in those early days and the home player had finished at least two hours before James Braid approached the last green. Braid's putt narrowly slipped past the left edge of the hole and the local crowd carried Hilton to the presentation ceremony on their shoulders to receive the Claret Jug for the second time.

A Hoylake member also had an influence on the Club's second Open. Alex Herd, the eventual winner, was persuaded to play the new Haskell ball by John Ball. Herd had seen Ball's prodigious distance with the new ball and managed to get the Club's Professional to sell him the entire stock of four balls! Harry Vardon refused to play with the new ball and lost the championship by one stroke.

Hoylake has been a good hunting ground for popular foreign players. Arnaud Massy, a Basque from South-West France, became the first Continental European to win the Open in 1907. Walter Hagen triumphed in 1924, Bobby Jones in 1930, and Peter Thomson completed his unique 20th Century hat-trick of consecutive Open victories in 1956.

JH Taylor won his fifth and final Open Championship at Hoylake in 1913. By then the event had seen the start of the foreign invasion of quality overseas players including John McDermott, who had won the US Open

in 1911 and 1912, but the gales on the second day suited Taylor's compact swing which produced a lower trajectory than many of his peers.

Ulsterman Fred Daly won the 1947 Open, but there was late drama when US amateur Frank Stranahan, needing an eagle at the last to force a playoff, landed his six iron a mere two inches from the hole. Many people still recall Roberto de Vicenzo's win in 1967. Partnering Gary Player in the final round, Player three-putted from a short distance at the old tenth hole whilst de Vicenzo secured a birdie. On the old sixteenth, de Vicenzo cut his drive but then hit a superb three wood on to the green over the heart of the out of bounds area to save the day.

Whilst today's third and eighteenth have the most famous out of bounds, many players have also been caught by the trees that cut into the left of the eighth hole. The best views on the course are found from the eleventh to fourteenth holes which look out across the Dee Estuary to Hilbre Island and the Welsh hills in the distance. The thirteenth is a particularly good short hole known locally as Alps after the large sand dunes which can come into play off the back tees. The closing stretch from the sixteenth feels very long and suits players who are accurate with fairway woods and long irons.

It was great news that a way could be found to continue Hoylake's proud Open traditions!

WINNERS AND RUNNERS-UP IN HOYLAKE'S EARLY OPENS

YEAR	CHAMPION	WINNING SCORE	RUNNERS-UP SCORE	RUNNERS-UP
1897	Harold Hilton (A)	314	315	James Braid
1902	Alex Herd	307	308	James Braid / Harry Vardon
1907	Arnaud Massy	312	314	J H Taylor
1913	J H Taylor	304	312	Ted Ray
1924	Walter Hagen	301	302	Ernest R Whitcombe
1930	Bobby Jones (A)	291	293	Leo Diegel / MacDonald Smith
1936	Alf Padgham	287	288	Jimmy Adams
1947	Fred Daly	293	294	Reg Horne / Frank Stranahan (A)
1956	Peter Thomson	286	289	Flory van Donck
1967	Roberto de Vicenzo	278	280	Jack Nicklaus

ROYAL LYTHAM & ST ANNES

10 OPEN CHAMPIONSHIPS

Lytham may not be one of the most beautiful Open courses, but it has witnessed some of the greatest events in golfing history including Bobby Jones's miracle shot in 1926, the first leg of Tony Jacklin's double in 1969, and Seve Ballesteros's successive victories and recovery heroics in 1979 and 1988. The course and the clubhouse ooze nostalgia.

The Club was founded in 1886 by a Scot, Alex Doleman, together with Talbot and JAS Stretton Fair. The first course was laid out near the small town of St Annes but there were problems with long-term security of tenure. The Club therefore identified the present location for the new course, laid out by George Lowe, the Club's Professional and expert club maker, which opened for play in 1897. Interestingly, the lease issues could probably have been resolved as most of the land occupied by the old course later became the home of St Annes Old Links which has now celebrated its own centenary.

Today's course at Lytham is shaped like a thin triangle, bounded on one side by a railway line which stretches along the entire length of the course and threatens any sliced tee shots at several holes. The shape has also led to the unusual configuration which starts with a par-3, the only Open course to do so, and then continues with two more short holes before the turn. Over the years Herbert Fowler, Harry Colt, Tom Simpson and Ken Cotton have all advised on changes to Lowe's original layout, but early golfers would still recognise today's course although distances have been lengthened considerably. The seventeenth hole has acquired a challenging dog-leg whilst the eighteenth remains a daunting

prospect with its green positioned directly beneath the clubhouse windows.

The organisers had taken an act of faith in holding Lytham's first Open Championship in 1926. The links were shorter than many of the existing Open courses but the greens were known to be superb and the location and local accommodation were thought to be good enough to trial the course for a major championship. At one stage, the General Strike threatened the whole event causing many Americans to consider cancelling their visit, and Bobby Jones was only persuaded to play after he was heavily and unexpectedly defeated in a match against Andrew Jamieson in the Amateur Championship at

Above: The clubhouse viewed from the final fairway with the Dormy House to the left

Muirfield without winning a single hole! This defeat was only a temporary setback and he soon returned to form, defeating Cyril Tolley by 12&11 in the Walker Cup singles at St Andrews before travelling down to Sunningdale where he played a near-perfect Open qualification round which caused the bookies to offer unprecedented odds of three-to-one for Jones to win The Open itself.

Today's visitors staying in the Dormy House can imagine the excitement amongst the throng of American journalists who had travelled all the way to Lytham to witness Jones's heroics in the days of prohibition back in the US! After three rounds at lunchtime on the final day, Jones was just two shots behind his playing partner and fellow American Al Watrous, the Professional from Grand Rapids. The two left the links for a lunch break back at the Majestic Hotel and when they returned, Jones realised he had left his player's badge behind and was forced to buy a 2/6d entry ticket as the gate staff did not recognise him! Back on the course in the final round, Jones was still two shots behind Watrous with just five holes to play, but by the seventeenth tee he had drawn level. Watrous negotiated the difficult dog-leg well and was safely on the green in two shots whilst Jones pulled his tee shot into sand some 170 yards from the green which was hidden from view behind inhospitable scrub land. A plaque marks the spot where Jones played his next shot. With no room for error, he took an old mashie-niblick (approximately an eight iron) and found the heart of the green. Watrous was so disconcerted that he three-putted leaving Jones to win the hole and ultimately the championship. Jones's club hangs in the clubhouse together with his famous portrait painted by JAA Berrie who also features in the history at Wallasey.

Lytham had to wait more than a quarter of a century before The Open finally returned to the Club in 1952. Few Americans made the trip and Bobby Locke took the opportunity to emulate Harry Vardon and James Braid by winning The Open for a third time in four years. Peter Thomson won the 1958 Open to complete an unparalleled run in his last seven years of second, second, first, first, first, second, first; the like of which may never be repeated. Several of Thomson's nearest challengers were defeated by the hazards at the eighteenth. Christy O'Connor Senior was bunkered, costing him a play-off place and the same fate befell Eric Brown who found the sand off the tee and took a double-bogey six leaving only Welshman Dave Thomas to contest the 36-hole play-off which Thomson won by four strokes.

The Americans were back in force for the 1963 Open, but this was ultimately won by the left-handed New Zealander, Bob Charles who had one of the smoothest putting strokes of all time. British honour was finally restored by Tony Jacklin in 1969 when he beat Bob Charles by two shots and then went on to win the US Open at Hazeltine the following June, thus becoming only the third British player after Harry Vardon and Ted Ray to have won both titles.

Above: *Eighth fairway at Royal Lytham (photograph by Eric Hepworth)*

three rounds, but Seve swept all competition aside with a superb last round 65 which is remembered as one of the greatest final rounds to win a major championship.

Tom Lehman won the 1996 Open which can now be seen as a 'changing of the guard'. Ernie Els bunkered his tee shots in the final round at the sixteenth and eighteenth holes and had to settle for a share of second place, whilst Tiger Woods was the leading amateur in what was his last tournament before turning professional. Woods' prodigious striking was evidenced at the par-5 sixth hole which he reached in two shots with a three and a nine iron. David Duval won the 2001 Open, but many people will recall the sad mix-up which caused Ian Woosnam to suffer a two-shot penalty for having too many clubs in his bag when he was well in contention.

A local golfer, Donald Beaver, suffered a more severe penalty whilst playing in a Club competition. He thinned a bunker shot near the eighteenth green and the ball was discovered lodged in the ivy on the clubroom windowsill. Beaver took off his shoes to observe the 'no spikes' rule, walked through the main entrance and into the clubroom, opened the window, stood on the sill and then played a deft chip shot down onto the eighteenth green. His pleasure turned to disappointment when the Secretary informed him that he would have to be disqualified for leaving the course during play!

In addition to the Open Championships, Lytham has hosted the Curtis Cup and many other top ladies' championships as well as two Ryder Cup matches in 1961 and 1977. Both were won relatively easily by the visitors, but the Americans nearly missed the chance to retain the Cup in 1961 as they lost it on the way to the course. The trophy was eventually tracked down by a local golf writer who spotted a likely box tucked away in the corner of the parcel office at the nearby St Annes railway station.

Gary Player triumphed in 1974 by breaking par in all four rounds, and his victory meant that he had won The Open in three different decades. Although his lead was rarely threatened, many will still recall his left-handed putt played inches from the clubhouse wall on the last hole. Seve Ballesteros emulated Player's four sub-par rounds in 1979, but Ben Crenshaw had been in contention until a double-bogey six on the seventy-first hole whilst Ballesteros seemed to miss every fairway; his recoveries from a car park and other wild parts of the course have entered golfing folklore. Ballesteros clearly loves the course as he started the 1988 Open with three straight birdies and was five-under-par after ten holes. Nick Price and Nick Faldo had moved into contention after

Visitors are encouraged to spend a night in the Dormy House and enjoy a full English breakfast in the clubhouse dining room before treading in the famous footsteps around the course.

ROYAL ST GEORGE'S

13 OPEN CHAMPIONSHIPS

Writing in 1890, Horace Hutchinson identified the frustrations which had caused Dr. Laidlaw Purves and fellow Wimbledon player Henry Lamb to seek a top class golfing venue on the South Coast. Golf on Wimbledon Common was restricted to three days per week by the Conservators and Hutchinson reported: "...the ground is far from perfect. In fact, it is almost an insult to the game to dignify it by the name of golf. Rather may we call it a wonderful substitute for the game within so short a distance of Charing Cross."

Purves and Lamb had started their search for a southern equivalent of the St Andrews links at Bournemouth, and must have begun to despair of finding suitable land when Purves and his brother, a keen archaeologist, arrived in Sandwich town. Legend tells that in 1885, Purves climbed the tower of St. Clement's Church and saw the distant dunes and flat grassland which looked like ideal links land.

Purves negotiated a lease from the Earl of Guildford, and Henry Lamb and Robert Anderson, another Scot, helped Purves form the Sandwich Golf Association on behalf of the Club. Purves named the course St George's after England's patron saint in the belief that he had finally discovered the perfect southern links to complement St Andrews.

The inaugural meeting of the Club was held at the Metropole Hotel in London in May 1887 and the first golfing competition took place a few days later. Purves's layout was well received and Hutchinson wrote that: "The first five holes are so good that, in our opinion, they are nowhere excelled...there is, moreover, far severer punishment for devious driving

and for topped shots than at St Andrews." The initial layout included a number of blind shots over bunkers, the most famous of which required a full drive over the Maiden sand dune.

Early members were generous with prize money and in 1888 Hutchinson reported that the Club had hosted: "...as representative a gathering of professional talent as had ever been seen in golfing history." In 1894 a potential players' revolt over the

Above: View from the eighteenth fairway to the starter's hut

Left: Joshua Crane's 18-inch putter and one-handed putting style was not a success and he **did** not qualify for the later rounds of an early Open!

size of the prize fund for the Open Championship was narrowly averted when an additional £30 was added to the traditional pot of £100, and Sandwich hosted the first Open Championship to be held south of the Border. The event marked the emergence of the Triumvirate of JH Taylor, Harry Vardon and James Braid. Taylor won the Championship by six shots from the big-hitting Douglas Rolland who had acquired his strength whilst working as a stonemason.

From the outset, the St George's Grand Gold Challenge Cup has been one of the most prestigious prizes in amateur golf. John Ball Junior won the first four competitions, Harold Hilton succeeded in 1893 and 1894, Freddie Tait won in 1896, 1898 and 1899 whilst more recent and legendary winners have included 1913 US Open winner Francis Ouimet in 1923, and Jack Nicklaus in 1959.

Henry Lamb was a fine golfer who won many scratch medals, but history also remembers him as the inventor of the 'bulger' driver which led to the eventual demise of the sleek look of earlier straight-faced drivers. HSC Everard wrote that: "As inventor of the bulger club, his name stinks in the nostrils of all who see a thing of beauty in the delicate curves of a real thoroughbred head." Others, however, were keen to share the notoriety. Willie Park Junior wrote to Golf magazine in 1890 claiming that he had invented the bulger and correspondence continued from both sides before interest subsided.

Sandwich continued to host successful Open Championships in the early 1900s and both Harry Vardon and Walter Hagen were double-winners. Although Vardon may have been slightly biased by his success, he referred to Sandwich as the best golf course in

the world! Jack White from Sunningdale won his only Open Championship in 1904 in an event featuring some astonishingly low scores. James Braid's third round of 69 included a 31 on the outward nine holes (five 3s and four 4s), whilst White's final round of 69 was just good enough to win by one shot despite Taylor's final round of 68 which was an Open record and remained unsurpassed for many years.

In 1930, St George's hosted the Walker Cup which was won fairly easily by the US who defeated Great Britain by 10-2. Bobby Jones was Captain of the US team in the year in which he achieved his unique Grand Slam of the old Majors of golf (the Amateur and Open Championships of the US and Great Britain). The 1934 Open Championship was won by Henry Cotton playing some of the greatest golf ever witnessed in an Open tournament. His opening round of 67 was followed by a 65 giving rise to the famous Dunlop 65 brand which lasted for more than half a century.

Although Sandwich had built a terrific golfing heritage, it became apparent that certain changes were required including the removal of several blind shots together with the lengthening of the course. Alterations made first by Alister MacKenzie and later by Frank Pennink included extensive changes to three holes (the third, eighth and eleventh) whilst tees were moved to make the fourth and fourteenth fairways more visible.

The famous short hole by the Maiden dune is no longer played blind over the steepest part of the hillock. Whilst course improvements were necessary, access problems were also improved by the construction of a bypass which eased traffic congestion through the narrow and historic streets of Sandwich town. As a result, the Open was able to return to Royal St George's in 1981 after a break of more than 30 years.

Very few Opens at Sandwich have been won with scores below par over 72 holes. The combination of wind, deep bunkers, lightening fast greens and rolling fairways has defeated most challengers. The main exception occurred in 1993 when the course hosted one of the greatest-ever Opens which turned

Main: *A player emerging from the deep green-side pot bunker at the par-3 sixth hole known as The Maiden.*

Below: *Extract from the 1888 course map showing the blind tee shot over The Maiden. 'The Unknown Sahara' hints at early conditions away from the fairways! (Courtesy of Royal St George's Golf Club)*

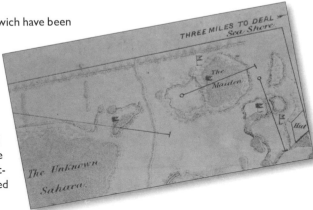

THE OPEN CHAMPIONSHIP						
1894	J.H.Taylor	84	80	81	81	— 326
1899	H.Vardon	76	76	81	77	— 310
1904	J.White	80	75	72	69	— 296
1911	H.Vardon	74	74	75	80	— 303
1922	W.Hagen	76	73	79	72	— 300
1928	W.Hagen	75	73	72	72	— 292
1934	T.H.Cotton	67	65	72	79	— 283
1938	R.A.Whitcombe	71	71	75	78	— 295
1949	A.D.Locke	69	76	68	70	— 283
1981	W.C.Rogers	72	66	67	71	— 276
1985	A.W.B.Lyle	68	71	73	70	— 282
1993	G.Norman	66	68	69	64	— 267
2003	B.Curtis	72	72	70	69	— 283

Above: *View back towards the clubhouse from the right of the first fairway, near the area reserved for the tented village during recent Open Championships*

Inset: *Honours' Board - Hagen's victory in 1922 was the first time that a native-born American had won the British Open. Americans then had ten straight wins until Henry Cotton's triumph at Sandwich in 1934*

into a showdown between the top three golfers in the world at the time, Bernard Langer, Nick Faldo and Greg Norman. Gene Sarazen, who was in the UK to celebrate his historic win at neighbouring Prince's some 61 years earlier, told Norman that he had just witnessed the most awesome display and the greatest championship in his 70 years in golf.

Golf on a peaceful day at Sandwich provides a perfect contrast to the noise and excited galleries surrounding the course during the major championships. On warm Spring and Summer days, the shutters of the clubhouse are thrown open and the noise of the skylarks and crows adds a special flavour to the surroundings.

As Henry Cotton once remarked: "The turf gives lies one dreams about. The ball is always lying a treat, so with the larks singing and the sun shining on the waters of Pegwell, it is a golfer's heaven."

Reg Whitcombe made it five British wins in a row when the Open returned to Sandwich in 1938. The competition was originally planned for neighbouring Deal just three miles down the coast, but disastrous flooding led to the change of venue. Bad weather continued to dog the Championship and the exhibition tent was totally destroyed by overnight storms. The bad weather continued throughout the following day causing some of the highest scores in Open history.

Irishman Harry Bradshaw, came close to winning the 1949 Open, losing to Bobby Locke in a play-off. Famously, during his second round he was unable to claim relief for his ball which had lodged in a broken beer bottle and he dropped two shots. Sandy Lyle therefore became the only post-war British winner of an Open at Sandwich when, in 1985, he won by one stroke despite a bogey on the final hole.

ROYAL BIRKDALE

8 OPEN CHAMPIONSHIPS

Birkdale's place amongst the world's great courses is assured. The fairways are laid out beautifully through undulating and sandy dunes and each hole feels like a separate campaign requiring few of the blind shots which are characteristic of some of the other seaside courses around the coast. The Club has witnessed some of the most memorable events in golfing history.

Birkdale's golfing origins date from July 1889 when nine gentlemen met at 23 Weld Road, Birkdale, the home of JC Barrett, JP, and agreed to the construction of a 9-hole layout over land to be leased at a cost of £5 per annum from Weld Blundell, who became first President of the Club. RG Hayward was elected as first Captain and the formal opening took place in October with the new Club agreeing to adopt the basic rules of West Lancashire Golf Club which was located a few miles down the coast at Blundellsands.

The original short course had its limitations and protracted negotiations with Weld Blundell eventually led to a move to the present location in 1897. Despite his Presidency, the landlord had been cautious about agreeing to a long lease of up to 21 years in case golf turned out to be another passing craze like ping pong and quoits! During the disruption, Birkdale's entire golfing membership was elected to honorary membership of neighbouring Southport (later renamed Hesketh) Golf Club, epitomising the strong historic and co-operative relationships which have bound the old Lancashire clubs over the years.

Today's fourth green has witnessed a number of different golfing buildings. The hole was originally the eighteenth, and the first formal clubhouse was a converted pavilion, purchased from Waterloo Lawn

Tennis Club. Unfortunately, the Club had misunderstood the geography of its lease and the building had to be demolished as it had been erected outside the legal boundaries. The replacement, purchased for £200, was located to the seaward side of the same green and had originally been intended as a hospital in Ormskirk before being dismantled and moved to Birkdale. The building which remains by the green today was originally the Professional's shop and is now used by the artisan golfers.

Southport Corporation deserved great praise for the success of golf in the district. In 1922, the Club was offered the freehold of the links for £19,000 but the price was too high for the members and the Corporation stepped in to buy the land from the landlord. Showing great foresight, the new landlord offered the golfers a long, 99-year lease, provided that the course was remodelled and a new clubhouse constructed in order to create a

Above: The well-bunkered eighteenth green and famous Art Deco clubhouse viewed from the right of the fairway

world-class golfing venue. Course architects Hawtree and Taylor take credit for redesigning the course between the sandhills rather than over them.

The replacement clubhouse is one of the country's best Art Deco buildings and created great interest when it was first opened in July 1935, being described as: "... a ship sailing amidst a mountainous sea of sand dunes." The view of the outside is impressive whilst the view from inside looking out of the large, gracefully curved, windows over the surrounding links is even more remarkable.

The war years set back the Corporation's hopes for immediate success at the improved course, but rapid progress was made soon afterwards. The British Amateur Championship was held in 1946, the inaugural Brabazon Trophy followed in 1947, and both the PGA Matchplay Championship and the Curtis Cup were hosted by Birkdale in 1948.

The long-awaited first Open Championship at the Club was played in 1954, just a few years after Birkdale had become one of the later English clubs to become Royal. It was hoped that Ben Hogan would defend his title won the previous year at Carnoustie, but in the end only a few Americans made the journey and the stage was set for the Australian, Peter Thomson to win the first of his three consecutive Opens, defeating Bobby Locke, Dai Rees and Syd Scott by one shot. The Australian had been runner-up in the previous two years and Pat Ward Thomas wrote: "... there was a sense of inevitability about Thomson's victory. His poise and assurance were remarkable in a young man of 24, his swing classic in its simplicity and beautiful rhythm, and his attitude to the ebb and flow of fortune, that of a great competitor."

The next Open in 1961 was badly affected by atrocious weather. A number of marquees and temporary buildings were blown away before the golf had even started, and further gales led to play being abandoned for a while. Arnold Palmer scored a remarkable 73 during the worst of the storms and his round included a penalty shot when his ball moved in a bunker. Only Palmer had seen the movement and his honesty was rewarded in the later rounds when he performed two of the most remarkable shots in Open history. In his third round at the sixteenth (now seventeenth) hole, the ball drifted into thick rough behind a bush with no apparent route to the pin apart from a small gap through the branches. Undeterred, he laid the blade wide open on a sand wedge and the ball rose, spun and finished a few inches from the hole. His playing partner, Kel Nagle, joined in the cheers.

Even more audaciously, Palmer was again in trouble in the final round on the fifteenth (now sixteenth) hole, having driven under a small bush approximately 140 yards from the green. The sensible play was to hit a wedge out sideways but Palmer reached for a seven-iron. The crowd saw him change his mind but instead of playing for safety Palmer changed up to a six-iron, demolished the bush, and found the green. He won by one shot from Dai Rees, proving that fortune does sometimes favour the brave. Many commentators credit these two shots by an American as being amongst the most important in the development of British golf. As well as cementing the Palmer legend, his success encouraged other world-class Americans to compete in the Open in order to pit themselves against the best. As Michael McDonnell wrote in his book 'Great Moments in Sport': "After Palmer, they all came."

Changes were made to the links in the 1960s to lengthen the course and to cope with the large galleries being attracted to the Open. In particular, a new hole, the twelfth, replaced the old, par-3 seventeenth, which had produced bottlenecks amongst the spectators and was also unpopular with the players who disliked facing a short hole so late in the round.

1965 was a remarkable year at Birkdale as the Club managed to host the Open Championship and the Ryder Cup in the same Summer. One of the strongest ever international fields arrived at Birkdale for The Open in which Peter Thomson achieved his second victory at the venue, joining the illustrious band of the Triumvirate (Braid, Taylor and Vardon) by winning the Championship at least five times. Welshman Brian Huggett and Irishman Christy O'Connor Senior were Thomson's closest pursuers, finishing two shots behind. The Ryder Cup stayed in American hands with the US running out easy winners by seven clear points.

Much greater drama occurred when the Ryder Cup returned to Birkdale four years later. The British team was leading by 13-11 after the morning matches on the last day and needed three and a half points in the afternoon (out of eight) to bring the Cup back across the Atlantic for the first time in twelve years. The afternoon matches remained closely contested and ultimately two decisive matches remained on the course, Huggett against Casper and Jacklin against Nicklaus.

As the wind stiffened, Huggett, trying to sink a 30-foot putt for a win at the final hole slid his attempt four and a half feet past. Hearing a roar from the previous green, Huggett presumed that Jacklin had won his match and that he had to sink the return putt to win the Ryder Cup. The Welshman duly sunk the putt to halve his match but in fact the roar was for Jacklin who had sunk a 55-foot putt for an eagle to level his match.

The two Open Champions moved to the last hole under unbearable pressure. Both players managed to find the green in two shots. Nicklaus hit his attempted birdie putt four feet past the hole whilst Jacklin left his winning attempt an agonising two feet short. In the circumstances, the next putt was not straightforward but Nicklaus conceded for a half, leaving the match tied for the first time in its history. Jacklin had played near immaculate golf throughout the competition which will forever be remembered for Nicklaus' act of great sportsmanship.

Overseas players have won the most recent five Open Championships and Birkdale has still to applaud its first British winner. Lee Trevino defeated the memorable Mr. Lu (Liang-Huan Lu) by one shot in 1971, and Tom

Watson joined the distinguished group of five-time Open winners in 1983. Johnny Miller, Ian Baker-Finch and Mark O'Meara complete the Birkdale winners' list although the 1998 championship will also be remembered for the brave effort of Justin Rose who finished tied fourth, the best result in the Open by a British amateur since Roger Wethered in 1921.

Ladies have played a significant role in the development of golf at Birkdale. The first lady members were elected in 1890 and their section has remained an important and integral part of the Club. The Ladies' British Open Amateur Championship was one of the first important events hosted by the Club in 1909 whilst Birkdale has now become a regular venue for the Women's British Open Championship.

As expected, the course is beautifully maintained and many of the holes, including all of the par-3s, are memorable. The short seventh is one of the most photogenic and includes a doughnut-shaped hazard which must produce some alarming lies for unfortunate golfers lying close to the edge of the bunker furthest from the green! Following changes in the 1960s, Birkdale now has an immensely long finish. Visitors play three par-5s in the last four holes although the Professionals have to play the 472-yard closing hole as a four which helps add to the drama on the final hole in major competitions.

Above: *The beautiful, circular hazard at the par-3 seventh hole. The drive is from an elevated tee and the whole green appears to be surrounded by bunkers*

ROYAL CINQUE PORTS

DEAL

Inset: Supporters watching a close match at the nineteenth hole during a recent Halford Hewitt competition. The green is visible from the clubhouse and is guarded by a small stream ensuring a stiff challenge in tight matches

The links at Deal occupy a historic stretch of the Kent Coast. Julius Caesar landed nearby 2,000 years ago and the Cinque Ports, including Deal, date back 1,000 years. Henry VIII was closely connected with the existing castles at Deal and neighbouring Walmer.

The East Coast Mercury newspaper mentioned plans for a golf course in 1890, and the first documented meeting was held at the Union Club in Walmer in February 1892. Major General Graham acted as Chairman and other attendees included Lt. Col. Shewell, Major Hungerford, Captain Eccles and three civilians. The meeting heard that rights to play golf at Sandhills had been obtained from the Deal Corporation, Lord Northbourne and the Ordnance Department.

The first course, of nine holes, was opened in the Spring and Graham won the first competition with a gross 18-hole score of 109, net 95. The clubhouse, which is still occupied today, was opened in November 1892 and over the next few years the Club hosted several important events. The first professional competition was held in 1894 immediately following the first Open Championship to be held in England at the neighbouring St George's Club in Sandwich, and was won by Sandy Herd with four, 9-hole rounds of 38, 42, 40 and 41 (aggregate 161). Herd won £15 with James Braid winning £2 and Andrew Kirkaldy, who had finished third at Sandwich, £1.

Deal has had close relationships with St George's over the years. One famous connection occurred on a Winter's day in 1898 when Freddie Tait, who had won the 1896 Amateur Championship at Sandwich,

backed himself to play a gutta ball in forty teed shots from the St George's clubhouse to the Cinque Ports clubhouse. He was to hole out by hitting any part of the building. Eyewitnesses confirm that he holed out with his 32nd shot which went through a window and startled a serving maid cleaning silver who had to be mollified with part of his wager winnings!

The course was expanded to eighteen holes in 1898, and although further alterations were made by James Braid in 1919, the first three holes and the last three of today's course still use the original greens laid down by Henry Hunter in 1892. Discretion determined that changes were required to the original short fourth hole as the tee shot was played blind from near the sea, over a bank and onto a green hidden in a hollow. Doug Green, who was a member of the greenstaff for fifty years until 1984, told of how his grandfather remembered: "... there were more holes-in-one than enough as the caddies (who had walked ahead from the third green) nudged the tee shots into the holes to earn

Above: *View from the pebble beach, across two fairways to the clubhouse which was completed in 1892*

gold sovereigns from their grateful gentlemen." The fourth green today is clearly visible from the tee although onshore gales can still make the hole a tricky proposition.

By 1900, the Club had begun to host small invitation challenge matches for large prizes, and in 1905 Harry Vardon and JH Taylor beat Braid and Herd in a foursomes match for what was then a huge purse of £200. Vardon's game, and in particular his putting, seemed to be affected by Deal and he was rumoured to prefer playing at Sandwich although in April 1908 he wrote: "... the more I play at the Deal course the more I like it and am glad to see it has been added to the Championship courses." James Braid remarked that he rated Deal as the best course that he had played in England whilst Ben Sayers commented that: "... the Deal course is the best golf course ever I played on."

In 1908, Deal hosted the annual England against Scotland Professionals' match. The fixture had started in 1903 with a win for Scotland, but England had won the previous two events leading up to Deal. The match was effectively decided in the morning

when England won the foursomes by nine matches to two with one half, and in the afternoon chief interest surrounded the match in which Braid and Herd halved with Taylor and Vardon. Contemporary articles described the record of this 'Quartette' and it was only later that Herd was excluded from the group which became known as The Great Triumvirate. At the time Braid and Taylor came out bracketed first in international matches with Herd's record matching that of Vardon.

Deal's addition to the Open roster in 1909 arose from a perceived need to balance the Scottish/ English courses. At the time, Scotland had three courses (St Andrews, Prestwick and Muirfield) whilst England only had two (Sandwich and Hoylake). This was thought to be unfair to travelling English golfers. Deal had severe competition for the honour from Westward Ho! which was supported by St Andrews and it may have been Deal's extra length which persuaded a majority of the Committee to vote for the Royal Cinque Ports Club.

Further fame nearly came to Deal in 1908 when the Olympic organisers agreed for a tournament to be played over Cinque Ports, St George's and the neighbouring Prince's courses. However, at the last moment, The R&A refused to sanction the event, perhaps fearing a potential loss of control over the rules and conduct of the game.

Sea flooding in 1908 briefly jeopardised Deal's first Open, but a public subscription raised £850 to rectify the problems and in 1909 a record 204 entrants took part with James Braid and Arnaud Massy being viewed as likely favourites. Players were allowed to use a rubber-cored ball rather than gutties for the first time, and in the end JH Taylor won comfortably by four shots from Braid with an aggregate of 295, winning the Gold Medal and a first prize of £30 out of a total prize fund of £100. The tournament was judged to be a success and Cinque Ports was promised the 1915 Open although the Great War prevented the event from being staged until 1920.

Several courses lay claim to the best Walter Hagen story, but Deal would seem to have a fair case. Hagen's flamboyant reputation had preceded him across the Atlantic and when he and Jim Barnes

arrived at Deal for a practice round before the 1920 Open, they went into the clubhouse to change shoes before commencing play. They were met by an over-eager head locker steward who informed them that, as Professionals, they would have to use the Professional's shop as a changing room in future. Having made a brief visit to the shop to introduce themselves, the two golfers decided that their rented Austro-Daimler limousine would make a better changing room!

Hagen and Barnes were met at the eighteenth green by the Club Secretary who was initially apologetic about the earlier misunderstanding, but then went on to reaffirm that Professionals were not allowed to use the clubhouse facilities. Horrendous weather affected Hagen's game in the Open and he trailed in near the back of the field but still maintained his upbeat attitude until, in his own words: "... it took Deal's little Mr. Secretary to finish me off." "I'm sorry you didn't do better, 'Eye-Gen', he gloated, "but golf over here is very difficult. I do hope you'll come back some future year and try again." "Don't worry about me," said Hagen, "you'll see my name on that cup!". In fact, Hagen went on to win four of the next nine Opens.

The 1920 Open at Deal was won by George Duncan who overturned a thirteen shot deficit with Abe Mitchell after two rounds. Mitchell's excellent first two rounds of 73 and 74 had included a hole-in-one at the eighth but he slumped to a disastrous third round 84 and Duncan's great fightback was attributed to his purchase of a new driver in the exhibition tent. Mitchell finished in the top five of the Open on five occasions over a 20-year period and was often described as the finest player never to win the title.

In 1922, Deal suffered another of its great floods and was dropped from the Open roster but by 1923 it had recovered sufficiently to host the British Amateur Championship which was won by Roger Wethered, husband of the famous Joyce. Great excitement surrounded the semi-final when a crowd of three thousand watched Wethered beat the American, Francis Ouimet, who had previously won

the 1913 US Open at the age of 20 and, much later, became the first American Captain of The R&A.

By the mid-1920s, Deal's London membership had become significant and during one Summer it was believed that rumours of the course's difficulty were preventing players from making the journey down to the Coast. The Club therefore sent a postcard to all members explaining that the rough had been dealt with and that the course was in great condition! This may have been wise marketing because in 1925 the Public Schools Golfing Society decided to hold its fledgling competition in Deal. The 1924 event had been organised by GL 'Susie' Mellin, an Old Malvernian who was also a Cambridge soccer and golf Blue, and the competition that year had taken place over several months on a knockout basis culminating in Eton defeating Winchester in the final at The Addington.

The 1924 competition had been adversely affected by the crowded nature of the London courses and Halford Hewitt, who was Treasurer of Deal at the time and an old boy of Charterhouse, offered to donate the cup which would be played for over a long weekend at Deal in 1925. 'Hal' Hewitt became Captain of Deal in 1929 and 1930 as well as in the war period between 1943 and 1945.

The Halford Hewitt old boys' cup has grown into one of the world's most successful foursomes competitions and is held in early Spring when the weather can be atrocious. The competition attracts 640 golfers representing 64 schools plus numerous supporters and the first two rounds are now shared

ROYAL

1902	BRITISH LADIES AMATEUR CHAMPIONSHIP
	Miss M.Hezlet beat Miss E.Neville at 19th
1909	OPEN CHAMPIONSHIP
	J.H.Taylor 74-73-74-74-295
1920	OPEN CHAMPIONSHIP
	G.Duncan 80-80-71-72-303
1923	BRITISH AMATEUR CHAMPIONSHIP
	R.H.Wethered beat R.Harris 7 and 6

between Royal Cinque Ports and neighbouring Royal St George's in order to complete the tournament on time. The early years of the Halford Hewitt Cup were dominated by Charterhouse, Eton and Harrow but other teams including Tonbridge have started to challenge more recently. Many foursomes matches are settled on the eighteenth or nineteenth green, both of which are protected by streams and are easily visible from the clubhouse balcony; there can be no hiding place in tight games.

Throughout its history, Deal has enjoyed close ties with royalty. In the early 1900s, HRH The Prince of Wales, later Edward VII, played regularly on his visits to Deal and he was President of the Club from 1905-1907. King George V accepted the Patronage in 1910 and continued until his death in 1935, and Deal's right to use the Royal title was reconfirmed by King George VI in 1949. Prince Andrew, Duke of York, accepted Patronage in 2002, and his first role was to present the winner of the 'Queen Elizabeth, the Queen Mother Cup' which the Queen Mother had presented to Jack Aisher, the long-time President of the Club, at Walmer Castle in July 2001. In her role as Lord Warden of the Cinque Ports, the Queen Mother had once told the Club that she thought that Cinque should probably be pronounced as sink, as in 'kitchen sink', although her Private Secretary added that she would not wish to be dogmatic about it!

In many ways it is a miracle that golf is still played at Deal. Floods again prevented the Club from holding the Open in 1938 when the event was moved along the road to Sandwich, and they also ruined the Club's chances of hosting the event in 1949 when Sandwich again came to the rescue. The devastation this time was so great that the course did not recover in time to hold the planned Ryder Cup match which was therefore moved to Ganton.

By way of variety, Deal was unable to host the planned English Open Amateur Strokeplay Championship in 1974 because of the petrol rationing crisis and Moortown near Leeds was chosen as a more 'fuel efficient' venue. The worst floods of all occurred in 1978 and 1979 and a new sea wall was finally constructed in 1981.

Today, Deal remains a final qualifying course for the Open Championship when it is held at Royal St George's and it also continues to host other important national and international events including the Brabazon Trophy.

The great Bernard Darwin was Captain of the Club in 1930 and his thoughts still carry a resonance today: "Deal is a truly great course, I incline myself to think the most testing of all Championship courses... this smiling corner of the earth's surface has for me something that no other spot, not even perhaps St Andrews, can quite equal."

HALFORD HEWITT CUP

1924	Eton	beat	Winchester.
1925	Eton	"	Harrow.
1926	Eton	"	Winchester.
1927	Harrow	"	Rugby.
1928	Eton	"	Charterhouse.
1929	Harrow	"	Charterhouse.
1930	Charterhouse	"	Uppingham.
1931	Harrow	"	Winchester.
1932	Charterhouse	"	Rugby.
1933	Rugby	"	Harrow.
1934	Charterhouse	"	Watsons.
1935	Charterhouse	"	Shrewsbury.

PRINCE'S

The origins of Prince's, Sandwich, share similarities with those of neighbouring Royal St George's. Both links courses were founded by London-based golfers seeking less crowded and more challenging links away from the city and its surrounds.

The original golf course at Mitcham Common, a few miles to the South of London, was laid out by the Prince's Club Ltd in 1891, but the Conservators of the Common reserved the entitlement for the public to walk and exercise their rights over the land. The course was planned by Old Tom Morris of St Andrews and Tom Dunn, the Professional of the then highly-regarded Tooting Bec Golf Club.

By 1905, membership of the popular Mitcham Club had reached 700, but following its purchase by businessman Sir Harry Mallaby-Deeley, the Member of Parliament for Mitcham, the Club became more exclusive and the cry was heard of: "Mitcham Common for Mitcham people." As an attempted compromise, the Mitcham Village Golf Club for local players was founded under Sir Harry's presidency. However, this did not provide a solution and the matter ended up in the High Court where it was decided that Mitcham Common had been preserved for the community as a whole and that any agreements between the Conservators and the Prince's Golf Club were ultra vires. In 1924, Sir Harry decided to donate the clubhouse and the Mitcham links to the Conservators in order to resolve the problem.

It is little wonder that Sir Harry and his friends, including fellow Cambridge University colleague Percy Montague (PM) Lucas, were keen to start another course away from the hassles of the London common. Mallaby-Deeley identified suitable land immediately adjacent to the well-

established Royal St George's course in Sandwich, and the Earl of Guildford donated the land to the golfers with the proviso that at least £2,000 was spent on the construction of the course.

The 1902 Amateur Champion Charles Hutchins was engaged to assist Lucas lay out the new course, and this was completed in 1906. The prolific golfer and former Prime Minister, AJ Balfour, was elected as the Club's first Captain and drove the first ball in the Founder's Vase in June 1907.

Balfour and Hamilton-Deeley ensured that the Club was well-regarded from the outset. Golf Illustrated reported at the time that the formal opening of the new seaside course was an event of great importance in the golfing world. The architects had been able to take into account the greater distances covered by the new rubber-cored 'Haskell' balls, and the article continued: "the great and outstanding glory of Prince's golf course is the situation and character of the putting greens. The flags do not simply occur, like telegraph poles, as they do on many modern courses, for no other apparent reason that it is so many yards from the last teeing ground. Each hole thus forms a separate campaign." The journal concluded that: "...the result is a links so ideally perfect that criticism is disarmed."

Although the Club was highly fashionable in the early years, the founders had been keen to encourage a wider class of players, including ladies and juniors, and this cause was helped when the Club hosted the 1912 English Ladies' Open Championship. Just as the course was reaching its prime, the Great War saw the links taken over for coastal defence and training with barbed-wire entanglements and anti-aircraft batteries. Lucas

Above: *Open Champion Gene Sarazen with the claret jug following his win at Prince's in 1932 (Courtesy Prince's Golf Club)*

Main: View of the ninth green on the Himalayas loop taken from the clubhouse balcony. The white cliffs of Pegwell Bay are visible in the distance.

Above: Laddie Lucas, aged five, on his way to winning the Juvenile Challenge Cup for golfers up to the age of thirteen at nearby North Foreland Golf Club in 1921. His prize was the Laddie Lucas Spoon (effectively a 3-wood) which Abe Mitchell, the famous Professional at North Foreland had specially made for him by his personal club maker (Courtesy Prince's Golf Club)

kept the greens cut throughout the war and the Argyll and Sutherland Highlanders billeted in the clubhouse nicknamed Percy's young son as Laddie.

Laddie became a fine golfer at an early age and he was able to develop his skills after the war whilst the course was returned to its old glories. Prince's hosted the 1922 Ladies' Open Championship, won by Joyce Wethered, and in 1932 the course had its finest hour when selected as the venue for the Open Championship. The three days, with 36 holes played on the final day, produced ideal golfing conditions and Gene Sarazen led after each round and won by five shots in a record low score of 283.

Laddie's golfing career blossomed in the 1930s and he was the leading amateur in the 1935 Open at Muirfield, but his golf career and Prince's advance were halted by the return of war to Europe. The links were again requisitioned and the course was virtually obliterated by battle training. The famous golf sponsor, Lord Brabazon, likened its use for target practice to: "throwing darts at a Rembrandt."

The hostilities did not keep Laddie out of the golfing spotlight. Eventually decorated as Wing Commander PB Lucas, CBE, DSO, DFC he served as a fighter pilot and after one sortie was forced to land his damaged Spitfire close to the Prince's links which caused a senior member to proffer the immortal rebuke: "in the rough again Lucas!" Fortunately, Laddie was not seriously injured and he returned to golf after the war and captained the British Walker Cup team in 1949.

The Club was slow to recover after the end of hostilities, but eventually finance was made available by Sir Aynsley

Bridgland and major reconstruction commenced, hole by hole, in late 1949 under the control of John Morrison and Sir Guy Campbell.

Damage had been so great that the Club decided to build a brand new links, although seventeen of the original greens were incorporated into the new layout featuring three loops of nine holes. This approach was not popular with everyone and Henry Longhurst, writing in The Sunday Times in 1971, conjectured that: "...they should surely have constructed the original course that had made Prince's famous and which so many of its old friends would remember." Today's clubhouse is situated inland from the shoreline whilst the original building was situated right next to the beach.

Whilst it is true that Prince's does not enjoy the same sense of historic continuity as neighbouring Royal St George's, the complete redesign did enable the Club to construct a course which was a realistic challenge for Club and society golfers whilst at the same time being capable of hosting major championships. Many of the greens are set slightly above the fairways placing a premium on accurate iron play, and only thirteen of the 27 holes are protected by greenside bunkers.

Played off the back tees in windy conditions and with high grass in the rough, the course provides a very tough test of golf.

The Club has hosted four Final Qualifying competitions in the last 25 years when the Open has been held at neighbouring Royal St George's, and it is fair to say that Prince's is now rebuilding its position towards the top of the list of great courses in the country.

EARLY SEASIDE LINKS

The Victorian railway system played a vital role in carrying golfers from the cities to the wide open links on the coast. Golfers' Halts were built on many lines and the game helped drive the development of a number of holiday towns including Hunstanton, Littlestone, Silloth on Solway, Skegness (Seacroft) and Southwold. Golfers were taken to Rye (below) by the Rye-Camber tram which stopped at the Golf Links Station.

Hayling 1883
Formby 1884
Southwold 1884
Hesketh 1885
Cleveland 1887
Littlestone 1888
Littlehampton 1889
Berwick upon Tweed 1890
West Cornwall 1889
Burnham & Berrow 1890
Hunstanton 1891
Wallasey 1891
Royal West Norfolk 1892
Silloth on Solway 1892
Rye 1894
Seacroft 1895

HAYLING

THE SANDEMAN FAMILY

Hayling owes the success of its golf Club to the early efforts of the Sandeman family who are best known for their famous ports and wines. The first meeting of the Hayling Island Golfing Club was held in August 1883 at Whinhurst on South Hayling, which was the home of Lieutenant-Colonel John Glas Sandeman. The original Committee unanimously elected themselves and included three Sandeman brothers as well as two further relations by marriage, Major Alfred Lynch and Captain GJ Lynch Staunton. Fleetwood Sandeman was elected the first Captain and served in that role for the first fifteen years through to 1897. The Lieutenant-Colonel was unanimously elected as Honorary Treasurer and, shortly afterwards, Miss Maud Sandeman was appointed first Captain of

the newly formed Hayling Island Ladies' Golfing Club with another Miss Sandeman acting as the first ladies' Club Treasurer.

Aside from the Sandemans, key early members included The Rev. J Cumming MacDona, who had travelled south from West Kirby near Hoylake, in order to Chair the inaugural meeting, Captain George C Wylie, F Crawford, who played off scratch, and Captain Ronald Alexander who drew an early sketch of the course and its characters. The Club's first Professional, Joseph Lloyd of Hoylake, nicknamed: "The General", was appointed in 1883 at a rate of 18 shillings per week. It is likely that the Reverend would have known about Lloyd from his West Kirby connections.

The Rev. MacDona, Fleetwood Sandeman, and a non-golfing brother, Albert George Sandeman, shared an interest in importing and breeding Arab horses. For a time, the Beach Common was also the site of an annual race meeting which was no doubt well patronised by the Sandeman family.

The first course of nine holes was situated on Beach Common, just to the east of the current course and in front of what was then the Bay Hotel. The first clubhouse was at Whinhurst, the Lieutenant-Colonel's home, but the Club soon relocated its headquarters to the hotel.

London Scottish members were frequent visitors to Hayling in the early years and must have felt at ease. The Portsmouth Times in November 1884, reporting on the dinner at the Autumn Meeting, noted that: "the ladies were escorted home after dinner by the members of the Club, headed by Mr. F Crawford playing spiritual reels and marches upon the bagpipes, upon

which national instrument of the cradle and home of golfing, he is an accomplished performer." Hayling's golfers today play annually for the London Scottish Cup, presented in 1898 by stalwart members from the club on Wimbledon Common.

The original course was soon expanded to eighteen holes in a westerly direction and the extended links were first used in the Club's Autumn Meeting of 1884. The land used for the new nine holes was leased to Fleetwood Sandeman personally, and it was not until 1894 that the relevant leases were transferred to the Club.

Early handicaps were quite flexible. Colonel T Duff Cater played off a handicap of 50 on the Saturday of the 1884 Autumn Meeting but he still came last with a net score of 149 and his handicap was extended to 100 for the Monday medal round which enabled him to finish in mid-field with a net score of 106! F Crawford, playing off scratch, managed to beat the Colonel by 3 shots.

The Club shortened its name to Hayling Golf Club in 1890, and two years later Vardon and Braid visited the Club and played an exhibition match. Open Champion JH Taylor was engaged in 1905 for a fee of £11 to recommend improvements to the layout, and some of the classic links feel enjoyed today must be credited to Taylor. In 1909, the first two holes were still played at the Beach Common end of the links and part of

the thirteenth and fourteenth holes were played on the far side of the road at the ferry end of the course. After the Great War, course architect Tom Simpson made significant changes which brought the course closer to its present boundaries. In facilitating these arrangements, the tenth hole was extended by 235 yards, a new eleventh hole was constructed and new greens were laid at the twelfth and thirteenth holes.

The course at Hayling is approximately fifteen miles by road from Portsmouth, but less than half a mile by ferry and there is still a small clubhouse by the existing thirteenth green. This was built to assist Portsmouth based golfers from the Services who decided to take the ferry across the mouth of the estuary from Eastney in Portsmouth in order to play the course.

The Club has had a number of famous visitors. In July 1935, the Prince of Wales and the Duke of Kent took time away from the Royal Yacht Victoria and Albert on which they had been preparing for the Naval Review at nearby Spithead. The newspapers chronicled that: "the Duke of Kent found a spot of trouble in the shape of lost balls, and to crown it all, his shirt which he had taken off, got lost on the course." It must have been a hot Summer! Bobby Locke first visited Hayling in 1936 as a 19-year-old amateur and won the Club's Easter Open Championship with a two-round total of 144. 23 years later, and as the proud winner of four Open

Championships, he returned to the Club and set a new course record of 65.

Hayling has hosted several English Ladies' Closed Amateur Championships and in the 1936 final, the famous Wanda Morgan beat Miss Wade 2&1.

On commencement of the Second World War, the course to the west of the seventh fairway was requisitioned to help defend the nearby naval base at Portsmouth. The course was hit by a number of German bombs and many of the craters are still visible today, particularly to the right of the ninth and fourteenth holes. During the war, the old thirteenth green became completely buried by sand and the opportunity was taken in the course of post-war repairs to build a new green closer to the Ferry Clubhouse. A new fairway was also constructed and the hole has lost some of its former venom. The nickname Widow referred to a massive sand dune bunker which used to capture many tee shots and it was said that: "Once trapped by the Widow's clutches, it was difficult to escape."

Hayling Ladies' Golf Club was founded in 1884 and is believed to be the third oldest ladies' club in the country. Their first competition was held in July 1884, and had 21 entrants although only seven cards were handed in. Miss M Sandeman won the first prize and Mrs J Bell,

the mother of the Bishop of Chichester, was runner-up. The local press reporting on the Winter 1884 ladies' meeting noted that most of the competitors appeared in the new uniform of scarlet jackets: "the appearance of which on the green imparted a gay and warming effect to what was otherwise a dull and bleak day." At one time there was a separate ladies' course but this seems to have been short-lived. Male chauvinism affected life at Hayling as at many other clubs in late Victorian times. In 1899, the minutes record that: "At an Extraordinary General Meeting (after the completion of the clubhouse) it was carried by a majority vote that the ladies would not be invited into the clubhouse for afternoon tea."

Jack Smith served as the Club's Professional for 53 years. He became Assistant Professional to his brother in 1912 and took over the main role when his brother retired in 1921. Amongst Hayling's male golfers, Ian Patey stands out as the most successful. He won the English Amateur Championship at Royal Mid-Surrey in 1946 and was runner-up in 1950 as a result of which he was made an Honorary Life Member of the Club. Members play annually for the Patey Salver which was presented by Ian in 1963 in memory of his father, AP Patey, who was Honorary Secretary from 1939-1949 and played an important part in helping the Club to survive during the difficult war years.

The links are situated on unusual terrain. The topsoil is relatively thin but the course drains extremely well as there are huge shingle deposits immediately below the surface which help Hayling to be an all-weather course. The Club is frequently open for play when other courses are closed due to frost and water-logging. The habitat has also led to the course being established as a Site of Special Scientific Interest. Unusual flowers found on the course include two rare orchids as well as Childing Pink which is a native dwarf carnation and Little Robin which is a member of the geranium family.

Short-eared owls are regular Winter visitors to the links and Dartford warblers have bred in recent years. Wheatears are visible on their Spring migration and yellow wagtails and ospreys have been seen on Autumn migration. Golfers need to keep an eye out in the rough for adders.

The most memorable holes on the course feature at the far end of the links. The round starts quietly with an opening par-3, but as at many coastal courses, the wind can have a huge impact on club selection and it can take anything between a short iron and a driver. The sixth hole, par-4, is only 434 yards off the back tee but the stroke index one is deserved. The hole is often played into the wind and there is a water hazard just short of the green occupying a cutting which was made during the preliminary work on a railway line which was never completed.

The par-5 seventh stretches across the full width of the peninsular and leads play across to the beach side of the course and the start of the classic corner. The short par-4 eighth requires a blind second shot to the pin over a sand dune, and the ninth has a well-positioned bunker which catches most people trying to take the tiger line to the green. The short par-4 tenth looks like a birdie opportunity, but the green is quite narrow and crooked shots are penalised whilst the par-3 eleventh green is surrounded by bunkers and the hole is often played into the teeth of the wind.

The drive from the twelfth tee on the Desert hole is still quite daunting although some of its former devilry has been lost. The hole is played parallel to the beach, with out of bounds on the left and trouble either side of the fairway. The thirteenth continues in the same direction and is a classic hole, tempting long drivers to try for the green but exacting a heavy penalty for all but the luckiest gamblers. The elevated scrubland to the left of the fairway is treacherous and the second shot to the green needs to be hit carefully as the green slopes away from the fairway and out of bounds lurks close behind.

The par-5 fourteenth is another testing hole and shorter drivers treat it as a double dogleg, explaining its local nickname of the Banana hole. Scrubland and a lateral water hazard are both well positioned to trap players trying to take the tiger line rather than staying on the fairway. The drive at the fifteenth hole has to clear thick gorse and a water hazard occupying the old railway cutting, although there is more room behind the vegetation than appears at first sight. There is trouble on both sides of the eighteenth hole but it is certainly best to avoid flirting with the out of bounds down the left hand side of the fairway.

Hayling is an excellent golf course providing conditions to test the best golfers. The new clubhouse is beautifully designed and the views on a clear day are stunning. The Club is right to assert that it is: "one of the best courses in the South of England."

Main: View from the clubhouse roof towards the seventeenth green. The red flag is just visible behind the bunkers. The water-filled gravel pit is now a nature reserve where more than 65 species of birds have been recorded

Above: The Bay Hotel features in the background of this drawing by a founding member, Ronald Alexander. The Secretary, Harry Liddell is shown on the left. The Captain, Fleetwood Sandeman, is pictured below the lady players. Further Sandemans, including The Colonel and the Hon. Treasurer appear to the bottom right (Courtesy Hayling Golf Club)

FORMBY

Above: Jose Maria Olazabal (left) beat Colin Montgomerie 5&4 in the final of the 1984 Amateur Championship (Courtesy Formby Golf Club)

Below: The clubhouse viewed from a bunker on the eighteenth fairway. The original clubhouse was burned down in 1899 and the replacement was completed in 1901 with the clock tower being added in 1909

Formby Golf Club lies along the famous Lancashire Golf Coast and is characterised by the fir trees which line the links-like fairways, protecting the course from the worst of the winds which blow in from the nearby Irish Sea. A fir tree features as the Club's emblem and the woods contain a rare population of red squirrels. The main course is played in a large anti-clockwise circle with the central area being occupied by the links belonging to the separate Formby Ladies' Golf Club.

The early story of golf at Formby is hazy as most of the records were destroyed in a clubhouse fire in the late 1890s, but it is known that a group of 24 local businessmen founded the Club in 1884. JS Beauford was one of the founding members and was Captain in both 1887 and 1892. A number of early members were associated with the shipping industry which had been booming in nearby Liverpool.

The initial 9-hole course was rented from a tenant farmer during the Winter months for a fee of £10 per season, whilst the links had been expanded to eighteen holes by 1896 following the purchase of Sutton's Farm.

Willie Park and James Braid both advised on early changes to the enlarged course and major changes were made during the 1970s to combat sea encroachment including the construction of the new seventh to ninth holes, designed by Donald Steel, which took the course away from the shoreline.

Formby has hosted many important competitions including three Amateur Championships in 1957, 1967 and 1984, whilst the biggest event so far has been the two-day 33rd Curtis Cup match played during June 2004 over the main course between the leading lady amateurs from Great Britain & Ireland and the USA. The Americans retained the trophy 10-8 in front of galleries of 8,000 per day.

The ladies' course is shorter than the men's, measuring approximately 5,370 yards, but the fairways are narrower and the greens smaller, placing a premium on accuracy rather than distance. In 1998, the Junior World Championship was played over both courses and Greg Norman and Tom Watson walked with their sons. Norman later wrote of the ladies' course: "...over 100-years-old and still your course can stand the test of time. What a beautiful course. It clearly shows that courses do not have to be 7,000 plus yards to be formidable."

The ladies' links have also hosted the British Girls' Championship and several Girls' Home Internationals as well as the British (men's) Seniors' and the inaugural Ladies' Seniors' championships.

The Ladies' Club is proud of its independence. They have a Captain (not 'Lady Captain'), a separate clubhouse and their own Greenkeepers although some specialist machinery is shared between the two clubs. The front extension to their clubhouse is widely referred to as the

Monkey House as that is where most of the chattering has been done over the years!

Whilst Norman and Watson have walked around Formby, other golfing greats have competed over the main course. Jose Maria Olazabal beat Colin Montgomerie in the final of the 1984 Amateur Championship whilst other champions have included Sir Michael and Lady Bonallack, Sam Snead and Diana Fishwick. Harold Hilton won the Club's two scratch Spring medals a total of 20 times and fellow Hoylake member John Ball also features on the honours' boards.

The main lounge contains an unusual exhibit. The story of the hippo's original journey to Formby is strange enough, but its subsequent 'holiday' away from the Club bears repeating as it also encapsulates golfing history during the war. The story is told in the book 'Convoy is to Scatter' by Capt. Jack Broome, RN.

"...our motor boat had some petrol. Ignoring the risk of German invasion in the next few hours we left Gladstone Dock, unobserved, bound for Formby Golf Club. The course was netted with barbed wire, pocked marked with tank traps, the Club house, now a sand-bagged fortress, was in military hands, but there was still a golf course. A remarkable obstacle race was followed by a riotous dinner with the Army in occupation....as we descended the stairs to leave, there, in a glass case, was the open mouthed for'd end of a hippo, breaking surface through the wired reeds of a plastic swamp. We all agreed it looked sad and wan..... With great care we withdrew him from his case....In Liverpool we were treated with a full scale air raid, out of which sprang a tense young policeman who immediately ordered us off the road. We pleaded a wounded aunt in the back; he lifted the rug, flashed his torch into the cavernous mouth, and gave us no further trouble."

The story goes on to recount how the hippo was taken aboard a Royal Navy boat and survived a Luftwaffe bombing raid in the Norwegian fjords before being returned to the Club. "The local Admiral, an ardent golfer and member of Formby Golf Club had heard the story. I was summoned and threatened with Court Martial. Having got that off his chest, the Admiral cooled and settled for an instant return of Hippo - and a personal apology to the Golf Club Committee from all concerned."

Formby is unusual in having only three par-3s. The course starts with three tough holes stretching away from the clubhouse and bordered by threatening out of bounds on the railway line to the right of and immediately behind the protective pines. The railway was of great benefit to the development of golf along this section of the Lancashire Coast and the full story has been told in the book 'Links Along The Line', written by Harry Foster.

The course contains a large number of bunkers; some are particularly noticeable from the tee on the thirteenth hole where four sand traps appear to occupy the majority of the fairway at around 200 yards. Fortunately, the sand is of excellent links quality leaving no excuses for poor recovery shots.

Writing in 1910 in his book, 'Golf Courses of the British Isles', Bernard Darwin's description of Formby is still apposite today: "...we finish with a good two shot hole on to a fine big green in front of a fine big clubhouse. The greens are beautifully green; they are likewise very true and keen enough without ever being bare and hard. The lies, too, are excellent, and it is altogether one of those courses where the player's fate is entirely in his own hands. If he plays well everything will conspire to help him on his way, but he has to play really well-good, sterling, honest golf, there is no mistake about that at Formby."

The Club has a small Dormy House which can accommodate up to ten people in two single and four twin rooms for golfers wishing to extend their stay, and the two courses will provide an enjoyable challenge for all players planning a holiday amongst the Lancashire coastal links.

Top: Pines and grassy banks guard the approach to the seventh green

Above: The much-travelled hippo is a feature in the lounge

SOUTHWOLD

REVERTED TO 9 HOLES – 1953

Below: The historic buildings of Southwold viewed from the links

The town of Southwold enjoyed an early act of benevolence. In 1509, William Godyl left the local common and marshes to the people of Southwold 'forever', and the land is therefore administered by trustees who are able to determine how the land should be used.

The first meeting of the Club was held in January 1884, and at that time the only other golf clubs in East Anglia were Cambridge University, Felixstowe and Great Yarmouth, with Aldeburgh starting later the same year. Following permission from Southwold Corporation and the trustees, a 9-hole course was laid out. Unusually, the Club was formed as the Southwold Golf and Quoits Club. The rules proposed reduced subscriptions for 'quoits-only' members, but only one

original subscriber opted for this arrangement and the Club then dropped all mention of quoits, although a separate club did continue to play the game in the town for a number of years. The Field magazine carried details of Southwold's first internal golf competition in August 1884, but the game did not take off in the early years and play was mainly restricted to a few enthusiasts on the Committee who had to cut the grass on the course themselves, and at their own expense, before they could play a round.

In 1891, Southwold Corporation's Amusement Committee challenged the Club to make the links more widely known so that additional visitors would be encouraged to visit the town, and the Club was reinvigorated in that year. Unfortunately, a couple of early golfing visitors had a succession of difficult experiences at the Club which caused them to write to The Truth, a late 19th Century journal which sought to highlight injustices. The journal wrote: "If there is a golfer with a temper that nothing can ruffle, and if he has a sense of humour which nothing can satiate, let such go to Southwold during the month of August. By the end of that time, the visitor will have learned that the Draconian severity of the rules of the Southwold Golf Club put into the shade the stately strictness of the code of the Royal and Ancient of St Andrews."

The visitors' first mistake, causing them both to be disqualified, was to play a competition round, for which they had correctly paid an entry fee, without also entering their names on a notice board in the clubhouse. Next, one of the visitors entered a medal round and marked his score for each hole but failed to add up his total for the second circuit of nine holes, and was thus deemed to have made a 'no-return'. On a third occasion, one of the visitors entered the clubhouse briefly in mid-round to get a light for his pipe and was promptly disqualified for 'taking shelter' during a competition.

The same visitors also observed that local fox-terriers seemed to take a particular liking to visitors' golf balls. On one occasion, a dog picked up a ball situated close to the flag on a green and dropped it back down the fairway from where the visitor had to replay the shot. On another occasion, the dog's owner initially denied that the animal had stolen the ball but subsequently realised his mistake and returned the ball to the visitor, but not until after he had given up the hole. The Truth refused to publish the Club's side of the story and so the defence was taken up by Golfing Magazine which was more knowledgeable about the etiquette of the game. Tongue in cheek, it quipped that it had heard that Southwold had trained a special type of terrier which only removed visitors' balls, and support for the Club was also forthcoming from as far away as Liverpool and Edinburgh.

The Liverpool correspondent lamented the visitors' lack of knowledge about the rules and etiquette of the game and concluded: "He should carry about a code of regulations to suit himself whenever he goes to the country on holidays. But his code need only comprise one law, viz., 'I shall do what seems unto myself right, and shall pay attention to no man.'"

In 1892, with an act of early independent thinking, the Club decided to adopt a club uniform of a green jacket with gold buttons which was identical to that worn by the Suffolk County Cricket Club. In 1896, conformity prevailed and the uniform was changed to a red jacket with green facings. Perhaps the first move had been influenced by Club member Frank Penn, who played cricket for Kent and England. Penn topped the national batting averages every year between 1880 and 1884, and in 1880 featured in the first official test match between Australia and England which was played at the Oval.

By the mid-1890s, it was clear that serious golf clubs had standardised a round over eighteen different holes and so thought was given to the expansion of the links. Relationships with the Corporation and other users of the common were strained at times. Cow keepers and

fen reeves were reputed: "to watch the cutting of modest greens with jealous eyes" and one of the Municipal Fathers objected to the construction of a third bunker on the course on the grounds that the two which were already there were rarely used! In 1899 and 1900, the Club asked several well-known Professionals, including James Braid, JH Taylor and Harry Vardon, to give their views on how the existing course could be expanded over the adjoining marshland. Braid had already visited Southwold when he played W Aveston from Cromer in September 1898, but the Club's records show that Braid's quote for the work of eight guineas was beaten by Harry Vardon who quoted seven pounds ten shillings. During the match with Aveston, Braid had caused a sensation by driving the ball an estimated 300 yards which was a huge distance considering the capabilities of the old clubs and balls.

It is unclear from the archives whether any of Vardon's ideas were actually carried out as the main work in 1901/2 was based on a report from yet another famous Professional, Tom Dunn, who had the idea of accessing appropriate land on the marsh by constructing a bridge over the nearby railway cutting which served the town until the line was closed in 1929. The Borough Council

Top: Green at the par-4 eighth/seventeenth hole. The road to the right of the green leads to the clubhouse and also to the small Southwold Harbour visible in the distance, which is situated on the River Blyth. The waterlogged land behind the green was formerly part of the course before catastrophic flooding in 1953

Above: Founding member John D Garrett

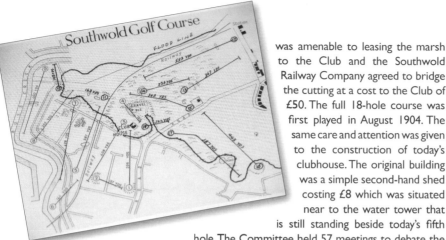

Southwold Golf Course

Above: Diagram of the course showing the extent of the flooding following the 1953 disaster. In essence, the holes to the right of the floodline are still in use whilst those to the left have never been recovered from what is now marshland. After the flood, an additional hole was constructed on the Common on the seaward side of the road to the clubhouse, and the holes were renumbered accordingly

Inset: Cover of the Club's first members' directory. The Quoits section did not take off and the word was soon dropped from the Club's name

was amenable to leasing the marsh to the Club and the Southwold Railway Company agreed to bridge the cutting at a cost to the Club of £50. The full 18-hole course was first played in August 1904. The same care and attention was given to the construction of today's clubhouse. The original building was a simple second-hand shed costing £8 which was situated near to the water tower that is still standing beside today's fifth hole. The Committee held 57 meetings to debate the style and cost of the new clubhouse before it was finally opened in 1894. Fortunately, the hard work has stood the test of time and today's building still houses the original honours' boards hidden behind those featuring more recent winners of the Club's competitions.

During the First War, the nine holes on the marsh were turned over to grazing and the remaining holes on the common were closed in 1917. However, the whole course was brought back into use during 1919. Any hopes that the Club had harboured of acquiring further land to avoid future problems with the Corporation over playing rights on the Common were dashed during the 1930s when the then Honorary Secretary absconded with most of the Club's funds. The Committee had to issue emergency debentures to make good the loss and prevent insolvency.

After the Second War, the Club devised a new category of member to help boost finances. 'Scholastic members, including assistant schoolmasters and mistresses', paid a reduced rate which covered them for play during school term-time only. The Club did not receive final compensation from the War Damage Authority until 1952, and it hardly had time to spend the money before a calamity struck it, and indeed much of the East Coast of England. Towards midnight on 31st January 1953, a combination of north-westerly gales and high seas caused the River Blyth to burst its banks, and the marsh was flooded to a depth of eight to ten feet. At first, the Club was optimistic that the marsh holes could be recovered, but discussions and negotiations

continued for years and in 1959 the Club was forced to concede that the land had been lost forever.

In an unusual continuation of the historic and separate roles of early Professionals across the country, the Club's own Professional, Brian Allen, is still responsible for both tuition and course maintenance.

Although today's course has only nine holes, it offers a combination of nostalgia and excellent greens in an attractive setting. Both short holes are interesting. The par-3 first slopes uphill and plays longer than it looks off the back tee, whilst the view from the tee of the par-3 closing hole over the pit to the clubhouse would be recognisable to Braid if he was still playing today. The best hole is probably the par-4 eighth which requires a good long iron to hold onto the green which is set in a photogenic corner of the course with views out across the marsh towards Southwold Harbour.

The Truth may have been a little unfair to the Club in the early days and visitors today certainly have no need to worry about receiving a warm welcome!

1884.

SOUTHWOLD
GOLF AND QUOIT CLUB.

Hon. Treasurer:
ARTHUR R. GRUBBE.

Hon. Secretary:
DONALD R. GOODING.

Committee:

JOHN D. GARRETT	FRANCIS H. VERTUE
ARTHUR E. DECK	W. GAUSSEN
J. B. GOODING	

WITH THE

HON. TREASURER & HON. SECRETARY.

HESKETH

ARNOLD BENTLEY AND THE HITLER TREE

Hesketh was founded in 1885 as Southport Golf Club by the well-heeled residents of the town which was described by a journalist at the time, writing in the satirical journal The Liverpool Porcupine, as: ".... the richest town in the world in proportion to its population." Southport boasted sixteen railway stations, many used by residents to commute the 20 miles into booming but grimy Liverpool.

The founding group included representatives of two competing landowners, the Hesketh Estate and the Scarisbrick Estate Trust, and the Club was an early beneficiary of enlightened landlords recognising the benefits that the game could bring to their property interests. An initial links was laid out by JOF Morris who was the second son of Old Tom and younger brother of Young Tom, over land leased from Colonel Edward Fleetwood Hesketh. The course meandered amongst a few cottages used by fishermen and shrimpers, and the original clubroom was located in the nearby New Inn which was notorious locally, under its previous name of The Fleetwood Arms, from its connection with smuggling.

Unfortunately, the New Inn Links were subject to occasional inundation from the sea and, more alarmingly for members, they were also located close to a rural slum known as Little Ireland. The New Inn was the frequent venue of drunken brawls which was not in keeping with the pretensions of the golfing members. On one occasion, this juxtaposition featured in the local newspaper under the headline 'Extraordinary Conduct of a Golfer'. A coroner was using the clubroom in the Inn to preside over an inquest into an apparent suicide in nearby Little Ireland, but the golfer insisted on using the premises for changing in the usual manner whilst the hearing was in full swing.

Not surprisingly, in 1888 the Club moved to a new building at the furthest end of the links from Little Ireland, and in 1892 the AGM agreed to move to a new course, Moss Lane Links, provided by the Scarisbrick Trust. The Hesketh Estate was stung into action and soon demolished Little Ireland. It then gambled successfully on tempting members back to an improved and enlarged layout incorporating some of the popular features of the original New Inn Links and the Club was renamed as Hesketh Golf Club.

The Hesketh Estate benefited from the efforts of Charles Bibby of the famous Liverpool shipping family who had married the eldest Hesketh daughter and heir. As a clear sign of allegiance to his new family, he obtained permission from Queen Victoria to change his name to Charles Hesketh Bibby Fleetwood-Hesketh! Members transferred to the new Hesketh Golf Club and Charles was made Honorary Life President and

Inset: Photograph of the Prize of the Nations won by the English team at Baden-Baden in 1936 (Courtesy of Hesketh Golf Club)

Captain: "in recognition ...of the development of golf locally, having at the same time the best interest of the residential district at heart."

The 1920s and '30s were a golden age for Hesketh. J Rayner Batty was Captain in 1920 and 1921 and became the Founder and first President of the English Golf Union (EGU). Southport Corporation encouraged the development of the game and sponsored the annual £1,500 Southport Professional Golf Tournament which attracted excellent golfers and low scoring, including 68 by Henry Cotton in 1932 and Reg Whitcombe's 64 in 1934.

The clubhouse has a special room dedicated to the Bentley brothers who were known for their style and panache. They had a flat in Park Lane, London, and a permanent table in the bar at the nearby Dorchester Hotel. Harry won the English Amateur Championship at Deal in 1936 and played in three Walker Cup teams, whilst younger brother Arnold won the same competition in 1939. Between 1928 and 1950, they won 50 of the 80 scratch competitions played at the Club. The brothers were close friends of Henry Cotton which accounts for Harry's success in winning the Monte Carlo Open in 1948 and 1949 where Cotton was the Professional.

In 1936, Arnold and Tommy Thirsk represented the EGU in the Prize of the Nations tournament, consisting of eight individual medal rounds and played as an exhibition sport in tandem with the 1936 Berlin Olympics. Jesse Owens had already disappointed Hitler's hopes for the games and the Fuhrer was delighted to hear from foreign Minister, Von Ribbentrop, who was himself a low handicap golfer, that Germany was leading the tournament. Hitler set out for Baden Baden to present the trophies personally and had to be intercepted when the English pair stormed to victory in the final afternoon rounds. Arnold's individual prizes included a plaque, emblazoned with a swastika, and a fir tree which was planted outside the clubhouse and has thrived due to personal 'watering' by members during the war years!

The first two holes and the last five, played around the clubhouse, are the oldest and still the best. The fifteenth, played over a large sand dune towards Emmanuel Church, is the signature hole whilst the others, set out on recovered estuary land, have a quality parkland feel but are still an enjoyable test of golf. If the wind blows, as former Masters' winner Larry Mize discovered during his successful qualifying round for the 1998 Open at Birkdale, the course is a stiff challenge for the best Professionals.

Main: The clubhouse, built on an old sea cliff, viewed from the seventeenth hole. The player in the foreground is walking up the eighteenth fairway. Arnold Bentley's famous 'Hitler tree' is in front of the flagpole

Above: The younger of the two Bentley Brothers, Arnold, won the English Amateur Championship in 1939. In 1936, playing with Tommy Thirsk, he shared a feat with Jesse Owens of disappointing Adolf Hitler (Courtesy Hesketh Golf Club)

CLEVELAND

LINKS AND STEEL

Golf on the Coatham Links in Redcar was started by a group of former footballers who had first turned to hockey for exercise in their middle age before meeting Captain Williams who was Head of Coastguards at Redcar. Williams had previously been based further north at Alnmouth on the Northumberland coast where he had become interested in golf being played over the links next to the village. The hockey players were soon converted to golf and the Club was founded in May 1887, becoming the first course in Yorkshire. Williams was elected inaugural Captain in recognition of his pioneering role and Cleveland was also helped in the early days by Doctor McCuaig who had already played a major role in establishing the club at Seaton Carew on the other side of the Tees Estuary.

The original 9-hole course was extended to eighteen holes in 1890 and Old Tom Morris visited Cleveland in the late 1890s to advise on alterations. By 1901, the links measured 5,210 yards with a Bogey of 86 reflecting the difficulties caused by the abundance of rough and sand throughout the course. The Kirkleatham Estate retained mineral rights over the land and large quantities of sand were removed on a regular basis leading to constant changes to the look and challenges of the course.

Following the bombing of nearby Hartlepool during the 1914-18 war, a large gun was placed at the far end of the course, four holes were closed for play and competitions were suspended. The new clubhouse which had been requisitioned by the War Office for billeting troops burnt down, and the Club emerged from the war with a ruined course, no clubhouse and no funds to carry out repairs. Priority was given to repairing the links, but flooding closed the course for six months in 1927 whilst in the 1939-45 war, the RAF used part of the course for a rifle range, an unexploded bomb removed the old fourteenth from play and lives were lost when mines were exploded between the then second and sixteenth holes.

Below: This remarkable early photograph shows the Captain playing from a deep and ragged bunker at the old sixth hole in 1908. The houses in the background occupied by former steelworkers have been demolished. A contemporary writer described the links as: "no green and all bunker" and observed that: "...only the cleek and the sand-iron and the niblick can persuade the ball to play."

Changes continued after the war. The light railway used to transport sand across the course was re-sited on several occasions and a famous sand mound known as Majuba was removed as a feature following the purchase of the land by the Redcar Corporation in 1956. FW Hawtree designed several new holes in the 1960s and most recently three replacement holes have been designed by Donald Steel with financial assistance from The R&A.

A new clubhouse was opened in 2002 by Sir Michael Bonallack as the Corporation wished to develop part of the course lying nearest to the town.

Whilst coping with all these changes, the Club has also given sanctuary to a lost community. The village of Warrenby was built in 1873 to provide new homes for workers who were able to walk to work at the nearby steel works along the River Tees. Shortly after the 1914-18 war, six young men from the settlement started to play golf on a regular basis at the Warrenby end of the course and the Club decided to prosecute them for trespass. The case was thrown out by the Court in Middlesbrough but the Club then pursued the matter all the way to the High Court in London which found in favour of the Club in the not surprising absence of the defendants. The fines were never paid and in 1921 the Club relented and agreed that an Artisans' Section could

be formed with limited playing rights. The artisans had course maintenance obligations and individuals paid an annual membership fee of five shillings. The settlement at Warrenby was pulled down and the villagers relocated in the 1960s following the recommendation of the Regional Planning Officer, but the Artisans' Section lives on as a part of the main Club and the old cups are still played for on a regular basis.

Cleveland has been played by many famous golfers. Reigning Open Champion Harry Vardon won the Yorkshire Professionals' Championship in 1896 with rounds of 75 and a record-equalling 73, a number of top Professionals fought through wind and snow during the northern qualifying rounds of the Daily Mail Professionals' Tournament in 1937, and in 1958 the Central Council of Physical Recreation helped to arrange for Bobby Locke to play in an exhibition match. The Cleveland Salver scratch competition for Category 1 amateurs has attracted a host of emerging players including Howard Clark and Gordon J Brand.

Cleveland is the only links course in Yorkshire and the recent changes and improvements have persuaded The R&A that the Club is now a suitable venue for important open competitions. The industrial backdrop adds to the character of the links and when the wind blows the course is a tough challenge.

Main: *The drive at the second tee showing the extensive sand hills and the Corus steelworks in the distance*

Above: *County golfers and Cleveland stalwarts Cyril Roddam and Frank Robson met in the 1922 final of the Club's Calcutta Cup competition. The match was all square after seventeen holes, Roddam hit his tee shot at the old par-3 eighteenth to within two yards and Robson holed his tee shot to win the match by one hole*

LITTLESTONE

HOME OF THE POLITICIANS

Like many old English seaside courses, Littlestone owes its early success to the expansion of the Victorian railway system and patronage from London.

In 1884, Londoner Henry Tubbs purchased The Warren from the New Romney Corporation. This land had been granted to the town of nearby New Romney by Queen Elizabeth I in 1563 and Tubbs' original interest was to establish a marine town at Littlestone which at the time consisted of just a coastguard station and a few related cottages. He was encouraged by Robert, later Sir Robert, Perks, a Director of the Lydd Railway Company which extended its line to New Romney in June 1884.

Littlestone's Marine Parade, consisting of a hotel and a number of tall houses, was laid out in 1886, but the rest of the new development did not take off as planned. Nevertheless, two years later, Tubbs and twelve colleagues, including Laidlaw Purves of Wimbledon fame, met at a hotel in London to discuss the formation of a golf course on the land immediately behind the sea at Littlestone on the Romney Marshes. The founders moved at lightning speed and the first course must have been extremely rough.

In March 1888, E Butchart, the club maker from Wimbledon was appointed as Professional and the first golf event was held that Whitsun. It was won by Purves with a score of 93 playing off scratch. JM Cripps was second with 131(115 net), indicating that Purves must have been in a class of his own. At the Club's first AGM in August, Purves was appointed as first Captain and the Rt. Hon. AJ Balfour became President. Between 1887 and 1891, Balfour was Chief Secretary for Ireland, he became Leader of the Opposition between 1892 and 1895, and Prime Minister between 1902 and 1905 during which

time he continued to play off a single-figure handicap.

Purves was an ophthalmic surgeon who practised in London. He had a significant influence over the spread of golf in England, and in addition to his responsibilities at Wimbledon he was a prime mover in the establishment of Royal St George's at Sandwich in 1887 before moving his attention along the coast to Littlestone the following year. He had the honour of being the first Captain of both clubs at the same time and was a great enthusiast for the rules of the game. He persuaded the Club to adopt Wimbledon's rules as The R&A had not yet gained full acceptance of their standard set. The Club flourished from the start and membership rose from 79 in 1891 to 612 by 1905.

In 1894, the Club hosted the Ladies' Golf Championship, the first-ever held under the official

Main: View across the putting green to the prominent old water tower which is now a private dwelling

auspices of the Ladies' Golf Union. The event was played over a 9-hole course laid out especially for the event, and was won by Lady Margaret Scott who beat Issette Pearson in the final 3&2, thereby repeating her success in the inaugural event held at Royal Lytham & St Annes the previous year. Local press commented that this course was irreverently nicknamed 'the Hen Run'.

The special peaceful appeal of Victorian golf at Littlestone was captured by an article in a September 1895 edition of Golf Magazine which described how: '... the fine bracing air, the absence of brass bands and minstrels, those mosquitos of all seaside places, leads one to believe that Littlestone is the only place left among the hundred and one health resorts by the sea within easy reach of London where quiet repose and good golf is to be found'.

In the early 1900s, Littlestone enjoyed exclusive patronage. In addition to Balfour, Herbert Gladstone MP, the younger brother of the Liberal leader, was Captain in 1896/7 and became Home Secretary between 1906 and 1910. His friend, Herbert Henry Asquith, frequently visited Littlestone and became Captain in 1907/8 and Prime Minister between 1908 and 1916. For a brief period in 1908, the Club had the Prime Minister as Captain and the Leader of the Opposition as President! Perhaps the most accomplished sportsman amongst Littlestone's politicians was the Colonial Secretary, Alfred Lyttelton KC. MP, who was Club Captain in 1902/3. He played cricket for England against Australia and also represented England at Association Football and racquets as well as being amateur tennis champion.

The presence of so many senior politicians did not go unnoticed by the suffragettes, and in 1909 three members of the Women's Social and Political Union

attacked Asquith at the door of the clubhouse. Reports at the time noted that they were excluded from the premises by the Home Secretary, Herbert Gladstone. Women were struggling for equal rights at a local as well as national level. Littlestone hosted the Kent County Ladies' Championship in October 1909 but ladies were not allowed in the main clubhouse. The local newspaper reported that: "...the weather was terrible. A terrific gale with pouring, driving rain. One of Littlestone's worst productions. The rule (excluding ladies from the clubhouse) was rigorously enforced and those ladies who came from a distance endured great discomfort in being obliged to eat their lunch on the balcony outside in the cold and drenching rain." The suffragettes were a serious threat to golf courses in the 1910s, and during 1912/3 they caused damage to twelve courses including Sheringham and Sandwich, using chemicals to burn slogans into greens including 'Votes for Women' and 'Votes or War'.

Mary Watson, daughter of the Club's long-time Professional, David Herd, wrote eloquently of early Edwardian Summers at Littlestone: "...the families, including small children and many nannies often stayed for the whole Summer with the menfolk joining them at the weekends. It was quite an event on Friday evenings for the local people, especially caddies, to meet the 7pm train just to see which gents had arrived so that they knew if they would be sure of a job the following day. Golfers were met at the station by their own carriages or the local horsebus before the arrival of the motorcar." In 1902, Herd's brother Sandy, won the Open Championship at Hoylake playing the new 'Haskell' ball and another brother, Fred, had won the American Open in 1898 in the first year that the competition had been extended from 36 to 72 holes.

The Club was an important source of employment for caddies and there were usually twenty or more in employment during Summer weekdays and many more at weekends. The Club flew a blue flag when extra assistance was required. Average pay was one shilling and sixpence for a morning round plus a six pence disc entitling a lunch of bread and cheeses which was served at the kitchen door of the clubhouse. Pay was less for the afternoon round and a different coloured disc provided

CAPTAINS.	
1888-89 W. Laidlaw Purves.	1899-1900 W. Trower.
1889-90 W. Laidlaw Purves.	1900-01 W. Trower.
1890-91 Wᵐ R. Dockrell.	1901-02 A.T. Lawrence, K.C.
1891-92 James Bannon.	1902-03 Hon. A. Lyttelton, K.C. M.P.
1892-93 Lestocq R. Erskine.	1903-04 F. Hugh Lee.
1893-94 F. Faithfull Begg.	1904-05 H. E. Johnson.
1894-95 R.H. Hedderwick.	1905-06 Sir R.B. Finlay, K.C. M.P.
1895-96 W.E. Maclagan.	1906-07 F.W. Hollams.
1896-97 R.Hon. Herbert J. Gladstone, M.P.	1907-08 R.Hon. H.H Asquith, K.C. M.P.
1897-98 Hon. J.B. Lubbock.	1908-09 Sidney A. Boulton.
1898-99 A.J. Stanley.	1909-10 Ernest Baggallay.

an entitlement to tea. Caddies were graded as either 1st or 2nd class, the latter being mere 'bag carriers'. Before the days of rubber and wooden tees, the Club provided containers of sand and water at each teeing ground so that the caddies could make a teeing mound.

The Great War had a devastating effect on the Club. Membership fell from 500 to 300 through death in action and resignations, and the course itself became badly damaged by rabbits. The military took over the course during the war for training, and in 1919 the Club invited annual tenders for the concession to kill rabbits which was won, for a sum of £30, by a Mr. Catt, the proprietor of the local Station Hotel. As a further contribution to the war on rabbits, Captain Somerset Webb made a gift of ferrets to the Club.

In the 1930s, Noel Coward bought 'Goldenhurst', down the road from the Club at Port Lympne. He became a member of Littlestone in 1931 and Herd commented later that Coward was the only person he had been unable to teach because he was quite incapable of connecting club and ball. When a friend asked Coward how the lesson had gone, the apocryphal response was: "My dear, it made me cry."

The Depression years in the 1930s brought hardship to many Clubs. The neighbouring Greatstone Golf Club collapsed in 1931, and in 1933 the Club's Artisans' Section was established, enabling former Greatstone members to use the Littlestone course at certain times. The course closed for six years during the Second World War and Littlestone was heavily affected by the air battles. There were over 70 plane crashes in the locality between 1940 and 1944, and a Hurricane is still said to be lying buried on the course. A German bomber crashed by the water tower which is still a prominent feature alongside the course. In June 1944, the German flying bomb attacks on London commenced and anti-aircraft defences were moved to the coast. A number of guns were deployed on the course and some sites are still visible today.

Littlestone has tried to keep pace with technology. In the 1920s, Harry Colt's partner, Dr. Alister MacKenzie, was invited to modernise the course. Many of his recommendations caused heated debate amongst the members, and his design for two of the course's signature holes, the sixteenth and seventeenth, were

not implemented until 1931, under the supervision of Abercromby. Further changes have been made following advice from Frank Pennink, Peter Alliss and Donald Steel. Members wonder whether MacKenzie's design, along with Bobby Jones, of the thirteenth tee shot at Augusta, with its angled water hazard, may have been inspired by the eleventh hole at Littlestone.

Although the course is flat, few golfers find that it is easy to play. The wind is often a factor and the greens are small and are likely to penalise poorly executed approach shots. Players should keep an eye out for rare birds. Short-eared owls and hen harriers can sometimes be seen over the marsh and other interesting sightings have included woodcock, stone curlew and, during migration time, cranes (more than 100 in 1982), marsh and Montagu's harriers.

The course is a pleasure to play although golfers need to arrive by car (or use the Romney, Hythe and Dymchurch miniature railway!) as the main railway line from Ashford to New Romney was closed in 1967. Visitors and societies are welcome during the week although it should be noted that four-ball matches are discouraged in order to keep the game moving.

Main: An early photograph of the Club's President, the Rt. Hon. AJ Balfour, completing a round at Littlestone

Above: Caddies received their remuneration partly in meal vouchers. The top two discs were presented for lunch and the lower two were used to purchase tea

LITTLEHAMPTON

NAUTICAL GOLF

Littlehampton Golf Club is bordered by the River Arun and its yacht harbour to the east, and the dunes, beach and English Channel to the south, providing an ideal setting for a coastal links course. For many years, the main route to the Club and the only access from the town was by ferry from Littlehampton across the river. A toll-operated swing bridge was opened in 1908 but two boatmen, Jimmy and Peachey offered an alternative row boat service at tuppence return with up to fourteen passengers per journey. Generations of golfers, including the Duke of York, later King George VI, have waited their turn on the ferry steps. The first clubroom was situated in the ruined fort which lies covered in ivy beside today's

second tee. The building was constructed in 1853 to counter the threat of a French invasion up the River Arun, and was manned by a garrison of 60 soldiers. By 1891, thoughts of invasion had waned and the fort was abandoned by the military and became available for alternative use. The first Club pavilion was built close to the fort in 1894 and remained in use until 1985 when it was destroyed by fire and replaced by today's clubhouse constructed further inland.

The Club was founded by two local solicitors, Richard Blagden and Upperton Lear, who recognised that the old rifle range across the river would make an ideal golf links. Early success was guaranteed when the Duke of Norfolk agreed to become the President, and this close and long-standing family connection later became a vital ingredient to the survival of the Club. The first medal was played over the new 9-hole course in May 1889, and the first issue of Golf magazine in September 1890 commented that the difficulties of the (then) first hole: "are probably equalled by few in the United Kingdom. The whole course is at this time of year still encumbered by grass, but in the course of another month or so, and during the next six months, it is well worth playing on, especially as the greens are particularly good and true." Early golfers did not have the luxury of mown fairways during the Summer months.

The course was extended to eighteen holes in 1893, and by 1898 Golf Illustrated was able to describe the course as: "one of the best 18-hole courses in the South of England." In 1923, Hawtree & Taylor made significant improvements to the course, reducing the number of inland holes which Taylor

described as being: "much too like those of an inland course" and re-routing them through 'tiger-country' nearer the dunes and the beach. The Club reached its zenith in the 1930s and a cartoon by Mel for Sporting and Dramatic magazine in 1934 includes a drawing of a portly member, Aubrey Troughton, who was the Secretary of the Badminton Club in Piccadilly. Troughton had a cottage near the fifteenth green and when the flag was flying on Sunday mornings and other special occasions, golfers were encouraged to pop in for a quick pink gin or two before finishing their rounds.

In 1939, the course was requisitioned by the War Office and the Admiralty, a line of concrete blocks was built along the shore boundary, and mines and barbed wire covered the links. Later, the course was ploughed up by tanks preparing for D-Day and the future for golf looked bleak. By 1946, the Club was broke and despite generosity from the landlords, the financial difficulties continued into the 1950s and the Club was threatened with liquidation. In 1956, as a last resort, the Committee approached the President of the Club, Bernard, 16th Duke of Norfolk, who agreed

to rescue the Club. In January 1974 his stewardship had a happy ending when the Club was transferred back to the members as a going concern.

Most of the first eleven holes are routed through the land lying close to the coastal dunes whilst the middle part of the course is notable for the River Rife which flows into the Arun. The opening par-4, with out of bounds to the left, leads out to the dunes and can be difficult to reach in two with the prevailing south-westerly blowing across the fairway. There is an excellent view back across the River Arun to Littlehampton from the elevated second tee and after a brief turn inland, the course offers an attractive test of seaside links golf between holes six and ten. The fourteenth is a difficult hole with out of bounds lying to the right of the Rife which flows close to the right-hand side of the fairway, and the eighteenth is an excellent closing hole played to a green in front of the clubhouse guarded by well positioned bunkers on either side of the putting surface.

Littlehampton provides an interesting mix of links and parkland golf in a nautical setting with the sounds and smells of the seaside close to hand.

Main: The seventh tee is situated in an elevated position close to the beach. The drive at the ninth has a similar feel

Above: First Captain, AJ 'Archie' Constable

BERWICK -UPON- TWEED (GOSWICK)

SPLENDID ISOLATION

Below: View out to sea from the second tee

Goswick is an excellent and unpretentious links course situated in splendid isolation near the sea, some five miles south of the town of Berwick-upon-Tweed, close to the East Coast boundary between England and Scotland. Berwick's proximity to the home of golf meant that its citizens were eager to have their own links, but heated debate took place over the choice of original location.

Berwick now has a local course, Magdalene Fields, situated within five minutes' walk of the town centre, but this spot was not considered suitable in the Victorian days before the invention of mechanised mowers.

The inaugural meeting of the Club was held at the King's Arms Assembly Rooms in Berwick in October 1889. The Mayor, Captain FM Norman, RN, chaired the gathering at which it was agreed that Tom Dunn, the Professional at North Berwick should inspect both Magdalene Fields and Goswick and then give his opinion on which location should be developed. Dunn chose Goswick and commented that Magdalene Fields had too much 'luxuriant grass' which would not get cut in Summer and would therefore limit play to Winters only. In an early example of frugal membership, T Darling complained of the unnecessary expense of taking Dunn's advice as: "anyone who has played over St Andrews links did not need a Professional to tell them whether Goswick links were more suitable for golfing than Magdalene Fields. Any reasonable man knew that!" Darling was reassured by the interim Secretary that a 'gentleman' had settled Dunn's fees.

Not surprisingly, Goswick turned out to be an inconvenient location in Victorian times as it could only be accessed by bicycle, pony and trap, or by train if the railway company could be persuaded to co-operate. Nearby Windmill Hill station had been opened by the North Eastern Railway Company in 1885 to serve a small farming settlement, and in 1898 the company agreed to rename the station

as Goswick. The Club itself has endured a number of unwieldy names to help prevent visitors from arriving at the wrong location. An early EGM agreed a change to 'Berwick-upon-Tweed Golf Club Goswick Station'. Local rail services ceased in 1958 and the Club has since dropped mention of the station, but it has retained a long formal title whilst branding itself more simply as Goswick Golf Club which still causes occasional puzzlement to visitors travelling by car as the actual settlement of Goswick no longer exists! For many golfers, their first view of the course has been from a train window of the King's Cross to Edinburgh express as it tears past the course at speeds of more than 100mph. On one sombre day in 1947 the train crashed and the clubhouse was used to treat the wounded before they were taken to hospital.

The original 9-hole course was laid out by James Braid over land provided by Sir William Crossman

MP, and the lengthening to eighteen holes in 1894 was celebrated by a 36-hole match between Sandy Herd and Willie Fernie which Herd won despite Fernie setting the course record with 72 in the afternoon round. Braid played two rounds against the better-ball of two sets of local players in September 1901, and The Daily Express arranged for Abe Mitchell to play a similar format when he played at Goswick during his 'galloping tour of the North of England'. Mitchell remarked that: "it struck me as one of the few absolutely natural seaside courses in this country" although he added that it needed more length. This challenge was taken up by the Club in 1930 when Braid was paid eight guineas to advise on major changes to thirteen holes whilst Frank Pennink helped with further improvements in 1964.

Bernard Darwin was also a great fan of the course and wrote that it was: "one of the most

naturally magnificent pieces of golfing ground that ever swam into the ken of the golfing explorer. With those glorious ranges of sand dunes, and that ideal seaside turf, money and a skilled architect in combination could do anything. Meanwhile, in default of millionaires, Goswick will presumably remain much as it is, that is perfectly delightful." Darwin would be pleased that the Club has retained all its positive natural attributes and is still a joy to play. Flocks of geese fly noisily over the links to the local nature reserve and it is difficult not to cast a wistful eye out towards the sea across huge dunes which would make further great golfing country.

The course opens with a strong right dog-leg par-4 known as Copse Corner, with the view to the green being shielded by a small conifer plantation. Most of the course is then played over true links land in two loops of nine holes, but the same trees come into view at the intriguing closing hole which is a very short par-4 played to a well-guarded green positioned in front of the clubhouse.

Goswick is a small and friendly Club which has not hosted many championships, but the reason has been one of access and accommodation rather than the quality of the course. The pleasure of playing a natural links in uncrowded conditions makes this a trip to be recommended.

WEST CORNWALL

THE LEGENDARY JIM BARNES

West Cornwall is another club which owes its success to the enthusiasm of a vicar. In fact, two clerics were involved at the Club. At the outset, the Vicar of Lelant, RF Tyacke was supported by WH Hughes from the Parish of Marazion across the peninsula at Mounts Bay.

The first meeting was held in December 1889 and the two churchmen were joined by Captain C Lack and three civilians who agreed to build a 9-hole course on the Towans at Lelant. At the time, the only other course in Cornwall was the Royal Cornwall Golf Club at Bodmin which has not survived. This leaves Tyacke's course as the oldest in the county, and he was closely involved with the Club throughout the remainder of his life, acting as Secretary until he died in 1901.

The first course was laid out by John Allan, the Professional at Westward Ho!, and the Club agreed to pay Mr. Olds, the tenant on the Towans sandhills, a contribution of £2 per annum as compensation for the loss of grazing land. Olds also supplied a man one day per week to keep the greens in order at a cost of two shillings and sixpence per week.

Members of the Royal Cornwall Golf Club living to the East of Truro were able to join the Club for ten shillings per year on the understanding that West Cornwall members living west of Truro or east of Plymouth would be received on the same basis by the Royal club at Bodmin.

A short ladies' course of 1,537 yards was constructed in 1892 and the main course was extended to an 18-hole layout, then measuring 4,436 yards, by 1896.

The road to the right of the par-3 first hole leading down to the church used to be 'in bounds' and a local newspaper, reporting on an exhibition match in 1902 between the Open Champions Braid and Taylor, noted that: "Braid began by making a wonderful recovery after being in the road with his drive, holing in 3 to Taylor's 4."

Sheep were the original fairway mowers and early minutes note that the tenant had agreed to increase the number of sheep grazing on the course up to 100, and then later to 120, provided the Club agreed to feed them in the event of a drought.

The Club will forever be associated with one of Britain's greatest, but least known, golfing heroes. James Martin (Long Jim) Barnes was born in Lelant Village in 1887 and started out as a caddie, being paid six pence for an 18-hole round. Between 1902 and 1906 he acted as the assistant to the Club's Professional, Fred Whiting, and although the Club did not have a formal Artisans' Club for caddies and other local golfers until 1920, it is clear that Barnes developed his skills on the course and impressed the members because they awarded him a testimonial when he left for the US at the age of 19.

Above: View from near the clubhouse towards Lelant Church with the short par-3 fifteenth hole, surrounded by twelve bunkers, in the foreground. The first hole runs down to the church on the right of the picture

JAMES MARTIN "LONG JIM" BARNES

BRITISH OPEN CHAMPION 1925
U.S. OPEN CHAMPION 1921
U.S.P.G.A. CHAMPION 1916
WORLD CHAMPION OF GOLF 1921 ~ 1925

BORN IN LELANT. JIM BARNES SPENT THE EARLY YEARS
OF HIS ILLUSTRIOUS GOLFING CAREER
ON THE LINKS OF THE WEST CORNWALL GOLF CLUB,
DURING THE YEARS 1909 TO 1925
HE WON ALMOST EVERY TOURNAMENT IN THE UNITED STATES,
INCLUDING THE U.S. OPEN AND P.G.A. CHAMPIONSHIPS.
HE COMPLETED THE BIG THREE BY WINNING THE BRITISH OPEN IN 1925.
WHEN HE BROUGHT THE TROPHY TO CORNWALL.
THIS PLAQUE, PROUDLY DONATED BY MEMBERS AND PERSONAL FRIENDS,
COMMEMORATES HIS LONG ASSOCIATION WITH WEST CORNWALL

Main: View from an exposed part of the course across the Hayle Estuary which opens out into St. Ives Bay

Above: Early picture of golfers playing on the first green in front of Lelant Church. The boy caddie is carrying two sets of clubs although the players themselves do not look much older

Inset: Jim Barnes is the unsung hero of British golf. He was born in Lelant Village in 1887 and gained his skills and love of the game whilst caddying as a boy. He left for the US in 1906, aged 19

Barnes took up American citizenship and became the Professional at Tacoma, Washington in his early 20s. He rapidly became a legend, winning the inaugural USPGA competition in 1916 and again when the event was held for a second time after the War in 1919. He won the 1921 US Open by a 9-shot margin, and in 1925 he returned to the UK and won the British Open following which he visited Lelant to show the trophy to members of the Club.

Barnes returned again to Cornwall in 1955 and recommended a number of course alterations which were accepted. During the same visit he played the course in par using only a three iron. When he died in 1966 at the age of 79, the New York Times reported that he was: "the Ben Hogan of his Era."

Members playing the eighth hole in 1984 were witnesses to one of the strangest holes-in-one in golf. Two four-ball groups were playing on the par-4 hole measuring over 300 yards in hard, running conditions. One of the members was in the process of putting when a tee shot from a fellow member, Stephen Elliott in the group behind, shot across the green and went straight between the putting member's legs, hitting his putter and then his ball, before ricocheting into the hole.

West Cornwall is laid out over classic seaside links-land, with fine views across the Hayle Estuary and St. Ives Bay. Although the course is not long, a number of holes penalise poor or timid shots and the wind is probably the course's greatest defence.

The first hole is a tricky par-3, heading down to St. Uny Church which has been an unchanging landmark since the first days of the course. From the second tee, it is difficult to work out where to hit the ball without the benefit of a course-planner guide. Sand hills seem to run along the entire right-hand side of the fairway but a well-positioned tee shot brings the green into sight, positioned uphill at the back of a small break in the dunes. The third hole is a challenging par-3 whilst the fourth requires a very tight drive across the corner of the St. Uny churchyard, which in windy conditions seems almost impossible to control. Further trouble lurks behind the green with a road which is out of bounds.

The fifth to seventh holes are played on the other side of the railway and hug the estuary shore-line. The drive at the short fifth has to be struck perilously close to the railway line with the prevailing wind tending to blow the ball towards the out of bounds, whilst the sixth hole has out of bounds all along the left side and behind the green which is set right back against the shore and causes many golfers to play into the bunkers placed just short of the green.

The par-4 ninth hole is the most difficult on the outward nine, requiring a well-hit tee shot to an elevated green. Big trouble awaits the approach shot down the bank to the right of the green. The tenth has a blind tee shot and the eleventh is an excellent hole, requiring a blind second shot over the top of a ridge situated some 80 yards from the green and with a hidden bunker to the left of the green waiting to collect under-hit approaches.

The par-4 fourteenth is the most difficult hole on the inward half and golfers tempting to cut out the dog-leg do so at their peril. The short fifteenth is guarded by twelve bunkers whilst the par-5 sixteenth also offers a challenge with its left to right sloping fairway and trouble to the right of the green.

The traditional clubhouse contains several tributes to the memory of the greatest locally-born golfer, Jim Barnes.

BURNHAM & BERROW

HOME OF THE WHITCOMBES

The championship links at Burnham & Berrow have survived with a classic traditional layout of nine out and nine back although many improvements have been made over the years under advice from experts including JH Taylor, Burnham members Herbert Fowler and Hugh Alison, Harold Hilton, Alister MacKenzie, Harry Colt, and more recently, Frank Pennink. Challengingly, the prevailing south-westerly wind blows across all the holes so there is no respite on a windy day.

Here as elsewhere, the Church features prominently in the early history of the Club. The Reverend Canon Kennard, a Roman Catholic priest and one of a golfing family dynasty at Royal North Devon arranged for the Westward Ho! Professional, Charles Gibson, to lay out the first 9-hole course for the Burnham Golf Club close to the lighthouse which still stands near the beach. Kennard persuaded Walter and Thomas Holt, owners of the town's brewery and its largest employer, to help finance construction of the course over Burnham Warren.

The Lords of the Manor allowed the golfers to lease the land for seven years at a rent of £10 per annum, but this caused local consternation. Golf was seen as a rich man's sport, played by wealthy Burnham residents and visitors making use

of the well-established railway link to the town. Berrow Village lay less than a mile away but was inhabited by relatively poor residents, many of whom relied upon the Warren for subsistence grazing, hunting rabbits and sand abstraction. There was frequent early vandalism but fortunately the Club reacted sensibly and a change of name to Burnham & Berrow helped to gain local acceptance. The game also appealed to the young men in the village who gained employment as caddies and sought to copy the playing style of the Club's first Professional, the young JH Taylor, who had been convinced to accept the job recommendation from Kennard and Gibson by his mother. Taylor stayed for only eighteen months before moving on to Royal Winchester, but he had helped to light a fuse, and within five years the problem had become one of unauthorised play by local villagers!

Above: The present twelfth green next to Berrow Parish Church. The hole was diverted from the north-east to the south-west of the church during the 1970s to overcome danger to the public

Inset: CF Penruddock, Captain of Oxford University and a Burnham member, preparing to ring the all-clear bell by the seventeenth hole in the 1926 Varsity match

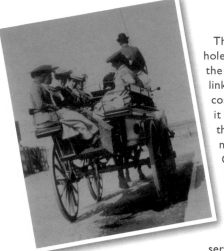

The course was extended to eighteen holes in 1897 and stretched out as far as the church. At the same time, two further links had been constructed along the coast to the south of the main course and it is easy to understand how threatened the local villagers must have felt by the new game. The Burnham Ladies' Golf Club was formed in 1892 and in 1897 it merged with the Mid Somerset Golf Club which played over land immediately to the south of the main course. The men's and ladies' clubs co-operated closely with men serving on the Committee of the ladies' club whilst the main course hosted major ladies' competitions including the Ladies' British Open Amateur Championships in 1906, 1923 and 1938. Sea erosion finally caused the ladies to abandon their separate course in 1948.

Berrow Village can lay claim to producing the largest number of successful English professional golfers from one small settlement. Within the first 20 years, eighteen golfers became Professionals including the Whitcombe brothers who were born in the cottages next to Berrow Church, and the Bradbeer brothers, four of whom qualified for the final two rounds of the 1928 Open Championship at Royal St George's. Village baker George Bradbeer and his wife, Helena, had fourteen

Top: Competitors in the 1906 Ladies' British Open Amateur Championship were conveyed to the course from the Queen's Hotel by horse and trap

Inset: The clubhouse was built in 1910. The nearby lighthouse can be glimpsed over the roof of the building

children in total including ten boys, nine of whom became professional golfers with seven of them working during the 1930s at Basingstoke, Porters Park, Hendon, Saunton, Calcot Park and Hindhead, as well as Burnham itself where Robert Bradbeer became the Professional in 1919, serving for 20 years before finally succumbing to the long-term effects of the gassing which he suffered during the First World War.

Fred Bradbeer took over from Bob in 1938 and held the position for 30 years and Richard, Bob's son, then served through until 1979 when he moved to Royal Birkdale. During the Second World War, the family's Club tradition was in the safe hands of a Miss Bradbeer who served as caddiemaster between 1941 and 1947. More recently, the Club's strong professional lineage has been continued by Brian Barnes who joined the Club in 1954 as a 9-year old whilst his father, Tom, was Club Secretary.

The Club hosts the annual West of England Amateur Championship which is one of the most prestigious competitions in the region. The event dates back to 1912 when a visitor from Lahinch in Southern Ireland suggested that Burnham would be an ideal venue to host a tournament similar to the South of Ireland Amateur Championship. The Golf Committee followed up the idea enthusiastically and arranged for Mappin and Webb, the famous jewellers and silversmiths, to design a new trophy. The Hon. Michael Scott won the competition on four occasions, including in 1934 when he defeated Cyril Tolley in the final, and the winners have included many international players. Oxford University has been a traditional supporter of both the Club and the championship and the Club still hosts an annual match against the university.

Burnham and Berrow has hosted many international matches and senior competitions, but an extraordinary result in the first round of the 1938 Ladies' Open Championship is still remembered more than 60 years later. Gloria Minoprio, who made an annual appearance in the championship, dressed in trousers to the consternation of the

LGU, and perhaps more outrageously, using only one club, a cleek, (a shallow-faced, hickory 2-iron) managed to win her match against her South African opponent who had travelled half-way round the world just to play in the competition! More recently, well-known faces have included Justin Rose and Luke Donald playing for England in the Men's Home Internationals and Jose Maria Olazabal, Colin Montgomerie and Jesper Parnevik who took part in the 1982 Boys' Championship.

Changes to the coastline have largely been kind to the Club. Due to the receding sea, land owned has increased from 210 acres in 1928 to more than 500 acres by the turn of the Millennium allowing the construction of the separate 9-hole Channel course designed by Fred Hawtree.

Burnham is a true championship course with exceptional greens and fairway irrigation which has not detracted from the traditional links challenge.

The course measures nearly 6,800 yards off the back tees and the frequently windy conditions mean that few players have ever tamed it. Visitors are able to stay in a comfortable Dormy House which helps to maximise time available for golf.

Above: *Berrow Parish Church moulds in with the course*

Inset: *Ladies playing from the old fifth tee, behind the current sixteenth, during the 1906 Championship*

HUNSTANTON

BOB TAYLOR'S UNIQUE ACHIEVEMENT

Above: *Holcombe Ingleby, a newcomer to Norfolk and previously the Honorary Secretary at Royal Eastbourne, was the first Captain and served for four years from 1891*

Inset: *Players dressed for the wind and waiting to tee off at the first hole in front of the clubhouse. The colourful beach huts add to the character of the course and lie to the right of the eighteenth fairway*

Hunstanton is a well-established and successful seaside championship course having hosted the Ladies' British Open Amateur competition on six occasions between 1914 and 2002 as well as being a regular venue for important men's events including the English Amateur and more recently the Brabazon (British Open Amateur Strokeplay) Championships. Since 1963, Hunstanton has hosted the finals of the annual Grafton Morrish tournament for Public School Old Boys' teams which was instigated as a new competition for those schools not eligible to play in the Halford Hewitt which is restricted to the originating 64 schools.

The town of Hunstanton grew with the opening of the railway line from King's Lynn in the 1850s and its location next to the Wash means that it enjoys an unusual reputation as an east coast resort with views of westerly sunsets. The inaugural meeting of the Club was held in the town's Golden Lion Hotel in March 1891 and was attended by just seven people including The Rev. HD Barrett, vicar of St. Edmund's Parish Church,

Dr. CR Whitty and G Carrick from Wisbech. Hamon le Strange, the local landowner who could trace his ancestry back to the Norman Conquest, was elected President in his absence and despite the low turnout the meeting decided to press ahead and appointed George Fernie from Troon to lay out the first 9-hole course, permission having been received from WC Dodman, the tenant of Caley Hall Farm. John Hughes from the club at Great Yarmouth, where he had learnt the game under Willie Fernie, the Open Champion in 1883, was appointed as the first Professional.

The Club had a slow start, partly because of almost immediate competition from the new Royal West Norfolk club at Brancaster, a few miles further east. A number of Hunstanton's founders and early members helped encourage the Brancaster club including Hamon le Strange who advised the neighbouring squire, Simms-Reeve, and Holcombe Ingleby, the Club's first Captain.

An article in the Lynn Advertiser in January 1912, written to celebrate the Club's 21st Birthday described how: "The beginnings of the club were modest in every way. The links were a wilderness of marram grass in the drier parts, and rushes in the damper hollows, and were honeycombed with rabbit warrens. The tenant, Mr. Dodman, used to let the shooting for a substantial sum."

The Duke of York became Patron of the Club in 1900 and continued in this role after he became King George V in 1910. Despite this connection, Hunstanton is not a 'Royal' club unlike the three other early Norfolk clubs at Brancaster, Cromer and Norwich. This may have been due to the Club being too timid in its approach to the matter and not asking the direct question. In most

cases, the Royal title was granted along with bestowal of Royal Patronage. In 1910, and following the Duke's coronation, Hamon le Strange wrote to the Privy Purse Office noting: "The Committee have asked me to ascertain whether they may be authorised to use His Majesty's name as their Patron; they hope that his mark of favour may be accorded to them." The Club received a response in March 1911 which simply noted that: "the King is pleased to continue his patronage of Hunstanton Golf Club."

The Club experienced an early lesson in 'caddie-power' and in diplomatic solutions. Fred Matsell was a village boy who started caddying as an 8-year-old and joined the groundstaff when he was twelve. He became spokesmen for the caddies and incurred the disapproval of the Committee and was suspended when he lobbied for an extra penny per round. Matsell responded by standing on the public road next to the first tee and blowing a bugle whenever a golfer tried to tee off. His suspension was soon cancelled by the Secretary who took the view that he was more trouble off the course than on it! Fred went on to become a loyal servant of the

Club. In 1915 he was appointed as Head Greenkeeper and altogether he worked for the Club for more than 50 years with his son following in his footsteps.

Harry Vardon, Braid, Taylor, Sandy Herd and Jack White all played at Hunstanton around the turn of the century and Braid was invited to make improvements to the course in 1907. Bernard Darwin described how Braid: "left a cunning trail of bunkers behind him!" The Club's first hosting of the Ladies' British Open Championship was held in May 1914, just before the outbreak of World War One, and was won by Miss Cecil Leitch who defeated the US ladies' champion, Gladys Ravencroft, 2&1 in the final.

John Hughes retired from the Club in 1920 and is also remembered as the man who helped create a 9-hole course at nearby Sandringham where he taught golf to the Royal Family and played with four future kings, Edward VII, George V, Edward VIII and George VI. The renowned James Sherlock succeeded Hughes as Club Professional and shortly after his arrival represented Great Britain against the US Professionals at Gleneagles in 1921 in the fixture which evolved into the Ryder Cup.

Main: The present clubhouse was constructed in 1910 and replaced the original wooden building (photograph by Bob Laughton)

Inset: The traffic light system on the eighteenth fairway helps to warn golfers of pedestrians using the footpath which is partially concealed by the sand dunes

THIS SEAT COMMEMORATES A UNIQUE ACHIEVEMENT BY
R. J. TAYLOR
WHO HOLED IN ONE AT THE 16th HOLE
ON THREE SUCCESSIVE DAYS
EASTERN COUNTIES FOURSOMES MEETING
1974

Main: The par-3 seventh hole has a tight landing area and a cavernous bunker in front of the green is edged by railway sleepers

Above: Hamon le Strange, the squire of Hunstanton Hall, was an enthusiastic supporter of the early Club and was elected first President

Inset: A commemorative seat celebrates a feat which may be unique in the entire history of golf

Writing a tribute in The Daily Telegraph, Leonard Crawley remarked that: "few made the science of hitting a golf ball sound simpler." He had thirteen holes-in-one over a long career and members play annually for the Sherlock Cup which he donated after winning it outright as Midland professional champion.

In 1974, the Club witnessed a most extraordinary golfing achievement. Playing in the Eastern Counties Men's Foursomes, a visitor, 30-year-old Bob Taylor holed in one on three successive days at the 188-yard sixteenth. Taylor used a one-iron on the practice day, and following a switch in wind direction, a six-iron in two rounds of the formal competition.

The course is laid out on either side of a central grassy sand ridge which runs parallel to the shoreline. The first eight holes run in a rough north-easterly direction to the extremity of the course, and the prevailing south-westerly wind means that scores need to be built early in the round. The thirteenth has attracted much discussion over the years as it is the reverse of most 'two shot' holes with the fairway finishing some 100 yards short of the green requiring an accurate tee shot and a well-flighted approach.

Hunstanton has been happy to embrace modern technology to help improve safety. At the blind par-3 fourteenth hole, a traffic light system has been introduced with players changing the lights to 'Go' as they leave the green on their way to the next tee. An even more ingenious system has been installed on the eighteenth fairway. The public has a right-of-way across the course to the beach and the footpath is partially obscured by the central ridge. The Club has therefore installed an electronic sensor which turns a set of traffic lights from green to red when a pedestrian passes through a sensor on the path. It may not be traditional, but it is certainly sensible and more practical than a bell which may not be heard in windy conditions.

The Club has an enviable reputation for the true nature of its greens and it is still fair to echo the words of Sir Peter Allen, writing in his book 'Famous Fairways', who ventured that the course was the best in all England between the Tweed and the Thames.

WALLASEY

DR. FRANK STABLEFORD

Wallasey has survived innumerable problems and is now an excellent course providing a stiff challenge to top golfers seeking to qualify for the Open Championship when it is held at nearby Hoylake. The future was finally assured when the course was bought outright by the Club in 1995. Before then, sand inundation, gales, war needs and new club and ball technology had made a huge impact on the original course laid out by Old Tom Morris and RW Kirk, the Professional at Hoylake. Just four greens remain from the first links.

The original grounds of 240 acres have shrunk to 140 acres over the years and a number of top-class architects and famous golfers including Alex Herd, Harold Hilton, James Braid, JH Taylor and Fred Hawtree have all used their skills on the course.

The Club was founded in 1891 by eight golfers, including RW 'Pendulum' Brown and James Cullen who were both members of the Royal Liverpool Club at nearby Hoylake, and who believed that their home course was becoming overcrowded. Some less charitable historians have also suggested that Wallasey was chosen because it was slightly nearer Liverpool by train, allowing less time to be lost away from the office! The landowners, Frederick and Heath Harrison, were amenable to the course being laid out over the sand hills which early photographs portray as one huge bunker! The course was some distance from the nearest settlement and the first clubhouse stood isolated amongst the dunes. The only road led to the railway station, and the Club had to lay 600 railway sleepers to improve access across the sand.

The first professional match was held in 1897 when Harry Vardon scored 77 and 76 to win the £10 first prize, with Alex Herd finishing second. James Braid and

Willie Fernie were also in the field. In 1908, a crowd of 1,500 people watched Braid defeat Vardon 2&1 in an exhibition match.

The St. Nicholas, or Harrison Memorial Church across the road from the first tee has played an important part in the history of the Club. The church was built by the Harrison brothers in memory of their parents, and the building includes a stained-glass window depicting golfers which was designed by John Berrie, a Wallasey member, who also painted famous portraits of Bobby Jones and Frank Stableford. The window was funded by Hilda Wilde as a tribute to her husband, Herbert, who was also a member. Golfers used to attend a special early Sunday morning service, leaving their clubs in the church porch, whilst the bell ringers would later replenish their thirst in the clubhouse. The tower was used as a vantage point

Main: The final green is a fine finish to the round and putts are scrutinised by members sitting in the clubroom

Above: Dr. Frank Stableford was Club Captain in 1933

for spectators during the qualifying competition for the 1930 Open which featured Bobby Jones and Henry Cotton, and disaster nearly struck when a smouldering discarded cigarette set fire to the roof. Fortunately, the fire brigade managed to save the building which Bobby Jones had visited during his stay in Wallasey.

A famous painting of Jones in his blue sweater was completed at the Club by John AA Berrie, RA, who persuaded Jones to sit for half an hour on Sunday morning, the day before the Open. Jones recalled that he was kept happy with whisky and soda, and he was so pleased with the result that he signed the picture and dated it 15 June, 1930. The portrait hangs in the main clubroom and the same artist painted a replica which is on display at Augusta. Another Wallasey member, Jock Liddell, sat for the body in the picture wearing Jones's sweater and he was later presented with the top by the great man.

Wallasey is famous for its connection with the invention of the Stableford scoring system. Frank Barney Gorton Stableford MRCS, LRCP, was an excellent golfer before he joined Wallasey in 1914. Playing off plus-1, he won the club championship at Royal Porthcawl in 1907 and broke the amateur course record at the same club in 1909 with a gross 71. He became frustrated at failing to reach the fairway on a number of Wallasey's tough par-4s when they were played directly into the wind

ON THIS HOLE
Dr. FRANK STABLEFORD
DEVISED HIS
POINTS SCORING SYSTEM

**THE FIRST STABLEFORD COMPETITION
WAS PLAYED AT WALLASEY
ON 16th MAY 1932**

and realised that many golfers tore up their cards after playing only a few holes. Golfers worldwide have reason to be grateful for his idea!

The doctor was made a life member of the Club in 1953 and in his letter of thanks he recalled: "...when I offered my system of scoring to the Club, the Council thought it much too complicated but after the first competition, the enthusiasm was nearly out of bounds." Sadly, the doctor's eyesight failed in later life and when he could no longer see the balls on the snooker table he decided that the fun had gone out of life and he was found dead from a gunshot wound with his pistol by his side.

ROYAL WEST NORFOLK

Royal West Norfolk is a special and unusual Club and is situated next to one of the most beautiful beaches in England. Access is via a tidal causeway and golfers can be cut off from the mainland during certain high tides. Despite, or perhaps because of, many Royal connections, it has retained an informal and low-key profile. There are no signposts to the Club in Brancaster Village, no reserved parking spaces for the Captain and Committee, no competition honours' boards and no rules about the wearing of jackets and ties. Dogs are actively encouraged to accompany their golfing owners around the course and during the author's visit a small terrier devoured a whole rabbit of about its own size in front of the clubhouse!

There is now a long waiting list and, once admitted, members are expected instinctively to do what is right. A minute in 1932 noted that: "It was the object of the Committee to elect as members of the Club none but gentlemen in every sense of the word, that is, men of integrity and honour." However, high social standing was not necessarily an advantage. The Club's centenary book includes a possibly apocryphal story concerning a lady who enquired about membership for her husband and herself. "My husband" she volunteered, "is a Sir." The Secretary was out but the Steward was on hand with a helpful response: "We happen to have a waiting list just for Sirs."

The Club was founded in 1891 by Holcombe Ingleby who spotted the land whilst journeying along the road to Burnham Norton with his brother, Herbert. Ingleby had been the Honorary Secretary at Royal Eastbourne for two years before marrying into

a wealthy Norfolk family and moving to East Anglia. He was also the first Captain of the club at nearby Hunstanton, serving for four years. He persuaded the Lord of the Manor, WH Simms-Reeve, to allow golf to be played over the dunes and marshes although the squire had never seen the game being played and knew nothing of the rules. Perhaps this lack of knowledge helped to persuade the locals that the game was not a threat to their grazing rights over the common land. The King's Lynn Advertiser in February 1892 reported on a meeting between the golfing founders and the local village commoners. In replying to a question about the safety of livestock,

Above: The clubhouse is extremely vulnerable to tidal storms and must rank as one of the most remote in Britain. On the positive side, it enjoys one of the most dramatic outlooks anywhere in the golfing world

Main: A narrow sandy channel separates the clubhouse from the first tee and leads down to the beautiful beach

Above: The much-decorated Earl of Leicester was Club Captain in 1912. The Coke Family live at nearby Holkham Hall which is open to the public

Reeve was able to respond, to general laughter, that he had made enquiries and found that the game was: "played at a walk and a very slow walk at that, and that ladies played it and no one hurried because the men wanted the girls to keep up with them."

The locals were placated and tensions were eased further when villagers were given limited playing rights and organised themselves into the Brancaster Workmen's Golf Club which has since become the Brancaster Village Club, open to locals living within the boundaries of Brancaster and Brancaster Staithe.

Horace Hutchinson helped to advise on the layout of the course and was appointed as first Captain, and HRH the Prince of Wales became the Patron, establishing a Royal link with the Club which has continued into the modern era. The Sandringham Estate lies nearby and several generations of Royals have enjoyed playing over the links with four members of the Royal Family serving as Captain. Ingleby drummed up early support for the Club by writing to his contacts from his Athenaeum Club address in London, comparing the new course favourably with the well-established links at Sandwich and Westward Ho! His campaign was successful and within a year membership had reached 270.

Early matches between the Club and the village golfers were popular and produced some memorable encounters. In 1928, the Prince asked to play for the Club and the villagers fielded 72-year-old Bob Lake as one of his opponents. By lunchtime, Lake and Charlie Large, the Course Greenkeeper, had beaten the Prince and his Equerry, the Hon. Piers Legh by 4&3. Lake played with five clubs and wore hob-nail boots and working clothes whilst the Prince was reported to have 32 clubs and wore very long, colourful and baggy plus-fours. Lake enjoyed a few beers at lunchtime but there was a similar result in the afternoon when he won his singles match against the Prince by one hole. "I told him he needed more practice, and, even more important, more patience on the greens. He just walked straight up to his putts and hit them. I think he took my advice kindly." In 1931 the Dukes of Gloucester and Kent played in the fixture as well as the Prince.

Beer clearly flowed freely and a villager recalled the aftermath of these matches. "Everyone excepting us boys retired to the clubhouse. We made our way up the beach road and waited patiently at the bridge to see the next part of the action. Just before the bridge, the road turns fairly sharply to the right whereas straight ahead there is a muddy creek, full of water at high tide. About two hours later, the village golfers, their clubs over their shoulders, riding their bicycles, would come rather unsteadily up the beach road, weaving from side to side. Invariably one or two of them failed to negotiate the bend and rode their bicycles into the creek, which we thought was hilarious, and, to do them credit, so did most of the victims because, when we helped them out, we often received a few coppers."

Little has changed at the Club since these bygone days and it is easy to imagine the friendly banter. Members still favour matchplay over medal rounds and four-balls are not allowed on the course. Many of the holes have changed little since the original layout in 1891 with the most memorable being the par-5 eighth hole which requires two precise shots over different sections of the harbour, and the par-4 ninth which also offers two separate opportunities for a watery grave. Slicers might be advised to play when the tide is out as balls can often be played from the saltmarsh once the waters have receded.

The course is a virtual nature reserve in its own right and the Club's former Professional, Ray Kimber, was a well respected ornithologist. He observed many rarities on or near the links including ivory gull, alpine accentor, nutcracker, rustic bunting and bluethroat.

The Club co-hosts the annual Grafton Morrish Public Schools golf competition with the neighbouring club at Hunstanton and this event has introduced many players to the joys of golf along the Norfolk Coast.

The wind is a constant challenge and a reminder of the Club's vulnerability to the elements. Over the years the sea and the dunes have advanced inland and the original tees for the first two holes have been lost to the sea whilst the original second hole has had to be abandoned. The Environment Agency has adopted a policy of managed retreat for the coastline and the Club is only allowed to use soft defences, including geotextile fences, rather than the familiar large hard boulders. Fortunately, the new technology seems to be working although a large North Sea surge like that suffered in 1953 could still change the situation dramatically. The clubhouse remains especially vulnerable, and whilst the offshore sandbar of Scolt Head is providing some extra protection for the eastern end of the course, it is possible that the clubhouse may be outflanked by sea inundation from the south-west.

Pat Ward-Thomas, the well respected golfing journalist who wrote for Country Life for many years, was Captain of the Club in 1980 and summed up the perennial fascination of the course in an article entitled: 'A course to last a lifetime.' "A golfer can pursue the game's challenges there in a setting of severe beauty that has escaped all but natural change since the beginning of time."

Below: View from above and behind the ninth green looking across the harbour to the village of Brancaster Staithe

SILLOTH ON SOLWAY

CECIL LEITCH AND WILLIE WHITELAW

Above: William Whitelaw, Willie's grandfather, was Chairman of the railway company which owned the Club and hence became Silloth's Patron (Courtesy Silloth on Solway Golf Club)

Right: The road to the clubhouse from the town passes a small port which belies the peace to be found on the links

The Carlisle & Silloth Bay Railway and Dock Company line was opened in 1859 by Carlisle industrialists looking for an efficient port for their goods. However, early revenues were disappointing and the line was soon sold to the Scottish-based North British Railway Company. Around the same time, Dr. John Leitch, a Scot from Fife, became GP and Medical Officer for the town. He played a form of golf with his sister, Moncrieffe, on what is now the village green, to the east of the docks, in the early 1870s.

The Scottish owners of the railway decided to develop Silloth as a resort and were quick to appreciate its golfing terrain. Willie Fernie, who was to win the Open Championship in 1883, was engaged to lay out a pay and play links near to the Leitch's course. Unfortunately, green fees were disappointing out of the main season and it was decided to try again using more promising golfing terrain to the west of the docks. This time, money was no object and the company hired Davie Grant, a Professional at North Berwick and the brother-in-law of Ben Sayers, to lay out the course. Grant was assisted by Mungo Park who became the Club's first Professional. Later improvements were implemented by Willie Park Junior and Alister MacKenzie.

The railway company hoped that an express train would enable golfers from Edinburgh, Hawick, Langholm, Carlisle and Lockerbie to play golf during a day trip to Silloth. Free use of the links was offered on a trial basis and golfers were promised that: "The salubrious and invigorating breezes which prevail all Summer are charged with more ozone than one can enjoy in any other part of England." The links at Silloth were a pleasant contrast to the cramped course at Dalston near Carlisle which had been formed by Scottish doctors based in the town and was only available during Winter months. The railway company therefore effected a merger

between the Carlisle and Silloth clubs in an attempt to boost passenger traffic and bring Summer golf to Carlisle's members.

The Club's early Professionals suffered from the lack of golfers. Park and his successor, Stranach, soon moved on, and Hugh Kirkaldy, the Club's second Open Champion, was appointed in an attempt to maintain the high quality image of the course. Kirkaldy beat JH Taylor in an exhibition match over four rounds in 1896, but tragedy struck when Kirkaldy died in the Spring of 1897 aged only 29. Tom Renouf from Jersey took over from Kirkaldy, and the Club believed it had found the ideal Professional who was good enough to play the visiting giants of the game without expecting a champion's wage. Shortly after his arrival, Harry Vardon beat Renouf by 7&6 over 36 holes, and in 1902, special trains were laid on to carry spectators to watch an important four-ball match between Vardon who scored 70, James Braid, 75, JH Taylor, 77, and Renouf, 80. In the afternoon's foursomes, Braid and Taylor, representing the 'mainland', beat Vardon and Renouf of Jersey 2&1.

Renouf's successor, Alex Brown, had a further challenge to overcome. Jack 'Wingy' Scott was a caddie who had lost an arm in an accident. Wingy achieved local notoriety when he beat another one-armed golfer, John Haskins from the Hoylake Village Club, 3&1 in a 72-hole match played over Silloth and Hoylake in 1909 for a prize of £20. Wingy used his fame and experience to offer himself as caddie, coach and seller of second-hand golf balls to such an extent that Brown believed his own living as a Professional was at risk. The Club withdrew Wingy's artisan's ticket but he continued to undercut the Professional's price for golf balls and Brown finally gave up the fight and resigned in 1911. John Shanks was then appointed and stayed for 33 years, having presumably come to some sort of understanding with Wingy!

Silloth has played an important role in the history of ladies' golf in England. Dr. Leitch had passed on his love of golf to his five daughters, four of whom played off scratch or better. The girls practised on their own private miniature course near the village-green dressed in sailors' suits and using Tate and Lyle syrup tins as makeshift holes. In 1904, the four sisters occupied the first four positions in the Club's team for an important representative game against Penrith, and in an away match against Moffat, the young girls were met off the train by the opposition Captain who remarked that: "You needn't have brought your caddies, we do have our own you know!" The four sisters all won their matches against both teams.

Unfortunately, Dr. Leitch died in 1896 and was not able to enjoy his daughters' later triumphs. May Leitch played several times for England and won the Golf Illustrated Gold Cup at Bushey by two shots from younger sister Cecil. Edith played off plus-fifteen at one stage and won the English Ladies' Championship in 1927 at Pannal, but the family name was made famous worldwide by Cecilia 'Cecil' Leitch who won the Ladies' Championship on four occasions with her idiosyncratic palm grip. Her fame was heightened by the interest shown in her success by the suffragettes. As well as playing handicap matches against some of the leading male players including Harold Hilton, she also attracted admiration by breaking the overall Silloth course record, for men and women, with a score of 72 playing off the men's tees. The outbreak of war in 1914 curtailed her sporting triumphs but she achieved a rare hat trick by winning the last Ladies' British Open Amateur Championship before the war which was held at Hunstanton, and then the next two championships at Newcastle, County Down in 1920 and Turnberry in 1921, when she beat her great rival Joyce Wethered in the final. Cecil was self-taught and Wethered once remarked that: "...to have allowed myself to watch her strike the ball with her forceful and individualistic swing would have destroyed my own sense of rhythm."

Above: The Rt. Hon. The Viscount Whitelaw KT, CH, MC, but known to all at the Club as 'Willie' (Courtesy Silloth on Solway Golf Club)

Cecil recovered sufficiently from serious injury to reach the final of the Championship again in 1925 when she lost to Joyce Wethered at the 37th hole in front of a crowd of 10,000 people at Troon. She later reflected that this was one of her greatest golfing experiences. Retirement beckoned but she decided to compete in the 1926 championship at Royal St David's at Harlech where she achieved victory on Welsh soil to complete a unique record of wins in all four home countries. Cecil became the Ladies' President of Silloth in 1922 and continued in the office for 55 years. She played a major role in helping the Club to host the Ladies' British Open Amateur Strokeplay Championship in 1972. The event was due to be played at Newcastle, County Down but was switched at short notice due to the security problems in Northern Ireland at the time. In 1976, the Ladies' Open Amateur Championship was hosted by the Club following which Silloth has now become established as a regular and challenging venue for top quality ladies' events.

Silloth's other famous player could trace his roots back to the early days of the Club although The Right Honourable, The Viscount William Whitelaw played his early golf at Nairn in the North of Scotland. Willie was born in Morayshire in 1918 and when his father died shortly afterwards, his grandfather, also William, stepped in to help his mother with Willie's upbringing. The older William became Chairman of the London Northern Eastern Railway (LNER) in the 1920s, and thus Patron of the Club which was still owned by the railway company. Silloth finally bought the course for its members in 1937 and the railway closed in 1964 as part of Dr. Beeching's cuts.

Willie was a shy boy and his grandfather thought that the game would help the young man to develop confidence with a wider social experience. Seldom can guardian influence have worked better. On his way to becoming Deputy Prime Minister, Willie won a Blue at Cambridge playing off scratch and helped Winchester to win the Halford Hewitt trophy in 1948. He became a Walker Cup selector in 1952 and Captain of The R&A in 1969/70. Silloth honoured him with the office of President between 1977 and his death in 1999. He was known to everyone at the Club as Willie, and Margaret Thatcher once remarked memorably that: "every Prime Minister needs a Willie." In his obituary, the Guardian newspaper, which was no supporter of the Tories, wrote that: "Charm was the essence of the man and it was recognised by thousands of people who never met him."

The course has continued to win plaudits. The fairways are particularly springy whilst the dunes are covered in heather which punishes any wayward shots. If he was alive today, Bernard Darwin would surely repeat his summary of 1925; "I never more violently fell in love with a course at first sight."

RYE
HOME OF THE PRESIDENT'S PUTTER

Rye deserves a special place in the history of English golf through its connections with Harry Colt, Bernard Darwin and the Oxford and Cambridge Golfing Society which plays for the President's Putter in the middle of Winter each year over the excellent and well-draining links. The nearby town is a fascinating medieval coastal settlement which has become isolated from the sea over the centuries as the shoreline has grown through the favourable effects of long shore drift. The course has been built on the sand dunes which have accumulated over a layer of shingle which accounts for the excellent drainage and Rye does not need preferred lies or Winter Rules as plugged balls are almost unknown.

Harry Colt was involved from the early days at the Club. The inaugural meeting was held in November 1893 and was attended by nine enthusiasts including three solicitors, two doctors, two reverends and the manager of Lloyds Bank in Rye. Several of the founders had connections with the town of Hastings, ten miles west of Rye, where Harry Colt was serving in a solicitor's office. Colt had won a golfing Blue at Cambridge University when he captained the team in 1890, and his skills were undoubtedly known to the emerging golfing community on the South Coast. The Clubs at Sandwich and Littlestone had been established successfully and the founders identified that the dunes near Camber Sands, two miles to the east of Rye town, would be suitable for golf.

The Rector of the nearby village of Iden, the Rev. JL Bates, and his son the Rev. GL Bates, gave early impetus to the Club. The enthusiastic younger Bates had played golf at Cambridge University in the early 1890s and even persuaded his father to build a 9-hole course in the rectory's garden. The first course built in the Spring of 1893 on Camber Sands was surveyed and laid out by Alexander, the Professional from Littlestone. Rye soon appointed Littlestone's Assistant Professional, H Gosbee, as its second Professional

and Greenkeeper at a salary of £1 per week following the fairly rapid departure of the big-hitting Scot, Douglas Rolland, who had been attracted from the 9-hole course

Left: American author Henry James became a social member in 1898 and lived in the nearby town. He did not play golf but was particularly fond of the Club's teas

Below: The clubhouse viewed at dusk with shadows accentuating the fairway humps

Main: Evening light
and perfect links land

Above: David Lloyd George
driving at the short seventeenth
(now eighth) hole during the
Parliamentary Handicap meeting

at Limpsfield in Surrey at a salary of twenty five shillings per week. The Club made a concerted effort to improve the course in Spring 1894 and paid for two more Scottish Professionals, Ramsey Hunter, the first Professional at St George's, Sandwich and Peter Paxton from the links at Eastbourne, to advise on improvements. Rye advertised for members in a December 1893 edition of Golf magazine, and asked for subscriptions to be paid to the Rev. Guy L Bates at 'The Parsonage, Iden, Sussex'. It would seem that Rye took a calculated risk about the character of its early membership as interviews were not mentioned at the time.

The Club was officially opened in February 1894 and Harry Colt, who was elected first Club Captain, immediately set about planning for a more permanent course stretching up to 6,000 yards in length. Membership increased rapidly thanks to improved access facilitated by the new steam tram which started in July 1895. A platform was constructed near today's thirteenth hole

and the line was soon extended onwards to the beach at Camber Sands to cater for Summer holidaymakers. The Club had to subsidise the line for running trams on Sundays and during the Winter months, and by the 1920s, further economies were required following increased competition from the motor car. The steam engine was replaced by a more efficient and smaller petrol tractor and the line struggled on until 1939 when it was finally closed to passengers, although it continued in use for military supply purposes during the war.

Increased traffic along the road from Rye to Camber Sands required a succession of changes to the links and the fifth and twelfth holes are now the only original fairways on the course. The links used to stretch north of the road and also eastwards of the coastguard cottages behind the current third green, but Rye has been fortunate that extra land continues to be recovered from the sea. By the 1920s, Colt had become a renowned golf architect and the Club asked him to advise on the necessary modifications. No doubt proud of his first layout at Rye, he advised that it would be best to move the road as the Club now owned the course and the land to the north of the road! Unfortunately, this proved to be prohibitively expensive, and following advice from James Braid that the course would indeed need to be altered, first Tom Simpson and later Sir Guy Campbell were employed to make the necessary changes.

Like Littlestone along the coast, the Club developed early links with well-known Parliamentary golfers. The Hon. Alfred Lyttelton and the Hon. Arthur Balfour both joined the Club in 1895 and Rye hosted three annual Parliamentary Handicap competitions which attracted other noted politicians including David Lloyd George. The Club also established strong early connections with the Bar and most significantly, in 1899, the newly formed Oxford and Cambridge Golfing Society accepted an invitation to play their home matches at the Club. The strength of Oxbridge golf in the 1920s was demonstrated in 1923 when the Society played against the visiting American Walker Cup team at Rye in a day of foursomes and four-balls which ended in a halved match. The first competition for the President's Putter, which was open to members of the Society, was held in January 1920 and it has become a matter of pride and tradition that the tournament has continued to be played in most years at the same venue and time of year.

The first wooden putter to display the winners' balls was presented by the first President of the Society, John Low, and had been used by Hugh Kirkaldy when winning the Open Championship in 1891. Famous winners have included three British Amateur champions, EWE Holderness, Cyril Tolley and Roger Wethered as well as Laddy Lucas, Bernard Darwin, Leonard Crawley, Gerald Micklem, George Duncan, golf architect Donald Steel and England cricketer Ted Dexter. Crawley's knowledge of the course was excellent as he used to live in one of the old coastguard cottages by the third

green. The most memorable encounter occurred in the 1926 final which ended in a declaration of joint winners when Roger Wethered and EF Storey were still level after six extra holes and had to surrender to Winter darkness. Donald Steel once wrote in Country Life that: "The strength of the Putter, apart from taking place at Rye, on incomparable Winter links, is the spirit it evokes in all those taking part", whilst Bernard Darwin once described the event as: "one of the few really sacred festivals of golf."

Darwin was probably the greatest golf writer of all time. He was also a very good player and the Club celebrated his enormous contribution to the game by making him Club Captain for the second time at the age of 80 in 1956, exactly 50 years after his first appointment. He retired from full-time writing for The Times in 1953 and became a resident in the Dormy House next to the course. By then, he suffered from arthritis and had ceased playing golf, but he was still an enthusiastic supporter of both the Club and the President's Putter. The clubhouse has furnished a special Bernard Darwin room in his memory.

Rye is predominately a foursomes course and four-balls are not recognised and have no standing. It is difficult to play as a casual visitor but the Club treasures the history and traditions of the game and keen golfers should jump at the chance of accepting an invitation to play with a member, many of whom live away from Rye and therefore play the course on an irregular basis.

Above: The Rye-Camber tram ran along the coastal side of the links and there was a special Golf Links Station

Inset: The President's Putter is the famous annual golf tournament of the Oxford and Cambridge Golfing Society

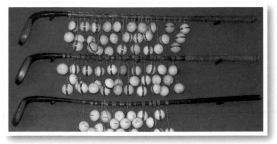

SEACROFT

NOTTINGHAM ANCESTRY

Above: In 1989, local girl Helen Dobson had one of the most remarkable years in the history of ladies' golf (Courtesy Seacroft Golf Club)

Inset: Storm clouds gathering behind the heavily bunkered sixth green

Seacroft is a delightful links course lying close to Skegness on the east coast of England and situated just north of The Wash. Successive Earls of Scarborough were responsible for the development of Skegness following the arrival of the railway to the town in 1873 when the population was only 349. By 1895, more than 2,000 people lived in Skegness. Following encouragement from the 10th Earl, an open meeting was held in August 1894, chaired by Admiral Buckle, to discuss the formation of the Skegness Golf Club. The Rector of Skegness, the Rev. CP Disbrowe was appointed Honorary Secretary and the first 9-hole course was funded by the Earl and laid out under direction from Tom Dunn of Wimbledon. Although the course attracted players from across Lincolnshire, a number of businessmen in the City of Nottingham had more ambitious plans for the dunes. The railway had helped to establish Skegness as the prime seaside resort for Midlanders, and a consortium from Nottingham leased a large tract of land, including the original course, and instructed Willie Fernie from Troon to lay out a full eighteen holes.

Many of the original Skegness members joined the new Seacroft Golf Club, but control was exercised from Nottingham. In 1907, an exhibition match was staged between Arnaud Massy, the new Open Champion at Hoylake, and the runner-up, JH Taylor. Golf Illustrated covered the match and was full of praise for the extended course, noting: "It is hard to speak in terms of too high praise of one of the best seaside courses one could hope to play over", whilst The Daily Telegraph acknowledged the Nottingham connection as well as the characteristic landscape which has survived through to modern times: "Seacroft is primarily the sea links of the Midlands'. It is

very happily situated. The links are real links, a narrow strip between the sea and the sown, and they run straight along the low undeviating coastline, west of the waves and just beyond their sound." Skegness has accumulated extra land from long-shore drift over the last 100 years and the course is now rather further from the sea.

During the Second World War, much of Skegness became a Prohibited Area and access was only gained by special permit. An 18-foot-wide anti-tank ditch was dug across the course complete with concrete and wooden obstructions, and a local rule was introduced in October 1942 to the effect that: "A ball lying on the bank of the tank trap or immediately in front of the same, may be thrown back, and if in the tank trap or on the far bank may be thrown forward without penalty." The Club continued to be busy as servicemen were offered half-price green fees, and honorary social membership was granted to officers of all the Army regiments billeted in the area. By the end of the war, membership had fallen by more than two-thirds to just 156 and green fee income was

only 10% of pre-war levels. Fortunately, local membership increased quickly from 1945 onwards and the axis of the Club moved away from Nottingham to Skegness.

Seacroft's best player emerged only in recent years. Helen Dobson was born in Skegness and took up golf at the age of six. In 1984, aged 13 and playing off a three handicap, she scored 74 in a monthly medal and her progress continued apace. She won the British Open Girls' Championship in 1987, and in 1989 had perhaps the greatest individual year in ladies' amateur golf, winning titles including the Ladies' British Amateur Open at Hoylake, the Ladies' British Open Amateur Stroke Play Championship at Southerness, the English Ladies' Close Amateur championship at Barnham Broom, and the English Girls' competition at Edgbaston. Not surprisingly, she was voted the Avia Watches Woman Golfer of the Year. Fortunately for the Club, she still had time to return to her roots and help the junior team from Seacroft to win the Lincolnshire County trophy. Dobson turned professional in 1991 and in 1993 she became only the third British woman to win a tournament on the US professional tour.

The course is quite narrow, being laid out over land leading towards the Gibraltar Point National Nature Reserve. This is well-known as a vantage point from which to observe the Spring and Autumn migration of rare birds. The outward and inward nines are divided by a central ridge of dunes, with the sixth and twelfth holes being played in the reverse direction to the rest of their respective halves. The fairways are tight and undulating and many of the 75 bunkers on the course are deep and demanding.

The first nine holes would still be familiar to Willie Fernie, but holes eleven to sixteen have been built over land acquired during the 1920s, aided by a £5,000 loan from John D Player who was a director of the famous tobacco company. The original back-nine occupied a much smaller and tighter area. Out of bounds lurks unnervingly close to the right-hand side of the second fairway and the second shot is hit to a plateau green which is more than 40 yards long. The middle part of today's course is unusual with holes nine to fourteen inclusive being alternating par-5s and par-3s, whilst the round finishes with two strong par-4s measuring over 400 yards. The final green has tricky borrows and is known in the Club as 'three-putt territory'. Asked to comment after playing Seacroft in 1957, Dai Rees replied: "Don't let them alter the course, it was just right as we played it", and in 1992 Donald Steel noted that Seacroft has stood the test of time better than most long-established courses.

Above: *View from the clubhouse down the first fairway to the large sycamore behind the green*

ROOM ON THE DOWNS

Whilst coastal links were viewed as the best golfing territory, a number of clubs were established within reach of the railway to take advantage of the springy turf on the open downs. The grass was frequently kept under control by grazing sheep. Players at Goring & Streatley (below) need to consider the slope during club selection as they descend from the hills towards the end of their round.

Guildford 1886
Royal Eastbourne 1887
Brighton & Hove 1887
Marlborough 1888
Royal Winchester 1888
Salisbury & South Wilts ... 1888
Minchinhampton 1889
Long Ashton 1893
Goring & Streatley 1895
Gog Magog 1901

GUILDFORD

HISTORIC TIES WITH PAU

Guildford is the oldest golf club in Surrey and plays over quick-draining and chalky common land on the Merrow Downs which are situated a couple of miles to the east of the town centre. The land was formerly part of the large Onslow Estate and the 4th Earl of Onslow became the first Honorary President of the Club in 1889. Successive Earls continued the tradition through until 2001 when the first elected President was chosen from within the Club's playing membership.

Between 1752 and the middle of the 19th Century, the Downs were also the site of Guildford Race Course and a number of prestigious Royal Plate races were run over the grounds.

Notices on the Common are worded to the effect that until Michaelmas 2038, golf can only be played with the express authorisation of Guildford Golf Club or Guildford Ladies' Golf Club.

The Club was founded in 1886 by Colonel W Bannatyne, Major W Pontifex and EL Hooper with support from the Earl of Onslow. The Club has a unique connection with Pau Golf Club in France which describes itself as 'Le St Andrews du Continent' and was the first club on mainland Europe. Pau was formally founded in 1856 by British holidaymakers who are reputed to have included a few of the Duke of Wellington's Scottish soldiers who remembered the area from their long march home after the Peninsular War in 1814.

Pontifex, together with two other early Guildford members, Colonel Hutchinson and Archdeacon Sapte, were founder members of the golf club at Pau. As a consequence, the two clubs have held a number of

events over the years to celebrate the connection, and the clubhouse at Guildford contains a large, fading photograph of the three founders at Pau. Pontifex was also a member at Blackheath and he became President of Pau Golf Club in 1894, eight years after he founded the Club at Guildford.

The original six holes at Merrow Down were rapidly expanded first to twelve, and then to eighteen, and by 1889 the course measured 4,600 yards. Although major changes in layouts have occurred over the years, the chalkpit has appeared as a feature from the earliest days as a succession of course designers have sought to incorporate the pit as a novel challenge. It features in three holes on the 1891 course whilst today's players need only to survive the drive at the fifteenth hole.

Above: *View of the Guildford clubhouse looking down from an area of common land on Merrow Downs which was once used as part of the course before the playing area was moved a short distance further east*

Lt Col W. Bannatyne
1887

The earliest rented clubhouse at the bottom of the Common in Downs Road was soon replaced by an impressive two-storey building on the opposite side of the Common and up the hill in One Tree Hill Road. This building is remembered in a fading photograph hanging in today's clubhouse. Almost immediately, the members were offered a plot of land in private fields back down on the more convenient, lower slopes of the Common, and the current clubhouse was built in what is now High Path Road. Lord Onslow, who owned most of the surrounding land, was persuaded to buy the new building in One Tree Hill Road from the Club at market value and recently, the Club has made major improvements to the Victorian clubhouse whilst preserving the original character. Peter Alliss officially opened the upgraded building in 1998.

The first two Captains were competent golfers and both had an eighteen handicap. Colonel Bannatyne was the first winner of his own Challenge Cup in

1887 with a net score of 91, and Major Pontifex won the same cup in the following year with a net 86. The early Club was clearly well-patronised with titled Captains including Lord Albert Seymour in 1889, the Rt. Hon. St. John Brodrick in 1897 and 1898, the Rt. Hon. The Earl of Onslow in 1907, and the Rt. Hon. Lord Alverstone in 1910 and 1911.

As a counter to this exclusivity and remembering that the Club was playing over common land, a separate club, the Guildford Town Golf Club, was formed in 1919 to allow less well connected local golfers to play the game. The Town golfers had restricted playing rights over the course and these arrangements continued until 1974 when the two clubs finally amalgamated.

Guildford lady golfers have been a strong and intrepid force over the years and it is perhaps no coincidence that Laura Davies, one of the country's best lady golfers of the present generation, learnt her early golf at Guildford and very soon graduated to playing off the men's tees. The ladies enjoyed a separate links until around 1900 when they were allowed to play on the main course, and there is an early photograph in the clubhouse showing a ladies' county match between Kent and Surrey being played at Guildford in heavy snow. The newspaper remarks that: "Last week's sporting events were sadly interfered with all over the country by the snowstorms...It will be noticed from the golfing pictures that the ladies survived conditions which drove men into the pavilion."

In September 1922, the Club organised a charity exhibition match between the Club's Professional, G Cawkwell, and three former Open Champions, James Braid, Harry Vardon and Ted Ray, in aid of the Surrey County Hospital. The three visiting Professionals were paid six guineas each for the day and the notice for the match stated that: "collections will be made on the links to which all onlookers will be expected to contribute, and the whole of the sum will go to the Hospital."

No doubt the views of these prestigious visiting golfers were useful, as in 1925, the Club engaged JH Taylor and Fred Hawtree to make various improvements to the course. These included the construction of an additional, replacement hole on the eastern side of the course on the far side of Trodd's Lane, the elimination of several blind shots, and the construction of some additional bunkers. Like many older and successful Clubs, Guildford has been well served by a small number of Professionals. Most notably, GM Turner and then T Turner served the Club as father and son for more than 60 years between 1923 and 1985.

Today's course is not long by modern standards measuring just over 6,000 yards off the white tees, but the undulating nature of the ground and the figure-

of-eight layout ensures an interesting round. The first hole is an enjoyable start with the tee and green on the same level, but the entire fairway is positioned through a valley. The tee shot needs to avoid a pot bunker to the left of the fairway whilst a hooked ball will reach the public footpath on the left which is out of bounds.

The first par-3 comes next where appearances are deceptive, as 90% of players leave themselves short even though the hole measures only 126 yards. The first par-5 is the third and is stroke index one on the ladies' card. Fairway bunkers capture tee shots hit too far left, whilst trees feature at strategic points to the right of the fairway. The first three holes lead to the highest point on the course and the par-4 fourth hole provides the first realistic birdie chance as long-hitters can reach the green off the tee.

Holes six to nine are situated on the slightly newer part of the course on the opposite side of Trodd's Lane, and the tenth hole is rated stroke index two for both men and ladies. The fairway and green slope from left to right and need to be factored into both tee and approach shots. Holes eleven and thirteen are both par-3s with the latter the more challenging and requiring a long iron to a closely-bunkered green with variable breaks on the putting surface.

The fifteenth can be tricky for higher handicap players and includes the old chalkpit. The green itself slopes from back to front and requires a good approach shot to hold on the surface. The seventeenth is an attractive par-4 dog-leg played from an elevated tee down into a valley flanked by trees. The second shot has to be played back up the hill and therefore plays longer than the yardage.

Guildford has a good variety of golf holes set out over undulating terrain. In the right conditions there are also excellent views over four counties.

Above: *Another co-founder, Major Pontifex was the Club's second Captain. He was also a co-founder of the famous club at Pau in Southern France*

Inset: *Fading 1890s' photo of the old clubhouse located in One Tree Hill Road at the top of the Common*

ROYAL EASTBOURNE

BELVEDERE IN PARADISE

Above: Horace Hutchinson demonstrating why Harold Hilton described him as "probably one of the most unorthodox players in the ranks of first class golfers." Despite his idiosyncratic swing, Hutchinson had one of the finest records in amateur golf

Inset: Early picture of the Paradise hole taken around 1897

The Club's early history is closely associated with the Cavendish family who owned Compton Place which still stands on the southern edge of today's course. William Cavendish, 2nd Earl of Burlington, inherited the Dukedom of Devonshire in 1858, and over the next 30 years he played a major part in developing Eastbourne as a high-class seaside town with a good mixture of permanent houses and holiday attractions.

Several members of the Royal Family have stayed at Compton Place, including King Edward VII in 1903 and George V in 1935 and 1936. In the 1870s, the town supported thriving tennis, cricket, croquet and riding clubs, although these were largely Summertime activities. In 1886, an anonymous letter appeared in the Eastbourne Gazette seeking support for the establishment of a golf club: "...as there is very little amusement in the Winter here, anything to enliven and make the place more attractive is desirable." The challenge was accepted by two R&A members; a retired solicitor, Arthur Mayhewe, and his brother-in-law, James Wright, who had also been Captain in 1882 of the influential but subsequently-disbanded Royal Isle of Wight Golf Club at Bembridge.

The Duke agreed to build the first clubhouse and lease an area of his land near to Compton Place which was already known locally as The Links due to the nature of the sloping downs and the fields with their adjoining banks. Mayhewe helped to agree terms with Matthias Mockett who had grazing rights over part of the land, and the first 9-hole course was laid out during the late Summer of 1887 with the assistance of the reigning Amateur Champion, Horace Hutchinson, who had recently moved to live with his father in Eastbourne.

The first Officers gave the Club immediate credibility and gravitas. The Duke accepted the Presidency, which has stayed with the family ever since, and his elder son, the Marquis of Hartington MP, was the first Captain. His younger son and two other members of the family, together with two further peers of the realm, were appointed Vice-Presidents. The town's second largest landowner, Carew Davies, succeeded the Marquis as Captain and the Club's Council included Lord Vernon from Royal Wimbledon who knew the Duke through the proximity of their respective seats at Sudbury Hall and Chatsworth in Derbyshire. Lord Vernon's American father-in-law, FC Lawrence was also on the Council and was Captain of the famous French club at Pau. In 1887, HRH Prince Albert Victor of Wales became Club patron and Queen Victoria agreed that the Club could use the Royal prefix.

The new use of the links was not universally popular and an article in the local paper reported that: "...golfing holes have been destroyed, Club property stolen, cops erected at great expense maliciously damaged and on

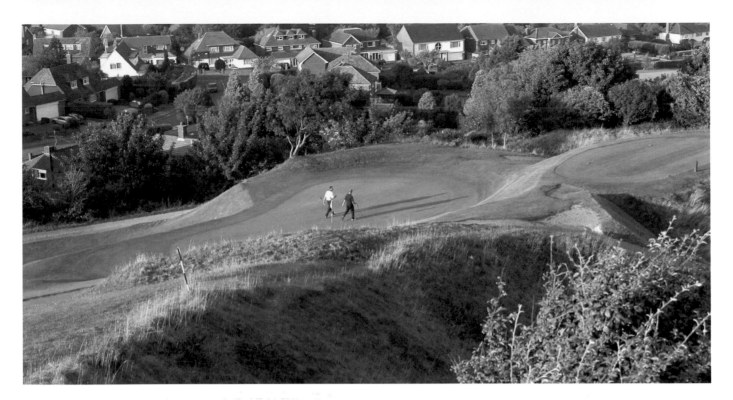

Sunday afternoon last, an iron roller, weighing a ton, was dragged 50 yards and run into the cattle pond. Three horses are necessary to draw it out." It went on to seek help from the public to track down the offenders. Mayhewe was an early proponent of winning hearts and minds, and in November 1888, the Eastbourne Gazette reported him as estimating that the Club was worth £6,000 per year to the economy of the town. Club membership grew rapidly and by 1894 stood at 350, 100 more than the maximum undertaking given by the Club to the Duke.

In 1890, the Duke moved the separate ladies' course to an area within the existing boundaries of the main course and this short layout is still used by the main Club today and is known as The Hartington. In the same year, Eastbourne College was granted a lease over a neighbouring part of the central area of the course for use as playing fields, and the school still uses this area for rugby and other sports. The main course was extended to eighteen holes in 1894 and subsequent changes have focussed on using more of the land to the north-west of

the chalkpit known as Motcombe Laine. The Duke also arranged for the construction of the present clubhouse to replace the original building which was demolished to enable the extension of Paradise Drive through to Compton Place Road.

Club members also helped the Duke with his charitable endeavours. Golf Illustrated in January 1910 reported that the Duke of Devonshire had sent a cheque for £18 19s to the Princess Alice Hospital being the proceeds of the sale of golf balls which in the previous year had been played out of bounds and into the grounds of Compton Place.

Membership declined dramatically during the Great War, and by 1931 the Club was running at a loss. An initial proposal to merge with the separate Royal Eastbourne Ladies' Club was rejected by a majority of the ladies who were happy with their separate existence on the shorter course. However, a number of their younger members wanted to play on the longer links and 43 joined the new ladies' section of the main Club in the first month. This loss of younger blood led to the rapid

Above: *View of the par-3 eighth green taken from the Downs above the third fairway. The area now covered by housing was the site of a large Army Convalescent Camp during the Great War*

Above: Modern view of the distinctive green on the Paradise hole with the Belvedere monument in the background. Until 1890, the green had sloped steeply and was almost unplayable in dry or frosty conditions

Below: Harry Vardon playing off Paradise Drive during a challenge match against JH Taylor in 1903. Vardon won the 36-hole match 6&4

decline of the Eastbourne Ladies' Club and, accepting the inevitable, it closed in 1937 with many more lady golfers joining the main Club.

Royal Eastbourne owes a debt of gratitude to F Eliot Williams OBE, who was Captain in 1938 and served in that role throughout the war years and again in 1951 and 1952. In one famous incident during the war, the Royal Artillery mounted an ack-ack gun near the eighteenth green and fired a shell through the gable immediately above the Secretary's office whilst aiming at low flying enemy aircraft! In an apologetic letter, the Commanding Officer confirmed that the aircraft had been shot down by another of his unit's guns. In 1941, the Home Guard established a permanent gun emplacement near the bunkers on the first fairway and later in the war the chalkpit was used as an Army rifle range.

Seven greens of the original 9-hole course built in 1887 are still used today, although the green next to the Belvedere had an important early alteration. Horace Hutchinson later described the reason for the change whilst writing for Country Life in 1920: "It is amazing to me now to think how ignorant we were in those days of the proper treatment of inland greens. We could plan the rest of the course well enough but

the great idea was to keep on rolling and rolling and rolling - the heavier the roller the better - until we had a surface round the hole so slick that if there was any gradient at all the ball would not stay near the hole even if you placed it there by hand...one device used to be to cut some jagged edges to stick out on the ball's surface, before driving off the tee for this hole. Thus jagged, the ball would not fly properly, but it was better to lose a shot owing to this jaggedness through the green, than to lose twenty on the putting green. On the rough edges of its scars the ball would come to rest even in Paradise."

The Eastbourne Gazette described the early perils of the Paradise hole in an article reporting the results of the monthly medal played in December 1887: "This hole was fully equal to the reputation for difficulty of access which its name implies, for, the hole being on sloping frozen ground, the ball that missed it trickled on indefinitely, till sundry (players) absolutely gave up all idea of ever getting it in at all." This seems to have been proved by a total of 11 no-returns in a field of 23!

Horace Hutchinson takes pride of place amongst Eastbourne's famous members. Following his early days at Westward Ho!, he went to Oxford University in 1878 and earned three Blues. In 1885 he lost in the final of the first unofficial Amateur Championship at Hoylake before beating Henry Lamb and John Ball in the official events in 1886 and 1887. By 1888, his Club handicap was plus-six but he still managed to win the Club's main gold medals on a number of occasions. Harold Hilton believed he would have achieved even more but for his regular bouts of illness, and Bernard Darwin attributed Hutchinson's success to: "his remarkable looseness of wrist, freedom of right hand and ability to adapt to difficult lies."

In 1920 at Muirfield, Cyril Tolley became the second Eastbourne member to win the Amateur Championship, defeating the American Robert Gardner in the final with a long putt at the 37th hole. Tolley played much of his early golf at neighbouring Eastbourne Downs Golf Club and later described how he had been playing so badly that year that he had concentrated on cricket and was only persuaded to enter the Championship at the last minute by fellow Oxford team member, Roger Wethered. Tolley won again at Sandwich in 1929, and in 1930 he came close to robbing Bobby Jones of his famous Grand Slam. Their fourth round match was all square after eighteen holes and Tolley lost on the next because Jones' ball had stymied Tolley's seven-foot putt. The stymie rule was eventually revoked in 1952.

Other notable golfers at Eastbourne have included three times Prime Minister Arthur Balfour, and several members of the Hambro banking dynasty. Sir Everard Hambro, Captain in 1893, was Chairman of the Bank for 48 years. He had a home in Biarritz and encouraged the young Professional, Arnaud Massy, to visit the UK in 1907 when he became the first non-British player to win the Open Championship.

Eastbourne's caddies were closely controlled by the long-time caddiemaster, FW Holly. The Club established a Caddies' Aid Association with a full-time instructor and a purpose-built workshop in which the boys were taught carpentry and boot repair. Eastbourne caddie contracts stipulated a basic weekly wage of six shillings but there were fines for a wide variety of offences including: "smoking in the workshop" (3d); "not going into the workshop when unemployed by the caddiemaster" (3d); "shouting or annoying a member or visitor" (1s) and "not wearing badge in conspicuous position or found without sponge" (1st offence 3d, 2nd offence 6d, thereafter a shilling).

Eastbourne's most famous golfing record occurred between the wars when Colonel FG Crompton, the Club Captain, halved the par-3 thirteenth hole in one shot whilst playing with the Assistant Professional, E Macey. Perhaps more unusually, in 1982 AB Paterson, a junior member, holed his tee shot at the eighth and then scored an albatross two on the par-5 sixteenth hole. One other golfing feat is unlikely to be repeated. In 1912, T Simpson wagered that he could drive a ball from the first tee and hole out at the Beachy Head coastguard station, some 3,500 yards away, in 50 strokes. In the end he needed only 30 shots, but the expansion of the town and modern health and safety requirements will probably prevent any attempt to repeat the wager.

The course has an unusual skew between the length of the two halves. The front nine is quite long with consecutive par-5s at the fourth and fifth holes and only one par-3 which does not arrive until the eighth hole. The back nine has four par-3s, including both the closing holes, and this distribution limits the ability of the Club to offer two tee starting points. The Club has, however, incorporated part of the Hartington course into a shorter circuit which has proved popular with the senior players who are known locally as the Ancient Royals. The third hole, played over the chalkpit, is viewed as one of the most difficult. Although the sixteenth fairway is wide, the out of bounds to the right still ensures that the new owners of Compton Place receive a regular haul of golf balls.

The chalky soil drains well all year, but the course is probably best played in Summer when there are beautiful views towards the Downs.

Above: Eastbourne hosted early challenge matches featuring leading Professionals. In the picture, taken during a match in 1907, JH Taylor is driving watched by James Braid (extreme right). Taylor won the match 4&3. The Downs are visible in the background and the early landscape was largely devoid of trees

BRIGHTON & HOVE

Above: The Dyke railway ceased operations in 1939. Before then it had played a significant role in the successful development of the Club

Inset: View from the tee down to the green far below on the famous sixth/fifteenth drop hole

Brighton and Hove Golf Club is located on a beautiful spur of chalkland known as Hangleton Down, a short distance north-west of Brighton. The course is now restricted to nine holes which is the same length as the original links laid out in 1887. However, for many years until the early 1960s, members enjoyed the benefits of a full-length course.

Apart from Blackheath, the area around Brighton is one of the earliest places where golf was played in England. The Prince of Wales, later to become King George IV, was associated with Brighton from 1783 and the Scots amongst his courtiers played the game locally whilst staying on the coast. Around the turn of the 18th Century, the Duke and Duchess of Fife played golf on rudimentary links on the cliffs at nearby Roedean, and later in the century the eventual founders of the Club first practised their game in the vicinity of the Kemp Town racecourse. Royal Blackheath possesses a famous poem dating back to at least 1826 which refers to Scots setting out from London: "...to establish at Brighton a wee Club of Golf." The poem goes on to extol the virtues of the Downs when compared with Blackheath and even dares to suggest that the links might be better than the venerable grounds at Leith in Scotland!

Devil's Dyke is situated just to the north of the Club and is reputed to be one of the deepest dry valleys in the world. An entrepreneur, William Thacker, bought the site of an old inn at the summit of Devil's Dyke in 1835, and by 1870 the Dyke had become a popular destination for day trippers from Brighton and neighbouring Hove. Thacker laid on horse-drawn

charabancs for the visitors to make the journey up the steep incline from the sea.

Two of the key founders were Hamilton Percival and Percy Willet. Both men lived and worked in busy Hove but used to walk the four miles up the hill to the undeveloped land on the Downs. Writing in 1897, Horace Hutchinson noted that a few golfers were playing at Hangleton as early as 1875/6 but that the game did not take off at the time because of the difficulty of access. However, in September 1887, the first train ran on the new Dyke Railway and the improved link from the coast led to a rapid increase in golfers prepared to journey up to the Downs. By the end of 1888, the Club had 129 members, growing to 375 by 1900.

The course was extended from nine to eighteen holes in 1891 and the Club held a professional invitation match for a £10 prize which was won by Peter Paxton. Other well-known golfers taking part included Douglas Rolland, Tom Dunn and Charles

Ramage. For 20 years, golfers actually had a second railway vying for their business. The Poynings steep grade railway was built up the northern slope of the Downs from Poynings village and there was even an aerial railway built across the nearby valley so that, for a while, the South Downs must have seemed more like a modern Swiss ski resort.

In 1895, the Club signed a sixteen-page agreement with the London, Brighton and South Coast Railway Company which included details of a bell to be fitted in the clubhouse and linked to the signal box at Dyke Station in order to warn golfers that the train was about to begin its descent to the Coast. The railway built a separate platform, Golf Club Halt, especially for golfers, situated about half a mile down the track from the terminus at Dyke Station.

The first President of the Club was Baron George de Worms JP, a wealthy retired businessman and also Chairman of the local Conservative Association. The Baron did not play golf but his two sons were capable, with Percy playing off a handicap of seven and Anthony off fourteen. Many influential early members shared at least one of three common connections through Harrow School, Trinity College, Cambridge and the

Carlton Club. Anthony Worms, Harry Farquhar de Paravicini and Lord Ernest Hamilton were all contemporaries at Harrow and the first two went on to Cambridge whilst Ernest Hamilton became the MP for North Tyrone and wrote widely on the Irish troubles. Harry de Paravicini was a good all-round sportsman. He was part of the pair which won the Public Schools' Racquets Championship in 1878, and he played cricket for Middlesex before becoming President of Sussex County Cricket Club.

Harry's younger brother, Percy, was even more talented, playing cricket for the MCC under the captaincy of WG Grace and football for England. He also won an FA Cup medal with Old Etonians who defeated Blackburn Rovers in the 1882 final in the era before the big professional clubs dominated the competition. The Paravicini brothers both married sisters of the Fourth Marquis of Chomondeley and Harry's wife, Lady Eva, was one of the founders of Brighton and Hove Ladies' Golf Club in 1891. The ladies played over a separate 9-hole links until the Second World War when their course was requisitioned by the MOD for a firing range. After the war, the ladies began to play over the men's course although the men

Main: The dew pond near the third/twelfth green looking back inland towards Devil's Dyke and the clubhouse

Above: Harry Farquhar de Paravicini, a founding member and President of the Club from 1928-1944 (Courtesy Brighton & Hove Golf Club)

Main: *Wind blown solitary pine at the fourth/thirteenth green*

Above: *Johnny (JEH) Gelston, Honorary Secretary, 1924-1969 (Courtesy Brighton & Hove Golf Club)*

were somewhat grudging in the early days of this new arrangement!

Baron de Worms died in 1912 and was succeeded as Club President by the Third Baron Sackville, Lionel Sackville-West, father of Vita, the well-known novelist, poet and gardener. This appointment was important as it helped secure playing rights over Hangleton Down which had been owned by the Sackville family for more than 300 years. The war years took their usual heavy toll on membership but there were a few lighter moments. In 1917, the members were advised that although the supply of alcohol was running short: "...an admirable substitute might be found in Oxo or bouillon" to which another member had added the helpful but slightly irrelevant comment that: "... dandelion tea is very stimulating"! Shortly after the war, in July 1919, the Prince of Wales played a round at the Club with his brother, the Duke of York, later King George VI.

The Club's future was greatly aided in 1926 by Colonel Sir Sidney Wishart VD, TD, DL, JP who had been Club Captain in 1925. Wishart purchased the course and some surrounding land from the Sackville Estate for £6,440 and then sold it on at cost to the Club in 1928 once it had succeeded in making the necessary financial arrangements. During the Second World War, the MOD requisitioned the land of the neighbouring Dyke Golf Club and the top half of the Club's course became unsafe for play although some stoic members formed the Brighton and Hove Emergency Golf Club

and continued to play over the remaining part of the course situated by the expanding housing estate to the north of Hove. The war left the Club saddled with debt and struggling for survival and it was forced into a series of land sales. By 1958, the Club could no longer afford to maintain all eighteen holes and it resolved to retrench back to a short course of nine holes playing on similar ground to the very first layout back in 1888. The report detailing the reduction was drawn up by Club members Peter Bray and Henry Longhurst, the famous golf commentator and author. This must have saddened Longhurst who was a great lover of the game. In an earlier year, shortly after the Club had finally arranged to install running water, he was reported to have responded: "I am resigning .We cannot have this Club desecrated by modernization!" Many older members speak fondly of Johnny Gelston, Honorary Secretary for more than 40 years between 1924 and 1969, who helped the Club survive the crisis times in the 1950s. He was a scratch golfer and liked to spend as much time as possible on the course, viewing paperwork as a necessary evil.

In restricting today's course to nine holes, the Club is helping to support a mini wildlife haven. Adders, slow worms and common lizards are all found in the rough and the grounds also support the rare adonis blue butterfly as well as the purse web spider, the only British relative of the tarantula family. Stoats and weasels are also residents, skylarks sing overhead, and the declining yellowhammer can still be seen.

Although today's course covers only nine holes, the Club has tried hard to vary tee positions so that different angles and club selection are encountered on the two circuits. The first/tenth and fifth are both testing long holes when played as par-4s and the par-3 eighth hole measures over 200 yards when played from the tee on the first circuit. The most famous challenge is the short sixth/fifteenth drop hole. The green is surrounded by bunkers and although purists will say that the hole is a bit of a lottery, it is certainly fun to launch the ball over the edge of the hill and then wait for the outcome. The course will be enjoyed by golfers who like to play in beautiful, often windy surroundings with far-reaching views.

MARLBOROUGH

TEACHERS AND JOCKEYS

Masters from the famous Marlborough College had a significant influence over the early development of the Club bearing out the historic and innovative sporting ethos of the school.

The initial prosperity of Marlborough was created by the wool trade, and in the 1600s the town was used as a staging point for tired horses and travellers on the main coach route between London and Bath. The western end of Marlborough High Street features a man-made mound which is fabled to be the burial place of Merlin, King Arthur's magician. The opening of the Great Western Railway linking London and Bristol allowed wealthy Victorians to send their children to boarding school and the College at Marlborough was opened in 1843, primarily for sons of the clergy.

Early conditions at the school were appalling, and in 1851 the boys staged their 'Great Rebellion' which was only resolved after two months and following the appointment of the Rev. Dr. Cotton, who had been at Rugby School with Dr. Arnold. Marlborough was the first school to introduce organised games with cricket and rugby from 1853 and hockey from 1874, and its annual rugby fixture against Clifton College is thought to be the oldest in the world. The College was also a founding member of the Football Association.

The sporting masters turned their mind to golf in 1888, and WH Macdonald, a house master at the College, persuaded the Town Council to allow golf to be played over the common just to the north of the main High Street. For centuries the 112 acres of the common had been used as the town's main pasture land and successive councils had been careful to restrict building development.

The Club and common have a very close connection with horse racing. The first official Jockey Club meeting was held on the common in August 1840, and race meetings were held annually until 1862. In 1888 and 1889, races were run over what is now the fifteenth fairway. Sir Gordon Richards, the great flat race jockey, was President of the Club for seventeen years from 1950. He did not have an official handicap, but this did not stop him from playing for small stakes with Keith Piggott, Lester's father. Richards won 4,870 races but had never won the Derby until, in one of the most popular moments in British sport, he rode Pinza to victory in his 28th and final attempt, in the same week that Queen Elizabeth was crowned and he was knighted.

The initial 9-hole course laid out in 1888 was typically basic. Six holes were cut on the common and three holes were set on Rough Down which is to the right of today's eleventh and fourteenth fairways. In 1912, an

Main: *The modern clubhouse which contrasts with the old railway carriages (next page)*

Above: *Club Professional in 1922, Charles Whitcombe played in six Ryder Cup matches, three times as Captain*

out by one shot to Walter Hagen at Hoylake in 1924. The Club's newfound credibility was confirmed in 1928 when the Prince of Wales, the future Duke of Windsor, played at the Club whilst visiting the area to inspect the Royal Wiltshire Yeomanry.

The course was used as an American Military Hospital during the Second World War and lack of finance to make the necessary repairs caused the Club to hand over its assets to the Borough Council which finally reopened the links in 1950 as a municipal course. The clubhouse consisted of two railway carriages used by the US forces billeted in the nearby Savernake Forest and purchased at a cost of £10 with a further £50 transport costs! The course in the 1960s was very rough and the Council was probably relieved to hand management of the course back to the members in 1964 when, for the second time, the Club took the brave judgement that investment was the best policy. A decision was taken to expand the course to eighteen holes by taking on a new lease to the farmland immediately to the north of the existing nine holes. The work was largely performed by Club members and it is no wonder that the project took nearly three years to complete. The extension was finally opened in August 1974 by Reg Swinton who was made a life member in recognition of his efforts in helping to transform the Club.

The course puts a premium on accuracy off the tee but it does not have any particularly long par-4s, thus meaning that in theory, most medium handicappers should be able to reach each green in regulation. The tee at the twelfth hole is built on a bronze-age tumulus, and the latter part of the course contains two of the trickiest holes. Trouble is found all round the par-3 fourteenth green and the tee shot at the fifteenth has to be hit to the left as the Rockley Road constitutes out of bounds all the way down the right-hand side. The round is finished off nicely by the par-5 eighteenth which is a right-hand dog-leg with well positioned bunkers around the green.

With a bit of luck and sensible course management, it should be possible to score quite well around the course. Perhaps reflecting its survival through adversity, the Club also prides itself in offering a friendly welcome to visitors.

extra hole was cut on the common replacing one of those on Rough Down. The Club had a slow beginning and by 1891 there were only 20 members, possibly only ten of whom actually played. By 1907, numbers had crept up to about 50 including a few ladies, and by 1913 about 40% of the membership was female. According to the Club's archives, the first Captain was not appointed until 1911 and this honour fell to AR Gidney, who was an Oxford Blue and a teacher at the College.

The course was used as a training ground during the First World War, but shortly afterwards, and somewhat bravely, the Club decided to invest in improvements to the layout. Course architects Tom Simpson and Herbert Fowler were consulted and the revised course, with all nine holes located on the common, was opened in March 1921. Eight of these holes are, with some modifications, still in use today.

The Club's prestige was enhanced by the appointment of Charles Whitcombe as Professional. Although he stayed only a short while, he had time to set a new course record of 67 for two circuits of the revised design. Charles and his two brothers, Reg and Ernest, were the sons of a Burnham Greenkeeper. Reg was the only brother to win an Open Championship, but Charles had good opportunities in 1922 and 1935 and Ernest lost

ROYAL WINCHESTER

JH TAYLOR'S EARLY DAYS

Golf at Winchester was well supported by senior and influential local people from the outset. The Hampshire Chronicle reported that a General Meeting to receive the Committee's rules and regulations was held in the Sessions Hall in October 1888. His Worship the Mayor, F Kirby, was in the chair and those present included the local MP, Mr. Richard Moss as President and the Earl of Northesk, who had his own course at Longwood, as first Captain. Many clergymen, Winchester College masters and Army officers from the local garrison were also in attendance and it was reported that 89 members had already joined the new Club.

The first course was laid out over Morn Hill, otherwise known as Magdalen Hill, situated on the Downs to the east of the city and between the main roads to Alresford and Petersfield. The site was very exposed and the only nearby building was the newly constructed Royal Victoria Isolation Hospital for Infectious Diseases. The Channel 4 Time Team excavated the site in 2001 and established that the area had previously housed the St. Mary Magdalene Leper Hospital as far back as 1130 when Winchester was one of the most important cities in Norman England. The Club rented the land from three lessors including James Stratton from nearby Chilcomb Village, and early golfers were entertained by the sight of the headmaster of Winchester College who used to arrive at the course on a Penny Farthing bicycle.

The site was not ideal as it was a significant distance from the railway station, players had to cross the main roads on two occasions, there was no furze or gorse much beloved of late 19th Century golfers, and no bunkers, although the course did have a deep ravine which added interest. In 1891, a ladies' course was laid

out in the same area and the women formed a separate organisation and ran their affairs independently of the main Club.

The Club's influence and wealth enabled it to attract top Professionals. The first appointment was Andrew Kirkaldy of St Andrews who had been runner-up in the 1879 Open before joining the Black Watch as a soldier at the age of 19 and serving in Egypt. He stayed for only six weeks before returning to Scotland as a playing Professional.

Fortunately, the Club then recruited an even better player. Before the advent of the professional circuits, ambitious golfers had to play challenge matches to get noticed. Often these games featured side bets

Main: *The modern clubhouse viewed from the practice area. The previous building burnt down in the 1990s*

Above: View from the clubhouse up the hill to the green on the short par-4 first hole which gives long hitters the chance of starting the round with a birdie. The green of the par-4 eighteenth hole is to the right of the picture and the clubhouse has a balcony giving excellent views of tight finishes on competition days

Inset: Picturesque downhill drive at the par-4 thirteenth tee which is located in an exclusive area near the city. The old clubhouse was situated in this area of the course before being relocated to its present site in 1966, as a result of which the holes on the course were renumbered.

and aspiring Professionals would finance the stakes themselves or find a willing sponsor. Whilst Kirkaldy was at Winchester, he was persuaded to play a 36-hole challenge match on a home-and-away basis against an unknown golfer, JH Taylor, from Burnham in North Devon. The match was facilitated by Mr. Adam Kennard who was a member at the Club and was later to become President, and his brother, Monseignor CH Kennard, President of the Club at Burnham.

Taylor impressed the Winchester members whilst defeating Kirkaldy 4&3, and when the Scot returned to St Andrews in 1892, the Club was happy to appoint Taylor in his place. JH won his first two British Opens in 1894 and 1895 whilst serving at Winchester, and his teaching was also an inspiration to members. In particular he gave regular lessons to Amy Pascoe who won the Ladies' Open at Hoylake in 1896. Miss Pascoe lived in Woking which is 50 miles from Winchester, but the two towns were well connected by railway. Other successful early members included Allan MacFie who had won the first Amateur Championship in 1885, and Rhona Adair (Mrs. Cutbill), the Ladies' British Open Championship in 1900 and 1903. Freddie Tait won the district's first County Championship which was played at Winchester in 1894.

In addition to his Club duties, Taylor ran a sports shop in the city centre with another golfing enthusiast named Cann which led to some confusion amongst the town's ecclesiastical golfing community. On one occasion a letter was sent to the Cathedral addressed to Canon Taylor and ordering clubs whilst at the same time expressing surprise that the Reverend Gentleman had time to make golf clubs and carry out his clerical duties! Cann replaced Taylor as the Winchester Professional when JH left in 1896 and served for three years before moving to Pittsburgh, USA, in 1899.

In 1893, Prince Arthur, the Duke of Connaught, who was the seventh of Queen Victoria's nine children,

became Patron of the Club, and from that time the Club used the Royal title. King George V reconfirmed the entitlement in January 1913.

In 1899, a letter appeared in the Hampshire Chronicle from Commander Grant-Dalton, RN, suggesting that a course should be built on Teg Down to the west of the city for the benefit of North and West Winchester residents. The Commander clearly started the ball rolling and in 1901 the golfers decamped across Winchester to a new layout designed by JH Taylor at Teg Down, taking a fourteen-year lease over 197 acres of undulating grazing land from the Ecclesiastical Commission. The word Teg is a local Hampshire word for sheep, describing the historic use of the land.

Royal Winchester enjoyed its greatest patronage in the early years at the new course. In addition to HRH Prince Arthur, the list of members included at least seven Lords, six admirals and eight generals. Unfortunately, the First World War had a devastating effect on golf at Winchester. The course was requisitioned for military training and the mounds near today's third and seventh holes are the remains of old rifle butts which add character to the course.

The Club purchased the freehold of Teg Down for £2,000 in 1929, but finances were parlous throughout the 1930s and in 1944 the lack of income during the war required the ladies to come to the rescue. They agreed to disband their separate organisation and merge with the men, at the same time contributing their reserves of £118 which were sufficient to stave off the immediate crisis. By 1955, matters had again become critical and an EGM was held on Christmas Eve to decide whether to liquidate the Club. The meeting was clearly heated as there were mass resignations from the Committee including the Captain, Secretary and Treasurer, as well as the Professional.

Whether by luck or judgement, this radical event led to a gradual change in fortunes and in 1962 the Club sold off its old clubhouse in Chilbolton Avenue, known locally as Millionaires' Row, and constructed a new clubhouse by the old sixth tee which was opened in 1966. The course was renumbered at that stage so that the first tee led away from the new building. Disaster struck the Club in the early 1990s when a major fire

almost completely destroyed the clubhouse. Most of the historic trophies were lost but a new and attractive building was completed in 1994 and the Club's trophy cabinet has been restored with accurate replicas of the original cups and medals. At least ten holes can be seen from the balcony.

Amongst Winchester's modern day golfers, Les Day's contribution stands out as remarkable. He won the Club's main scratch competition, the Challenge Shield, no less than fifteen times, and he has continued to play an active role in the Club's affairs through into the 21st Century.

The course is not long, measuring just over 6,200 yards off the back tees and unusually the layout has two back to back par-5s in the middle of the round. The tee shot at the ninth hole requires an accurate drive but the hole itself slopes downhill and it should be possible to get close to the green in two shots. The tenth hole is probably the best known hole on the course. Out of bounds lurks on the left of the fairway with woodland to the right. The green is elevated on the side of the valley and many golfers misread the approach shot and see their ball tumble into trouble on the left of the green.

The eleventh to seventeenth holes are played over a separate valley, out of sight of the clubhouse, and provide interesting and different views over an exclusive area of housing reminiscent of some of the West Surrey courses. The par-4 eighteenth hole is played from an elevated tee and the green is situated in front of the clubhouse from which excellent views can be enjoyed whilst sampling post-round refreshment.

Above: Photograph published in 1893 of members putting on the final green of the old course near Chilcomb to the east of Winchester. The building just visible above the caddies to the left of the picture is the Royal Victoria Isolation Hospital for Infectious Diseases.

Below: JH Taylor (second from right) together with Winchester members during his time as Club Professional.

SALISBURY & SOUTH WILTS

NEW COURSE 1895

Above: *The Daily Graphic included this view over Lord Pembroke's estate and towards Salisbury. The cathedral can still be seen from several holes today (Courtesy Salisbury & South Wilts Golf Club)*

Inset: *View across the original nine holes to the racecourse showing some of the old fairway hazards*

Salisbury and South Wilts Golf Club is situated on the hills just outside Salisbury and the magnificent old cathedral is visible from the course. The original club was founded as Homington Down Golf Club and the first course was located above Homington Village some three miles south of today's layout. The wife of Bishop Wordsworth of Salisbury is credited with the idea for the Club following the couple's return from a holiday at St Andrews. Several clergymen, including the Rev. P Miles, Vicar of nearby Odstock, the Rev. Douglas Kinnear MacDonald, who was the Club's Honorary Secretary and Treasurer between 1888 and 1901, and the Reverends EE Dorling and FW MacDonald were all early enthusiasts. Golf was very popular amongst the clergy during the 1880s and the Bishop of London gave his blessing to the healthy activity.

The course at Homington was laid out over land near Dogdean Farm and golf was played with the permission of the farm's tenant. Golfers used Homington Cricket Club's pavilion as a clubhouse. Unfortunately, the farm was sold to a Mr. Tyrrwhit-Drake in 1894 and the new owner proved less obliging, fearing for the safety of his flock of sheep. Helpfully, Lord Pembroke and the Wilton Estate made alternative land available next to the racecourse on the Downs further north towards Salisbury. The reigning Open Champion, JH Taylor, was contracted to design a new course which was opened in 1895 as the South Wilts Golf Club. Lord Pembroke became the first President of the Club and continued in that role into the 1930s.

The Daily Graphic in October 1895 featured the new links at Salisbury, describing the layout including the use

of the racecourse grandstand as the first clubhouse. Early relationships between golfers and the racing community were strained. Salisbury is the home of the Bibury Club, the oldest racing club in the country. The sport was so well established locally that Queen Elizabeth I is said to have watched racing on the course three months before the defeat of the Spanish Armada in 1588. In order to give the golfers some early credibility, Lord Pembroke introduced Lord Radnor, Lord James of Hereford and Sir Edward Tennant, Bart. MP, as Vice-Presidents of the Club.

The Ladies' Section was formed in 1900 and it is interesting to note that Mrs. Tyrrwhit-Drake was amongst the founding members although her husband had caused the Club to move from the original land at Dogdean Farm. Overall, the Club grew steadily in the early 1900s and by 1911 had grown to 110 members plus various Army officers from Southern Command. Until the First War, the Club played over a 9-hole course, although the circuit at the racecourse did have two separate tee off points at each hole allowing slight variety over a full round. After the War, the Pembroke Estate encouraged the Club to expand the course to eighteen holes and

persuaded a tenant, HA Woodford, to release 44 acres of agricultural land to enable the course expansion which was designed and supervised by Mr. Limouzin. These new holes lead down the hill from the racecourse to today's clubhouse.

The Club had severe financial problems during the late 1920s and the position was exacerbated by competition from the nearby High Post Golf Club which had also expanded from nine holes to eighteen, encouraging a number of members to switch allegiance. In 1933, South Wilts countered by forming an Artisans' Section which, with hindsight, probably saved the Club. Although Artisan members paid a lower subscription, many of them provided invaluable assistance to the Club, especially during the war years when they helped maintain the course using a Landrover supplied by American forces based at nearby Dinton. South Wilts is particularly indebted to TR Bennett, a tall, eighteen-stone former Lloyds Bank manager known as Big Ben, who became Secretary around 1948. In addition to bringing the necessary financial acumen to the job, he also spent many hours working on the course including mowing the fairways on the Club's tractor to save costs.

Today's members have 27 holes from which to choose. For a long time it had been apparent that the original nine holes running through the racecourse were less than ideal. Golfers were unable to play them at all on race days, and further restrictions applied on the days immediately before and after race meetings. The Club was also prevented from making some of the necessary alterations to the old holes which had become easier with improvements in ball and club technology. In 1972, work commenced on a third 9-hole layout immediately to the west of the existing course, and this was brought into play around 1974. Initially, the new nine was planned as a short relief circuit, measuring only 2,424 yards, but over the years the layout has changed and holes in this new area have now been lengthened and incorporated into the main course. The original racecourse holes are now treated as a separate practice course known as the 'Bibury' in honour of the Bibury Racing Club. The Club still incorporates the old holes into a few of its traditional competitions and South Wilts therefore has three different scorecards covering the Bibury Course (twice round the old racecourse holes), the Main Course (largely consisting of the holes created

Above: The player with the white hat teeing off at the par-4 downhill fifteenth hole has sliced his ball towards the out of bounds. This is marked by the trees lining an old Roman Road which linked Old Sarum and Dorchester

Main: The view of Salisbury Cathedral adds character to the course

Above: A drawing from the Daily Graphic showing extreme waviness on the original first green which the paper described as adding 'sporting character'! (Courtesy Salisbury & South Wilts Golf Club)

after the First War and in the 1970s) and the Old Course which was effectively the course before the 1970 additions.

The Club has had a number of interesting visitors. During the Second War, the course was played by a number of servicemen and visiting dignitaries including world heavyweight boxing champion Joe Louis, General Wavell, the Duke of Westminster, General Frieburg and Lord Chief Justice Goddard. In 1947, an exhibition match was held in aid of the Forces' Help Society and the Lord Roberts Memorial Workshops featuring the Club's Professional, Billy Elms, Peter Alliss, former Open winner Alf Padgham, and future champion Bobby Locke. Peter Alliss returned in 1966 when he played in another match featuring the Club's Professional, Arthur Illingworth, together with Tony Harman from neighbouring High Post and Dave Thomas who had been runner-up in the 1958 Open at Royal Lytham. Alliss and Thomas both beat the standard scratch of 68 by one shot.

Unusually, South Wilts is affiliated to the Stanley Golf Club in the Falkland Islands. Club member Airman Peter Scott hit the first ball at the Stanley Club

following the Argentine invasion in 1982, and the Island's Commissioner, Sir Rex Hunt, who was President of the Stanley Golf Club, presented Peter Scott with a seven iron, two dozen golf balls and, most usefully, an umbrella which had been forwarded by well-wishers from home. The Stanley course was originally built in 1937 by members of the British ex-Patriots Rugby Club who visited the Islands from the South American mainland in the build-up to the Second World War as a show of support for the Islanders.

Visitors wishing to experience the oldest part of the course at South Wilts will need to include the Bibury Course in their round, otherwise it is easiest to play the Main which starts with four difficult and largely uphill par-4s. Length is the main problem on the first two holes whilst the third is a dog-leg with a well-guarded green. The fourth hole is rated stroke index one. Golfers who like a solid start need to be patient over these early holes as shorter and downhill opportunities arise later in the round. The newer holes to the west still feel rather open and exposed as they march down the hill and back again, but the new thirteenth, constructed in the woods back near the top of the hill, is an attractive and testing addition to the course.

The last four holes on the Main Course play back downhill to the clubhouse, and golfers need to avoid the out of bounds of the old Roman Road which runs the entire length of these holes on the right-hand side. The eighteenth is an intriguing finishing hole being played over an old pit to a well-bunkered green in front of the clubhouse.

The Club has an unusual approach to most internal competitions which can be played at any time over four days, including the weekend. The idea is to encourage both midweek and weekend golfers to get involved but it is undoubtedly quite a complex arrangement for the Secretary and it also allows assiduous amateur weather forecasters to improve their medal chances!

The best views of Salisbury Cathedral are seen from the Bibury holes although the spire can also be glimpsed between the trees from a number of holes on the Main Course which measures almost 6,500 yards off the back tees and makes an enjoyable round in a friendly and generally uncrowded environment.

MINCHINHAMPTON

OLD COURSE

Golf on the Old course at Minchinhampton is a throwback to the game as it was played on English commonland more than a century earlier. The land is part of the Cotswold Area of Outstanding Natural Beauty and is situated on top of a hill with villages built from mellow Cotswold stone occupying neighbouring hills and valleys. In springtime, the land is covered in wild flowers including cowslips, wild thyme and rare orchids, and skylarks sing incessantly. Natural bumps and hollows provide the main golfing hazards. Some tee shots are blind and several greens are located at the foot of slopes whilst on other holes the base of the flag is hidden. Roads dissect the course, picnickers and walkers have right-of-way, and from the middle of May, cattle and horses graze on the course; the two animals are incorporated into the Club's emblem. Despite all these distractions, golf at Minchinhampton retains an historic charm.

The common is dotted with Scheduled Ancient Monuments some of which date back to the Neolithic period (3000-2500BC), and since the 14th Century the area has been quarried for limestone. Most of the grass has never been ploughed or treated with chemical fertilisers or pesticides and the common has been used for grazing for centuries. Numerous artificial rabbit warrens or 'pillow mounds' are visible around the Old Lodge Inn which was once the home of the warrener, and the combination of natural hazards means that artificial bunkers have never been required. The land has been owned since 1913 by the National Trust which manages to reconcile the needs of golfers with the interests of other users of the common.

Minchinhampton members have the best of both worlds. In the 1970s, it became impractical to play golf on Sundays during Summer due to the large number of picnickers, and Fred Hawtree designed a second course over disused farmland at nearby Avening. In the 1990s, Martin Hawtree designed a third layout known as the Cherington which has already hosted Regional Qualifying for the Open.

Most of the founders in 1889 were involved in the wool trade, and the first meeting was held at the home of the Playne family who had been Lords of the Manor of Avening since its separation from Minchinhampton in 1812. Arthur Twisden Playne owned the Old Lodge Inn and he arranged a room for the use of members.

Above: The Old Lodge Inn enjoys a prominent position on the common. It served as the main clubhouse for the Minchinhampton Golf Club before the golfers moved their headquarters to the new layout at Avening in the 1970s. The Old course winds in a clockwise direction around the Inn and today's clubhouse

Main: Players on the eighteenth green. The course is covered with daisies and dandelions in Spring prompting the golfer in red to use an orange ball. A modern wind turbine is visible behind the same player on the distant hills

Above: Lucien Davis drew this well-known picture of ladies playing on the common in 1890 for the Illustrated London News. The scene was re-enacted in 1989 during the Club's centenary celebrations and a photograph of the occasion hangs in the dining room of the Old course clubhouse (Courtesy Minchinhampton Golf Club)

Playne became the first Honorary Secretary and in 1893 the Club took over the tenancy of the entire Inn and a golf clubhouse was constructed in the Inn's garden. The Club purchased the freehold of the Old Lodge in 1920 from Arthur's son, William, who had served as the first Captain in 1890. A fire in 1946 destroyed the clubhouse and most of the Club's old records and memorabilia, but the adjoining Inn was saved and the Old Lodge was eventually sold in 1972 to help fund the new course at Avening.

The Club enjoyed early prestige and was well supported by lady golfers. In 1890, The Illustrated London News described the new game to its readers. In an article accompanying a drawing by its principal artist, Lucien Davis, the magazine reported: "The fair player in our artist's drawing is about to make the first 'drive' towards the next hole....Immediately in front of her lies a quarry full of stones and impediments of every sort. This may be cleared by a fairly good 'drive', but, alas! beyond it lies a pond; and, if this be avoided, then still farther on, where the ground dips, lurks the worst danger of all, in the shape of a road full of dreadful ruts; and only a golfer knows the despair in a closely contested game of seeing his ball lodge among a series of six-inch ruts."

In 1893, the Club played against a team from Stowell Park brought by the Earl of Eldon and led by his daughter, the reigning Ladies' Open Champion, Lady Margaret Scott, who played against the men off a scratch handicap. Minchinhampton won the match by 30 holes to 20, and immediately afterwards Lady Margaret played another eighteen holes against Issette Pearson who had been runner-up to Lady Margaret in the first two Ladies' Open Championships. The result in Gloucestershire was the same with Lady Margaret emerging the winner by 8 holes to 5 with five holes halved.

A Scot, George Brews, served as the Club's Professional between 1903 and 1923 having occupied the same role for nine years at Royal Blackheath. Two of his sons, Jock and Sid, worked for George as apprentices before leaving for South Africa where they enjoyed highly successful golfing careers. Jock was South African Open Championship four times in the 1920s, whilst brother Sid won the same championship on eight occasions. In 1934, he was runner-up to Henry Cotton in The Open at Sandwich. Whilst reigning South African champion, Jock was the first winner of the Club's own 'Commons Championship' which is open to all golfers, both amateur and professional, who were born or live close to Minchinhampton Common.

Golfers who prefer a modern challenge should play the Club's two new courses, but lovers of the game's history will enjoy the natural challenges set by the 'Course on the Common'.

LONG ASHTON

FINE VIEWS ON THE RIDGE

Long Ashton is situated on open hilly downland three miles south-west of Bristol and occupies a former part of the Ashton Court Estate. The first nine holes were laid out in 1893 for Winter play only by George Kingston, a Greenkeeper from the now defunct club at Portishead. The original clubhouse was constructed close to the current fourth green which is backed by a folly built to celebrate the Battle of Waterloo. The founders would recognise this section of the course along the ridge, although the Club has experienced subsequent extensions and major redesigns by a number of famous golf course architects including Dr. Alister MacKenzie and JH Taylor.

Long Ashton has shared a friendly rivalry with the Bristol & Clifton Golf Club for more than a century as the courses lie within a mile of each other. The latter was founded in 1891 by 38 golfers who elected the Duke of Beaufort as their first President. By contrast, Long Ashton was founded by just seven intrepid enthusiasts including the local headmaster and doctor, and the original membership was restricted to residents of the delightfully-named small parishes of Long Ashton, Barrow Gurney, Flax Bourton and Wraxall. Not surprisingly, these residential restrictions were soon lifted, and by 1898 about half of the 70 members came from Clifton and other parts of Bristol.

Sir Greville Smyth, the owner of Ashton Court, was the Club's first President, and annual subscriptions were fixed at ten shillings (50p) per annum for the head of each family. All other family golfers were charged five shillings each. The tenant farmer of Ashton Hill did not charge the Club for Winter golf, but in 1901, nine members opted to continue playing during the Summer and contributed a total of five guineas to cover the additional costs involved. The fairways were kept in shape by the tenant farmer's grazing livestock.

The course was extended to eighteen holes in 1905. In 1921, MacKenzie advised on various improvements, and in 1937 the current clubhouse was constructed at its new location whilst JH Taylor made recommendations on changes and rearrangements to the course. Long Ashton was quiet in the 1930s and rounds per week averaged around 100 compared with more than 1000 today. However, changes were afoot and a number of famous golfers visited the Club during the Depression years including Gene Sarazen, Abe Mitchell and Percy Alliss.

Above: Golfers playing to the fourth green which is backed by a folly planted with Scots pines by the Ashton Court Estate around 1818. It is thought that the landmark celebrated the outcome of the Battle of Waterloo

Inset: Photograph taken around 1908 of the clubhouse which superseded the original galvanised iron hut. The building was situated to the south of the present fourth green and is now a private residence

Main: *The tee shot at the short second hole is played across a minor road down onto a green within an old quarry*

Above: *Kitrina Douglas won the British Ladies' Open Amateur Championship in 1982. She went on to win her first professional tournament, the Ford Ladies' Classic at Woburn, in 1984, and subsequently obtained a PhD in psychology at the University of Bristol (Courtesy Long Ashton Golf Club)*

Bobby Locke raised the Club's profile further during an exhibition match in August 1950. Followed by more than 2,000 spectators, he remarked that the greens were the best that he had played on and that he: "wanted to roll them up and take them back to South Africa." The quality of the course attracted the televised Martini Tournament to Long Ashton in May 1966. The four-day event included a number of leading international players from the Professional tour and resulted in a tie on 275 between Peter Alliss and Bill Large who decided not to play off. David Snell shot the best round with a 65.

Quality Professionals returned to Bristol in 1969, 1972 and again in 1974 to play in the Coca Cola Young Professionals' Tournaments which the Club shared with Bristol & Clifton. Winners included Peter Oosterhuis and Dale Hayes, and Tony Jacklin was amongst the other players. More recently, the Club's own golfers have prospered. Andrew Sherborne and David Ray both progressed from the Club's junior section to play on the professional European Tour and in 1982, Long Ashton enjoyed a rare distinction when these two played in the same English International team at Royal Porthcawl. Long Ashton's ladies have enjoyed similar success. Ruth Porter was three-times English champion and played in three Curtis Cup teams, whilst Kitrina Douglas won the British Ladies' Open Amateur Championship in 1982 and became the BMW European Open Champion in 1992.

The course still bears testimony to a compromise struck between the Club and one of its senior members. The final fairway is crossed by a bank made by soldiers during the First World War, and in 1957 the Club President Joe Bennett agreed to buy a new carpet for the clubhouse lounge provided that the Green Committee agreed to dismantle part of the wall to reduce the hazard. Bennett's Gap remains although the carpet has long since been replaced! The front nine is the tougher, more undulating and more scenic part of the course, and includes the memorable tee shot into the quarry at the second. Golfers have a chance to repair their cards on the flatter back nine.

GORING & STREATLEY

THE SHOOLBRED MYSTERY

Goring and Streatley did not start with pretensions of grandeur. There is no record of early professional matches between the champions of the day and most of the founding members were wealthy locals living in the small, neighbouring and prosperous Thames Valley villages of Goring and Streatley which had a combined population of only 1500.

The Club was sensitive to friendly competition between the two villages and recorded its first headquarters in two separate public houses, Ye Olde Miller of Mansfield in Goring and The Swan in Streatley. The first clubroom on the course, some three-quarters of a mile from the nearer village, was a modest room in an old cottage situated close to the current second tee.

Contemporary journals refer to rudimentary golf being played locally from 1871, but the Club has settled on March 1895 for its official formation. According to the Golfers' Guide of 1897, the first nine holes were laid out by Tom Dunn over chalky downland owned by Ernest Gardner who became the Member of Parliament for Wokingham and Windsor between 1901 and 1922. Early golfers, who included a number of Army subalterns, enjoyed free use of the land on a grace and favour basis. Dunn's input is thought to have been commissioned and funded by Fredrick Shoolbred, a wealthy immigrant and London draper who had recently moved into a large house in Goring. Shoolbred and Gardner were both Master Drapers and members of the Guild. Mystery surrounds Shoolbred's later relationship with the Club. Local history records that he was refused membership, possibly because he was 'in trade' and it

is not surprising that Shoolbred reacted to the rebuff by building an 18-hole course on his own land further down Rectory Road at Warren Farm which he had purchased in 1895. He allowed everyone who was not a member of the Goring and Streatley Club to play free of charge and was happy to supply clubs and balls when required.

A more generous version of the affair was supplied by the daughter of Shoolbred's gardener who believed that he suffered from arthritis and found the steep slopes difficult to negotiate. The Club allegedly refused him permission to use his donkey cart whilst playing and so he decided to build his own links where he could set the rules! Warren Links did not survive Shoolbred's death in 1922.

Above: The par-4 eighteenth hole sweeps downhill towards the modern clubhouse. The green is situated between the two bunkers and a sliced approach onto the steep bank to the right of the green can leave a tricky third shot

Confusingly, the Reading Mercury & Oxford Gazette in October 1928 refers to the original nine holes being laid out: "with a little advice from Willie Park who had come from Musselburgh, via America, to found the Huntercombe Golf Club", but the latter was not founded until 1901.

Perhaps Park assisted Shoolbred with his own links or maybe both he and Dunn were involved with the main Club. Harry Colt advised on minor changes to the Club's course in the early 1920s whilst JH Turner, the Professional at Frilford Heath, was employed to design a further seven holes on leased land at the top of the hill on the south side of Aldworth Road. A succession of land purchases and swaps enabled the Club to buy the entire course during the 1930s leading to the emergence of the present layout.

Today's second hole is a longer version of the first on the original 9-hole course, the fourth on both layouts are similar whilst today's fourteenth to sixteenth holes are similar in layout to the old fifth to seventh holes. The course is situated in an area of outstanding natural beauty with excellent views north towards the Thames, the Chilterns and the historic Ridgeway Trail, and south across the Kennet Valley. The open nature of the downland course exposes golfers to the wind and the steep climb of 400ft between the second and fourth holes is a good test of fitness. Average golfers can feel like Tiger Woods whilst driving downwind at the fourteenth and fifteenth holes but care is needed at the 206 yard par-3 sixteenth which may need as little as a wedge!

The course record of 63 was set in 1956 by the Club's long term Professional, Roy Mason, and his son, Carl, became a junior member at the age of eight in 1961 and developed into a successful tournament player, winning the European Senior Tour Order of Merit in 2003.

Recently, magnificent red kites have moved into the area and are frequently seen quartering the Downs, adding to the feeling of space and well-being during a round at this friendly Club.

GOG MAGOG

RETREAT FOR CAMBRIDGE DONS

Whilst many new golf clubs formed in England at the turn of the 20th Century were aimed at wealthy businessmen and well-connected players living near major towns and cities, the history of the Gog Magog Golf Club, situated four miles south of Cambridge, tells a different story.

The annual Varsity match between Oxford and Cambridge had begun in 1878 and was an important influence in spreading the popularity of the game south of the Scottish borders. The resident graduate tutors, or dons, at Cambridge University became interested in the game as an escape from academia. In 1896 Gonville and Caius College purchased 220 acres of poor-quality farmland on the Gog Magog Hills to provide a golf course for the dons who had previously played on a rough course at Coldham's Common, close to the city centre. In 1899, W Duncan, the Professional at Coldham, laid out the first nine holes on the Gogs for a fee of £1, and a further nine holes were completed two years later.

The College bursar, Rev. JB Lock, played a key role in the early initiative and it was soon recognised that external revenue was needed to supplement income from the dons. The Club was formed to take over the running of the course and it accepted a lease from the College containing an important clause to the effect that: "the links should be used primarily as a place of recreation for the resident graduate members of the University", and that their enjoyment should not: "be defeated by reason of undergraduates or non-members of the University admitted to the Club." The spirit of this founding clause has echoed down the years and may explain why the Cambridge University

Golf Club tried to establish its own course at nearby Coton before settling its home at distant Mildenhall where all its members were allowed to play free of charge over the nine holes at Royal Worlington.

A number of undergraduates did play at the Club and discussion of a second relief course first started in 1902. Although interest in golf amongst the dons declined after the two wars, the Club continued to address the problem of supply and demand and the new 18-hole Wandlebury course now complements the original layout.

The inaugural Committee at the Club was led by Professor Sir German Sims Woodhead who was elected as first Captain and served for two years from 1901. His wife became the first ladies' Captain in 1903. Famous academic golfers over the years have included the economist John Maynard Keynes, who became

Main: *The clubhouse looks out onto the Gog Magog Hills, now the site of two championship courses*

Above: *Professor Sir German Sims Woodhead served for two years as the first Captain of the Club*

a member in 1908, and nuclear scientist Sir Ernest Rutherford who used to play a regular Sunday match with other eminent physicists from Trinity College. Bernard Darwin spent a brief time on the Committee in 1902 before moving away from Cambridge, but he may have played a role in arranging for Willie Park Junior to visit the Club in July 1902 to advise on the position and construction of bunkers.

Successive Committees were content to make their own changes to the course, and in 1922 the records reflect a certain pique when members requested that a golf course architect should be consulted. The minutes refer to the alterations recommended by the well respected J Abercromby as being 'trifling' and the resentment seems to have continued through to 1926 when the Secretary's response to a similar request was that: "it might be advisable to take the advice of a practical golfer like James Braid (five times Open Champion)." Whatever the sentiments at the time, the contributions of Park,

Abercromby and Braid all helped to add variety to today's layout which climbs steeply into the hills over the first two holes and then enjoys flat terrain before descending sharply again over the last two holes.

In recent times, the Old course has been played by a number of successful golfers. Club member and England international Russell Claydon won several important amateur championships in the late 1980s before turning professional, whilst Gog Magog now hosts the annual Lagonda Trophy which was won in 1992 by Lee Westwood with his mother acting as caddie. In 1996, Jason Boast lowered the course record by four shots to 60 in the first round of the Cambridge and Bedfordshire PGA competition.

Gog Magog has a large and enthusiastic membership which has enabled it to take the major investment decisions required to open a second course and a large new practice area, whilst remaining true to the original requirement that College academics should enjoy a welcoming golfing refuge.

...AND ON THE CLIFFTOPS

At a few coastal resorts, there was sufficient land along the clifftops to create courses over quick-draining soil and enjoying spectacular views. Erosion can be a problem and holes have been lost or are in jeopardy at Seaford Head (below), Sheringham, Cromer, and Mullion.

Cliff Edge

SEAFORD & SEAFORD HEAD

TWO HISTORIC COURSES

Seaford Golf Club's history involves two different courses and it should be possible to play a full round at both during the Summer as they are little more than a mile apart. The Club's first course was founded on Seaford Head where the South Downs chalkland meets the sea, producing the famous south coast White Cliffs. Seaford and Eastbourne share the honour of being the first towns to establish formal golf clubs in Sussex in 1887.

The inaugural meeting at Seaford was held in early August and the founders included Edward Bedford, who also played a leading role in the founding of Peacehaven Golf Club at neighbouring Newhaven, John Fletcher Farncombe, who was Honorary Secretary between 1888 and 1894, 'Father of the Club' Arthur Jack, Austen Leigh who was a descendant of the authoress, Jane Austen and who became Vice-President of the Club between 1896 and 1910, and J Robertson Reep from London who may have played the most important early role. The Right Hon. Viscount Hampden, PC, GCB was first President

and Major William Webb Turner the first Captain, serving for three years between 1888 and 1891.

The initial course at Seaford Head of twelve holes was laid out by Thompson, the Professional at Felixstowe. To complete a full 18-hole round, golfers had to play the first five holes a second time and then an extra hole back to the first on-site clubhouse, based in the cottage belonging to the shepherd. The building has since been demolished, but used to be situated by today's fifth green which was previously the closing hole. The course was extended to eighteen holes in 1889 and further changes were made in 1899 when three new holes were added at the top of the hill on the site of the Roman Camp. A number of existing holes were combined and hence lengthened.

The Club had an initial fourteen-year lease over the course from the owner, Launcelot Harison, who was made an honorary member, and he reserved the right to allow the grazing of sheep over the land. The shepherds were required to remove sheep 'in the line of play' when requested by golfers, and the Club rules specified that: "No unnecessary damage shall be done to the turf, nor shall any driving of sheep that may be grazing on the links be permitted, other than by request made to the shepherd or other person in charge of the flock." In addition to the Club cottage, the golfers also rented rooms where the Secretary was based at the former Bay Hotel in Pelham Road in the middle of Seaford Town, approximately half a mile from the course.

Unfortunately, strict laws stipulated that members were not allowed in these premises outside licensing hours and there was also a rule forbidding card games or any form of gambling.

At the end of 1887 there were 46 members, of whom seventeen were noted as not being local, and membership grew rapidly so that by 1903 there were nearer 400 members with a majority living away from Seaford. There is no doubt that the railway helped to fuel this increase. The directors of the London, Brighton and South Coast Railway encouraged London-based golfers to use the trains, and one of their employees, Allen Sarle, was made an honorary member of the Club in 1888 in recognition of this assistance. Three more railway employees were similarly rewarded in 1903. Although membership was booming, the Club continued to be handicapped both by the unsatisfactory clubhouse arrangements in Seaford Town and by various problems with the course owner who had different views on course layout and building development. The Club therefore took the radical decision to move location a mile inland to Bullock Down, East Blatchington. The decision was approved at the Club's November 1905 AGM and the move to the new course, designed by Open Champion JH Taylor, was completed in the Autumn of 1907. His Honour Judge Scully, the son-in-law of the Speaker of the House of Commons and Club Captain between 1904 and 1907 played a leading role in ensuring the successful relocation.

The opening of the new course was celebrated by an exhibition match featuring three Open Champions; course designer JH Taylor, James Braid and Jack White together with the Club's Professional, Joe Cheal. The four golfers averaged 80 strokes in their morning rounds and Braid and White beat Taylor and Cheal in the afternoon four-ball match with a better-ball score of 70 against their opponents' 74. The move to East Blatchington was not popular with all members and a number of golfers, mainly Seaford residents, decided to continue to play at Seaford Head. They formed the Seaford Links Golf Club which was later renamed as the Seaford Head Golf Club when it was taken over by Seaford Urban District Council in 1928. The course has stayed under local authority ownership ever since.

Although Taylor's original holes at East Blatchington have been renumbered and the course lengthened over the years, there has only been one major revision. In 1911, the present seventh hole was constructed and today's excellent dog-leg seventeenth was made by combining the original sixteenth and seventeenth holes. It is likely that the original course had much more gorse and that the fairways were considerably narrower. In addition to the new men's course, Taylor

Wind can play an important part in golf at both courses. At East Blatchington, the best views looking inland across rolling downs are found on the long par-4 thirteenth hole which has out of bounds to the left, although this should not come into play too often. The finishing holes ensure that the course leaves the best till last. The par-5 sixteenth can play extremely long in windy conditions. The seventeenth is less than 400 yards but is rated as stroke index four and is considered by many to be one of the finest holes in the county. The tee shot looks daunting. A long bank of gorse bushes lies immediately in front of the tee to catch any topped drive, and the correct line is to aim for the barn on the left-hand side of the fairway at the apex of the dog-leg. This is the hole that was created out of two of Taylor's shorter holes back in 1911. The eighteenth is another dog-leg and requires the tee shot to be aimed at the left-hand side of the fairway to open up the second shot.

Returning to the original course on the cliffs, Seaford Head must rank as one of the best municipal golf courses in the country. Green fees are good value, the course is historic, and the views from the top of the cliffs are quite outstanding. The course is also situated in an area of Special Scientific Interest and the fifteenth, sixteenth and seventeenth greens all lie within the boundaries of a late Bronze Age or early Iron Age sea fort which has been attacked from the south by coastal erosion of the cliffs. Due to its historical importance, it is classed as an Ancient Monument. Excellent views open up from the thirteenth hole onwards and the drive from the eighteenth must rank as one of the most dramatic in the UK.

Above: View across the Downs from the greenside bunker at the 11th hole at East Blatchington

Inset: View at sunset taken from the 17th green at Seaford Head

designed a separate 9-hole ladies' course which was used until 1917 when it was commandeered during the war for agricultural purposes and was not subsequently recovered. The ladies now play over the main course.

In the early 20th Century, Seaford became recognised as an educational centre of excellence. By 1929, the town had 35 private schools, nearly all of which were boarding, and a number of London-based golfers used to visit Seaford by train at the weekend to see their children and take the opportunity to play golf. The Club flourished at the new course and in 1925 took the important decision to purchase the freehold. However, the Second World War heralded a drastic downturn in fortune and in 1956 the Club undertook a sale and leaseback transaction with Miss Alida Dormer in which she purchased the freehold of the clubhouse and the course and leased them back to the Club for 99 years at an initial annual rent of £300 per year. The significance of this arrangement was that, along with improvements to the clubhouse, Miss Dormer established a Dormy House facility in the clubhouse allowing up to 20 guests to stay overnight in comfort. The Club bought back the course and the clubhouse activities from Mrs. Snow (nee Dormer) in 1968 and visitors can still make arrangements to stay in the Dormy House today.

ROYAL CROMER

THE CURTIS SISTERS AND THEIR CUP

The course at Cromer is situated close to the coastal village of Overstrand which became one of the most exclusive resorts in Victorian England following the arrival of the railway in 1876. The London journalist, Clement Scott, christened the area 'Poppyland' after the blankets of indigenous wild flowers, and influential visitors to the district included Lord Alfred Tennyson and Oscar Wilde who played golf with Lord Alfred Douglas whilst writing 'A Woman of No Importance.'

A Scottish holidaymaker, Henry Broadhurst, realised that the bracken-covered sandy cliffs near the lighthouse could be converted into a golf course, and he arranged a lease from Lord Suffield who entertained the Prince of Wales on a regular basis. Broadhurst and George Fernie, the Professional at Great Yarmouth, designed the first 9-hole course which was focussed on the cliff tops and in the dell known locally as Happy Valley, situated immediately below the lighthouse. The first clubhouse was constructed from timber and corrugated iron rescued from an old butcher's shop, and the building was reassembled at the foot of the valley where it reminded locals of a small Chinese settlement.

In 1891, Old Tom Morris advised the Club on changes including the construction of three new holes incorporating land covered by today's first and eighteenth fairways. Six holes on the extended layout were played twice to complete a full round and Morris visited Cromer again in 1895 to extend the course to eighteen separate holes. The round still started and finished in Happy Valley, and Harry Colt advised on further improvements in 1911

which were implemented by JH Taylor during the following two years.

Although the Club survived the Great War, by 1925 the course had fallen into disrepair and a member described its condition during a heated AGM as disgraceful. James Braid was then engaged to advise on further changes which included extra bunkers as well as the lengthening of holes and the construction of two new greens.

The local community had to be educated about the gentle new game and a journalist from the Eastern Daily Press reported in September 1887

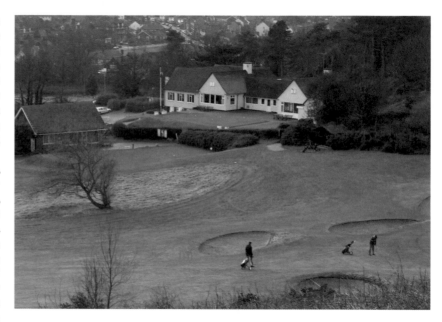

Above: *View down to the clubhouse and players on the final fairway taken from the elevated sixteenth tee*

how he had been assured: "that the game was health giving and was perfectly innocent and harmless, its pursuit being unassociated with panting of wild animals and writhing fishes."!

The Prince of Wales agreed to become Patron of the new Club on Christmas Day 1887 and the course was officially opened the following week. The first Captain was the Rev. HC Rogers who presented the Club with seven medals. Less than half of the original 78 members lived locally and founding members travelled from as far as Brighton, Newcastle and Edinburgh. The railway company built a Links Halt platform to serve both the golf course and the

Royal Links Hotel which towered over the course for many decades until it was destroyed by fire in the 1940s. Many of the founders were influential and included the Earls of Rosebery and Fife, Barons Suffield, Cromer and Carrington and several knights and MPs. The Patron did not play golf at Cromer, but other members of the Royal Family did participate including Alexandra Princess of Wales (later Queen Alexandra), Prince Arthur (the Duke of Connaught) and Princess Victoria. James Barrie, the Scottish creator of Peter Pan played at the Club and donated a prize putter whilst Herbert Asquith and Arthur Balfour were also seen on the course.

JH Taylor and Sandy Herd made their usual guest appearances and on a visit in 1907 Taylor was suffering from "an acute quinsy abscess" which was having a severe effect on his game leaving him three-down after the morning round. Fortunately, Club Captain Major HC Dent was a member of the Royal Army Medical Corps, and he lanced the abscess on the spot. Taylor swallowed half a pint of hot milk with a little stingo in it and then fought back in the afternoon round to square the match. He returned the favour at Royal Mid-Surrey several years later when he presented Dent with a new driver.

Cromer was fortunate to enjoy the early services of Percy M Lucas, the father of Laddie. Percy was Club Captain in 1893 and then acted as Secretary until 1902. Although there was no official county championship, he was probably the best amateur golfer in the region. In the 1960s, Laddie visited Cromer and presented the Club with 27 of his father's medals which are on show in the clubhouse. Also on display is a letter written to a misbehaving member in the 1930s by a later Secretary: "Dear Sir, Lest the susceptibilities of our visitors, on whom we depend for support, be offended, the Committee asks me to request that your expressions of disapproval at a shot not wholly successful may be couched in more moderate language than heretofore. Yours Truly, J Barrow, Secretary."

The founders included twelve lady golfers and Cromer has a special place in the history of the women's game following its hosting of the British Ladies' Championship in 1905. The tournament was preceded by three days of international matches between England, Scotland, Ireland and, for the first time, a team from the United States which included the Curtis sisters, Hariot and Margaret.

Although the first official Curtis Cup match between the US and the British Isles did not take place until 1932 at Wentworth, the Curtis sisters first suggested donating a cup after the success of

Above: Henry Cotton played an exhibition match at Cromer against the better-ball of (from l-r): Enid Wilson; Mme. Rene Lacoste and Joyce Wethered (Courtesy Royal Cromer Golf Club)

the match at Cromer. In the Open Championship itself, Bertha Thompson from Beverley and East Riding beat Miss Stuart from Royal Portrush 3&2 whilst Great Britain beat the team from the US in the preceding international fixture by six matches to one. The only American victory was by their Open Champion, Georgianna Bishop, who defeated the reigning British Open Champion, Lottie Dod, whilst Margaret Curtis was beaten by May Hezlet from Ireland and Elinor Nevile defeated Hariot. Although both teams were extremely strong, the matches were not accepted as official internationals as the teams were restricted to those individuals who happened to be present for the Open Championship.

Much of the Norfolk coastline is under attack from the sea although the problem at Cromer is a little different as the sandy cliffs have collapsed in places due to the actions of subterranean streams. Today's second and third holes were constructed in the 1970s to replace holes near the cliff edge which had tumbled onto the beach below or become unsafe. The current layout, completed by Frank Pennink, still allows for bracing seaside golf with excellent views. The fourteenth (Lighthouse) and fifteenth (Valley) holes are the most spectacular, but the outward half is a tougher golfing challenge with four long par-4s and only one short hole. Peter Alliss, Tony Jacklin and Nick Price have all tested their skills at the Club which gives a warm welcome to visitors.

Left: Top quality lady golfers from the United States assembled in Cromer for the 1905 Ladies' British Open Amateur Championship and associated international matches. From l-r: Ethel Burnett (later Mrs. Chas Clark); Miss Georgianna M. Bishop, Miss Frances Griscom; Miss Harriot S Curtis (at rear); Miss Griscom's sister (centre, wearing hat); Miss Emily Lockwood (became Mrs. WM Wood); Miss Molly Adams (became Mrs. Edward C Wheeler-in front); Miss Margaret Curtis

CHURSTON

Below: The par-3 seventeenth requires a firm shot to the heart of the green. Trouble lies short and to the right

Churston Golf Club is situated on top of the cliffs at the southern end of Torbay, on a long strip of downland turf six miles from Torquay. Although only two of the original holes have survived, the Club deserves inclusion amongst the ranks of historic English courses because of its early influence over the career of Ted Ray who is still one of only three Britons, alongside Harry Vardon and Tony Jacklin, to have won both the British and United States Open Championships. A fourth Briton, Cornishman Jim Barnes, also won both championships but took American citizenship before winning the titles.

Ray moved to Churston from Jersey in 1899 as a 22-year-old and started as the Club's Professional on a salary of thirteen shillings per week which also covered his additional roles as caddiemaster and caretaker of the clubrooms in the Harris' Railway Hotel. He received an increase of five shillings per week in 1901 for additional responsibilities supervising two Greenkeepers. The Committee encouraged Ray to enter the Open Championship each year and gave him a week's leave of absence and £5 expenses for each event. In 1903, Ray became the Professional at Ganton where he continued to improve steadily, coming third in the 1908 Open before finally winning it at Muirfield in 1912. The following year he accompanied Harry Vardon to the United States where they tied with the unknown American, Francis Ouimet, in the US Open at Brookline. Ouimet went on to win the play-off but in 1920 Ray returned to America with Vardon and this time succeeded in winning the US Open at Inverness.

Churston started as a rough 9-hole course laid out over the Galmton Warborough Common on the inland-side of the Great Western Railway, about 400 yards from Churston Station. The small tees and greens were maintained by one man employed for one day per week and the clubhouse consisted of rooms rented for £15 per annum from the landlord of the Harris' Railway Hotel. Lord Churston was one of the founding members and he personally contributed the £200 required to clear the ground and make the extra tees and greens when the course was extended to eighteen holes in 1896. The holes on the common were a hazard to walkers and other users and Lord Churston then arranged for the Club to develop sixteen new holes on his private estate which enjoyed superb views over Torbay. Harry Colt and Fred Hawtree made competing bids for the development and Colt won the contract to develop the new course which was ready for play in the Autumn of 1924. Colt was conscious of who was paying the

bills and observed: "...a reasonable amount to spend on the construction of the course would be £5,000, and personally I have every expectation that the Club should be a complete financial success...In my opinion, the outlay would be amply justified by the increased value of the surrounding land for building purposes."

Characteristic Colt features on the course are well illustrated at the par-3 seventeenth requiring an accurate tee shot to an elevated and sloping green which is well protected by greenside bunkers. The first and eighteenth holes are original remnants of the old course and the first has now been changed from an easy par-4 to a very testing opening par-3 measuring over 240 yards off the back tee. The front

nine stretches away from the clubhouse past large houses and out into the countryside towards Brixham Harbour, and although mature trees surround the far end of the course, it is still possible to see beautiful views across Torbay towards Paignton and Torquay. The Paignton and Dartmouth Steam Railway runs regular trains from Paignton to Kingswear and the noise and clouds of steam add a nostalgic feel to a round of golf.

Today's players are unlikely to suffer the additional hazard encountered by golfers in 1972 who suffered frequent attacks by a buzzard which drew blood on several occasions. The Club wrote a letter to the Committee for the Protection of Birds at the Home Office noting that: "...unless something is done someone will either lose an eye or perhaps lose their life from tetanus as one knows the claws of buzzards are very liable to be infected." It seems that the Home Office was slow to react because the Western Daily Press then reported that Bazil the Buzzard had been shot with an air rifle by a golfer and that the RSPCA had been called to treat the injured bird. At least the Home Office was able to close its file, noting that: "... the bird concerned was found injured and has been removed from the vicinity of the Club. It would appear, therefore, that the matter is now resolved."

Main: View from the clubhouse looking east to the first green and the eighteenth tee with Torbay in the distance

Above: The Club's first Professional and Open Champion Ted Ray (left), pictured with Frank Bowers who served in the same role at Churston between 1912 and 1950 (Courtesy Churston Golf Club)

Inset: This picture, taken around 1900, shows the first clubhouse attached to the old Harris' Hotel which was located next to Churston Station

NEWQUAY

ROYAL PRINCES LEARN THE GAME

Below: View from the tenth tee back down the eighth fairway

Newquay Golf Club occupies a magnificent stretch of exposed sandy links land on the cliffs between the main town and Fistral Beach which is world-famous for its surfing connections. Seagulls and skylarks add to the holiday feel. The late-Victorian Headland and Atlantic Hotels dominate the views and surfers often cross the course in penguin-like wetsuits on their way back to town. The two hotels presented the Club with Challenge Cups which have been played as annual open events for more than 100 years.

Before the arrival of the railways, Newquay was a small town reliant upon farming and fishing for employment. Around 1890, Silvanus Trevail founded the Cornwall Hotels Company with the idea of creating a fashionable resort to rival those on the south coasts of

Devon and Cornwall. He completed the Atlantic Hotel on one of Newquay's rocky outcrops, but work on the Headland Hotel was disrupted by locals who rioted over concerns that they would lose the use of the land for grazing and drying fishing nets. The Headland was eventually completed using labour imported from Redruth, but the protests saved the links from housing development. Silvanus suffered from depression and eventually shot himself in the lavatory of a train.

The Club was established in 1890 by HF Whitefield who became the first President and the original course stretched out past the Headland Hotel as far as the old lifeboat slip. The first pavilion was situated nearer the Atlantic Hotel.

The present clubhouse, known as The Towers, features a four-storey lookout tower as well as an old Catholic chapel which now serves as the Club's archive room and overspill bar. The house was built in 1835 as a seaside residence for GWT Gregor, who also let the building to wealthy families for holidays whilst he was staying at his inland home. In the 1950s, the Committee considered building a new clubhouse as The Towers was thought to be a white elephant, but the Club has retained the building which must rank as one of the most unusual clubhouses in the world.

Newquay Golf Club soon became successful and fashionable. Golf Illustrated reported in June 1902 that: "... the Club has been most successful in the Cornish Amateur Championship carrying off all the trophies, a feat never before achieved in Cornwall." In the early 1900s, the Royal Princes spent several holidays in Newquay and were frequent visitors to the course where they learnt the game and watched a number of

exhibition matches featuring the top Professionals of the time including James Braid, who held the course record of 68, JH Taylor, Harry Vardon and Alex Herd.

In August 1902, Herd and Braid represented 'Scotland' in a thirty six hole foursomes match against the English team of Vardon and Taylor and were victorious 4&3. Golf Illustrated rubbed in the result by revealing that the Scots were also 1-up on the bye. The Prince of Wales and the Duke of York were both made Honorary Life Members of the Club.

Early golfers were an enthusiastic breed. The Christmas Meeting in 1907 started on December 23rd with an open event consisting of 36 holes of foursomes, followed by eighteen holes on Christmas Eve, eighteen holes of strokeplay for ladies only on Boxing Day, and further competitions for both sexes on each of the following two days. A handicap limit of eighteen applied to all the open events and the Committee reserved the right to alter handicaps at its discretion.

Ladies featured prominently as members from the outset, although the Club did not establish a formal Ladies' Section until 1919. In the 1930s, their prizes were often obtained on approval from Harrods and included a silver cigarette case, antique brooches and glass powder bowls. The Spring Meeting prizes included a golf club valued at a guinea and silk stockings worth three shillings and eleven pence per pair!

Harry Colt made improvements to the course adding dog-legs and repositioning a number of bunkers. Today's course enjoys excellent seaside turf although some of the challenges have been removed since the times of an early advertisement which promised: "the turf is good (and) the bunkers and hazards are all natural consisting of sand pits, mine shafts and stone walls"! The first nine holes form an outer clockwise circle whilst the inward half includes several changes of direction so that the wind blows from a different direction for most tee shots. Although the course is relatively short, greenside bunkers are demanding and accuracy is the key to a good score.

Above: The young Prince of Wales and Duke of York pictured with top Professionals outside the first clubhouse (Courtesy Newquay Golf Club

Left: A surfer walking back from Fistral Beach to the town along the sunken footpath which dissects the course

SHERINGHAM

THE INCREDIBLE HENRY CRASKE

Many things have changed at Sheringham since the first nine holes were opened in 1891, but the founding fathers would still feel at home. The course was expanded to eighteen holes in 1898, the Grand Hotel has disappeared as a landmark, the cliffs have continued their march inland, and the old lifeboat station has disappeared from the middle of the course. However, the natural vistas remain the same and steam trains still run nearby. The view from the fifth tee is one of the most spectacular sights in English golf.

The town of Sheringham developed along with the Victorian railway system. Great Eastern opened the line from London to nearby Cromer in 1877 and a second line to Cromer via Peterborough was completed in 1887 by the Great Northern & Midland Joint Railway Company, leading to the rapid growth of hotels and holiday homes along the coast. The Liberal politician and first working-class MP, Henry Broadhurst, was a founder of the club at nearby Cromer in 1888, and Golf Illustrated in 1892 reported that the new golf Club

at Sheringham was entirely due to Broadhurst: "who has shown a keen desire to introduce the march of civilisation into this (until recently) remote region."

Broadhurst persuaded the Upcher family of Sherringham Hall to provide the land and arranged for Tom Dunn, the Professional at his London golf club, Tooting Bec, to lay out the first 9-hole course in September 1891. The Rev. AH Upcher became the first Captain in 1892, and members of the family acted as Club Presidents until 1985. The course was open for play at the Easter Meeting in Spring 1892. Dunn was assisted in his work by 13-year-old Ernest Risebro who carried his clubs and became the Club's first official caddie, earning a badge inscribed 'No. 1 Caddie'. Tom Dunn's son, Gourlay, was appointed as first Professional and Risebro became his assistant and continued to act for two subsequent Professionals before taking over the role himself in 1907. He served for more than 50 years and finally retired in 1959. Risebro was an excellent golfer, becoming a life member in 1932 in an era when Professionals were still barred from clubhouses around the country. He once beat the reigning Open Champion, Jack White, 6&4 in a match held at Royal Norwich, and over his long career scored eighteen holes-in-one as well as twos at all the longer holes at Sheringham giving him a career eclectic score of 32 for the course.

Amazingly, Risebro's tenure was surpassed by the Club's Secretary, Henry Craske, who completed 70 years of service, including his time in the Army Service Corps, starting as Assistant Secretary (to his uncle) in 1903 and becoming the full Secretary in 1919 through until his death in 1973. He was also a fine golfer and in 1927 won the Norfolk Amateur Championship held at

Sheringham with gross rounds of 74 and 79. The Club's centenary publication conjectured that: "Such single-handedness will not be repeated. Here is a record of service unassailable, nationally or internationally. Never again will a Secretary be appointed so young and stay so long. It will not be permitted, none will endure it, its quiet steady, civilisedly human tempo will not recur."

In 1890, Sheringham was a major fishing village with up to 250 boats regularly taking to sea. Given the nautical community, it is no surprise that Capt. RF Scott was one of the Club's early members until his death in Antarctica in 1912. Other early seafaring members and explorers included Admiral of the Fleet Sir John Jellicoe, who became First Sea Lord shortly after the Battle of Jutland, and Sir Ernest Shackleton who journeyed with Scott towards the South Pole during the Discovery expedition in the Summer of 1901. The clubhouse lounge contains a magnificent picture of a stormy sea as if to commemorate these early adventurers.

In 1898, the course was extended to eighteen holes and a professional tournament was organised featuring several top players including JH Taylor, who was the only player to beat the bogey of 80 over both rounds, and Harry Vardon who was runner-up. James Braid and Jack White were the only other players to break 80 in one of their two rounds. Taylor defeated Braid 5&4 over two rounds in August 1901, and in September 1908, the top players returned to Sheringham and played a rare foursomes format, winning the approval of Golf Illustrated which commented that the match: "... was so complete a success that it is hoped that other clubs will repeat the experiment." In keeping with the early traditions of quality and exclusivity, in 1898 the Club contracted with Harrods of London to build a two-storey extension to the clubhouse at a cost of £584.

The Club survived the First World War although the fifth hole, overlooking the 'German Ocean', was taken over by the military, and the first hole was played twice to complete a full round. One of the greens was also used by wounded soldiers from the Red Cross Hospital for games of bowls. Most newspapers were cancelled as an austerity measure, but the Club continued to receive The Tatler and tradesmen from the town were granted temporary membership during Winter months under the auspices of New Sheringham Golf Club. In 1916, military personnel were allowed to play on Sundays although the exemption was restricted to Winter months after 1pm.

Ladies' golf features strongly in Sheringham's history. The Club has hosted the English Ladies' Close Championship on three occasions and in 1920, Joyce

Main: *Westerly view from the tee towards the fairway bunkers at the spectacular par-4 fifth hole known as Fulmars after the seabirds which nest on the cliffs to the right of the fairway*

Above: *From l-r, JH Taylor, Arnaud Massy, James Braid and Harry Vardon at the Club in September 1908*

Wethered left her mark on golfing folklore. She started the competition slowly, scoring 94 in the qualifying round which was played in cold, windy conditions. The 89 of the favourite, Cecil Leitch, put the difficult conditions into context. The two fought their way through the knockout rounds, and in the final Miss Leitch was six-up at the 21st before Joyce Wethered started her remarkable comeback. The ground was very hard and the ladies were hitting prodigious distances. Miss Wethered drove the old twelfth hole which measured 296 yards, and Miss Leitch was also pin-high but just off the green. Commentators agreed that Miss Wethered's game was built on total concentration which was helpful as Miss Leitch had her own band of vociferous supporters. The seventeenth green lay close to the railway, and just as Miss Wethered addressed her putt to win the match, a train thundered past. The putt went in and Joyce is forever celebrated as saying: "What train?" The hole bears that name today.

More recently, the course has been played by several Open Champions including Gary Player and Lee Trevino who played in the Bernard Matthews' Pro-Ams in 1979 and 1980. Trevino was warm in his praise for Sheringham, noting: "This is a great course you have here and it's exactly the sort of place I would come to practise for The Open...and maybe that way I'll beat Tom Watson!"

The sea is visible from many holes and the wind is often a major factor, causing mis-hit shots to balloon alarmingly. Slicers must beware the cliffs which dominate the right-hand side of the course on the outward nine, and the railway which has a similar influence over the last four holes. The character of the course was beautifully described by Bernard Darwin. "One cannot get out of one's head the agreeable illusion that there is not merely a whole parish, but a whole world to hit into. If a man is not encouraged to open his shoulders by those green and breezy spaces, then his case is a sad one indeed."

Above: *Fifth green at Sheringham (photograph by Eric Hepworth)*

MULLION

ST. WINWALOE CHURCH

Below: Approaching the green at the uphill par-3 eleventh hole. The tenth green is behind the lady golfer and the famous old St. Winwaloe Church on Gunwaloe Beach is visible in the background

Mullion golf course enjoys one of the most beautiful and exposed locations in England and is built on the Towans which slope dramatically down towards Church Cove. The famous old church of St. Winwaloe and its separate tower are protected by a rocky knoll from the Atlantic storms which often threaten to engulf the mound. The 'Church of Storms' has been a place of worship since the 5th Century and there was a major settlement near the beach a few hundred years later. The tower dates from the 13th Century and the church was built in the 15th Century.

The Club has enjoyed mixed fortunes. After a quiet beginning it became the height of fashion in the 1920s and '30s without enjoying significant support from the local working population. After the Second World War, visitor numbers declined and the Club was liquidated in the 1950s. Fortunately, the course was saved and is now well patronised by both locals and visitors. Mullion has an enlightened attitude towards its juniors who have priority on the course on Saturday mornings.

William Sich was the pioneer behind the Club. His family owned several estates in Essex as well as the Lamb Brewery in Chiswick, and Sich was elected as first Captain, serving for 23 years. Major contributions were also made by an early Honorary Secretary, WA Fawcus, and Charles Turley Smith who rented rooms near the course. Turley Smith played host to many golfing friends from literary circles and high society including James Barrie, Arthur Conan Doyle, AA Milne, AP Herbert, Lady Cynthia Asquith, Sir Hugh Walpole, Bunny Austin, Jack Hobbs, Douglas Bader, Barnes Wallis and the Wethered family. Between the wars, the road near the Club was lined with their chauffeur-driven Rolls Royces and Bentleys.

The Club bought the course in 1925 raising funds through debentures, and it was the holders, fearful for the continuing return on their investment, who precipitated the liquidation in the 1950s. Mullion

had not been run on a commercial basis and members from the founding families were paying the same annual subscription of one guinea which applied in 1895. The National Trust bought the land for £3,000 and the game would have died but for the intervention of LR Francis who was the proprietor of the Polurrian Hotel. The liquidator allowed use of the grass-cutting machinery and the holes nearest the road were brought back into play. The honours' boards were sold to the National Trust which then donated them back to the golfers.

The clubhouse was sold to the Youth Hostel Association and green fees were collected in an honesty box placed at the entrance to the course. By 1966, matters had improved, a new clubhouse was constructed from a pair of old garages and the

Above: Severe problems lie immediately behind the tenth green.

Inset: Inauguration of the original first tee which was positioned on the far side of the stream in Poldhu Cove. The tee shot had to be hit up a precipitous slope and the location was soon abandoned in favour of an easier opening hole located on top of the Towans

course was expanded back to eighteen holes. The new layout was celebrated with a match between Dai Rees, Peter Alliss, Bernard Hunt and Norman Sutton.

In 1895, the first tee and original clubhouse had been situated on the far side of the stream in the valley behind Poldhu Cove. The stream forms the boundary between the parishes of Mullion and Gunwalloe and the Club was named Mullion although no part of the course is now located in that parish. The tee shot up the steep hill over impenetrable rough was soon abandoned in favour of an easier start on top of the Towans. Early golfers also faced other daunting hazards whilst playing the four holes situated near the church in Gunwalloe Cove. The twelfth hole was known as the Chasm, being played from a tee near Winianton Farm over Dollar Cove to a green by the cemetery. The hole was immortalised in the imaginary case of 'Rex v. Haddock', subtitled 'Is a Golfer a Gentleman?' written for Punch by AP Herbert as part of his series of Misleading Cases

in Common Law. The magistrate agreed that the extreme circumstances causing the defendant's expletives at the impossible Chasm hole could not have been contemplated when the Profane Oaths Act was drafted in 1745, and that he could therefore leave the court without a stain upon his character.

Coastal erosion and an increased concern for public safety halted the old golfing high jinx around the church, but Mullion still offers a combination of exhilarating views and memorable holes. The downhill par-4 sixth measures 300 yards but can be reached from the tee. Players on the green are requested to call down the game behind but must beware of aerial bombardment. The par-4 seventh is a classic two-shot hole with out of bounds threatening from the tee, whilst the dog-leg tenth requires an accurate second shot off a sloping fairway over a deep pit to a green which is well protected by bunkers on its upper side. The church and the Atlantic rollers form a riveting backdrop to many holes.

NORTH FORELAND

LORD NORTHCLIFFE'S HERITAGE

North Foreland is built over quick-draining chalk land just a stone's throw from the white cliffs overlooking the sea, and must surely enjoy the best drainage of all English courses. Mud is unheard of and the fairways and greens are fast-running and true.

The first nine holes were laid out in 1903 under the initiative of a solicitor, Sir William Capel Slaughter, and the Club was initially known as Kingsgate Golf Club after the neighbouring village and nearby bay of that name. 28 of the 100 or so members in the inaugural year had London addresses, reflecting the role of nearby Broadstairs and the Thanet Coast as a weekend and holiday retreat. The Rt. Hon. Lord Avebury was first President and a local surgeon, Dr. Hugh Raven acted as Secretary. The real impetus was provided by newspaper baron Lord Northcliffe who soon purchased the original Club and some adjacent land. Money was no object and he hired the top golf architects Fowler & Simpson to extend the course to eighteen holes whilst changing the name to North Foreland Golf Club, recognising the influence of the adjacent residential area and the world-famous lighthouse. Northcliffe would have been spurred on by the success of fellow newspaper baron Lord Riddell at Walton Heath, where Herbert Fowler had designed the Old Course in 1905.

Northcliffe was born as Alfred Harmsworth in 1865 and was the oldest of thirteen children. He rescued The Evening News in 1894, set up The Daily Mail in 1896, The Daily Mirror in 1903, The Sunday Observer in 1905, and rescued The Times

in 1908. He became the youngest ever peer of the realm in 1905, and when he died in 1922, he bequeathed three months salary to each of his 6,000 employees.

In addition to the main course, the Club enjoys an 18-hole 'approach and putt' course. The main honours' boards in the clubhouse reflect the importance attached to competitions held on this second layout which also hosts an annual open juvenile championship with past winners including Henry Longhurst and Laddie Lucas.

Below: A Winter's view across the course and the cauliflower-fields to the North Foreland lighthouse which has been signalling the southern approach to the Thames Estuary and warning of the treacherous Margate Roads since 1499. It was the last manual lighthouse in the UK to be automated when the Duke of Edinburgh presided over the ceremony in November 1998

Fowler and Simpson advised against the construction of sand bunkers on the two courses as they believed that the wind would rapidly remove sand from the hazards. Northcliffe's response was to build a small railway up from the sandy beach to ensure a steady supply of replacement material was available to the patient greenstaff!

Northcliffe appointed Abe Mitchell as the Club's playing Professional on a five-year contract between 1920 and 1925 whilst Ernie Coles acted as teaching Professional. At the end of his contract, Mitchell intended to live in America and play on the US tour, but he was persuaded to stay in the UK by Samuel Ryder who offered him a generous salary to become his personal coach and the first Professional for Ryder's new course at Verulam in St. Albans. Mitchell and Ryder helped establish the

biannual Professionals' match between Great Britain and the United States, and Ryder arranged for Mitchell to be modelled as the golfer on the lid of what became the famous Ryder Cup trophy. Whilst he was alive, Lord Northcliffe ensured that his national newspapers carried detailed results of the Club's competitions which helped to maintain its high profile.

North Foreland's successful image was maintained by Diana Fishwick who had won several of the Club's post-war Open Championships including the Peace Cup in 1926 and the Whitsuntide Cup on three occasions whilst playing against a field largely consisting of men. In 1930, she won the British Women's Open Amateur Championship at Formby, defeating the American champion, Glenna Collett, 4&3 in the 36-hole final at Formby.

Much of Broadstairs was evacuated during the Second World War as Thanet was seen to be on the frontline, and part of the course was covered with barbed wire, slit trenches and bomb craters as well as being used as a battle school and for ammunition storage. JSF Morrison was engaged after the war to return the course to a full layout.

Today's course is often busy but visitors are welcome and the Club hosts an Open Week in June each year with up to eight different events open to men and women with an official handicap. North Foreland was also the venue for a recent regional qualifying event for the Open Championship when it was last held at Sandwich, and visiting amateurs will be sure to enjoy the same open fairways, limited rough and bracing views of the sea which is visible from all eighteen holes.

BAMBURGH CASTLE

The beautiful course at Bamburgh Castle was established as a summertime resort for wealthy Newcastle families and the Club still retains an August 'year end' reflecting the time when families returned to the city from their holidays on the coast.

Golf had been played in 1896 on a rough 9-hole course on the other side of the village near the castle, but the Club itself was formed at a General Meeting held at Bamburgh Castle in February 1904. Lord Armstrong, nephew of the first Lord Armstrong and owner of the castle, was elected as President and he built today's clubhouse and leased the building to the Club on favourable terms. He also leased the land for the course from his friend George Cruddas, and transferred playing rights to the Club whilst honouring the Cruddas family's wishes by stipulating that there should be no play on the Sabbath. This was finally changed in the 1960s, but there are still no competitive matches on Sundays.

The course was formally opened in August 1904 by Lord Armstrong, and the first shot was struck by his young daughter, the Hon. Winifreda Watson Armstrong. The first Lord Armstrong, William George, was a great and pioneering engineer and his energies

Main: The very narrow fourteenth green offers spectacular views of the castles at both Bamburgh and Holy Island. This picture shows Bamburgh Castle and the view has changed little in 100 years (see lower picture)

Main: Tricky drive at the short, downhill par-4 seventeenth hole with out of bounds to the right of the wall. Longer hitters may be able to drive the green. The clubhouse is in the far distance

Right: Early player driving at the first hole. The sea is to the right of the steep slope

led to the development of the well-known Armstrong Siddeley and Vickers Armstrong engineering groups. He purchased the castle in 1894 and when he died the property passed to his nephew who continued with the renovations. The castle sits on top of a spectacular basalt outcrop overlooking the sea which has been fortified since the 6th Century. The present building dates back to shortly after the Norman Conquest and is recognised as one of the finest castles in England.

For many years, the Club had a reminder of the great engineering strengths of the founding family. A large rock face is visible to the left of the third tee, and until the early 1920s players had to contend with quarry blasting whilst they were playing. A small railway ran down to a dock at Budle Bay behind the fourth green and a local line-of-sight rule was used to help golfers impeded by railway trucks crossing the fairway. The course was also grazed by sheep until the 1960s, and for a while after the Second World War the very existence of the Club was in jeopardy due to petrol rationing and the absence of a local railway station which prevented many members from making the journey up from Newcastle. The first Captain, Arthur Hugo Leather Culley, served for nineteen years from 1904 and then a succession of Captains each acted for two years until the unusual tradition changed to the more normal annual appointment in the 1970s. The Club's survival owes much to a few energetic and well-connected golfers including the Souter and Dalgleish families, and Bamburgh's good sense in welcoming women from the outset ensured that many ladies were also able to help the Club emerge from the difficult times.

Bernard Darwin summarised much of what is so memorable about the course when he wrote in 1910 that: "there is surely no lovelier view from any golf course...the noble Castle of Bamburgh itself, Lindisfarne looming across the water on Holy Island and the Farne Islands in the distance...The golf too is delightfully amusing, especially the shorter holes, where we seem to be leaping like chamois from rock to rock..." Darwin must surely have been remembering the par-3s at the first, eighth and fourteenth holes. The eighth is perhaps the most dramatic, requiring a mid-iron shot over a big valley to a green which is partially hidden between two rocky outcrops. The course is not long, and depending upon the wind direction, big hitters have a chance of reaching several of the par-4s in one shot. This is particularly true at the downhill seventeenth, but out of bounds looms all the way down the right-hand side whilst weaker players may be trapped by the heavy gorse lying to the left of the narrow fairway.

The Club gives a warm welcome to visitors and it is a course where families and players of all standards will enjoy their round.

Above: Lord Armstrong played the central role in the formation of the Club. The first Lord Armstrong bought Bamburgh Castle in 1894 and when he died in 1900 the property was taken over by his nephew (pictured above - Courtesy of Bamburgh Castle Golf Club)

Below: View from the second tee across the deserted bay towards Holy Island

EARLY HEATHLAND COURSES

Before the advent of heavy machinery for course construction and maintenance, heathland offered the only other practical location for golf. Much of this land was located away from both the cities and the coastal resorts and many of the early heathland clubs started out as relatively small ventures. Much of the impenetrable gorse and heather has been cleared on most courses since the early days.

Aldeburgh	1884
New Forest	1888
Royal Ashdown Forest (left)	1888
Sutton Coldfield	1889
Berkhamsted	1890
Woking	1893
Woodbridge	1893
Royal Worlington	1893
Crowborough Beacon	1895
Rushmere	1895
Hankley Common	1897
Broadstone	1898
East Berkshire	1903
Piltdown	1904
North Hants	1904
Hindhead	1904

ALDEBURGH

CHAMPION OF EQUALITY

Aldeburgh is a challenging course with a long history of relatively equal rights for lady members. The Club is a regular host of the English Ladies' Close Championship and the men's card is particularly tough as there are no par-5s to encourage longer hitters.

Scot James Anderson, known to his friends as Skelton, was the prime mover behind the formation of the Club at Aldeburgh. He was married to Dr. Elizabeth Garrett Anderson who did much to champion women's rights in the UK. She was the first lady doctor in England and was later to become the first female English mayor when she was appointed to that role in Aldeburgh in 1908. Anderson himself was a successful businessman, being Chairman of Anderson Green, a constituent company of the P&O Shipping Group and which pioneered the first direct steamship route to Australia. His brother-in-law, Herbert Cowell QC, succeeded him as Club Captain and served for four years between 1885 and 1888.

James Pettit, the owner of nearby Red House Farm, and Joseph Flintham, tenant of Aldeburgh Hall Farm, both played important roles in allowing early golfers to play across their properties. Anderson also helped to obtain co-operation from the railway and another Scot, George (later Sir George) Gibb was a fellow founding member who became General Manager of the Great Eastern Railway. Gibb persuaded the railway to give golfers a travel concession on the route out of London from Liverpool Street Station although this applied only to the third-class carriages and would not have appealed to the better-healed members.

Anderson's final coup was to persuade the Lord of the Manor, Thomas FC Vernon Wentworth, who owned

most of the heathland used by today's course, to allow access to golfers. Following these successful land negotiations, the Club obtained the services of John Thompson, the Professional at Royal Wimbledon, and reigning Open Champion Willie Fernie, the Professional at nearby Felixstowe, to lay out a full 18-hole course including six holes to the south of the Saxmundham Road which were already in use as a fledgling layout.

Joseph Flintham died in 1905 and the new landlord of the 60 acres at Aldeburgh Hall Farm covered by the first six holes, served notice on the Club that he was no longer willing to allow access over his land by golfers. Clearly the situation had become untenable as one Committee member was quoted as saying: "I have met many fools in my life but never such an egregious ass as this one." The Club's only option was to approach Captain Vernon Wentworth to ask a further favour by requesting the use of additional acreage on his land to the north of the Saxmundham Road. Fortunately, the

by bringing his dog into the clubhouse. The Honorary Secretary was obliged to write to the offender noting: "It is very annoying indeed when old members, who know the rule perfectly well, infringe it, and particularly at a time when, as you know, there are in the air very difficult questions to be solved and a single mistake (and a very grave one) that you made might be likely to prejudice the Club in the eyes of Captain Vernon Wentworth. It seems incredible to me that you could have any excuse whatever for doing what you did do. Whether the dog belonged to the keeper or whether it did not does not affect the case at all. You had it and it was with you."

During these negotiations the Club was well-aware of the need to maintain Vernon Wentworth's goodwill. The Committee resolved to give his shepherd an annual Christmas box of £1 and in one year a further gratuity of 5 shillings: "...for his civil behaviour to members of the Club whilst playing round the Links." However, by 1909 the Committee must have been feeling more confident of their position because in that year they agreed: "... that in consideration of the unsatisfactory way in which the shepherd has conducted himself, the Committee gives him ten shillings as a Christmas donation and, if he will do his utmost to keep his sheep off the greens during the coming year, the Committee will increase the donation to 20 shillings."

Shortly after the Club resolved the land issue, it was faced with a further problem. In 1910, a spark from the kitchen chimney set fire to the thatch on the clubhouse roof and the building was completely destroyed. The Club was again indebted to its President who helped finance the replacement building as well as further bunkering on the course suggested by Taylor.

Bernard Darwin was an early fan of golf at Aldeburgh. Writing in the 1920s he described it as very much like one of the best Surrey courses: "...so that one might imagine that the course had been transported whole from the neighbourhood of Woking on a magic carpet." He continued: "...the last time I was at Aldeburgh, I got into more bunkers in a short space of time than I had ever done anywhere. And yet they are all strictly fair and they do not bear at all hardly on the weaker brethren."

initial reaction was promising although the Captain commented that he found it hard to imagine how a suitable course could be designed on the available land.

Heartened by this response, the Club sent a telegram to JH Taylor requesting him to redesign the course and to provide the necessary gravitas to persuade the Captain that the new layout would be appropriate.

Taylor was accompanied by fellow Open Champion, Willie Park Junior, and together they produced a layout which has many similarities to today's course. The seventh hole has a typical Taylor-inspired fairway bunker which traps many a seemingly good tee shot. Whilst the Club was still waiting anxiously for a response, the situation was apparently jeopardised by the actions of a senior member who broke a strict rule

Main: Distant view of the clubhouse at dusk

Above: Founder James 'Skelton' Anderson

In 1923, Vernon Wentworth agreed to allow the Club to purchase the freehold of the course and the clubhouse for £8,000 which was funded by the issue of £60 debentures exempting the holders from the payment of their annual subscriptions. In 1925, the Club also purchased twelve acres of land at Aldeburgh Hall Farm which is now used as part of the separate 9-hole River Course situated to the south of the Saxmundham Road.

Aldeburgh's best-known golfer was a lady, Joy Winn, whose first golf lesson was from James Braid. By 1913, she was playing off scratch which she improved further to plus-3 in 1922. In 1938, she narrowly missed winning the English Ladies' Close Championship which was hosted by Aldeburgh when she was defeated on the 35th hole by Elsie Corlett. She was elected as Honorary Vice-President of the Club in 1980. Amongst the men, Vic Longstaffe was a successful player and one of six founding members of The Moles Golfing Society. The Moles still play fixtures today against Oxford University and other senior Clubs, but it is doubtful that they will have had a greater day than that witnessed by non-playing Captain Longstaffe in 1926 at Woking when, in a friendly match, The Moles defeated the bulk of the American Walker Cup team which included Bobby Jones, Francis Ouimet and Jess Sweetster who won that year's Amateur Championship at Muirfield.

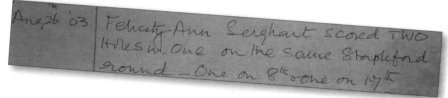

Aug 26th '03   Felicity-Ann Sieghart scored TWO Holes in One on the same Stapleford ground — One on 8th & one on 19th

The Club first hosted the English Ladies' Close Championship in 1930, but its next visit in 1938 was played in September under the shadow of war following the Munich crisis. Several players decided to withdraw during the competition, and Aldeburgh member Lady 'Yoey' Eddis, who was six times the County Lady Champion and who reached the quarter-finals of the competition, was engaged in distributing gas masks to the villagers when she was not actually playing a match on the course. During the war, the course was closed and trenches and other obstacles were laid to make it unsuitable as a landing strip for enemy aircraft. Afterwards, German POWs were employed to help reinstate the course.

Aldeburgh's best-known Professional was James Sherlock. Bernard Darwin once described him as: "...the steadiest player in the world" and he was considered to be one of the best teachers of the game as well as being a famous club maker. He won the British Professional Matchplay title in 1910 and played ten

Main: The famous horseshoe bunker at the par-3 fourth hole with its "seas and cliffs of black timber"

Above: Entry in the Club's record log. Felicity Ann Sieghart was 76-years-old when she achieved the feat

Above: Fire destroyed the original clubhouse in 1910 when a spark from the kitchen chimney ignited the thatched roof. The only water supply was from a pond more than 300 yards away

Inset: Mabel Potterton making a full swing whilst driving at Aldeburgh around 1903 showing that ladies' play had evolved past the short-course game

times for England in the regular fixture against Scotland as well as representing Great Britain against the United States at Gleneagles in 1921 in a pre-Ryder Cup fixture.

The Club's record book has been in use since 1892 and records many holes-in-one, but Aldeburgh must be one of the few Clubs to have documented two separate occasions where a player has scored two in the same round. Perhaps predictably, the first occasion was performed by James Sherlock; but more remarkably, the feat was repeated in 2003 by 76-year-old Felicity Sieghart at the eighth and seventeenth.

Out on the course, the large red building to the left of the fourteenth fairway has played an important role in the lives of Aldeburgh and its golfers. Founding member James Pettit owned Red House Farm and the course now stretches over land which formed part of the farm. More recently, the house was home to composer Benjamin Britten who lived there with his long-time partner Peter Pears. Britten spent much of his later life helping to raise funds for the rebuilding of the Maltings at nearby Snape and he died in the house in December 1976.

Aldeburgh prides itself as a two-ball course to help keep the game moving and four-ball games are not generally allowed. The clubhouse has a great view of the course with the two nines fanning out to the west and east. Gorse is in bloom throughout the year and acts as a reminder that straight play is vital.

With no par-5s, golfers need to plan their strategy carefully and the layout of the course makes it almost certain that the wind will be both helping and hindering at various points in the round. Locals advise to put on an extra layer of clothes in Winter as the East Coast is particularly exposed to winds from Siberia!

The third hole has been redesigned to prevent long hitters from trying to cut the corner of the dog-leg and accidentally hitting a hook onto the neighbouring Saxmundham Road. The short fourth is famous for the huge horseshoe bunker which surrounds the front of the green and is backed by hundreds of old railway sleepers. Writing in the 1920s, Bernard Darwin described the hole as: "...a quaint and frightening hole that you can't forget, with an undulating green which is a 'right little, tight little island' wholly surrounded by sandy cliffs, seas and cliffs of black timber."

The fifth and sixth holes are two of the toughest par-4s on the course and only the par-3 eighth provides a respite before the turn. The Professionals rate the long eleventh as one of the most difficult holes and both Darwin and Sir Peter Allen in his book 'Play the Best Golf Courses' rate the dog-leg fourteenth very highly. It seems amazing that Harry Weetman managed to drive the green on this hole in an exhibition match back in 1952 without the benefit of a modern driver.

Both the sixteenth and eighteenth holes are testing par-4s and provide a worthy finish to an excellent course. Winter visitors to Aldeburgh are encouraged by members to return again in late Spring when nightingales can be heard singing from the thickets in their beautiful natural surroundings.

NEW FOREST

GOLF AMONGST THE WILDLIFE

The New Forest Golf Club's course at Lyndhurst spreads over the heath which was once known as the Old Lyndhurst Race Course. The Club shares a common ancestry with the Forest Course at Bramshaw which is several miles away across the Forest. In February 1889, a few golfing enthusiasts met at Glasshayes, the home of Colonel Alexander Macleay, to formalise playing arrangements. In particular, permission was to be sought from the Commissioners for Woods and Forests based in Whitehall, London, to make the necessary modifications to the virgin heathland.

More than a century later, the Club still shares a number of common issues with the Bramshaw Club in having to reconcile the wishes of its golfing members with the requirements of the Conservators of the Forest and of the Forest Verderers. Macleay became the first Captain and President of the Club, but Philip de Crespigny, who founded Bramshaw and his co-founder, Captain HC Aitchison, also played a vital role in the early days at Lyndhurst.

For a time, the two courses operated as one 'Club', and monthly medals were alternated between the two courses. Writing in Country Life in 1907, de Crespigny described how the first course at Lyndhurst of nine holes was situated on the racecourse site indicating that the original grounds were similar to today's. This course then fell out of favour due to the difficulty of the heather, and a separate 9-hole course was constructed across the road around the Lyndhurst Cricket ground. The seventh hole on the original links was nicknamed Nil Desperandum, reflecting the hazards involved.

By 1907, the course had been expanded to eighteen holes, using land on both sides of the Southampton

Road. Golf played in difficult conditions in the formative years was a minority interest at Lyndhurst, and perhaps there were some early cases of handicap protection as the minutes in August 1891 noted that: "owing to the different other attractions of the Summer, the links at both Bramshaw and Lyndhurst have been practically deserted but this is only to be expected - the long grass and heather being certainly against low scoring and the glare of the hot sun is sure to tell its own tale on the round." Perhaps to encourage play in the difficult conditions, the Club introduced a local rule in May 1902 stating that: "players may take shelter during a competition provided their cards are handed in in the morning before 1.30 and in the afternoon by 5.30."

Above: 15,000 troops from the Seventh Division camped out on the course for a fortnight in October 1914 before setting out for their landing at Zeebrugge. Three weeks later, all but 3,000 had perished in the battles at Ypres

Reginald Hargreaves was another prominent early member and also a good cricketer, playing for Hampshire. He will forever be remembered around Lyndhurst for his connection with Alice in Wonderland. Author Lewis Carroll first met Alice Liddell on a boat trip in Oxford when she was 10-years-old and he is said to have based his fantasy stories around the beautiful girl. Alice later married Hargreaves in Westminster Abbey and moved to Lyndhurst after the wedding where she lived for more than 50 years. She is buried beside her husband in St. Michael's Church in Lyndhurst.

Following the death of Philip de Crespigny in 1912, a decision was taken to separate the two courses back into two distinct clubs although relationships continued to be cordial. The First World War had a dramatic effect on the Club. 15,000 troops mustered over the course in 1914 before their dreadful journey to Ypres. By 1919, the Club was in dire straights and members were asked for extra voluntary contributions to keep it going. Permission to use the cricket club side of the road was withdrawn in the 1930s and the Club continued as a 9-hole course playing over the grounds approximating to the original course on the racecourse side of the road.

The course was again commandeered for troops in the Second World War, and by 1946 the Club had only 43 members. The minutes noted that members thought it was better to have a good 9-hole course than an indifferent 18-hole layout, and it was not until the Club was effectively rescued by a professional golfer, Peter Swann, in the late 1950s, that arrangements were made to extend the course back to the full eighteen holes.

The New Forest course is best visited in Summer when the gorse and heather are in full bloom as the ground can get boggy and waterlogged in Winter months. The 585-yard par-5 third hole is undoubtedly the most testing on the course being a double dog-leg with out of bounds on the left. The hole is so long that in Winter it is divided into three (holes 3a, 3b and 3c) to compensate for taking the waterlogged seventh and ninth fairways out of use.

Although the course has seven par-3s, the eighth is 250 yards long and merits a single-figure stroke-index whilst the fourteenth is also over 200 yards and plays longer than it looks. The course will be enjoyed by all golfers who like a pleasant rather than difficult round over pretty and relatively flat terrain.

ROYAL ASHDOWN FOREST

THE CANTELUPE AND ABE MITCHELL

The beautiful Old Course at Ashdown Forest near Forest Row in Sussex currently hosts a Regional Qualifying day for the Open Championship. Streams, heather, bracken, undulations and grassy pits are all natural hazards positioned to trap golfers of every standard, and many players have completed a round without realising that there are no artificial sand bunkers on the course.

A December 1888 edition of The Field noted that a meeting was being held at the Brambletye Hotel that day to discuss the formation of a links course on Ashdown Forest. The Rev. AT Scott took the lead in selecting the ground and the Rev. JBM Butler, the Rector of nearby Maresfield and a Commissioner of the Forest, gave his support provided there was sufficient interest to start the Club: "...on a dignified and stable basis." Vital support was received from the 7th Earl De La Warr, Lord of the Manor of Duddleswell and owner of Ashdown Forest. Archdeacon Scott had the foresight to involve the local community from the outset, and in 1892 he helped to form what is now the second-oldest Artisans' Section in England, the Cantelupe Club, named after Viscount Cantelupe, the eldest son of Earl De La Warr.

The mutual interest of village and Club was demonstrated in 1890 by the presentation of the Forest Row Challenge Cup to the Club by 80 inhabitants of the community who wrote: "We think this is a fitting opportunity to congratulate you on the success and proportions of the Club. We are sensible of the great impetus it has given to the trade of Forest Row and hope it may long continue to be prosperous and flourishing."

Golf in the early days at Ashdown Forest was beautifully described in a May 1889 edition of the Sussex Daily News: "There is nothing more charming than an English Common, with its dark masses of heath, lit up here and there (looking like an oasis in the desert) by a patch of vivid green, the well cultivated patch of some squatter who long ago, before the time of Conservators, managed to build a hut on the Crown land and by gradual encroachment got possession of a comfortable estate. There is no mistaking common

Above: View of the approach shot over the stream to the par-5 fifth green from the right of the fairway. The tee for the tricky par-3 sixth hole is situated immediately in front of the house

Inset: HRH The Duke of Cambridge was Commander-in-Chief of the British Army from 1862-1895. He played his first golf shot in Ashdown Forest

land with its furze bushes, garnished with their golden blooms; the straggling geese on their way to the gurgling brook or unhealthy morass; the shaggy pony or donkey tethered in the neighbourhood of some gaily coloured van of the wandering gypsy; the healthy looking but ragged youngsters and the piles of wood faggots and osiers stacked around the mud huts. Ashdown Forest is particularly characteristic and from the Home Green, the eye wanders over a charming and varied extent of undulating country."

The paper went on to describe the first Spring Meeting of the Club. "Early in the morning the visitor looking across the Forest could admire the light and shade of the hills. The canny Scotchmen everywhere and their speech, added to the sight of brown heath and shaggy wood, made one think that one was really in the bonny land. Later on, competitors were seen returning, some bearing traces of how they had left the track and wandered into some of the accommodating bogs which abound on the Forest." In February 1891 the paper reported that: "After an

interregnum of two months, Golf has once more resumed its sway and during the past week or so, the red coat has been seen on what was erstwhile an Arctic expanse, traversed only, on its higher ridges, by the enterprising tobogganer."

Early changes were made to the original 1889 course following completion of the present clubhouse in 1895. In particular, the old first, second, and eighteenth holes were abandoned and replaced by the present layout which allows excellent views from the lounge balcony of the first and last holes.

Royal Ashdown is fortunate today to have a second course, the West, which owes its origins to the Ladies' Section. The Ashdown Forest and Tunbridge Wells Ladies' Golf Club was formed in 1889, less than six months after the formation of the main Club. A contemporary journalist wrote that: "to my mind there are few Clubs in the South so well regulated as the Ashdown Forest LGC. Miss Andrews, Miss Birch, Mrs. Green, Mrs. Lucas and many others insist on golf being played without any slips or deviations."

Miss Birch was Ladies' Captain for the first five years and was the sister of the first Honorary Secretary of the main Club. In October 1891, she had the honour of marking the card of Mrs. Cecil Green who performed one of the earliest ladies' competition holes-in-one at the fourth on the second circuit of the ladies' course which was at that time restricted to nine holes. Mrs. Green had taken an eight at the same hole earlier in the day!

The ladies' course was enlarged to 18 holes in 1932 and became the longest course in the country designed specifically for ladies' golf. The opening was celebrated by an exhibition match between four of Britain's greatest amateur lady golfers, Cecil Leitch, Joyce Wethered, Diana Fishwick and Wanda Morgan. During the Second World War, Ashdown Forest was used for Army training and the ladies' course slipped into disrepair so that by 1945, only three or four holes remained in play. In 1965, the main Club and the new owners of the nearby Ashdown Forest Hotel arranged to restore the old ladies' course to eighteen holes and these joint arrangements

continued until 2003/4 when the Club took full control of the West.

The Anderida Golfing Society is affiliated to the Club and has played over the West Course for many years. The holes on the West have recently been renumbered and the eighteenth hole, criss-crossed twice by a stream, now makes a superb finishing hole. The Cantelupe Club has produced some great golfers, and perhaps the most famous were Abe Mitchell, Alf Padgham and the Seymour Brothers. Mitchell was described by JH Taylor as the finest player never to win an Open. At least ten members of the Mitchell family were fine golfers including Tom, Charlie, Harry, Frank and Arthur. Alf Padgham was PGA Match Play Champion in 1935, won The Open in 1936 and played in three Ryder Cup teams. B Seymour won the PGA Match Play tournament in 1921, and his brother Mark was runner-up in 1931. Another Cantelupe member, Jack Smith, won the Long Driving Competition which took place before the 1922 Open. Forest Row may lay claim to producing more great golfers per head of population than any other village in England.

The Royal Club has also enjoyed some fine golfers. Freddie Tait was one of the earliest members, taking part in the Club's first Spring Meeting in May 1889, finishing second playing off scratch, whilst in November 1890, he shot a remarkable 76 which was well documented by all the national newspapers. Tait won the Amateur Championship in 1896 and 1898 and came third in the Opens of 1896 and 1897. Frank Pennink was English Amateur champion

in 1937 and 1938 and played in the winning 1938 Walker Cup team, and Horace Hutchinson, winner of the Amateur Championship in 1886 and 1887 was Captain of the Club in 1905.

Ashdown has been famously served by its Professionals. Jack Rowe, who was born at Westward Ho!, served for 55 years and was Captain of the PGA in 1922/3. Following his retirement in 1947, Rowe was succeeded by Hector Padgham, who continued in the role for more than 40 years. The Club therefore had only two Professionals in nearly

Main: *View from the elevated first tee taken at 8pm in July and featuring a five-ball group during a play-off in the 2004 Regional Qualifying competition for the Open Championship. The eighteenth green is towards the top left-hand corner and the first green is in front of the white house in the middle right of the picture. The crescent of bracken in the middle of the fairway collects many poorly hit tee shots*

Inset: *Captain of the Club in 1905, Horace Hutchinson was the first Englishman to be Captain of The R&A*

Top: Abe Mitchell was a famous member of the Cantelupe Club. He was described by JH Taylor as the best player never to win an Open

Below: Cecil Leitch facing a tricky lie during the exhibition match celebrating the extension of the ladies' course in May 1932. Club Professional Jack Rowe is standing between Joyce Wethered and Wanda Morgan

a century. Before Jack Rowe's appointment, it is believed that the post was held briefly by Hugh Kirkaldy who won the 1891 Open whilst attached to the Club.

Ashdown has also entertained some famous visitors. HRH The Duke of Cambridge, cousin to Queen Victoria and Commander-in-Chief of the British Army from 1862-1895, visited Forest Row during troop manoeuvres in May 1893 and was persuaded to play his first-ever golf shot. He arrived at the first tee on horseback from his tent pitched on the nearby ladies' course, dressed in full battle regalia including his cocked hat with plumes and ceremonial sword. Fortunately, the shot was a success and the Duke was sufficiently inspired to help the Club achieve its Royal prefix in June 1893.

In October 1897, the Club hosted a professional match for a purse of £28. James Braid and Douglas Rolland, who were first cousins, tied for first place and shared the winning purse of £15. Jack Rowe came third. Interestingly, the local press reported that Braid hit his second shot to the final green out of a bunker, and an entry in the suggestions book dated May 1901 and signed by 20 members pleaded: "...that the sixth and ninth bunkers shall be filled with proper sand (sea) instead of 'concrete' as at present.". Perhaps fortuitously, Royal Ashdown no longer has any bunkers in deference to the Conservators of the Forest. In May 1936, the great Bobby Locke won the Club's inaugural Winkley Smith Open Challenge Bowl. Locke's morning card was particularly rare as he scored four on all eighteen holes.

There are three further highlights in the Club's golfing calendar. Royal Ashdown has played an annual match against the Oxford and Cambridge Golfing Society for more than a century since the inaugural match in 1900, whilst the match against The Moles has been running since 1921. The principal internal competition is the Founders Cup which was presented by Archdeacon Scott in 1924 and is played as a knockout competition over the four days of the Easter weekend. The final is played on Easter Monday and is well supported by members who follow the game around the course.

Ashdown Forest today has many of the same views as described by The Sussex Daily News more than a century ago although the living conditions have vastly improved! Unusually, the first and eighteenth fairways on the Old Course cross each other, although it is rare for golfers on either hole to be inconvenienced. Players need to be aware that the area close behind the first green is out of bounds. The second hole requires a blind tee shot over a steep hill and this can be particularly difficult when played into a low Winter's sun, but the outcome determines whether the green can be reached in two shots.

Care needs to be taken at the third hole to avoid the out of bounds behind the green. This can be a challenge when playing an approach shot in wintry

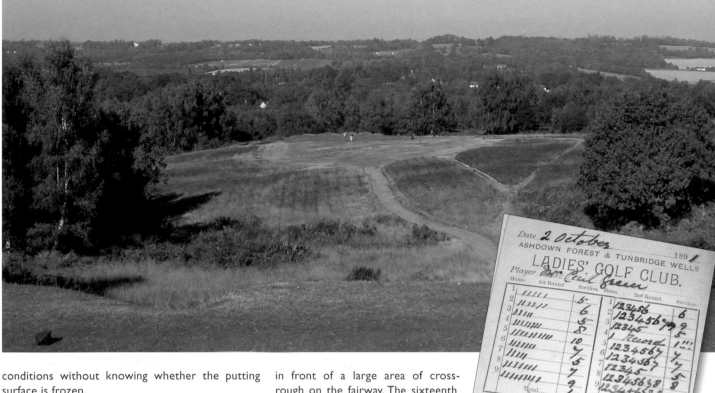

conditions without knowing whether the putting surface is frozen.

The fifth and sixth greens are both protected by a stream and the latter is one of the best holes on the course as danger lurks from the water on three sides of the green. In 1902, a frequent visitor to the Club, Lionel Ridpath endowed the hole with the sum of £5 plus annual interest at 5% to be paid to any member who holed in one during one of the three main annual competitions. The challenge was finally achieved in 1947 by a member who received a reward of £35 for his skill. The Club is still happy to reward members who repeat the feat during key medal rounds.

The par-4 seventh is an uphill dog-leg and is justifiably stroke index one. Attractive views of Coleman's Hatch Church can be seen from the next fairway and even better views can be seen from the tee on the par-3 eleventh which is situated at one of the higher points on the Forest. It is almost a pleasure to have to wait to play! The par-5 twelfth is an excellent hole and, depending upon the wind, a decision has to be made on whether to lay up in front of a large area of cross-rough on the fairway. The sixteenth and seventeenth holes have ruined many a medal card. The former is a long uphill par-4 with heather protecting the front of the green and the seventeenth is a very long downhill par-4 which normally requires an accurate long iron to the green to achieve par.

Bernard Darwin wrote of Ashdown's Old Course that: "...it is not quite like any other of my acquaintance, and I never knew anyone who played on it and was not fond of it." The Club's own Frank Pennink made a telling observation which is still true today, that: "The yardage bears no resemblance to the length the course plays." For many years, Royal Ashdown has been rated as one of the top 100 courses in the UK. The Old course is best known for two-ball and foursomes pairings, although four-balls can be played at certain times with prior arrangement. Societies can now enjoy playing over both the Old and West course in the same day.

Main: Panoramic view from the par-3 eleventh tee. The hole measures 249 yards

Above: Mrs. Cecil Green scored one of the earliest ladies' holes-in-one. The card also shows the tally system used to mark down every shot as it was played

SUTTON COLDFIELD

Above: TA Vaughton's Christmas card for 1916 is optimistically entitled 'Dormy', and shows the old seventeenth green viewed from the Roman Road which crosses the course. The British soldier looks confident whilst the Hun is stuck in the stream (Courtesy of Sutton Coldfield Golf Club)

Right: View of players on the tee at the short par-3 second hole, Spinney, taken from behind the green. The posts and wire keep grazing animals off the putting surface

Golf had been played in Sutton Park to the north of Birmingham for several years before the Club was founded. In 1882, Robert Ward was given permission to play by the Sutton Corporation on payment of an annual fee of a pound, and the first course was laid out near the Town Gate.

The area was once part of a Royal hunting ground and the park was given to the people of Sutton Coldfield during the 16th Century by Henry VIII following persuasion by Bishop Vesey. Commoners have animal grazing rights and the Club erects posts and inter-connecting wires around every green to protect the putting surfaces.

In 1889, Ernest Peyton founded the Club by circular letter, noting that: "... there is nothing to show non-players that the game is being played in earnest and ...until some trouble is taken by golfers themselves to provide the necessary putting greens etc, little sympathy will be shown by other frequenters of the

Park with their game." The Rev. WCR Bedford was appointed first Captain and two more men of the Church were members of the inaugural Committee. The course near Town Gate was soon abandoned in favour of a layout forming part of today's course located on the other side of the park and closer to Streetly Station. The existing clubhouse was built in the late 1890s on private land just outside the park and across a small rutted track, and members watched the golf from a second-floor balcony. The track has grown into a busy road, tall trees now screen the course from view and the balcony has been closed for safety reasons so that the clubhouse seems rather disconnected from the course.

Early golfers were unpopular with other users of the Park and there were calls for 'municipalisation'. In January 1908, The Birmingham Daily Post conjectured why: "...a certain number of gentlemen have power to play over Sutton links because they are in a position to pay a large subscription yearly?" However, local opinion was swayed by WH Hatton who responded that: "as a ratepayer....I object to the municipalisation of the golf links. I am not a golfer but see no harm in golf being played in the park so long as it is played at the expense of members...and under the restrictions of the Corporation. On the contrary, I think it has attracted a class of residents who add to the prosperity of the town. I do, however, object to paying rates for other people's golf." The threats had unnerved a number of golfers who arranged for Harry Vardon to construct the picturesque course at nearby Little Aston. The two clubs started as rivals but many golfers became members of both.

After the First War, Dr. Alister MacKenzie suggested major changes to the course and told the Committee: "The land on which the present course is situated is almost the best heathland I know for golf. It is a wide open moor similar to Walton Heath but in some respects superior, that is more wooded and has much better sand." He continued: "...if the suggested alterations are done ... there will not be a single weak hole on the course, and there is no reason why it should not compare favourably with the best inland course in Britain, and be vastly superior to many seaside ones." The Committee's heads were turned by such enthusiasm from the well-known architect and only six of the pre-war holes remained after MacKenzie had completed the project. Henry Cotton played in a charity match during the Second War and commented that the course was: "in the same category as Sunningdale - similar turf with plenty of heather and trees." The peaty nature of the soil has led to some dramatic effects from Summer fires which rage on the neighbouring heaths. In 1976, the fires spread beneath the surface of a number of fairways creating holes which were several feet deep.

Although the course is laid out over common land, the Club has hosted a number of important events including the Midland Open and the Second City Tournament with fields including Mark James, Sandy Lyle and Nick Faldo. Entrants for the 1950 Penfold Mixed Foursomes included five Open Champions; Henry Cotton, Alf Padgham, Fred Daly, Max Faulkner and the leading lady, Jessie Valentine. More recently Vijay Singh, Sam Torrance and Laura Davies were amongst the players in a pro-am to celebrate the Club's centenary in 1989. The Club's best known golfers were John Morgan, who played in three successive Walker Cup teams in the 1950s, and John Beharrel, who won the British Open Amateur Championship in 1957 whilst still a junior member of the Club.

Sutton Coldfield provides a good combination of woodland and heathland golf. Mature oaks provide tight lines on holes nearer the clubhouse, whilst in mid-round the fairways are more open but fringed with thick gorse and heather. Unusually, the fifth to seventh holes are three consecutive par-5s. The back nine is tighter than the front and includes the dog-leg eleventh which is one of the best holes in the Midlands, and the par-4 twelfth which features a stream in front of the green. MacKenzie would be pleased that his changes have stood the test of time.

Main: *Second shot to the green at the long par-4 third hole. The marker on the right shows the line from the tee*

Above: *Thomas Albert Vaughton was Club Captain during the First World War. He was a good artist and his pen and ink drawing entitled 'The Griefs of a Green's Committee' shows that grazing animals have always been a part of the golfing scene at Sutton Coldfield (Courtesy of Sutton Coldfield Golf Club)*

BERKHAMSTED

TOP PLAYERS WIN THE TROPHY

Below: Evening sunshine highlighting the trees lining the fairways

Visitors playing along Berkhamsted's attractive tree-lined fairways will be surprised to learn that the founders laid out the skeleton of the current course over open common land which was heavily grazed by sheep and rabbits preventing young saplings from taking root.

The Club was founded by George Gowring who had recently moved from Eastbourne College to become headmaster of the new Berkhamsted Junior School. Gowring had seen the new course built over common land at Eastbourne giving him the experience to repeat the formula near his new home in the company of a few teaching colleagues including the Rev. TC Fry and novelist Graham Greene's father, CH Greene who were successive headmasters of the long-established Berkhamsted Senior School.

The founders received permission from Lord Brownlow to cut back gorse on the common in order to build a rough 9-hole course. As local interest grew, they also leased the sloping farmland known as Farmer Dwight's Fields lying between the common and the station in the valley below. However, these field holes were soon abandoned and development of the course was concentrated on the higher common land despite the extra journey which that entailed. Willie Park Junior advised on the layout on the common during the 1890s and the Club moved the original clubhouse up to the common in 1896. Gowring, who by then was Honorary Secretary, had paid for the building out of his own pocket and he lent a further sum to the Club to fund the move, receiving title to the building as security.

In 1904, the Committee encouraged members to register a unique ball mark for a fee of one shilling per year. The Professional had a hand-operated press in his shop to enable members to stamp balls with their identification, and when a ball was found and returned to the Professional he then offered the original owner a chance to buy it back for 4d before it was placed in the second-hand ball box which was open for general purchase. The Professional paid finders either 2d or 3d according to the quality of the ball, and all members and caddies were required to return all finds. Clearly some found balls were still being re-sold outside these arrangements, and the 1914 Club Rules appealed to members that: "it will greatly strengthen the hands of the Committee if members will kindly inspect the list of found balls, which will be posted weekly on the notice board, and will redeem any belonging to them as early as possible."

Harry Colt provided occasional advice on the course layout from 1909 onwards and CJ Gilbert, who was in charge of the Green Committee, invited the renowned Greenkeeper Peter Lees from Royal Mid-Surrey to visit the Club and coach Ernest Roberts and his greenstaff on the art of laying turf. After the war, James Braid advised on further changes and the stretch between the fourth and seventh holes bear his hallmark.

JH Taylor, Harry Vardon, Ted Ray, James Braid, Abe Mitchell and Henry Cotton (who was Professional at the neighbouring Ashridge Club), all played exhibition matches at Berkhamsted and Cecil Leitch was a regular visitor. In her diary for April 1921, she noted a score of 72, against a scratch of 74 and recalled that her Sunday green fee was 2/6d with a further 9d for a first-class caddie. The Prince of Wales was a regular visitor in the 1920s and 1930s and was briefly Club Patron following his coronation as Edward VIII in 1936. However, King George VI did not continue the royal patronage following Edward's abdication. The Queen Mother, Lady Elizabeth Bowes-Lyon, also played regularly at Berkhamsted as a young woman and she later recalled the help and advice which she had received from Arthur Mayling who had established the Club's Artisans' Section.

Another artisan, Harold Rance, won the second National Artisans' Championship at nearby Burnham Beeches in 1925, and his skills as a scratch golfer led the Club, on more than one occasion, to increase the handicap of every other member by one shot rather than reducing Rance which might have hampered his chances elsewhere! By 1956, Rance had won 50 top trophies at the Club and the early-Spring Berkhamsted Trophy was founded in his honour and received immediate backing from The R&A as the first event on the amateur calendar, giving the Walker Cup selectors an early guide to form. Well-known winners have included Peter Townsend, Sandy Lyle, Peter McEvoy, Gary Wolstenholme and Luke Donald.

Three roads and a number of bridle paths and old sheep tracks cross the course but the overall atmosphere is very peaceful and deer can often be seen scuttling for cover. There are no sand bunkers but trees, gorse, bracken, grassy undulations and the occasional pond all protect against low scoring, and good drainage enables the course to be played in all seasons. The par-4 ninth hole is particularly memorable, requiring a drive towards the clubhouse over a busy but well protected road lying deep in a wooded valley below the tee.

Top: Early members pictured outside the original clubhouse which was then situated next to Berkhamsted Castle, nearer the town. From l-r: Sir James Thursfield, RH Ling, GK Hext, Mrs. T Stafford-the first Captain of the Ladies' Section, founder GH Gowring, E Mawley and CH Greene who became headmaster of Berkhamsted School in 1910 and was the father of the famous novelist, Graham Greene

Above: Harold Rance was responsible for setting up the annual open Berkhamsted Trophy for leading amateurs (Courtesy Berkhamsted Golf Club)

WOKING

DARWIN'S STAR OF SAND AND HEATHER

Woking is the oldest of the Surrey heathland courses and lies in a famous area of golfing country to the west of London. The land was not conducive for farming; indeed, in 1724, Defoe described the area as: "a vast tract of land which is not only poor, but even sterile - much of it sandy desert and one may frequently be put in mind here of Arabia Deserta." From these unpromising beginnings, Woking has developed into one of the most prosperous districts in the country.

Bernard Darwin was a Club member for more than 60 years and he referred to the course at his spiritual golfing home as: "the star of sand and heather."

A new railway between Southampton and London opened in 1838 and a small station was built at Woking Common on the empty heathland. However, the area remained a backwater until the 1850s when London ran out of burial space! Cremation was illegal and the Burials Act banned virtually all burials in the City. Following an

Act of Parliament, a group of businessmen established the London Necropolis and National Mausoleum Company and purchased almost 2,300 acres of common land near Woking for a huge national cemetery. Bodies were brought in by barge on the nearby Basingstoke Canal, and a train known colloquially as the Stiffs' Express left daily at 11.35 from Waterloo in London to Woking carrying bodies and family mourners.

The Necropolis Company overestimated the amount of land required for burials and in 1892 it readily accepted the request from a group of 100 London-based barristers from the Inner and Middle Temples to lease enough land to start a golf Club. The ubiquitous Tom Dunn laid out the course and the Club soon widened its membership to include other well-connected golfers. Early members included Prime Minister AJ Balfour who was Captain in 1904/05, national amateur golfing hero Freddie Tait whilst he was stationed at nearby Aldershot Barracks, 1925 Amateur Champion, Robert Harris, and 1896 Ladies' British Open Champion, Amy Pascoe who helped the Ladies' Club to achieve an early pre-eminence in regional competitions.

Woking was fortunate in the choice of two early Captains, Stuart Paton, whom Darwin christened 'The Mussolini of Woking' for his ability to get things done, and John Laing Low who became a well-known golf writer and major contributor to The R&A's Rules of Golf Committee. Paton and Low improved Dunn's somewhat simple layout. Redundant bunkers were removed and replaced by grassy hollows, undulations and subtle slopes were built into Dunn's flat, square greens, and tees were repositioned. The overall effect worked so well that in 1934 the Scot, Guy Campbell, the architect of the great West Sussex course at Pulborough, wrote favourably: "Woking possesses more good strategic holes than any other inland course."

The third hole has a beautifully positioned bunker just short and to the right of a sloping green and Paton added intrigue to the short par-4 fourth hole which is played alongside the railway line by placing a bunker in the middle of the fairway. Some commentators have considered the fourth to be the first strategic hole in English golf and Campbell wrote, with perhaps a touch of national chauvinism: "I never cease admiring the genius which created these holes, especially when one remembers that they were made long before the southern golfer had been educated up to this kind of thing."

Woking has important connections with two of the country's leading golfing societies, The Moles and The Seniors. The Moles Golfing Society was formed in 1911 by a group of young golfers from Aldeburgh, including Vic Longstaffe and Guy Howard, and it rapidly gathered a membership of formidable quality. In 1923, Woking hosted a match between The Moles and the visiting US Walker Cup team in which Club member Robert Harris defeated Jess Sweetser, who became one of the few golfers to win both the US and British Amateur championships. The Moles lost the match by 6½ to 8½ but gained revenge in 1926 when they overcame the full US Walker Cup team by 6–3, including a clean sweep in the morning foursomes against opposition including Bobby Jones, Francis Ouimet and Jesse Sweetser. The Americans recovered from the setback and won the Walker Cup at St Andrews a fortnight later by 6½ to 5½. Jones returned to top form with a huge 12&11 victory over Cyril Tolley, although Woking members Harris and Roger Wethered did score points for the home team.

The British Senior Golfers' Society was founded in 1926 by Colonel Francis Popham, Arthur Croome and JA (Jack) Milne and is open by invitation to golfers aged 55 and over. Horace L Hotchkiss had formed the American equivalent some 20 years earlier and similar societies also exist in Canada and Australia. Each society aims to promote 'friendly competition among senior players' and the new British club set out

to foster closer international relations with the other Seniors using a motto from the Aeneid which loosely translates to: "...they can because they think they can." The British Seniors began to use Woking as their home course in 1949, having moved from Stoke Poges, and the clubhouse displays many trophies demonstrating the warm and friendly links which have grown between the Club and the Society. The Societal colours of maroon and yellow are often seen in the Club bar as well as at more than 100 clubs around the country where the Seniors play annual matches. Several Woking members have captained the Seniors including Edward Blackwell, Bernard Darwin, Robert Harris and Jock Geils whilst Arthur Balfour was their first President.

Bernard Darwin, who was the grandson of the explorer Charles Darwin, features in the history of many English clubs. He joined Woking in 1897 having graduated from Cambridge with a law degree, and went on to pass his final law exams whilst working for a firm in the Temple

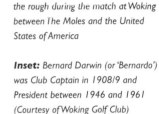

Main: Bobby Jones playing out of the rough during the match at Woking between The Moles and the United States of America

Inset: Bernard Darwin (or 'Bernardo') was Club Captain in 1908/9 and President between 1946 and 1961 (Courtesy of Woking Golf Club)

Main: View of the clubhouse taken from behind the pond at the eighteenth green. The grey heron just visible beneath the right hand bunker is a decoy positioned to dissuade real birds from eating the carp in the pond

Above: Stuart Paton, whom Bernard Darwin nicknamed 'The Mussolini of Woking', was Captain in 1902-1903 and President from 1937-1946 (Courtesy of Woking Golf Club)

Inset: John Laing Low was Captain in 1901-1902 and was a major contributor to the affairs of The R & A (Courtesy of Woking Golf Club)

before being called to the Bar in 1903. In 1907, he changed careers when he succeeded Arthur Croome as golf columnist for the Evening Standard before moving on to full-time employment with The Times, where he was encouraged by Lord Northcliffe, whilst also writing golfing articles for Country Life. Darwin was an excellent golfer although his appearance in the first British Walker Cup team to play in the United States was unexpected. He was in America to cover the event as a reporter for The Times when his Woking colleague, Robert Harris, was suddenly taken ill. Fate nearly withdrew Darwin's opportunity to play when he was struck in the chest by a ball whilst out on the practice range, but he recovered and went on to win his singles match although the team lost 8-4. Darwin's name lives on at the Club through the Bernard Darwin Trophy which is contested annually at Woking by senior golfers from the schools which played in the inaugural Halford Hewitt competition at Deal in 1925. The trophy itself is an old silver claret jug dating back to 1863 and was first played for in Scotland as the Gullane Prize. Darwin once reflected that Woking was: "...the best and pleasantest place to play golf that I have ever known."

The Club bears testimony to the effects of climate change on the environment. In earlier, colder Winters the pond to the left of the sixteenth green was used as a curling rink. The large round curling stones are still displayed in the clubhouse, and in 1903, the Club played a curling match against Wimbledon Curling Club which the home team won by 24-18. The game was clearly popular because a concrete rink was then built nearer to the clubhouse in the woods to the left of the first fairway, and this survived until the Second World War when it was converted into a rifle range. Like many southern heathland courses, the fairways at Woking have become enclosed by trees and the Club has carried out a major woodland clearance programme aimed at maintaining the heathland heritage of this exceptional course.

WOODBRIDGE

A CONVERT TO THE GAME

The formation of Woodbridge Golf Club was entirely due to Major Howey who lived at The Grange in the nearby village of Melton. Howey was a shooting enthusiast who also excelled at fishing and other country pursuits, and a colleague recalled that the Major had never played golf and had held the game in great contempt until being introduced to golf during a holiday in the South of France. On returning to England, the Major laid out a 6-hole course on parkland in front of his house, and then recognising the limitations of his private links he paid for the Scottish Professional from North Berwick, Davie Grant, to visit Suffolk and identify local land for a formal course. Grant had only to cross the bridge over the nearby River Deben before settling on the present heathland site which was being used as a working farm and he was heard to proclaim: "Yee've as gude turf for gowf here as yee'l find in all Scotland."

The other founders tried to agree a fair rent with the tenant farmer, but negotiations became protracted until the Major seized the initiative and agreed a three-year rental for shooting over the farmland with an agreement that golf could also be played without further payment. The golfers settled for this slightly precarious arrangement and the first 9-hole course was opened using the Cherry Tree Inn, next to today's first green, as the first clubhouse. The course was played in the reverse direction to the modern round. Within a year the golfers had second thoughts about stray bullets and the Club employed Thomson, the Felixstowe Professional, to rearrange and extend the course to eighteen holes whilst avoiding the rifle range. A new clubhouse, designed like a cricket pavilion, was

built next to today's seventeenth green on elevated land above a large pit at the fork of the road out of Melton.

In the early 1900s, the local press carried frequent correspondence concerning the conflicting interests of the patriotic Volunteers and the generally unpatriotic and grasping golfers. The matter was finally resolved in 1909 when the Honorary Secretary claimed that he had nearly been shot and the landlord, the Marquis of Bristol, agreed to close the range and move the Volunteers to a new site.

In 1908, the members enjoyed two new holes. 'Fatty' Fryer was a magnificent cricketer who took up golf relatively late but soon became a scratch golfer

Main: *Golfers waiting to tee off at the par-3 fifteenth hole known as the Punchbowl*

Above: *Major Howey was the inspiration behind the Club although he originally had contempt for the game. He was the first President and served until 1905*

Main: The green at the downhill par-3 ninth hole, known as Magazine, is well protected by bunkers

Above: A dramatic bridge was erected in 1910 over the Melton to Bawdsey road to allow golfers to walk from the old eighteenth (now seventeenth) tee to the green. The shot across the road was later abandoned for safety reasons

as well as the 'Greenmaster' at Woodbridge. He redesigned the seventeenth and eighteenth holes so that they required shots across the Melton to Bawdsey road and Bernard Darwin wrote of the redesigned seventeenth that: "...in the teeth of a strong wind, it is truly tremendous ...... unlike any other hole in golf. We have to carry a vast chasm, along which innocent wayfarers pass on their lawful business so that there is also, incidentally, the chance of an inquest at the end of it." Unfortunately, the increase in motor traffic required the Club to call in James Braid to redesign these two holes resulting in the current layout and the demise of the attractive footbridge built to carry golfers high above the road to the eighteenth (now seventeenth) green in front of the old clubhouse.

The old building was popular and survived until 1969 when today's clubhouse was constructed in a more convenient position for vehicle access. A Golf Illustrated article in 1927 described how a visitor might climb the zig-zagging rustic stairway to the old clubhouse and then pinch himself that he was not dreaming: "The whole of the countryside seems suddenly to have been transformed. Five minutes ago he was motoring through flat pastoral Suffolk and now, as at the touch of a magic wand, all is changed. Before his enchanted eyes roll heathery hills and dales worthy of Scotland or Yorkshire or Surrey." Bernard Darwin also wrote favourably about Woodbridge including it in the same company as the great inland courses at Walton Heath, Woodhall Spa and Ganton.

Over the subsequent decades, woodland has grown to obscure some of the views but the course is still a challenge. Gorse and heather line many of the fairways and a driver is not always advisable. The second hole is one of the most picturesque with a pond protecting the green, and a higher handicap member writing in the Club's centenary book suggested, tongue-in-cheek, that many players cut out this hole and go straight to the third. The last three holes all require two good shots to find the green. The sixteenth seems particularly long whilst the seventeenth is played at an angle and the green is situated at the top of a hill above a fairway gully. In the words of the same member: "...the layout of this hole was totally misconceived. Its only virtue is that it brings the nineteenth one hole nearer!"

ROYAL WORLINGTON & NEWMARKET

THE SACRED NINE

Royal Worlington has been described as the best 9-hole course in the world and a succession of famous and influential Cambridge University golfers, several of whom became prolific writers, has assured the Club of an important place in golfing history. Harry Colt, Bernard Darwin, Henry Longhurst, Gerald Micklem, Leonard Crawley, Halford Hewitt, Laddie Lucas, Dr. David Marsh, Patric Dickinson, Donald Steel and Ted Dexter all played at Worlington during their heyday. The superior quality of the course with its fast, true greens and well-draining fairways is due to a thin band of sand which also helps to explain why the address for this inland course is in Golf Links Road.

Formation of the Club was led by Capt. Baird of Exning Hall and Old Etonian Harry McCalmont who arranged for Tom Dunn from Tooting Bec to lay out the first course over land leased from another co-founder, William Gardner. Writing in the Club's Centenary book, 'The Sacred Nine', a phrase coined by Bernard Darwin, John Gillum notes that the original design was for eighteen holes but mystery surrounds the location of the lost nine. A reference in 1894 suggests that they may have been spun off into a short ladies' course but no trace remains to confirm the idea. An early match featuring Willie Park Junior, Douglas Rolland, Jack White and Hugh Kirkaldy helped to put Worlington on the golfing map, and White succeeded Tom Hood as the Club's Professional and Greenkeeper shortly afterwards, staying for two years before moving on to Mitcham. Much of the course remains unchanged although Harry Colt made some modifications including improvements to the fourth, eighth and ninth holes.

Left: *Racing enthusiast Harry McCalmont was co-founder of the Club and owned the famous horse, Isinglass*

The Prince of Wales became President and the Club became Royal in 1895. It is likely that the Prince did not play at the Club but realised that its proximity to the nearby racing community at Newmarket would be useful. Certainly, Harry McCalmont was well connected in racing circles as his most famous horse, Isinglass, won £57,455 over four years, the largest amount at the time to be won by one horse on English turf. Gardner attempted to sell the Club at an auction in 1901 as: 'Lot No.5, The Royal Worlington and Newmarket Golf Links', but fortunately the asking reserve was not reached and the members organised themselves and bought the land for £2,677. The connection with Cambridge University commenced the same year when the students began to use the course to practise and play their home

matches, travelling from Cambridge to the station at Mildenhall on the Great Eastern Railway. A Golf Links Halt platform was eventually built near to the course in 1922, but for the previous 20 years the students had improvised by throwing their clubs out of the train window as it passed by the course in order to lighten their load on the walk back to the links from Mildenhall Station. The railway was finally closed to passengers in 1962.

The Club's annals are full of stories about Cambridge golfers, many of whom went on to become members of Worlington itself. The students gave the Club an early indication of the quality to come in 1896 when their five-man team won the inaugural match against the Club by 32 holes to nil with Bernard Darwin captaining the students. He won all of his three matches for Cambridge in the university matches against Oxford in 1895-7, and was playing Captain of Britain's Walker Cup team in 1922 before becoming a Life Member of the Club in 1949. Leonard Crawley gained Blues at cricket and real tennis as well as golf and became a member of the Club in 1949, whilst Gerald Micklem took part in four Walker Cup competitions and was non-playing Captain in a further two matches. Other

successful Club members included the brothers Tom and John Blackwell who had the honour of captaining both the Club and The R&A, and Eric Martin Smith who startled the members, and presumably himself, by winning the Amateur Championship at Westward Ho! in 1931, succeeding Bobby Jones as champion. He became the MP for Grantham but died in his early 40s.

Sir Alexander Fleming was a member in the 1920s and used to play in a white jacket although history does not recall whether this was actually his lab coat!

Exotic cars and boisterous drinking were part of Cambridge student life during the inter-war years and two Club members, James Herbert 'Boxer' Cannon and John Morrison invented a drink, Pink Jug, which has become part of Worlington folklore and now features as the alternative Club emblem (to the Prince of Wales' feathers!). Taking a Victorian water jug of the correct shape, the mixture requires a bottle of champagne and tots of Benedictine, brandy and Pimm's No.1, together with a small amount of lemon and ice. The cosy clubhouse still echoes with the same fun and spirit today even if the measures are slightly more temperate! The Club is traditional but informal and visitors are made to feel welcome.

CROWBOROUGH BEACON

Crowborough is an exhilarating, natural course set high in the Sussex Weald in wild open countryside and enjoying far-reaching views across to the South Downs. The layout has changed since the early days and stands of trees have grown over part of the common, but it is still possible to envisage the founding members playing over the same rough heathland strewn with heather and gorse.

Crowborough was just a small village in the early 1890s and several of the founders, including the main instigator, George Langridge, a London-based merchant, lived outside the area. However, they were confident that the success of the nearby spa town of Tunbridge Wells and the proximity of a railway connection with London would enable Crowborough to develop as an inland resort. Lord Cantelupe, who later became the 8th Earl De La Warr, allowed golf to be played over land in the Manor of Alchornes, and Lady Cantelupe played the first tee shot on the new 9-hole course in October 1895 in pouring rain from under an umbrella held by her husband! After lunch, a more serious game was played between the reigning Open Champion JH Taylor and Jack Rowe, Professional at the recently established Royal Ashdown club on the other side of the forest. This resulted in a narrow victory for Taylor.

Crowborough immediately attracted a rising star to assist the Club's first Professional, A Jackson, who had laid out the initial course. Horace Rawlins learnt his trade as a player and clubmaker from Jackson, and in 1895, he travelled

to Newport, Rhode Island in New York, as a 20-year-old and became the first winner of the US Open Championship. Rawlins defeated a small field including Willie Dunn over 36 holes on the 9-hole course at Newport and won $150 out of the total prize fund of $335. On returning to England he played a 36-hole exhibition match against James Braid at Crowborough; four rounds of the new course. In appalling wet weather, Braid won the match by 5&3.

Within three years the course had grown to eighteen holes and Crowborough town was also expanding rapidly, boasting five hotels and many new villas, assisted no doubt by the fame of the Club and the good railway line to London. Unfortunately,

Main: Watery evening winter sunshine reflecting off the windows of the clubhouse viewed from the final fairway

today's journey time is still the same as the Victorians enjoyed 100 years ago! Club Vice-President, Lord Henry Nevill, negotiated subsidised rates for return train fares to London and Club members could hire a horse-drawn wagon to journey from the station to the course at a cost of two shillings. The Club issued many weekly and monthly green fee tickets confirming the early importance of the thriving town as an exclusive, inland, leisure and recuperation resort.

In 1907, the Club improved its rights to the course by purchasing the Manorial Rights of the Alchornes Manor from Earl De La Warr for £750, and further prestige followed in 1910 when world-famous novelist Sir Arthur Conan Doyle was appointed Captain, with his wife becoming Captain of the Ladies' Section the following year. Conan Doyle lived in Windlesham Manor, situated close to the course, and he could see the clubhouse from his study. It seems likely that many of the foggy scenes experienced in his books by Holmes and Watson on Dartmoor were inspired by the mists which sometimes envelop the course. Conan Doyle's son was killed in action during the First World War and the writer became interested in spiritualism. A local story relates that he arranged to meet his dead son on the fourth green exactly a year after he was killed. During 1910, green fees increased by 20% as additional visitors were attracted by his reputation and external income exceeded Club subscriptions despite a thriving membership of more than 500 people.

The Macey family features prominently in the Club's history and Macey Senior started as an assistant in 1906, before serving as the main Professional between 1912 and 1941. He was succeeded by his son, Charlie, who was celebrated

as an enthusiastic eccentric as well as a good golfer. He once completed the course in 314 strokes playing with a hollow plastic practice ball, and in 1944 he completed twelve rounds for charity in fifteen hours taking 948 shots at an average of only 4.4 shots per hole! On another occasion, he and a colleague played a challenge match of ball versus arrow over a 50-mile stretch of Hadrian's Wall against a team of archers, whilst a newspaper cutting from Perth, Western Australia reported that he had scored a hole-in-one at eight different holes at Crowborough.

The course is not long but fairways are quite narrow, the heathery rough is unforgiving, and several holes set a tricky challenge. Stroke index one comes early in the round at the long par-4 second hole which is played as a right-hand dog-leg with a pit short and to the right of the green. The par-3 sixth hole requires a carry of 160 yards over a deep pit to a small green, and it is easy to get blocked out from the green at the par-4 eleventh

hole by fir trees which stretch from the left-hand rough towards the middle of the fairway. The closing hole is all uphill and requires two full wood shots to the green situated in front of the large clubhouse. A recent visitor described the course accurately as a heathland masterpiece!

Above: The last rays of the day pick out players on the green

Inset: Ladies playing in front of the original clubhouse which was replaced in 1907

RUSHMERE

FIRST HOME OF IPSWICH GOLF CLUB

Above: *Founder James Edward Ransome was elected as first Chairman and Captain in 1895*

Inset: *Looking back from the green to the elevated tee at the par-3 fourteenth 'Pond' hole.*

Golf has been played on Rushmere Common near Ipswich for more than a century thanks to the early efforts of a few founders including the lawn mower magnate, James Ransome, and support from the club at nearby Felixstowe. However, the story nearly had an early conclusion. Dissatisfaction with public access over the course had been simmering and the matter was raised formally at Ipswich Golf Club's 1924 AGM. In October 1927, the Club moved from the crowded common to a prestigious new course at Purdis Heath designed by Hawtree & Taylor and built on private land just a short distance from Rushmere. The original clubhouse was sold to a Captain Forshaw, and Ipswich Town Council was offered the remaining period of the lease over the links for use as a municipal course. However, public funds were not available and it seemed unlikely that

the remaining golfers from the Artisans and the Rushmere & District Village Golf Club would be able to survive the departure of the main Club.

Despite occasional problems the villagers were generally in favour of golf on the common as it provided local employment and also helped protect the heath from less desirable activities including the dumping of waste. Employment of caddies was carefully regulated and in 1903 members and visitors were reminded to use official caddies and warned that: "Members or visitors employing one without a badge may render themselves liable to a summons before the magistrates and to a fine not exceeding £5 under the provisions of the Education Acts."

In 1921, the Secretary had to defend the Club which had employed an Ipswich man who was thought not to be sufficiently local. "This makes no difference to any Rushmere men at all. The man in question is a partially-disabled ex-service man who was put on in order that the Club might do a little to help find work for ex-service men by request of the Minister of Labour. If we got rid of this man we should not employ another in his place because we really do not want the extra labour."

In June 1901, The East Anglian Times gave a further insight of the interaction between golf and other life on the common. It reported on the Club's formal 'Smoking Concert' noting: "On Saturday.... there were sounds of revelry by night on Rushmere Heath, a place which at the dark hours is mostly given up to lovers and other seekers after natural history...."

Concern amongst the locals to see golf continue on the heath led to the formation of the Rushmere Golf Club which was paid £70 by Ipswich Golf Club to help it take up the old lease obligations over the common. Shortly afterwards, the new Club purchased the buildings of an old junior school standing next to the heath which became the new and current clubhouse. Golfers continued to suffer occasional problems from the public and in a well-documented story shortly after the War, a walker on the heath during a snow storm was startled by a frogman emerging from the pond at the fourteenth hole fully equipped with oxygen tank, flippers and goggles. The diver, who was a member, recovered more than a dozen flagsticks and as many green tee boxes, most of which had been thrown into the pond by boisterous spectators on their way to the weekly speedway races at the nearby Foxhall Stadium.

The Club has built close ties with Ipswich Town Football Club and Sir Alf Ramsay, who managed Ipswich between 1955 and 1963 before leading England to success in the 1966 World Cup, was a regular golfer at the Club. He is remembered as a quiet man who never drove a car and was happy to chat with members but not about football.

The course is built over quick-draining sandy heathland with large stands of gorse, old oak trees and patches of heather. The problem of public access has been improved on three of the newer holes on the front nine which have been built on seventeen acres of private land. The first half contains two challenging right dog-legged par-4s at the first and fifth, whilst the closing three holes are long and provide a difficult end to the round following three shorter holes, including the well-loved Pond at the fourteenth.

Above: The seventeenth green at the Punch Bowl is positioned at the bottom of a slope requiring a blind approach shot

Below: Early golfers on the original fourth green. Today's sixteenth is called Windmill but the building has disappeared

HANKLEY COMMON

JAMES BRAID EXTENSION - 1921

Below: View from the green back down the dog-legged fairway at the par-5 sixth hole, showing the typical lush fairways, heather and semi-rough together with pockets of fir trees

The founders of Hankley Common Golf Club in 1896 would find it hard to believe how well their original 9-hole layout has been transformed into one of the best inland courses in England even though seven of the original holes are still in use today.

The Scots-born Vicar of nearby Churt, Augustus William Watson, realised that the barren gorse and heather-strewn wasteland under Yagden Hill could be transformed into a rough links and he persuaded the local landowner and Lord of the Manor of Pierrepoint, Richard Henry Combe, to allow the use of his land at no cost to the golfers. In return, Combe was elected as the Club's first President although he had never played the game.

The initial layout in 1897 incorporated fairways and greens of mown heather and must have been treacherous. The first clubhouse was in the Duke of Cambridge, the public house situated near today's entrance to the course, and golfers would have seen an uninterrupted view of heathland.

Dr. (later Sir) Arthur Conan Doyle was one of Hankley's founding members and in 1898 he wrote 'The Ballad of the Hankley Fox', telling the story of a black-faced fox which always seemed to appear just as troops were about to arrest highwaymen who used to prey on the prosperous traffic passing along the Portsmouth Road. The Hankley Fox has been the Club's emblem for many years.

During the First World War, the land was used as a military training ground and, in 1915, King George V arrived on horseback to review the troops. Seven soldiers were billeted in the clubhouse refreshment room and were looked after by the Club's Professional, Charles Clare. One of the men, George Novell, later became the Club's first Greenkeeper.

James Braid charged a bargain fee of 5 guineas in 1921 to advise the Club on extending to eighteen holes, but the resulting full course still had weaknesses, especially the existence of six 'bogey 3s' including the old seventeenth and eighteenth holes. Harry Colt was called in during the early 1930s to advise on lengthening the course and his recommendations produced today's tenth, eleventh and twelfth holes.

The Club offered honorary membership to Canadian servicemen during the Second World War, but in one tragic case, a soldier deserted and set up shelter with his girlfriend who was then murdered. The serviceman was sentenced to death at Kingston Assizes in 1943. In another incident during the war, the Club's Greenkeeper, Charles Ranger, arrested a Luftwaffe pilot at gunpoint

in the caddie shed. The pilot had escaped detection for three days since being shot down over Haslemere.

In a reminder of the war, the forest to the left of the eleventh tee contains the remains of a solid wall which was used for military training by tank and gun crews and was built as a replica of the ramparts constructed by the Germans in Normandy. The surrounding area is still used by the MOD and signs on the edge of the course proclaim: "Out of Bounds to Troops" which is a neat reversal of the usual notices connecting golfers with out of bounds.

Seven of Hankley's sixteen founding members were women, and ladies have played an important role in the development of the Club. Elizabeth Fisher-Price moved to Hankley from the neighbouring club at Farnham and became Ladies' British Open Amateur champion when the competition was held at Ascot in 1949. She represented Britain in the Curtis Cup on six occasions between 1950 and 1960 and was part of the winning teams at Muirfield in 1952 and Prince's in 1956.

Fisher-Price's consistency was evidenced by a seven year unbeaten run as Surrey champion between 1954 and 1960, and she gave her name to the annual Elizabeth Price Scratch Open Foursomes competition which is held at Hankley Common and forms an important part of the golfing calendar in Surrey.

The great South African golfer and four-times Open winner, Bobby Locke, had a close association with Hankley Common. He was based in Farnham whilst playing on the professional tour and was made an Honorary Life Member of the Club. He was happy to play with members of all standards and often invited anyone who was looking for a game to join him. Elderly members recall that it was quite common to see as many as eight people all playing down the same fairway with Locke who achieved a course record of 63 in June 1961.

The course is not long, measuring a little less than 6,500 yards off the white tees, but this has not prevented Hankley Common from appearing frequently in the country's Top 100 lists. Several greens, including the fourth, fourteenth and seventeenth are small. The par-3 seventh requires an accurate tee shot across a valley to a two-tiered green protected by bunkers on either

side, and the par-4 eighteenth is an excellent finishing hole as the green is protected by a deep grassy hollow which makes it very difficult to hit with a fairway wood or long iron. Carries to several fairways off the new, mauve 'tiger' tees, particularly at the tenth hole, look intimidating.

In addition to its golfing attractions, the Club also plays an important role in wildlife conservation. The course lies within a Site of Special Scientific Interest and the Club owns additional land adjacent to the course meaning that the Course Manager has a dual role to prepare a first-class course whilst preserving and enhancing the surrounding habitat for wildlife. Rare birds visible from the course include Dartford warbler, woodlark and nightjar, and all six of the country's reptiles, including the sand lizard and smooth snake, are found locally.

The Scots pines dotting the course today are not indigenous so members and conservationists can be mollified when encroaching trees have to be felled to safeguard and improve playing conditions.

The open heathland views and the excellent fairway irrigation system mean that the course is a pleasure to play in all weathers and the addition of several new back tees should ensure that the course continues to provide a stern test of golf to players of all standards, including those seeking to use the course for Regional Qualification to the Open Championship.

Main: *View from the tee at the spectacular par-3 seventh hole showing the danger on both sides of its two-tiered green*

Above: *Early Club Professional Charles Edmund Clare as drawn by the well known artist and Hankley Common member, Philip Laszlo (Courtesy Hankley Common Golf Club)*

BROADSTONE
(DORSET)

Below: *View across to the green at the par-4 seventh hole which is rated as the hardest on the course. The right-hand side of the sloping fairway is divided by a thick stand of rough and shorter hitters are recommended to play their second shot to the small island of fairway in front of the wide bunker and then pitch to the green*

Broadstone was opened in 1898 as the private golf Club of Lord Wimborne whose Guest family had amassed a fortune from steel production in Wales. The Baron married Lady Cornelia Henrietta Spencer Churchill, Winston's aunt, in 1868 and the couple regularly entertained members of the aristocracy from their home at Canford Manor in Dorset. Golf supplemented shooting as entertainment for his visitors.

Lord Wimborne chose to develop the course on land lying between the Somerset and Dorset, and London and South Western railway lines and he arranged for a special platform halt for visiting golfers. The first clubhouse had been used as the Lord's hunting lodge and golfers took a wooden bridge over the railway to reach the first tee. The course was laid out by Tom Dunn who had designed the first municipal

course outside Scotland, on a limited budget at Meyrick Park in nearby Bournemouth where he then became the Professional. Money was no object at Broadstone as Lord Wimborne speculated that the combination of the railways and an exclusive course would help the hamlet to develop into a quality residential area. In retrospect, the initiative worked and smart houses now line the neighbouring Upper and Lower Golf Links Roads and Wentworth Drive.

Although earlier courses had been opened in Dorset, Broadstone rapidly became the premier club in the county and started as The Dorset Golf Club before a later name change to Broadstone (Dorset) Golf Club. Early membership was kept below 100, casual visitors were discouraged and the Club was regarded as unfriendly and elitist. It was once remarked that you could not slice a ball without hitting either a Cabinet Minister or a General. Winston Churchill once offered only a standard tip to his caddie and in a subsequent round he rapidly lost all his balls and the normally astute caddies seemed strangely unhelpful. On complaining to the caddiemaster, the official replied that perhaps Churchill had been off his game. Realising that the game was up, the future Prime Minister looked at the caddies and their bulging pockets before responding: "...perhaps you are right."

Dunn's heathland holes were well received but the middle part of the course had been built in flat parkland near Merley House and Bernard Darwin was particularly critical, describing the holes as very ordinary stuff indeed. He conjectured that: "...it is hard to understand why these park holes were ever made, because there is a glorious and apparently limitless

tract of heather waiting to be played over, only divided from the course by the railway." Stung by the criticism, Wimborne instructed Harry Colt to design nine replacement holes including seven to the west of the Somerset and Dorset railway line and Herbert Fowler was also engaged to add new pot bunkers as they had been widely acclaimed at Walton Heath.

The Club had always run at a loss and in 1930 the course was sold to Frank Toley whose father had developed a number of golf clubs around London and was known as The Playing Field King. Toley struggled to improve the Club's finances and a number of original members resigned as their privileged and secluded world was threatened by visitors prepared to pay green fees. Toley's wife took over the management when Frank died in 1940, and in 1951 her perseverance was rewarded when the Ladies' British Open Amateur Championship was played at Broadstone, being won by Kitty MacCann from Ireland. The members finally purchased the Club in 1974 and the closure of both railway lines, including one under Dr. Beeching's axe, allowed the Club to buy former railway land. This enabled improvements to the course and the relocation and construction of the new clubhouse which was opened by Peter Alliss. The consequent release of land for housing provided further finance, and members can reflect that the railways helped the Club both when they were operating and also when they were closed.

Course architect J Hamilton-Stutt directed recent improvements including the new lake in front of the third green, and the whole course is a feast of heather and gorse and is designated as an SSSI, harbouring rare heathland species including sand lizards and snakes as well as Dartford Warbler, woodcock and nightjar.

Good scores need to be made at the opening holes before the challenging stretch in mid-round which includes two tough par-4s at the seventh and thirteenth holes. Club member Lee James proved that the course helps top players to strengthen their game when he defeated Gordon Sherry in the final of the 1994 British Amateur Championship at Nairn.

Main: View of the approach shot over greenside bunkers to the par-4 thirteenth hole which Henry Cotton rated highly

Above: The second owner, Frank Toley, with his dog Par (Courtesy Broadstone (Dorset) Golf Club)

Inset: Players approaching the green at the uphill par-3 6th hole

EAST BERKSHIRE

TEACHERS OF WELLINGTON COLLEGE

Above: Ernest Alfred Upcott was one of the founding members from the staff at Wellington College

Below: An early postcard showing golfers in front of the old clubhouse confirms the Wellington College origins

East Berkshire was founded by a small group of school masters from Wellington College. Following Royal Assent from Queen Victoria and Prince Albert, the school was founded in 1859 to educate the orphan sons of soldiers as a permanent memorial to the Duke of Wellington who had died in 1852 and who was widely admired for his part in the defeat of Napoleon at the Battle of Waterloo in 1815.

Before 1900, the teachers played over a small 9-hole course within the college grounds, but as the game grew in popularity, land was identified for a full 18-hole course within walking distance of the college. The teachers formed the East Berkshire Golf Club Company with a plan to raise £5,000 from the sale of shares to fellow masters and close friends in order to purchase the 100-acre plot from Frederick Charles Ramsey. Only £3,400 was raised from the initial issue,

but the purchase went ahead and impetus was gained from the efforts of three masters, Dr. Henry George Armstrong, Ernest Alfred Upcott and the Rev. Henry Purefoy Fitzgerald.

Armstrong served as the first Club Secretary and Treasurer and was the Medical Officer at the college during the time when the whole school decamped to Malvern to escape a diphtheria epidemic which had killed two pupils. Upcott was an Oxford scholar, gaining three degrees including two with first-class honours, and in the official history of the college he was described as: "the most brilliant of Masters of the Golden Age, 1880-1920". Fitzgerald was another Oxford man who became a science teacher at the college and his interest and knowledge of horticulture will have been useful in the early days of developing the new course.

Although the Wellington College masters started the Club, its survival was due to another of the founders, W Howard Palmer, who became Chairman of the world-famous biscuit company, Huntley & Palmers Ltd. based in nearby Reading. The Club's small membership led to a financial crisis in 1909 and Palmer acquired the land for £10,000 and then leased it back to the Club at a nominal rent. This benefaction has continued through to the present day and in 1994 East Berkshire signed a new 99-year lease with the Palmer family.

The course was laid out by a Scot, Peter Paxton, who was the Professional at the fashionable Club of Tooting Bec in London. He was renowned for his ball-making skills and the 'Bramble' was endorsed by Harry Vardon. He was also an excellent club maker and his

Wellington College, East Berks Golf Club Links.

customers included the Duke and Duchess of York. It is a testimony to Paxton's design skills that the layout at East Berks has changed little in over 100 years. The course is relatively flat but interest is maintained by the heather, gorse, dog-legs, out of bounds and clever use of ditches which are well positioned at several holes to protect the greens.

The opening two holes provide a gentle start to the round and the first can be reached by long hitters, but most players will not receive a shot at either hole requiring an early test of concentration. The third is a tough par-4 and the Professional's advice is to treat it as a 'three-shotter'. The attractive par-3 fifth is regarded as the signature hole, but the most difficult of the short holes is the thirteenth which requires a clean shot through the trees and over a stream to a sloping green guarded by bunkers on either side. The second shot to the final hole is played across a road and golfers need to keep an eye out for cars and pedestrians.

The Club started the East Berkshire Stag competition in 1976 for amateur golfers with a handicap of six or better and the inaugural event was won by Sandy Lyle. Another golfing great, Bobby Locke, was a frequent

visitor to the Club and in 1964 he was near to the drama on the third fairway when a helicopter crashed close to the Reading-Guildford railway line. The Club's Assistant Professional, Arthur Roe, helped to drag one of the passengers away from the petrol covered wreckage.

Visitors in Summer will enjoy the fast greens and the smell of heather and pine as they contemplate the debt owed to the Palmer Family and the early masters at the nearby college.

Above: *Winter view of players on the green at the short par-4 first hole with the clubhouse in the background*

Inset: *The par-3 fifth hole is played through an avenue of trees. It is not long but danger lurks both to the left, which is out of bounds, and in front of the green which is guarded by a ditch. The course guide identifies that the position of the pin can make up to three clubs difference*

PILTDOWN

COUNT ALEXANDER MÜNSTER

Above: *Founder Count (later Prince) Alexander Münster*

Inset: *The old Professional's shop known as The Lodge is now a listed building and used as the juniors' clubroom*

The name Piltdown became famous in 1912 from what is now known to have been an archaeological hoax associated with an Uckfield solicitor who claimed to have found a skull proving a direct link between the evolution of apes and humans. In 1953, it was finally established that the skull was a clever combination of a human cranium and an ape's jaw. The Club's origins are equally exotic, starting with a German aristocrat, Count Alexander Münster, who was the son of Prince Münster of Derneburg, a former Ambassador in London and Paris. The Count married Lady Muriel Hay, the daughter of a Scottish Earl, and they had two sons. The family moved into Maresfield Park as tenants in the 1890s and the owner, Harvey Pechell, then bequeathed his entire 2,500 acre estate to Count Münster, including a farmhouse which is now the clubhouse and two fields now used for practice.

The Count and two other landowners, Lord Gage of Firle and George Maryon-Wilson, set about establishing a golf course which the Count hoped would persuade his German relatives to stay in the South of England whilst holidaying rather than venturing north to play on the well-established courses in Scotland. The Count was keen to repeat the success of the course at Forest Row on the other side of Ashdown Forest, and Royal Ashdown's Professional, Jack Rowe, was engaged to lay out an 18-hole course for a fee of one pound plus expenses.

The Münsters worked hard to develop the Club and introduced a number of prominent Europeans to the course whilst entertaining guests at Maresfield Park including Prince Henry of Prussia and also the Tsar of Russia who was reputed to have played in competition week in 1912. Princess Muriel became Ladies' Captain in 1913 but had to resign when their European utopia was shattered in the following year and the entire Münster family was forced to move to Germany, even though the Princess was a Scot and their two sons had been educated in Britain and spoke little German. The Münster's estate was taken over by the Public Trustee which enabled the Club to buy the clubhouse and practice area shortly afterwards. The family remained loyal to the Club and the Princess regained her British nationality when the Count died in 1922. The sons rejoined Piltdown and the younger man, Paul, became a scratch player.

The Princess ensured that ladies had equal rights from the outset and she also introduced a number of illustrious members including Lady Brassey, The Countess of Portarlington, Countess de la Warr, and most significantly upon her return from Italy in 1907, Lady Margaret Hamilton-Russell who, as Lady Margaret Scott, the daughter of the Earl of Eldon, had won the first three British Ladies' Open Championships in 1893-5. Lady Margaret had married her cousin, The Hon. Frederick

Gustavus Hamilton-Russell in 1897, and they founded a golf course together on the shores of Lake Como. She was lady Captain in both 1911 and 1914 and Cecil Leitch remembered that: "she was a gentle soul, very quiet on and off the course. Her manners were impeccable and she was universally admired." Lady Margaret had three famous golfing brothers, Denys Scott, Osmond and Michael, who had all developed their skills over the family's own 9-hole course at Stowell Park in Gloucestershire.

JH Taylor advised on early changes to Rowe's layout and the course now has no bunkers although they did feature in the original design. Despite the name, the Club is not situated on downland and it can become boggy in Winter although this is more than compensated for by the spectacular heather and gorse which flowers in the Summer and Autumn and exacts a severe toll on wayward shots.

Disputes over rights to the commonland feature throughout the Club's history. During the Great War there was vandalism on the course and the Greenstaff were paid to keep watch at night. On one occasion, the Club's mowers were thrown into Piltdown Pond. The Club purchased the freehold of the course from the two founding landlords in 1938, but this did not solve the underlying problems and matters smouldered on for decades. In July 1960, the greens were poisoned with sodium chlorate and despite rapid intervention by the fire brigade, they had to be re-turfed and seeded. Fortunately, times have changed and the Club now enjoys a more peaceful existence.

Piltdown has never rushed to make changes. Electricity was not installed until 1934 and mains water only arrived in 1956. The role of Club Secretary is still an unpaid honorary position. Henry Cotton played an exhibition match at the Club with Frank Pennink in 1955, and in his book, 'My Golfing Album', Cotton ventured to contrast the charming tiny cottages comprising the Piltdown clubhouse with the huge golf centre at Boca Raton in Florida which was the base for Tommy Armour and Sam Snead. Cotton described Piltdown as: "...very interesting to play and not nearly well enough known" whilst Henry Longhurst once told Peter Alliss that Piltdown was his favourite of all the Clubs of which he was a member. The same charm still exists today and although the cottages have been extended to allow more room for changing and entertaining, the course has retained all its natural heathland challenges.

Main: *The front of the two-tiered green at the par-3 closing hole is protected by a grass bunker with a steep slope*

Below: *View from the first fairway back towards the tee. The clubhouse is located behind the distant white posts*

NORTH HANTS

THE HAMPSHIRE HOG

Above: The original clubhouse and first 9-hole course were formally opened in May 1904 by Her Royal Highness Princess Alexander of Teck who tried her hand at driving off the tee. The Princess, who later became Princess Alice, Countess of Athlone, died in 1981 aged 97

Inset: The Hampshire Hog competition was inaugurated in 1957 and is now regarded as one of the main challenges in the amateur calendar

Right: View from the right-hand side of the third fairway to the new third green designed by Donald Steel in 2001

North Hants was established as a superior gentlemen's club on 130 acres of land leased from the Elvetham Estate by twelve residents from the village of Fleet. The location benefited from being close to an excellent railway station into London. Five of the founders were retired or serving Army officers who were no doubt keen to improve on the boggy surrounds of the original Army Golf Club links at nearby Aldershot.

The land had previously been leased by William Bloore of Vauxhall who used a part of the grounds to satisfy the sporting enthusiasm of his three cricketing sons. When Bloore moved away from the district, the founders negotiated a new lease from the landlord, Lord Calthorpe, who was enthusiastic about the golfing project. He had already built a golfing facility for his own Elvetham estate workers which later became the Hartley Wintney Golf Club.

The cricket pitch was soon transformed into high quality tennis and croquet lawns whilst James Braid was contracted to design a golf course which was opened by Her Royal Highness, Princess Alexander of Teck, one of Queen Victoria's many granddaughters, in 1904.

The new Haskell ball required Braid to lengthen the course in 1908, and Harry Colt was employed to make further significant improvements in 1913. The Club hit the front page of The Daily Mirror when they decided to speed tree felling with the use of dynamite supplied by the Nobel Explosives Company.

The spacious clubhouse with its eleven bedrooms remained open until 11pm on most nights of the week to accommodate Londoners staying over for golf and other sporting activities. The Tatler in October 1908 commented that the Club was: "...a charming reproduction of that type of country club which, though still too rare in England, had become so popular in the United States."

Beneath the surface things were less rosy. North Hants faced major competition from the new golf club at nearby Bramshot which had been designed by Open Champion JH Taylor and opened in 1905. Bramshot was one stop closer to London and its special railway Halt meant that golfers could alight straight onto the course. North Hants membership slumped from 215 to 175, and in 1910 the Club took the serious decision to suspend entrance fees.

The Great War caused the usual hardships but the Club was fortunate that the Elvetham Estate agreed to forgo rent, and after the war membership was boosted by a large influx of Army personnel, including Mess members, from the nearby garrison at Aldershot. This caused a change to the previously exclusive atmosphere. Tennis and croquet continued to be popular during the 1920s and '30s although golfers were heard to complain that the golf course suffered due to the inordinate amount of time that ground staff were spending on the courts and lawns.

Bramshot also continued to flourish, hosting The Daily Mail £1,000 Professional Tournament in 1936 which was won by Alf Padgham in the same year that he won The Open. However, the Second World War defeated the club and North Hants was able to survive the early years of reconstruction without competition from its former illustrious neighbour. Economies were required however, and the tennis and croquet sections were discontinued in 1948.

North Hants has reason to thank Reg Pearce for the idea of the Hampshire Hog competition which has brought the Club considerable kudos since its introduction in 1957. Pearce is remembered as a hard-drinking, pipe smoking, be-monocled dentist famed for his great charm and old-fashioned courtesy. On one occasion, he scored a hole-in-one at the par-3 fifteenth hole, which is close to the railway line, during a Sunday morning four-ball. Pearce recounted how a busy railway worker leant over the fence and told him that he was the first to get it in all morning!

The Hampshire Hog is a 36-hole hole amateur scratch competition which has been won by a series of well-known names. Michael Bonallack won the inaugural event in 1957 and repeated his success in 1979. Other winners have included Peter McEvoy, Bruce Critchley, Gordon Brand Junior, Sandy Lyle, Steven Richardson, Carl Mason, Gary Wolstenholme and Club member, Justin Rose.

Rose won a monthly medal in December 1993 at the age of twelve with a gross 74 whilst playing off ten. He repeated his success in the following April medal with a gross 72, and by June his handicap was down to five whilst still aged twelve. In July 1994, he

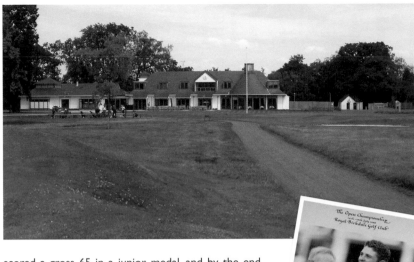

scored a gross 65 in a junior medal, and by the end of 1994 he was playing off two. The following year, he won the Hampshire Hog with a score of 134 (69, 65), setting a new course record whilst still aged fourteen. In 1997, Rose became the youngest player to appear in the Walker Cup and he returned a competitive medal card of 65 at North Hants in five consecutive years between the ages of thirteen and seventeen.

Fleet is situated in a flourishing part of the Thames Valley and the Club had been vulnerable to residential and commercial development threats. These worries were finally scotched in 1995 when a 999-year lease was signed, securing the long-term future of the Club. A small portion of the course was lost to allow access, but this allowed Donald Steel to redesign several of the early holes including the par-5 third which has become one of the signature holes on the course with the threat from the large lake to the right of the fairway.

The course was used by The R&A for Regional Open Qualifying between 1992 and 1997, and the Club continues to enjoy excellent fairways and greens which benefit from the quick-draining, sandy subsoil. The new par-3 opening hole provides a daunting opening challenge as it is often played into a prevailing wind, and the uphill sixteenth and eighteenth provide a couple of tough closing par-4s.

Main: *The modern clubhouse was built in time to celebrate the Club's centenary in 2004. The redevelopment required the first hole to be shortened to a par-3*

Above: *Justin Rose had an outstanding record as a junior whilst playing at the Club and few will forget his astonishing performance during the Open at Royal Birkdale in 1997. He is now an Honorary Member*

HINDHEAD

LITTLE SWITZERLAND

Hindhead Golf Club enjoys one of the most spectacular opening nines in the country. The course meanders through beautiful U-shaped valleys which are a feature of the area and were caused by melting glacial ice, giving rise to its description as the Little Switzerland of Surrey. Members need to be fit as the Club's historian, Ralph Irwin-Brown, once calculated that players must climb the equivalent of two Nelson's columns during each round. In the late Victorian era the views and scenery attracted many wealthy newcomers and also writers and painters to the hills around Hindhead and the Devil's Punchbowl. In 1897, the novelist and doctor of medicine Sir Arthur Conan Doyle moved into Undershaw near the summit and he must have hoped that the clean air would help his wife who was suffering from tuberculosis.

By 1896, golf was already being played some five miles away on the lower heathery moor at Hankley Common where Conan Doyle was one of the founding members together with the Squire of Grayshott, Alexander Ingham Whitaker, who captained the Hindhead

and Hankley Common Golf Club in 1898. The journey back uphill from Hankley by horse and carriage must have been difficult and a number of the members who lived in Hindhead and Grayshott decided to seek a more convenient location nearer their homes in the hills.

As Squire of Grayshott, Whitaker had already masterminded several major community projects in his village including the construction of St. Luke's Church, the Fox and Pelican Public House where he was assisted by the well-known Fabian, George Bernard Shaw, and the Grayshott Village Hall which was the biggest in Hampshire. He had grand plans for the new golf project but all the founders severely underestimated the effort and expense required to construct the course amongst the steep hillsides which were covered in gorse, bracken and heather, and strewn with stones. JH Taylor helped to identify the locations for tees and greens and clearly realised the enormity of the task lying ahead when he subtly remarked that the Club: "if properly managed" would be a great success. It was not until June 1906 that Taylor

and James Braid were eventually able to play an exhibition match to mark the formal opening of the new course. Braid won 3&2.

Whitaker and Conan Doyle both made large personal donations to the Club during the early funding crises, and perhaps not surprisingly they did not always see eye to eye. In 1907, the long-suffering Secretary, Edward Turle, minuted: "A Committee Meeting was called for September 1st but only the Secretary attended." Lady Louise Conan Doyle died in 1906 and two years later the writer and his new wife, Jean, moved to Crowborough Beacon, leaving the coast clear for Whitaker who became Club President in 1914. In January 1907, before he left Hindhead, the previous President, Sir Arthur, indulged in his other sporting pleasure, whilst at the same time upsetting Whitaker. He repeatedly skied down Churt Road from Hindhead Village, turning right at the clubhouse and then traversing across several fairways and down into Poor Devil's Bottom, which is now occupied by the fourth and fifth holes, before returning across the eighteenth green to the apparent annoyance of Club Captain Whitaker!

Despite the early travails, Hindhead soon became a highly regarded golf course which was visited by other top golfers including George Duncan, Abe Mitchell, Harry Vardon, Ted Ray, Alex Herd and Diana Fishwick. The Rt. Hon. David Lloyd George was elected an Honorary Life Member in September 1922 when he moved into his new home at nearby Churt, and the popular amateur golfer, PB 'Laddie' Lucas won the Club's scratch open competition, the Devil's Punch Bowl, in 1933. Dai Rees became the Club's Professional in 1938 and attributed his accurate driving to practise along Hindhead's narrow fairways. However he did not stay long after the war, noting that the town had slipped badly from its previous position as a thriving tourist or holiday town and regretting that: "many

hotels and big houses had been taken over by the civil servants for the country premises of banks and insurance companies, and had never regained their former status."

The course has two distinct halves. Holes two to nine wind through the beautiful and steep-sided valleys whilst the inward nine is located on more level ground giving glimpses of far-reaching views to the north. The Club has received recent recognition as a regional qualification venue for the Open Championship and overall it must rank as one of the prettiest and most underrated courses in the country.

Main: *Evening shadows at the ninth hole*

Inset: *The halfway hut above the ninth green is in keeping with the Club's reputation as Little Switzerland*

MOVE ONTO PARKLAND

Once mechanisation arrived, golf was able to move onto wooded parkland. At last it was possible to prune trees and keep control of grass on fairways during the fast-growing summer months without the help of grazing animals. A number of clubs, including Wildernesse, Porters Park (below) and Huddersfield were established in the grounds of large mansions.

Coventry.........................1887

Ilkley.............................1890

Wildernesse....................1890

Huddersfield...................1891

Burnham Beeches............1891

Harrogate.......................1892

Porters Park....................1899

COVENTRY

Coventry is one of the oldest golf clubs in the Midlands and was established by Harold Smith who summoned his friends to an inaugural meeting at the Drapers Hall in the city in April 1887. Smith, who was a keen cricketer and played at county level for Staffordshire, had seen the game at Blackheath whilst on a visit to London.

The first course of a few rough holes in a local field was soon superseded by a 9-hole course on Whitley Common which was laid out during Autumn 1887 by P Paxton, the Professional at Malvern in Worcestershire. Early players were not popular with other users of the common. The Freemen were concerned with the danger to grazing cattle and the Club was required to fit the holes with wooden blocks when the course was not in use. Players were required to wear traditional red jackets as a warning to the public.

Fortunately, early golfers enjoyed support from EH Petre who lived at nearby Whitley Abbey and became the first President of the Club. Inter-club matches began in 1891, and in an away fixture against Kenilworth,

there was drama when one of the Coventry players took the rule of play it as it lies rather too seriously. Following his ball onto an iced pond, he fell in and had to be rescued by fellow golfers.

The Coventry Ladies' Section was formed in 1892 making it one of the earliest ladies' clubs in the country. Their first 9-hole course was situated at Bulls Field Ground in an area of the city long since covered by factories. At the time, the grounds were also used by Coventry Football Club and North Warwickshire Cricket Club so the course could not be played during much of the Summer. The men allowed the ladies to play on Whitley Common when the Bulls Field was unavailable, and in due course a separate 6-hole ladies' course was built on the common.

In 1901, the Club expanded the main course to eighteen holes by incorporating the ladies' layout and including some additional land. In the meantime, public disruption was becoming more serious, especially on public holidays and at weekends, although greater danger was probably threatened by the Royal Artillery who used the common for field training! Conditions deteriorated further when the local council built a nearby sewage works and then opened a neighbouring rubbish tip, but the final demise of the otherwise well respected links at Whitley Common was caused by the death of the guttie ball as the course was too short for the new Haskell rubber-cored replacements.

The Club identified land at Finham Park, owned by Mr. Bromley Davenport, for a replacement links and Tom Vardon laid out the new course in late 1911. His famous older brother, Harry, helped with positioning the bunkers. The ladies' and men's sections

Above: *Harold Smith introduced golf to Coventry in 1887 and was Club Secretary until 1911.*

Inset: *View of the green at the attractive par-4 twelfth hole which was constructed in the 1960s as part of the course redesign by FW Hawtree at the time of the construction of the Kenilworth/ Warwick by-pass*

amalgamated during the move. Tom was an excellent golfer himself, coming second behind his brother in the 1903 Open Championship at Prestwick.

The clubhouse was opened in May 1912 and the opening of the new course was celebrated by a professional exhibition match between Harry Vardon, James Braid, Charles Wingate, from Olton, and Jack Bloxham from Leamington. Vardon won with a 68. Amongst Coventry's own early Professionals, Jack Burns and Hugh Kirkaldy were both Open winners, although not whilst they were serving at Coventry. Burns moved to Coventry for a short time after he unsuccessfully defended his Open title at Musselburgh in 1889, whilst Hugh Kirkaldy, the younger brother of the better-known Andrew, died aged only 32 in 1894. Kirkaldy liked the old course at Whitley Common but was less keen on the whining members. He once commented that: "players who could grumble and not enjoy the game there were not fit people to have clubs."

A young Archie Compston, who later came third behind Walter Hagen and Gene Sarazen in the 1928 Open at Sandwich, was the Professional in 1912/13, and Jack Bloxham took over from J Williams shortly after the First World War and served until 1938. Bloxham was remembered for his spicy language and several men banned their wives from receiving

lessons from him. He reportedly remarked to one lady that: "you'll never bloody play, you wriggle like a snake!" Coventry suffered a clubhouse fire, including the locker-rooms, shortly before Bloxham was due to retire and his pension was no doubt enhanced by the need to re-equip all the members with new clubs.

The Club survived a financial crisis in the mid-1930s and Albert Chavalier took over as Professional just before the war, partnering Henry Cotton in a charity match at Coventry in 1940 against the 1939 Open Champion Dick Burton, from Sale and G Robins, Hearsall, in aid of the Red Cross. These funds were sorely needed later in the year when the Luftwaffe bombed the city in November with the loss of 380 lives.

Six holes were commandeered during the war for food production, but enough of the course was playable in June 1945 to enable a crowd of 1,500 to watch another Red Cross charity match featuring Henry Cotton, his one-time assistant and Ryder Cup player Bill Cox, and two past and prospective members of the US Ryder Cup team, Horton Smith and Chick Harbert. Henry Cotton made a third appearance at Coventry in 1951 when he was paid £84 to play in an exhibition match to celebrate the restoration of the full course.

The last major change to the course occurred in the late 1960s when the Club was forced to relinquish two of its holes and the clubhouse to enable construction of the Kenilworth/Warwick by-pass. Fourteen acres of land were purchased on the opposite bank of the River Sowe to construct two replacement holes and the work was supervised by Fred Hawtree. Despite obvious concerns, the two new holes, today's eleventh and twelfth, have turned out to be beautiful additions to the course. The opportunity was taken at the time

to reverse the order in which the back and front nine were played and to re-number the holes.

The great commentator and writer, Henry Longhurst, formally opened the replacement clubhouse in May 1972. His early days as a player at Cambridge University were followed by more than 40 years as a weekly columnist for The Sunday Times. In one of his 'Letters from America', Alistair Cook surmised that Longhurst's commentating skills were so powerful because: "...human nature was his true topic." It was Longhurst who coined Cotton's nickname, ' Maestro'.

Between 1994 and 1998, Martin Hawtree helped the Club to reposition many of the bunkers. Today's course measures approximately 6,600 yards off the back tees and is a good test of golf. The third hole is played parallel to the River Sowe and offers a tight tee shot with water on the left and out of bounds behind the hole. Golfers may be lucky to see little owls hunting in daylight by the stream. The par-3 seventh hole is one of the most attractive on the course and requires a tee shot to be steered through an avenue of mature oak trees to a green surrounded by bunkers on three sides. Mishit balls striking the trees will inevitably be knocked down into the water.

The par-4 fourteenth hole is rated the most difficult as it is an uphill dog-leg right with a pot bunker and other trouble on the right which often prevents a

clear sight to the well-bunkered green. The closing holes include two long par-3s at the fifteenth and seventeenth holes. The slopes on the latter green make it difficult to judge where to aim the tee shot, and six times Ryder Cup player Peter Oosterhuis once referred to it as one of the most difficult short holes in the game.

The course has benefited from a major tree planting programme in the 1980s and is now attractive with the combination of trees, water, bunkers, dog-legs and sloping greens providing a good but fair challenge.

Main: *Ladies teeing-off at the tricky, downhill, par-3 seventeenth hole*

Inset: *Souvenir score card signed by the four Professionals who took part in the 36-hole charity match in 1940 in aid of the Red Cross. The four were a model of consistency, only once scoring more than five at any hole throughout the eight rounds (Courtesy Coventry Golf Club)*

ILKLEY

Below: *The view up to the elevated clubhouse from the eighteenth fairway would be recognisable to the original founders*

The attractive course at Ilkley is dominated by the River Wharfe which flows along the left side of the first seven holes making a nightmare start for golfers with a tendency to hook! The course is relatively level being built on the floodplain, but the surrounding hills and moors make a beautiful rolling backdrop. The river normally flows quietly, but as described in the Club's own history: "...it can quickly change into a rapid, roaring, powerful and sometimes violent torrent of water which gnaws away at the river banks and can cause havoc to the man-made barricades which attempt to deflect it from its chosen path."

The Club's first course was constructed high up on Rombald's Moor above the town and near the Semon

Convalescent Home under the direction of George Strath, the Professional at Hesketh near Southport. Strath had been approached by two businessmen from Ilkley, Ben Hirst and Alfred Potter, who had become frustrated with the seasonal constraints of tennis.

Harry Vardon's brother, Tom, became the Club's Professional in 1893, and he soon established a course record of 70 for two rounds of the difficult moorland course as well as a remarkable 32 for nine holes. By 1894, the Club had more than 230 members, many of them gentlemen from Leeds keen to escape the smoke of the city. The Club adopted an enlightened pricing policy, charging ten shillings per week to 'hackers' who were not members of a recognised golf club but only five shillings for members of other clubs.

In 1893, the Ilkley Local Board purchased the entire moor and all mineral, water and sporting rights from a Mr. Middleton for £13,500, and shortly afterwards the second hole was requisitioned for a reservoir. The Club feared for the future of golf on the moor and in 1898 the members started to play on the present river course back down in the valley which was also more convenient for the town. The course on the moor was taken over by golfing tradesmen and workers from Ilkley who formed themselves into the Olicana Golf Club which subsequently became the Ilkley Moor Golf Club in 1905.

Dr. Alister MacKenzie designed the second nine holes on the moor in 1913, and for many years the two clubs co-operated happily. When the Wharfe flooded, Club members could play on the moor whilst Moor Club members could play down in the valley when their course was covered in snow. The course

on the moor was finally closed in 1946/7 and a number of trophies were handed to the Club. A group of London businessmen failed in an attempt to reopen the upland course in the 1970s, and remnants of the old fairways and greens can still be seen during a walk over Rombald's Moor. Perhaps one day another group of golfing enthusiasts might be tempted to overcome the major obstacles lying in the way of rescuing a MacKenzie masterpiece.

Ilkley was one of the first clubs to introduce sand bunkers on an inland course, and the minutes of the time referred to them as having been 'erected'. Several were laid out as cross bunkers lying approximately 70 yards in front of the tees to capture topped drives. Interestingly, an early rule book of the Worcester Golf Club defined a bunker as being: "of whatever nature, water, sand, loose earth, mole hills, paths, roads or railways, whins, bushes, rabbit scrapes, fences or ditches or anything else which is not the ordinary green of the course." In 1908, Harry Colt helped the Club to abolish some of the cross bunkers and build new ones at the sides of the fairways, as well as to raise a number of greens, enclosing them on three sides by mounds with protective small bunkers.

A century before Colin Montgomerie brought international recognition to the Club, Ilkley celebrated the success of Miss KG 'Baby' Moeller who joined the Club on the moor at the age of eighteen in 1892. Within four years under the tutelage of Tom Vardon, she was playing off a handicap of plus-3 and she reached the semi-finals of the Ladies' Golf Championship at Hoylake, losing to the eventual winner, Amy Pascoe. Miss Moeller represented England in the international matches promoted by the Ladies' Golf Union in 1902, and the strengths and weaknesses of her game were summarised in a newspaper article covering the Yorkshire Championship at Lindrick: "Miss Moeller's driving was straight and for length like that of a member of the 'stern' rather than the 'weaker' sex...the only weakness exhibited was on the putting green and in the missing of short putts she only imitates the golfing champions."

100 years later, the Club produced two fine male professional golfers. Gordon J Brand played in the

1983 Ryder Cup and was runner-up to Greg Norman in the 1986 Open at Turnberry, whilst Colin Montgomerie developed into one of the world's top players with an unparalleled record on the European Tour. Colin's father, JD, was also a fine golfer and won the Club's scratch medal in 1979 with a two-round score of 146. Colin won the same medal three years later shooting 148.

Ilkley can be proud of its course. The occasional floods have produced the perfect subsoil for immaculate fairways and true greens, and the views from the clubhouse down onto the course and out over the town to the distant moors is evocative of all that is right about an English Summer's day.

Top: Ryder Cup Captain and honorary member Mark James displaying his bunker skills

Above: Early photograph of the course and the familiar clubhouse with sheep grazing in the background

Below: The final hole, viewed from the clubhouse

WILDERNESSE

TO KNOLE AND BACK

Inset: *The grand interior of the mansion which served as the second clubhouse whilst golf continued under the auspices of the Wildernesse Country Club*

The beautiful course at Wildernesse located in the village of Seal near Sevenoaks in Kent was one of the earliest inland courses constructed away from heathland. Interestingly, the Club does not know who masterminded the first layout, although it was clearly designed with skill and experience. Wildernesse has survived a number of serious reversals and now provides an excellent test of golf. In recent times it has hosted both regional Open qualifiers and a PGA Seniors event.

Few clubs can have experienced three different clubhouses in three different locations on the same course and all caused by changes in ownership or management.

A rough course was laid out before 1890 on land owned by a banker, Sir Charles Mills, who became the first Baron Hillingdon. His mansion in the village provided employment for nearly 100 people and had its own gasworks for indoor lighting as well

as a private laundry and a girls' orphanage which led to a ready supply of domestic servants. Lord Hillingdon built cottages for his workers as well as a new school and a village hall. He held frequent house parties at Wildernesse House which often featured cricket matches against top teams including the Eton Ramblers, I Zingari and the Band of Brothers. At the suggestion of a golfing relative, Lord George Hamilton, the earliest course was moved to its present location to the east of the mansion using a clockwise circuit around Chance Wood, and by 1892 the course had grown to eighteen holes. The Victorian tradition of playing in red jackets to warn of danger was only applied to visitors at Wildernesse, possibly to distinguish them from local members whose golfing abilities were thought to be more reliable!

The Mills family continued as Patrons and Presidents of the Club for more than 30 years, but in 1923 the golfers faced a dilemma. The mansion and surrounding grounds were sold to a syndicate which planned to sell off some land for housing whilst developing the mansion as a large and prestigious country house hotel with tennis and other sporting activities to complement golf. Members were faced with a stark choice between staying at Wildernesse but losing their identity and paying higher subscriptions, or moving to a new course to be designed by James Braid in the deer park at neighbouring Knole which had been offered on favourable terms by Lord Sackville. Perhaps not surprisingly, most golfers moved to Knole taking the original Club trophies with them as approved at the 1924 AGM. Some lady members decided to stay on at Wildernesse, but the grand plans for the country

club proved too ambitious and in 1927 the syndicate let it be known that they would have to sell off the golf course for further property development.

Fortunately, the course was overlooked by the house belonging to George Fawcett who lived at Wildwood in Seal Chart. Fawcett hated the idea of new housing and decided to buy out the syndicate whilst maintaining the country club as well as the golf course. Apartments and suites were available for weekend hire and some permanent residents were accommodated. The first Club Captain was appointed in 1927 and membership numbers were rebuilt from an influx of wealthy residents. However, members had no say in management decisions although continuity of play at Wildernesse was enough to attract some golfers back from Knole.

Gerald Micklem brought prestige to the Club by winning the English Amateur Championship in 1947 and 1953 and he later served on various R&A Committees with great distinction. Many observers give him credit for the success of the modern Open Championship which had a total prize fund of just £8,500 when he first became involved in 1963; this was proving insufficient to attract many top international players. He held the unofficial course record for many years, scoring 45 points during a Stableford competition in 1938 playing off a handicap of plus-1, which gave him a net 67 (gross 66).

Wildernesse finally became a members' Club in 1954 following the death of Bernard Fawcett. The mansion was sold to the Royal London Society for the Blind to help meet the family's death duties, but the golfers, including CE Mansell and Micklem, arranged financial help, including a loan from a local paper manufacturer, to acquire sixteen holes plus enough spare land to build two replacement holes and construct the current clubhouse. The course redesign was supervised by JSF Morrison and in the following decade JJF Pennink advised on the construction of two more new holes to replace those turned into the practice ground.

Today's course is a great test of inland golf. Woodland lines most fairways requiring accurate tee shots, most greens are protected by well-positioned bunkers, the bottom of the flag is often obscured, making the assessment of distance more difficult, and the greens themselves have subtle contours. Recent alterations have moved the competition tees further back into the woods to ensure that the Club continues to offer a tough challenge to scratch golfers. Tommy Horton survived the challenge whilst winning an event at Wildernesse on the PGA Seniors' Tour whilst the Italian Ryder Cup player, Constantino Rocca, added international flavour to one of the Open qualifying events hosted by the Club.

Top: Approach to the green at the par-5 eighteenth hole. The Club has had three clubhouses in different locations

Above: The first clubhouse still stands as a private dwelling

HUDDERSFIELD

FIXBY HALL

Huddersfield Golf Club lies 700 feet above sea level on a wide plateau of springy moorland turf near the top of Netheroyd Hill to the north of the town. The first layout was designed in 1891 by Tom Dunn of Tooting Bec over land at Fixby Hall, owned by the Thornhill Estate and rented for £50 per annum. The Club then defrayed part of the cost by sub-letting the land for grazing. The large mansion-like clubhouse is now Grade-2 listed and was once the home of Richard Oastler, a well-known Industrial Revolution reformer who helped stamp out the employment of child labour in mills and factories.

The Club attracted Alex 'Sandy' Herd from St Andrews to become the full-time Professional in the Spring of 1892. Sadly, Herd's wife died shortly before he was due to arrive which cast a shadow over his early times at Huddersfield, but Herd recovered well from the setback and later the same year he tied second in the Open Championship held at Muirfield and won by Harold Hilton. The new Professional gave further evidence of his talent by beating Harry Vardon over 72 holes 'home and away' at Huddersfield and Bury, and then finally confirmed his promise by triumphing in The Open for the first and only time at Hoylake in 1902 using the new Haskell ball.

Despite his youthful impatience, Herd had a long and successful career and won the British Professional Matchplay Championship in 1926 aged 58. Many observers believed that there was really a Great Quadrivium consisting of Herd as well as the famous Triumvirate. Herd married the daughter of the steward at Fixby Hall and moved to the new club at Coombe Hill in 1911, and then on to Moor Park in 1923. Bernard Darwin once wrote that: "I cannot conceive that Sandy ever had an enemy. If he lives to be 100 he will be the same fine, sturdy, independent ever-youthful creature."

Herd helped establish Fixby Hall as 'the home of Yorkshire Golf' and one of the Club's earliest Captains, Dr. FL MacKenzie originated the concept of the County Unions and was the first President of the Yorkshire Union when it was formed in 1893/4. The County's honours' boards are displayed in the Centenary Hall within the clubhouse mansion.

Dunn's original layout has been changed several times by a number of top players and architects including Herd, W Herbert Fowler, Dr. Alister MacKenzie and Donald Steel. The present twelfth and thirteenth holes were opened in 1969 following the sale of land adjacent to the present seventeenth hole. In the last few years, the Club has spent half a million pounds relaying all eighteen greens to USGA standards under the direction

of the architect Cameron Sinclair.

Gary Player has reason to remember his first visit to Fixby Hall in 1955. The course incorporates a number of ha-ha's or sunken walled fences hidden in ditches which had been built by the original inhabitants of the mansion to keep out animals without interrupting the views from within the building. Competing in the qualifying stages of the Professional Matchplay Championship, Player found his ball lodged against the ha-ha to the left of the eighteenth fairway and decided to hit his ball against the wall so that it bounced back behind him onto the fairway. Unfortunately, the rebound struck him in the face but he managed to complete the hole in seven, including a two-shot penalty, before going to hospital for treatment. Player returned to Fixby Hall in 1969 to play in an exhibition match including Peter Oosterhuis and remarked that he would like to carry the Fixby fairways around the world with him.

The course is laid out in two loops of nine which present different challenges. The outward half is significantly longer but is laid out over fairly level ground, whilst the inward nine is a tougher test of golf being built on the rolling slopes of the moorland ridge on the western side of the Hall. On a clear day, views of more than 40 miles can be seen from the marker post at the top of the hill on the eighteenth hole which requires a blind drive up and over the summit.

For many years the Club hosted the Lawrence Batley Seniors Tournament organised by the PGA as part of the European Seniors' Tour, and the Club has hosted a number of events for the Ladies' Golf Union and the English Ladies' Golf Association including the Ladies' Home International matches in 1994 and the British Ladies' Open Strokeplay Championship in 1998. The prestigious clubhouse, flanked in Spring by magnificent rhododendrons, is a fitting venue for important championships.

Main: The tee shot at the par-3 thirteenth hole is played from an elevated tee over dangerous rough and a sloping fairway

Above: Alex Herd posing with (left) Prince Edward, the Prince of Wales and Prince Albert, the Duke of York. The photograph was presented to the Club by Alex Herd's grandson in 1990 (Courtesy Huddersfield Golf Club)

BURNHAM BEECHES

NURTURING THE LACEYS

Above: *FCD Haggard was the founder and first Captain*

Below: *View from the second fairway of the clubhouse and players on the green at the downhill par-4 opening hole*

The rural area of Burnham Beeches lies 25 miles west of London and has survived thanks to the Corporation of London which purchased the woods and heathland in 1880 as an open space for its citizens to enjoy as a respite from the city pollution of Victorian England. Golf began in 1891 on rented agricultural land at Britwell Farm next to the Beeches, and many of the early players lived in London and used the Great Western trains out of Paddington.

The Club was founded by W Aitchison, WH Anderson and FCD Haggard, the cousin of Rider Haggard, the author of King Solomon's Mines. The first meeting was held in October 1891 at Burnham Infants School, and nearly half the inaugural members were ladies. Haggard was elected first Captain and he was followed in the role between 1894 and 1899 by the village doctor, Alfred Edward Wilmot who once wrote a postcard to the Club's solicitor in order to correct the impression that the Club would only allow sheep to graze on the course. In fact, he explained: "… the (only) exception we make are bulls…and cows with calf and horses."

In the early 1900s, more than a dozen teachers from Eton College and a number of Dukes, Lords and Ladies helped to give the Club an exclusive air. In 1903, Raymond Hervey de Montmorency was elected Captain at the age of 28 playing off a handicap of plus-4. He later played golf for England and became President of the EGU in 1935. During a sporting weekend in 1904, he is said to have scored 72 for Oxford University against Rye at cricket on the Saturday with every run being a four and then repeated the score of 72 on the golf course the following day hitting eighteen fours!

JH Taylor advised on changes to the course in 1902 and in 1907, the Club faced possible lease problems and Taylor was asked for his views on a move to Stoke Park. In a response which would have surprised Harry Colt who designed the famous course at Stoke Park the following year, Taylor thought: "…it was not suitable for a golf course as there are too many trees and, even if these were cleared, owing to the nature of the ground the golf would be of an uninteresting character."

In September 1907, many of the top Professionals played at Burnham during southern qualification for the News of the World tournament, but the day was a challenge for the large field which had to play two rounds. Golf Illustrated noted that: "Poor Tom Vardon played the last two or three holes by torchlight while the hole itself was marked by a bicycle lamp."

The house near today's twelfth green has its own golfing history. It was formerly occupied by a Greenkeeper, Arthur Lacey Senior and his two sons, Arthur and Charles, who learnt their golf on the course out of sight of the clubhouse. Young Arthur played in the 1933 and 1937 Ryder Cup matches at Southport & Ainsdale whilst Charles emigrated to America where he was helped by Walter Hagen and acted as assistant to Gene Sarazen. The highlight of his career was a third place finish in the 1937 Open at Carnoustie when Arthur finished equal seventh.

The course has been popular with players of other sports including cricket and football. Club member Walter Robins was Chairman of the England Test Selection Committee and suggested that the 1938 Australian cricket team should be made honorary members and the tradition continued through several Ashes series. Don Bradman played the course in 1948 and Richie Benaud's 1961 team included so many left-handers that they had to share clubs. A number of England football teams have stayed at the Burnham Beeches Hotel whilst

training at Bisham Abbey, and a succession of England strikers have played the course including Kevin Keegan, Gary Lineker, Alan Shearer and Michael Owen.

Luke Donald set a four round course record of 270 (67, 68, 66, 69) in a regional amateur event in June 1997, and an earlier Ryder Cup player, Ken Bousfield, shot 69 in 1938 whilst completing a round in 91 minutes as part of a commercial challenge. He played a total of six rounds in three minutes over twelve hours with an average score of 72.5 and was sponsored by the advertising agency, J Walter Thomson, to promote a brand of cocoa which he was required to drink between rounds to prove its assistance for stamina. A more potent drink was enjoyed by members in 1984 when the Club hosted the White Horse Whisky Challenge as part of the women's professional tour.

Burnham Beeches is a well-wooded traditional parkland course providing one of the best tests of golf within easy reach of Central London.

Main: The par-3 tenth hole features a huge bunker in front of the green which is faced with railway sleepers

Above: The Hon. HLW Lawson bought the course in 1909 and, as the second Lord Burnham, established a close link between the family and the Club

HARROGATE

CHARLES CRABTREE - PRESIDENT AND SAVIOUR

Harrogate Golf Club was founded by a Scot, Dr. Andrew S Myrtle, who was inspired into action by the success of the new club at nearby Ilkley which had opened in 1890. Harrogate's spa waters and other social attractions were a magnet for wealthy holidaymakers from all over Europe, but in 1891 many visitors had journeyed out to Ilkley to play golf up on the moors. Myrtle reasoned that Harrogate should have its own course which was convenient for the town, and the first nine holes were laid out by Willie Park Junior over undulating and difficult land at Irongate Bridge. The first tee shot was played over a quarry and the whole course was described with a sense of understatement as 'very sporty'.

The image of a salubrious game in pleasant surroundings was shattered in 1895 when the landlords, the Duchy of Lancaster, built a slaughterhouse close to the clubhouse. The members protested and the attention of the Committee was called: "to the need for some cover or shelter for the offal cart and manure pit at the end of the slaughter house, more particularly in the hot weather." Although the Committee arranged for 'Harvey the Joiner' to spend up to £4 on the erection of a palisade as a screen and also to build a shed for the offal cart, not surprisingly the stench remained and in 1898 the Club arranged to move to the present course laid out over land owned by the Slingsby Estate at Belmont Farm.

The new course was further from town but lay close to the Starbeck Station operated by the Leeds and Thirsk Railway Company. Sandy Herd from Huddersfield Golf Club set out the first eighteen holes and a medal was played over the new links in May 1898, less than eleven weeks after the lease was agreed. In the Middle Ages, part of the new course had been land attached to Knaresborough Castle and the ruins of the building are visible behind the fourteenth green. Sir Hugh de Morville and his fellow assassins of Thomas Becket took refuge in the castle for three years after their murder of the Archbishop in Canterbury Cathedral in 1170.

In 1908, a tournament was held to mark the opening of the extension to the clubhouse which featured reigning Open Champion, Arnaud Massy, who received a fee of 15 guineas, Harry Vardon (10 guineas), JH Taylor (£8) and Ted Ray (£5). Awful weather restricted the crowd and the press remarked that Massy was not playing up to form in the morning and appeared to be a little careless or off colour, whilst in the afternoon four-ball he was: "all over the course and generally appeared to be quite content to leave things to his partner, Vardon."

Numerous improvements were made to the original rushed design and following recommendations from Harry Colt, the course was altered into inner and outer loops of nine holes. Alister MacKenzie also advised on improvements, and his book 'Golf Architecture' includes the seventeenth green with the comment: "Approximate cost £180; an entirely artificial plateau green constructed on flat land. The comparatively heavy cost is due to the character of the sub-soil – heavy clay."

The Club purchased the freehold of the course for £5,250 in the 1920s and Myrtle's vision for golf as a boost for the town came to full fruition in the same decade. In 1929, the British Ryder Cup team practised on the course before the event at Moortown, and the Club entertained a host of celebrities visiting Harrogate as part of the social programme which included grouse shooting and racing at Doncaster and York. Private guests of Club Professional, Jack Crapper, included the Aga Khan, Douglas Fairbanks, Fred Perry, Gertrude Lawrence and Ivor Novello.

The Club played an important role in the formation of the town's highly regarded second course at Pannal in 1906 which was also designed by Sandy Herd. Most of the leading figures in the launch were Harrogate members including Pannal's first two Captains, Francis Barber who had been a Club member since 1898, and HE Harker. Both clubs had the same Honorary Treasurer, GG Stephenson. In a match against Dewsbury, six of the eight members of the Pannal team were also members of Harrogate, and by 1908 the combined membership of both clubs exceeded 1,000. From 1934 onwards, Barber had the unusual distinction of being an Honorary Life Member of both clubs.

After the Second War, the Club suffered a series of financial crises and would probably have failed without the support of a Leeds industrialist, Charles Crabtree, who took over personal responsibility for the Club's

borrowings and injected further funds, including £500 in Life Membership fees for four ladies who never visited the golf course. A photograph of Crabtree in the Club's history is captioned 'Captain, President and Saviour'.

In the 1930s, Harrogate's layout was described as being rather open and featureless, but the course has been improved immeasurably by the clever planting of trees which have matured to complicate the angles and approaches to many of the greens. Five of the last six holes measure 400 yards or more making a tough finish to an attractive parkland course.

Above: Classic follow through at the first tee. The picture shows the tree lined nature of the parkland course

Inset: In 1955 a ball driven from the thirteenth tee landed in the engine cab of a passing train and struck both the driver and the stoker. The ball ended up in York and was subsequently mounted with an eagle and presented back to the Club as a souvenir

PORTERS PARK

Above: CT Part served as first
Captain from 1899 to 1902. He lived
at Aldenham Lodge which had its own
private golf course, but the land was
eventually sold for executive housing

Below: View downhill to the
par-3 ninth green which is fronted
by a stream. The Pro's tip is "Back
of green is best"!

Porters Park is an attractive, undulating and peaceful parkland course lying close to Radlett railway station and within fifteen miles of Central London. An Irishman, Dr. Ross Smyth, was the catalyst behind the Club. He numbered several golfers and wealthy landowners amongst his patients including MP Grace who lived in the main property at Porters which had a cricket pitch in the grounds laid out by his famous namesake and probable relative, WG.

Charles Part and HJ Lubbock both played over private golf courses within the boundaries of their large houses. Smyth brought all the interested parties together and a course was laid out in Grace's parkland. They were soon joined by golfers from the existing club at nearby Colney Heath who had played on a 9-hole course laid out over common land, and a number of wealthy businessmen from the City of London also became members thanks to the proximity of the local railway station.

The tone of the Club changed in 1902 following Grace's sale of Porters, including the golf course, to Cecil Raphael who succeeded Grace as Club President and Patron. Raphael retained an entitlement to graze sheep in the park but was happy to extend the lease to the golfers. In return he negotiated the right to appoint up to four members of the Committee and he also risked the wrath of the local clergy by stipulating that caddies could work on Sundays. The Patron performed the dual role of benefactor and dictator for 20 years until 1923 when he offered the Club the opportunity to purchase the course and clubhouse for £18,000. Unfortunately, funds were not available and the land was purchased by Middlesex County Council. Shortly afterwards, Raphael resigned from the Club when his sons were asked to pay green fees whilst playing on the course, and it is likely that his final departure made life more comfortable for the Club's management! The Club finally bought the freehold to the land in 1979.

Porters Park enjoys a strong tradition for quality golf and has been served by several leading Professionals including James Bradbeer who was one of the famous golfing brothers from Burnham & Berrow, and then Eddie Whitcombe, from another golfing dynasty at Burnham. In 1938, more than 1,000 people watched Eddie, playing with his father Ernest, take on nephews Charles, and Open Champion Reg. Eddie was perceived as the underdog in the family and a music-hall song at the time suggested how: "Uncle Charles, Uncle Reggie and Dad should do a bit more for the lad"!

Many top Professionals played in the qualifying rounds of the News of the World matchplay tournament at

Porters Park in 1921, and in 1927 the Club hosted a competition which featured six Open Champions plus a young Henry Cotton. In 1932, Bradbeer partnered Abe Mitchell in a match against Arthur Havers and Ted Ray, losing 3&2. In 1967, the Variety Club of Great Britain arranged for a challenge match at the Club between Gary Player and Peter Thomson. Cecil Leitch won the Club's first Ladies' Open Meeting in 1912, and in 1924 she returned in her role as Captain of the Ladies' Medical Golf Association. Porters Park has also developed a number of its own top players, of which the best known is Peter Townsend who became a junior member in 1959 and went on to a successful career culminating in captaincy of the PGA.

Golf course architect CK Cotton served briefly as Club Secretary in 1945 and subsequently helped the Club implement various course improvements. The Head Greenkeeper, Martin Smith, became National Artisans' Champion in 1977 when Porters Park hosted the Sandy Herd Trophy, and the Club benefits from the involvement of a low handicap golfer in the daily routine around the course. Another artisan and former member of the greenstaff, Doug Brown, moved indoors, becoming locker-room attendant. Over a period of more than 30 years he used the position to raise large sums for charity and he was rewarded with the British Empire Medal in 1995.

The first hole is a driveable par-4 offering a positive start to the round, but the challenge soon begins as a stream cuts through the course which can affect play on at least five of the opening nine holes. The inward half is significantly longer and the second shot to the green at the finishing hole has to be hit over a deep valley which lies in wait to collect any under-hit approach shots. The course is generally in good condition as it drains well and benefits from restricted play.

Above: The clubhouse viewed from the left of the par-4 eighteenth fairway. The elevated putting surface is protected by a valley in front of the green causing many golfers to treat the hole as a par-5

Inset: The attractive statue of stag and hind celebrates the Club's centenary. The animals dominate the putting green in front of the clubhouse and look out across the first fairway

EARLY RYDER CUP COURSES

In addition to the matches held at Royal Birkdale, Royal Lytham and the more modern venues of Wentworth and The Belfry, the Cup has been played for at Ganton, Lindrick, Moortown (below), Southport & Ainsdale and Walton Heath.

Ganton............................1891
Lindrick..........................1891
Walton Heath.............. 1903
Southport & Ainsdale 1906
Moortown 1909

GANTON

Ganton lies about six miles from the sea in the Vale of Pickering in North Yorkshire and is one of the country's great inland courses. Founded in 1891 as the Scarborough Golf Club, the name was changed in 1903 to avoid confusion with the new Scarborough Town Golf Club which had opened on the coast.

The course was laid out by Tom Chisholm of St Andrews over a site chosen by the Club's first President, Sir Charles Legard. The sandy wasteland was unfit for agriculture but lay within walking distance of the small Ganton Station on the main railway line from York to Scarborough. Members were met off the train by their regular caddies, and at the end of the day a bell was rung inside and outside the pavilion to give a ten-minute warning for the return journey. The North Eastern Railway issued certificates to members which entitled golfers to subsidised first-class travel throughout its network.

In October 1891, the first Captain, the Rev. A Swayne, Curate of St. Martin's Church in Scarborough, had a lucky escape on the course. He was seriously injured when he fell heavily from a tree whilst trying to retrieve his ball and was taken to hospital unconscious but made a good recovery and resumed playing during his period of office.

Harry Vardon moved from Bury to become the Club's Professional in 1896 and later that year won his first Open title at Muirfield, defeating JH Taylor after a play-off. Taylor had received warning of Vardon's skills when they met at Ganton in an exhibition match in May. Writing in his autobiography, 'My Life's Work', Taylor admitted that he had underestimated his opponent:"The match had not been going long before I realised that he was a player who was something far above the ordinary. His placidity, his coolness, the unruffled nature of his game were such as to unsettle a much less nervy player than me...Little did I guess when I played him at Ganton that I was playing a man who was to make golfing history and develop into ... the finest and most finished golfer that the game has ever produced."

Vardon suffered a serious illness in 1903 and his role at Ganton was taken by another Jerseyman, the popular, pipe-smoking Ted Ray, who stayed at the Club for nine years, winning The Open at Muirfield in 1912 with Vardon in second place. Between them, Vardon and Ray won five of their seven Open Championships whilst serving as Club Professional, suggesting that Ganton's links-like qualities were ideal preparation for the Open venues.

Above: *Ted Ray followed Harry Vardon as the Club's Professional and served between 1903 and 1912*

Below: *View of the first tee on the approach from the clubhouse with the Yorkshire Wolds in the background*

tiered greens at the third, seventh and ninth holes and Tom Simpson.

In 1948, CK Cotton toughened the course in time for the following year's Ryder Cup. The Americans finished the first day 3-1 down after the foursomes, but then rallied strongly after a tough team talk from non-playing captain Ben Hogan to win the second day singles and hence retain the Cup. The tone was set by EJ (Dutch) Harrison who birdied four of the first six holes against Max Faulkner, starting 3,3,4,3,3,3. Even this onslaught was overshadowed in 1968 by Michael Bonallack who scored an approximate 61 in the morning round of the final of the English Amateur Championship, including an inward nine of 29 strokes.

The Club has produced a number of top Walker Cup players including Bill Stout 'the long-hitting Bridlington dentist', Alex Kyle, Clive Clark (who also played in the 1973 Ryder Cup), Rodney Foster, Michael Kelley, Martin Thompson (who was also Amateur Champion in 1982) and Jeremy Robinson. Peter Dawson turned professional and played in the 1977 Ryder Cup team. Tom Thirsk represented England together with AL Bentley from Hesketh in the Prize of the Nations Tournament held at Baden-Baden in conjunction with the 1936 Berlin Olympics, and his trophies are displayed in the clubhouse.

Ganton is not long but with only two par-3s off the medal tees the course is rarely mastered. However, Sir Paul Bryan MP had a day to remember in 1963 when he holed out in one at both the short holes. Stopping at the halfway hut to celebrate, one of his friends gave the news to Mrs. Henderson who was manning the bar and who did not seem too impressed: "Aye, well, he did choose the shortest holes!"

The course is famous for its free-draining gorse-lined fairways, excellent turf, fast, true-running greens and more than 100 deep and well-positioned bunkers. The Club has recently hosted both the Curtis and Walker Cups, and Gary Player once remarked that Ganton is the only inland course worthy of staging the Open Championship.

Many of the great golf course architects have contributed to Ganton's quality including Tom Dunn, James Braid, CK Hutchinson, Harry Colt who designed the fourth hole with its famous shot across a valley to a plateau green backed by thick gorse, Herbert Fowler, Alister MacKenzie who introduced

Above: *Sixteenth green at Ganton (photograph by Eric Hepworth)*

LINDRICK

Above: *Home players Christy O'Connor Senior and Eric Brown lost their first-day foursomes match against Mayer & Bolt 7&5, but both the Great Britain & Ireland players recovered to win their singles matches the next day*

Inset: *Large crowds at the final green during the 1957 Ryder Cup when the home team overturned the first-day deficit*

Golf Committees often cover the mundane, so it is possible to imagine the feeling of surprise and excitement which swept through the room at Lindrick in 1956 when the Captain apologised to his colleagues for keeping them in the dark and then announced that the Club would be hosting the Ryder Cup the following year! The decision had remained a well-kept secret since the moment when Sir Stuart Goodwin, a Sheffield industrialist, reached agreement with the PGA that he would sponsor the event at Lindrick. Goodwin was a member of the Club but was not on the Committee.

The decision also caused surprise away from Lindrick as the Club had no previous experience of hosting major events and the course was thought to be rather short for top competitions. In addition, the A57 ran through the course raising concerns over safety, and there were few local hotels capable of accommodating the large crowds which were expected to converge on South Yorkshire. Fortunately, Bernard Darwin, Henry Longhurst and Frank Pennink were all advocates of the course from previous visits with the Oxford & Cambridge and Seniors' Golfing Societies, and West Riding County Council agreed to close the main road during the tournament.

The match was a home triumph. After the first day's foursomes, the Cup seemed to be heading back to its usual home in America. Great Britain & Ireland trailed 3-1 and the papers were preparing their usual obituaries. At least concerns about the length of the course proved unfounded as none of the teams broke 70. On the second and final day the home team lost only one singles match, achieving what turned out to be the last victory before the change to include players from continental Europe. The Americans made no excuses and were full of praise for the course. Jackie Burke, the USA Captain commented that:"...the course is a golfing paradise. The turf is perfect and the greens flawless." Victorious Captain Dai Rees praised Lindrick for the demands it placed on the 'second shot' at the par-4s, although top players over the years have also struggled with some of the tee shots including Greg Norman who took fourteen shots at the seventeenth during the Martini International in 1982.

The Club did not gain any immediate financial benefit from the Ryder Cup, but it was appreciative of Sir Stuart's initiative and he became Club President in 1958. Buoyed by the success, Goodwin offered the course and his personal sponsorship for the 1960 Curtis Cup, and Henry Longhurst remarked that the crowd was: "the biggest I have ever seen watching women's golf anywhere in the world."

The Club started life in 1891 as the Sheffield & District Golf Club and was the brainchild of Harry Steel who died of typhoid in December of that year before he could enjoy the new course. The site was not in the most convenient location for Sheffield, requiring a train journey out of the city followed by a walk across fields or a ride by pony and trap. However, the founders chose wisely as the limestone base allows for excellent drainage producing good, springy turf. The first nine-holes were laid out in the reverse direction to today's course and included the third hole measuring 750 yards which was considered a 'Bogey-8'! Ben Sayers played the course in 1893 and described it as: "the longest 9-hole links in the Kingdom." William Jessop won the first 9-hole competition with a gross 74 (net 29) playing off a full handicap of 45, and the Club still plays for the Jessop Cup twice a year. The course was expanded to eighteen holes in 1895 playing in today's direction. The long third hole disappeared, but the Club created two 'bogey-5 and a half' holes where a five beat the 'Colonel' and a six lost to him. The last major alterations to the course were made in 1932 including changes to two holes which had previously been played directly across the main road.

The coaching guru John Jacobs grew up at the Club and played with Lindrick Artisans as a boy. He played in the British Ryder Cup team at Palm Springs in 1955, winning both his matches and he must have been disappointed when rigid selection rules prevented him from representing GB&I on his old home turf in 1957. The Lindrick Artisans celebrated their own centenary in 1999 and Cecil Leitch was the first President of the Lindrick women's Artisan Section which was one of the first to be affiliated to the LGU.

The success of the Ryder and Curtis Cup tournaments prompted the Club to continue staging top events including two Dunlop Masters championships and the Martini International as well as two Ladies' British Open Championships, amateur international matches, and regional qualifying for the Open Championship. Increased traffic on the A57 means that future events are likely to feature top amateur fixtures which attract smaller crowds, but members and visitors can still enjoy the quality conditions which were once lauded by the leading players in the world.

Main: *Waiting to play at the tough par-3 finishing hole, it is possible to imagine the tensions of the Ryder Cup*

Inset: *View from the fairway at the top of a steep bank down to the fourth green which has survived the recommendations of various golf architects and other observers who disliked the blind approach shot. The tee for the fifth hole which was the subject of an ownership dispute at the time of the Ryder Cup lies beyond the stream near the bottom right of the photograph.*

WALTON HEATH

OLD COURSE - 1903
NEW COURSE - 1907

Above: *Sir Winston Churchill demonstrating a rather upright follow through. According to Bernard Darwin, James Braid believes that Churchill, who liked to talk, may have been the inventor of the greensomes format*

Inset: *The fourth green on the Old Course taken from behind the famous fairway heather mound. The Club's Centenary publication, 'Heaven & Heather' won the 2003 US Golf Association International Book Award*

Walton Heath is not the oldest English club, but it can claim to be one of the most renowned. Throughout the last 100 years, a series of individuals have provided the Club with a rich history, including James Braid who was appointed as the Club's first Professional in 1904 and was still playing brilliant golf at Walton Heath until his death in 1950 at the age of 80.

Four past or future Prime Ministers were members at the Club before the First World War; David Lloyd George, Winston Churchill, Bonar Law and Arthur Balfour. In 1913, Walton Heath's membership boasted six Cabinet Ministers including the Chancellor of the Exchequer (Lloyd George), the First Lord of the Admiralty (Churchill), the Secretary of State for War (Col. JB Seeley), the Home Secretary (Reginald McKenna) and the Attorney General (Rufus Isaacs). It is easy to imagine how great affairs of state and war planning must have occupied the minds of players at the time.

Churchill was particularly fond of the opportunities for conversation provided by the game, and Bernard Darwin wrote that James Braid believed that Sir Winston may have invented the greensomes format, as it allowed him to talk to as many people as possible whilst still playing the game at a reasonable pace!

The Club was founded by the banker, Sir Cosmo Bonsor, who funded construction of the courses. He engaged Herbert Fowler, a relation by marriage,

to design the first layout which was rapidly followed by a second course, the New, which was built as nine holes in 1907 and extended to the full eighteen in 1913. Fowler was also a banker by profession before emerging successfully as a world-famous course designer alongside Simpson, Abercromby and Croome. Fowler had played cricket for Somerset and Essex and was a late starter at golf, taking the game up at the age of 35, although within a year he was playing off scratch.

George Allardice (later Lord) Riddell joined the Club as a Director in 1905 and had a huge influence in its successful development. He was the Managing Director (and later Chairman) of the News of the World newspaper group which had the biggest

circulation in the country. Riddell helped build a home, Cliftondown, for Lloyd George near Walton Heath and the two men were close friends for many years before falling out quite dramatically over policy towards Turkey.

Lloyd George joined the Club in 1907 and continued as a member until 1945. He became Prime Minister in 1916 when Lord Beaverbrook and others helped him supplant Herbert Asquith who was spending a lot of time away from London, playing golf on the famous Kent courses near his second home at Walmer.

A few years previously, Lloyd George had begun a 30-year affair with his secretary, who was 25 years his junior, Frances 'Pussy' Stevenson. Whilst staying at Number Ten, Lloyd George was accompanied by his wife, Margaret, but Frances was accepted as his hostess at Cliftondown. Lloyd George finally married Frances in 1943 following the death of his wife. Throughout the long affair, the newspapers, including The News of the World, kept the story quiet although journalists were amongst those who enjoyed hospitality at Lloyd George's country home!

Given the composition of the Club's early membership, it is not surprising that the Parliamentary handicap competition was a popular fixture. In 1932, the Prince of Wales reached the semi-final from a field of more than 100 when he was defeated by Lord Balfour, who in turn lost in the final at the first extra hole to Colonel Boore-Brabazon who later became Lord Brabazon of Tara. The following year, the Prince again reached the semi-final when he played against Lady Astor who had been the first woman to take her seat as a Member of Parliament in 1923. The Prince won 2&1.

For many years, The News of the World was the proud sponsor of the second most important professional golf tournament in the country. Riddell and his newspaper editor, Sir Emsley Carr, who was a scratch golfer and also a Walton Heath member, played a pivotal role in the creation of the News of the World Matchplay Championship

in 1903. James Braid was the auspicious winner of the inaugural event at Sunningdale which must have helped his appointment as Professional at Walton Heath the following year. Many such events were held at the Club, although other venues including Lytham, Hoylake, Birkdale and St Andrews were also used on occasion. Braid won the event three times and his record was eventually beaten by Dai Rees and Peter Thomson who both won four titles. Thomson's final win was at Walton Heath in 1967, just two years before the Championship was last staged.

James Braid was born in Earlsferry, Fife, in February 1870 and his first employment in the golf world was as a club maker at the Army & Navy store in London. He then became the Professional at Romford for eight years before moving to the new Club at Walton Heath in 1904. The Club has preserved Braid's old workshop and showroom as a small museum celebrating his golfing life.

Above: Players searching for a ball in the rough to the left of the par-3 eleventh hole on the Old Course

Inset: *Sir Cosmo Bonsor founded the Club and arranged for Herbert Fowler, who was related by marriage, to design the Old Course*

Below: *Lloyd George showing skill in transferring his weight through the ball. Fellow member and politician, Bonar Law, once described him as: "the most dangerous little man that ever lived" over his policy on Home Rule for Ireland, but the two men continued to meet and talk during their visits to the Club*

At one time, Braid employed seven assistants as club makers. They worked on the wooden clubs locally whilst the metal for the iron clubs was forged in Fife to Braid's specification before being shafted, gripped and finished at Walton Heath. His early irons were stamped 'Walton Heath - near Epsom', recognising the Club's proximity to the world-famous racecourse, but as Braid's fame spread, later clubs were simply stamped as 'Walton Heath, Surrey'.

Braid was the one-man handicapping Committee at the Club. Instead of watching new members hit the ball, he is reputed to have asked them to demonstrate their swing three times and then told them their handicap there and then! At the age of 68, he completed the New Course in 64, and when he was 78, he scored 74 playing on the Old. He achieved his eighteenth hole-in-one aged 79, and had the remarkable achievement of scoring a two

or better on every hole on both courses.

James Braid was Honorary Captain of the Walton Heath Artisans and both his sons, Harry and James Junior, were Artisan members. When Braid died in 1950, Bernard Darwin wrote: "Modesty, dignity, reticence, wisdom, kindliness...but I think there is another epithet that would come to most people's minds. They would call him, almost instinctively, a great man."

Braid is buried in St. Peter's Churchyard, Walton-on-the-Hill. His son, Harry, was also a good golfer, reaching a handicap of plus-1 and representing Scotland before captaining the Club for three years from 1953. Harry was following in hallowed footsteps as earlier Captains had included HRH The Prince of Wales, who became King Edward VIII in 1936, together with a subsequent succession of knights and lords. The King's first sporting love had been steeple-chasing, but following a health scare with King George V, Queen Mary asked her son and heir to the throne to play something safer. Braid and the Prince were often seen playing together at the Club.

More recently, the Club has played host to a number of important professional events. The European Open was first staged in 1978 over a composite course featuring holes from both the Old and New courses. The event was not enjoyed by Seve Ballesteros who had to borrow a set of clubs and missed the cut. His own clubs were later discovered in a locker in the clubhouse. Tom Kite won the Championship when it returned to the Club in 1980, and Paul Way became the first Englishman to win the event in 1987. Way had played Walton Heath regularly as a youngster and knew the greens.

In 1981, the Club hosted the Ryder Cup. The US assembled its strongest-ever team which

had won 36 Majors between them including Jack Nicklaus, Lee Trevino, Tom Watson, Hale Irwin, Johnny Miller, Tom Kite, Bill Rogers and Ray Floyd. In heavy rain and gusty winds, the US achieved one of their biggest ever victories despite the recent reinforcement to the European team provided by continental players such as Bernhard Langer. Both Tony Jacklin and Ballesteros were missing from the home side. Henry Cotton noted that the difference between the two teams was on the greens. "It was uncanny, everything the Americans touched went arrowing into the hole." Bernhard Langer recalled that Sandy Lyle was approximately nine under par playing against Tom Kite and still lost 3&2.

Ewen Murray, the golf commentator, described Walton Heath as: "The Greatest Club in the World." During the 1970s, Murray was Assistant Professional at the Club, serving under Harry Busson who some players regarded as the greatest ever club maker. In Murray's early days as a tournament Professional, Busson helped him cure a putting problem by 'borrowing' one of Braid's old putters out of the clubhouse. Murray won the event, the Northern Open at Dornoch, by five shots, and the putter was quietly returned to its rightful place on display!

In one sense Walton Heath has been unlucky. The M25 London Orbital motorway passes close to one side of the two courses and on a few holes the noise is a reminder of the modern world. Elsewhere, the golf is blissfully peaceful amongst the heather and it is easy to forget that the Club is less than fifteen miles from Central London.

Many of the holes are memorable, but the par-4 dog-leg twelfth hole on the Old Course deserves a special mention. Playing in a challenge match with Reg Whitcome against the South Africans, Locke and Brews, Henry Cotton took the direct route over the rough to the green and won the hole with a birdie. At the time, the shot was a sensation and was featured in many of the national newspapers and sporting journals. Despite modern technology, few visitors will risk repeating the shot!

SOUTHPORT & AINSDALE

Below: Abe Mitchell driving at the par-3 opening hole during his singles match against Olin Dutra in the 1933 Ryder Cup. Mitchell went on to win 9&8, but the hole caused calamity to the British team during the 1937 match when all four pairings lost the first hole after lunch, creating a deficit which was never recovered (Courtesy Southport & Ainsdale Golf Club)

Southport & Ainsdale, known widely as S&A, has a permanent place in British golfing history following its staging of two early and successful Ryder Cup competitions. During the 1930s, the neighbouring club at Birkdale was becoming established as the top course along the Lancashire Coast, but construction of its new clubhouse and course improvements were still in progress when a venue was being sought for the 1933 Ryder Cup. S&A had already hosted the annual professional tournament for the Dunlop Company, including the 1931 competition which was won by Henry Cotton, and so provided a natural alternative venue.

The Club's roots lie with members of the Grosvenor Bridge Club who arranged for the laying out of a 9-hole course over part of Birkdale Common, near Hillside Station, a short distance from the present links. The original name of Birkdale Grosvenor Golf Club was changed to Southport Grosvenor Golf Club following objections from Birkdale, and then changed again when the club now at Hesketh, which used to be called the Southport Golf Club, also objected! The final name of Southport & Ainsdale seemed to satisfy everyone although the course was in Birkdale and not Southport or Ainsdale!

The original course was soon abandoned in favour of a links laid out over land leased from the Weld-Blundell Estates and situated within part of today's course boundaries. The first clubhouse was built as two semi-detached houses on Liverpool Road at the Birkdale end of the course. Although these buildings still stand, road construction and residential development caused the Club to lay out six replacement holes, designed by James Braid, and to build the present, replacement clubhouse which was opened in December 1924.

The 1933 Ryder Cup was a sensation. Huge galleries of more than 20,000 attended the second day's play although many were less interested in the golf than in the prospect of catching a glimpse of the Prince of Wales who was in attendance to present the trophy. 250 stewards kept some sort of control with long bamboo poles topped by red flags, consequently becoming known as the Ainsdale Lancers.

At the end of the first day's foursomes, Great Britain and Ireland led by 2½ to 1½ and by lunchtime on the second day, at the halfway stage of the decisive eight singles matches, both sides were up in three games. The tension continued during the afternoon until it

was apparent that the final outcome hinged on the only match still out on the links featuring Easterbrook against the experienced American, Densmore Shute. At one stage, Shute was one up with only four holes to play, but Easterbrook holed twice from five yards at the fifteenth and sixteenth to square the match, and then negotiated a partial stymie at the seventeenth to remain level.

Everything boiled down to the eighteenth hole, and by then the entire crowd was thronging the fairway, leaving the two golfers only a narrow corridor to drive through. Not surprisingly, both players ended up in a bunker and both reached the green at the par-4 in three shots. At this stage local legend reports that US Captain Hagen, who had earlier beaten Lacey 2&1 in his own singles match, was still talking to the Royal visitor and was unable to get a message to Shute about the state of the overall match before the vital putts were taken. Shute's first putt was too bold and finished six feet past the hole, whilst Easterbrook also missed but left himself with a tap-in for a bogey. Shute was therefore left with a six foot putt to halve the match and hence retain the Ryder Cup which the USA had won two years previously in Scioto. Instead, he failed to hole out and so both countries had then won the Cup on two occasions. The 1937 competition was a much more one-sided affair with the USA winning 8-4, and the doldrum years for the British team continued until 1957 when Dai Rees and his team finally won back the Cup at Lindrick.

Further residential development after the Second World War required S&A to replace two of the holes used during the Ryder Cups, but fortunately the Club's future on the present course was secured in 1964 when the freehold was purchased from the Weld-Blundell Estates. The course is effectively land-locked, limiting scope for future lengthening or modification.

As well as playing host to famous international Professionals, the Club has a proud history of producing its own excellent amateur golfers. Dr. David Marsh won the English Amateur Championship in 1964 and 1970 and played 75 times for England as well as featuring in two Walker Cups. He was Captain of The R&A in 1990/1. Geoff Roberts won the English Amateur in 1951 and in earlier times, Sam Robinson, playing off a handicap of plus-5, had an outstanding record in the Lancashire Championship.

S&A is still a stern test of golf. Unusually for a Lancashire links, the fairways are edged by heathery rough and in addition to the famous opening hole, visitors will remember the blind shot over the huge hazard, lined by railway sleepers, at the par-5 sixteenth hole known widely as 'Gumbleys'.

Above: Arthur Havers playing a recovery shot from a bad lie during his match in 1933 against Walter Diegel which he went on to win 4&3 (Courtesy Southport & Ainsdale Golf Club)

Inset: Sam Ryder (centre) watching non-playing Great Britain Captain, JH Taylor (left), shake hands with US Captain, Walter Hagen before the 1933 Ryder Cup competition (Courtesy Southport & Ainsdale Golf Club)

MOORTOWN

Above: Dr. Alister MacKenzie designed the course at Moortown and was Club Captain in 1913

Below: The eighteenth green in front of the clubhouse is well guarded by bunkers on both sides of the putting surface

Moortown Golf Club near Leeds was the second course to be designed by the renowned golf architect Dr. Alister MacKenzie who built the layout over the heathery and boggy hillside of Black Moor which was potted with stagnant pools.

The founders took a significant gamble as the early course had major drainage problems and was located some distance from the nearest railway which was the normal mode of transport for golfers at the time. Players had to take public transport out of Leeds and then walk for over a mile across rough ground before they arrived at the Club. In 1911, Moortown and The Alwoodley golf clubs made a joint approach to Leeds City Council for the provision of electric trackless tramcars from Moortown Corner to Alwoodley, but the request was refused and the early members without a car had to continue to arrive by bicycle or on foot.

Despite the early challenges, the Club developed successfully and in 1920, Moortown was sufficiently

well established to host the Yorkshire Amateur and Team championships. In 1929, the Club's fame spread throughout the golfing world when it hosted the first Ryder Cup competition to be played in Great Britain.

Surprisingly, the initiative for the course was taken by a non-golfer, Frederick Lawson-Brown, who attended the Yorkshire Amateur Championship being held at the beautiful course at Ganton whilst he was holidaying in Bridlington. He realised that his home area would benefit from the creation of a similar, top quality venue. MacKenzie had recently completed the highly acclaimed course at nearby Alwoodley, and Lawson-Brown arranged for him to introduce the same novel features of wide, contoured greens and cunningly placed bunkers onto Black Moor. The Committee arranged for Harry Colt and Herbert Fowler to visit Moortown and review the emerging MacKenzie's work, and both expressed satisfaction with his design and construction.

MacKenzie was elected Captain for the year in 1913 and he continued overseeing various changes until the early 1930s when the Green Committee was finally happy to record that: "Seeing that the course has now been got more or less in its final form, the necessity for the office of Honorary Course Constructional Adviser no longer exists, and it is recommended that the present is a convenient time for Major MacKenzie to relinquish this office. That we tender to Major MacKenzie the very best wishes of the Committee for his services and that we ask him to accept an honorarium of £25 for services rendered, and that he will avail himself of the courtesy of the course till the end of the present year."

Kolin Robertson, a Moortown member and an employee at The Yorkshire Evening News, is credited with bringing the Ryder Cup competition to The Club. He had helped organise several Yorkshire Evening News Professional Tournaments at Moortown but they did not achieve a high profile and Robertson had greater ambitions for the Club and his employer. The Ryder Cup was played over Friday and Saturday in late April and Golf Illustrated described how: "the course was in perfect condition and the greens beautiful." 20,000 spectators attended over the two days with Great Britain emerging victorious 7-5. Charles Whitcombe, Archie Compston, George Duncan, Aubrey Boomer and Henry Cotton won their singles for the home team, but the most spectacular shot was played by the American, Al Espinosa, who holed in one at the eighth. The US Captain, Walter Hagen, was made an Honorary Life Member of the Club.

Following the Ryder Cup, Moortown hosted a succession of important championships including the Brabazon, won by Doug Sewell in 1957 and shared by R Foster and Sir Michael Bonallack in 1968, and three successive years of the professional Car Care International trophy during the 1980s with winners including Nick Faldo. In 1976, the Club hosted a PGA Cup match between the United States and a combined team from Great Britain and Ireland which was won by the visitors. The Captain in that year, Victor Watson, also caused a stir when he invited his namesake, the then Open Champion Tom Watson, to join him in a match with 36 invited guests and dubbed 'The Watsons versus the Rest of the World'. Henry Cotton and the Leeds United and England football manager, Don Revie, were amongst the guests.

Since the early days the course has become surrounded by houses, but mature trees have grown around the perimeter and it is easy to forget that Moortown now lies within an affluent suburb of northern Leeds. The layout of the par-5 first hole has changed little from the original design and it should be regarded as an early birdie chance, measuring only 500 yards off the back tees. The green at the second hole has been moved back by some forty yards since the Ryder Cup days and its recent change from par-5

to par-4 has made it a stiff test. Outside pressure caused the Club to build two replacement holes through the woods in the late 1980s, and the sixth which is played through an avenue of trees, is now rated as the most difficult hole.

The middle part of the course, and especially holes eleven through to fourteen, are more reminiscent of the heathland holes at nearby Alwoodley. Indeed, the map of northern Leeds contains a profusion of flags identifying the location of a number of neighbouring and high-quality golf clubs. The par-4 eighteenth is a classic closing hole and the tee has been pushed back to ensure that hooked drives do not hit the houses built alongside the course. The fairway has been widened to the right to encourage players to align more in that direction, and the bunkers by the green in front of the clubhouse have been modified and deepened.

The closing hole has seen its fair share of drama. Severiano Ballesteros once flew a nine iron right over the green and onto the practice putting area which is positioned in an old quarry next to the clubhouse, whilst Nigel Denham, playing in the English Strokeplay Championship, managed to hit his approach shot into the clubhouse. He played his next shot to the green through a window which was opened especially, but the rules have since been changed and the clubhouse is now out of bounds.

Top: Tee shot to the sloping green at the 10th hole named Gibraltar after an underlying sandstone outcrop

Above: A rare card signed by all members of both teams (Courtesy Moortown Golf Club)

THE ARCHITECTS ARRIVE

Many golf historians believe that the work by Willie Park Junior at Sunningdale marked the advent of true golf course architecture and he was soon followed by Herbert Fowler, John Abercromby, Harry Colt and Alister MacKenzie. James Braid, Tom Dunn and other great Professionals were also much sought after by new clubs wishing to enjoy their cachet.

Notts
Willie Park Junior 1887

South Herts
Willie Park Junior 1899

Huntercombe
Willie Park Junior 1901

Sunningdale
Willie Park Junior 1901

St Enodoc (Right)
James Braid 1890

Shanklin & Sandown
Tom Dunn 1900

New Zealand
S Mure Fergusson 1895

Saunton
Herbert Fowler 1897

Woodhall Spa
Colonel Hotchkin 1905

Worplesdon
John Abercromby 1908

The Alwoodley
Dr. Alister MacKenzie 1908

Left: *James Braid - Courtesy of Walton Heath Golf Club.* **Right:** *John Abercromby - Kind permission of The Addington Golf Club*

NOTTS

Hollinwell lies about twelve miles north of Nottingham and is one of the toughest and most attractive inland courses in the country. The name derives from a natural spring known locally as the Holy Well which gathers in a small pool of drinkable water before feeding into the lake at the eighth hole.

The City of Nottingham contains two of the earliest sites for golf in England. In 1864, John Doleman, from the famous Scottish golfing town of Musselburgh moved into the district, bringing with him a good supply of golf balls. The game was unknown in most of England so he found a suitable patch of land by the Queen's Walk in the middle of the city and played the mysterious game by himself. He soon started golfing on the other side of the River Trent, and every morning played with a club and ball between Wilford Ferry and the Trent Baths where he used to take a refreshing dip before another spell of golf. Doleman eventually persuaded a local Nottingham man to join him, at which stage the authorities told the two men that they should desist from playing the hazardous game so close to the general public.

During one of his morning rituals, Doleman met another Scot, John Harris, who had moved to the city from St Andrews to practise architecture, and a formal Club was finally established when a local vicar, the Right Reverend A Hamilton Baynes, arranged the inaugural meeting at his house. The Club gained early credibility through the inclusion of Nottinghamshire cricketers including Richard Daft and William Wright of Wollaton who became

the first President. The Reverend was appointed as the first Captain and Harris became Secretary and Treasurer.

The first course of seven holes was laid out with the agreement of the Public Parks Committee of the Corporation of Nottingham in the Queen's Walk Recreation Ground and nearby meadows, and the golfers promised not to interfere with the numerous football matches during Winter or with cricket which was played over the grounds

Above: View from the tee at the long downhill par-5 fifth hole to the green situated in front of the clubhouse

Above: John Harris, Founder and Captain, 1890

Inset: John Doleman played his first game of golf in 1837 and was Captain in 1891

during the Summer. The players suffered considerable barracking from passing members of the public who had no idea about the strange new pursuit. Doleman won the first medal of fourteen holes with what was described as a creditable total of 73 strokes. Within a few months, the players tired of the dull, flat and all-too-public course in the city, and moved to another 7-hole course laid out over Bulwell Common which was a sandy and gorse-covered tract on the outskirts of town. Most importantly, the course lay close to Bulwell Forest Station on the Great Northern Railway and the players were allowed to store their clubs in a cupboard below the stairs in the

stationmaster's house. Young Tom Williamson, the stationmaster's son, was made to sit under the kitchen table cleaning clubs, but this apparent abuse of child labour had a happy ending as Tom grew to love the game and eventually became the Club's Professional. Meanwhile, Mrs. Williamson and her daughter provided tea and light refreshments for the players and the railway family had clearly found a profitable sideline to supplement their main responsibilities.

The course at Bulwell Common was expanded to eighteen holes in 1894 and all was well until 1897 when Nottingham Town Council proposed to build a cemetery on the common. Although this idea was abandoned, the public had started to encroach again and the decision was taken to move even further out of the city to the sloping and bracken-covered land in the Kirkby Forest owned by the Ecclesiastical Commissioners which had been spotted by CR Hemingway whilst contracting for a tunnel for the Great Central Railway. The course was laid out by Willie Park Junior and opened for play in 1901. Not surprisingly, the lease stipulated that play was not allowed on the Sabbath. The old layout at Bulwell Forest became a municipal course which is still played today.

Almost immediately JH Taylor and Tom Williamson were instructed to lengthen the course at Hollinwell following the introduction of the new Haskell ball, and by 1906 it measured over 6,000 yards and had a bogey score of 81. Williamson made further changes in 1912, constructing what are now the first three holes in the triangle of land lying on the railway side of the approach road to the Club near to the old Hollinwell & Annesley Halt which was known as Hollinwell Golf Station to a generation of players.

The Club is now a green oasis, but writing back in 1910, Bernard Darwin was conscious that the course lay close to the heart of British industry: "... the factory chimneys are not so far away, but that the ball, which starts its career from the first tee a snowy white soon passes through a series of varying greys till it is coral black, unless its complexion is

renewed by the use of the sponge. The Southern caddie's simple and natural method of cleaning a ball is not here to be recommended."

Hollinwell has a long history of hosting professional tournaments, starting with the News of the World Matchplay Championship in 1906 which attracted all the top players to compete for £240 prize money. The highlight for the crowd was the match between the brothers Tom and Harry Vardon, but Alex Herd emerged as the overall winner taking the £100 top prize and the Gold Medal. In 1925, nearly 4,000 people watched the Daily Mail Golf Tournament and two bookmakers started to shout the odds from a position near to the first tee but were quickly evicted from the course.

More than 10,000 people attended the £3,000 Dunlop Masters Tournament in 1957 which was won by Eric Brown who defeated Peter Alliss, and competitors in the John Player Classic of 1970 played for the largest prize money which had ever been offered. In 1978, the Club hosted the Ladies' British Open which was won by the Australian, Edwina

Kennedy. Hollinwell has also hosted numerous top amateur events including the English Amateur and the Brabazon (English Strokeplay) Trophy. Sandy Lyle and Nick Faldo both featured in the 1975 Trophy which was won by the Scot.

Tom Williamson's rise from the stationmaster's son cleaning golf clubs under the table to becoming one of the game's top players was a heart-warming story. Like the great Harry Vardon, Tom started to play golf with pieces of branches before collecting a few old clubs together. His first ambition was to work on the railway but he failed an eye test and instead was sent to North Berwick in 1895 to learn club-making at the late JH Hutchinson's shop which became known as Ben Sayers. He was taken on temporary trial by the Club at the age of sixteen

Top: *The green at the par-4 eleventh hole lies at the top of a narrow valley*

Above: *The Hollin Well spring bubbles to the surface at the eighth hole and provides a refreshing drink*

Inset: The Rev. AH Baynes, Captain 1887/8

Below: View from the back tee at the par-4 eighth hole requiring a long shot over the spring water lake to the fairway

on a wage of five shillings per week, and stayed on at Hollinwell until his death 54 years later in 1950, which the Club believes is a world record for a Club Professional in full-time service. Tom was a Methodist by upbringing and kept a promise to his mother on her deathbed that he would never play golf on a Sunday nor drink alcohol until he reached the age of 60. He established another record by playing in every Open Championship between 1897 and 1947, coming fourth at Prestwick in 1914.

Williamson was a well-known club maker and was the first person to start numbering clubs, although his irons were numbered in the reverse direction to today's accepted norm, starting with One for a niblick. Tom was also a great teacher and his most famous and successful pupil was Miss Enid Wilson whom he started to teach at the age of fourteen. Miss Wilson won the Ladies' British Open in three consecutive years between 1931 and 1933. Brian Waites was another Professional at Hollinwell who managed to combine his Club duties with a successful record in tournaments. Shortly after his appointment in 1969 he equalled the Hollinwell course record, shooting 68 in the final round of the John Player Classic, and in 1983 achieved the highlight of his career, playing in the Ryder Cup match at the PGA National in Florida.

The view from the clubhouse is dominated by a steep ridge which towers above the first three holes. The course is built within the historic boundaries of Sherwood Forest and the second green is situated immediately below a large rock known as Robin Hood's Chair. The par-5 third hole is played downhill back to the clubhouse and the remaining holes are then included within the pre-1912 boundaries. The view from the back tee across the freshwater lake at the eighth hole is particularly memorable and it takes a shot of good length and accuracy to hit the fairway. The pond is alive with water birds and dragonflies in Summer. The Club has constructed holes 8A and 8B for golfers who prefer to return to the clubhouse without taking to the hills.

The tight par-4 tenth hole requires a blind drive across the corner of a right-hand dog-leg, and the eleventh hole is a beauty, being played up a narrow valley to a green nestling into a ridge. Many of the fairways are flanked by gorse bushes which make a unique sound as their seeds pop in the hot sun. The short thirteenth is played from the top of the hill down to a well-protected green, and several of the storm shelters in the upper sections of the course are occupied by nesting swallows which swoop low across the fairways. The par-4 fifteenth hole rises again to a green shut in by the hills, whilst the last three holes give longer hitters a chance to redeem their rounds. Hollinwell plays equally well in Winter and is a beautiful test of golf.

SOUTH HERTS

VARDON AND REES

South Herts Golf Club is located near Barnet within ten miles of Central London and is rich in golfing history. Harry Vardon and Dai Rees served as the Club's Professionals for a combined period of more than 70 years and the course has been used for practice by visiting American Ryder Cup teams, and on a number of occasions as a regional qualification venue for the Open Championship. Speaking as the guest of honour at the Club's annual dinner in 1986, Henry Cotton referred to South Herts as: "one of the back-bones of golf in Britain."

The roots of the Club date back to 1899 when a large group of members from the club at nearby Muswell Hill, which had been founded in 1893, believed that their course faced closure as a result of property development. They were also concerned that play was prohibited on Sundays. At the time, the land they selected for the new course was in the county of Hertfordshire, hence the name South Herts, although the county boundary has since been moved further north away from London.

Willie Park Junior laid out the first course of 5,580 yards and Sunday play was allowed although under a Club rule that: "No caddie or other servant shall be employed to carry clubs on the course on Sundays." By 1928, this had been relaxed slightly so that: "Only caddies over seventeen years of age may be employed

on Sundays." Vardon arrived at the Club in 1902 with the dual role of Professional and Greenkeeper and quickly set about improving the layout with help from Park, stretching the course to 5,814 yards. The Club acquired the land in 1928 for £21,500 and Vardon made further course improvements in the 1930s producing today's course which has stood the test of time. The dog-leg right par-5 fifth hole provides a good example of the changes as it was constructed out of two relatively short and simple 'Bogey' four holes on the original course.

Vardon never had a golf lesson but he was already three-times Open Champion when he arrived at South Herts from Ganton in 1902 and almost immediately won his fourth Open at Prestwick in 1903. Unfortunately, he then suffered a recurrence of tuberculosis and spent many months recuperating in Norfolk. He made an immense contribution during his 35 years at the Club, and South Herts was highly regarded as a result of his skills and reputation. One of his golf balls inscribed '1915 Totteridge Club Record–63' is on display in the entrance hall whilst the Club has the original signed card of his round in January 1923 when he repeated the score. In July 1924, Vardon, Braid, Herd and Taylor played an exhibition match to celebrate Vardon's 21st year at South Herts, and after his death in 1937, the latter three plus Ted Ray played at

Above: Dai Rees was Captain of the Great Britain and Ireland Ryder Cup team which scored a rare victory over the Americans at Lindrick in 1957 (Courtesy South Herts Golf Club)

Inset: The statue of Vardon looks as if the great man is still intent on playing the short par-4 first hole

the Club again in a memorial match timed to coincide with the unveiling of the Harry Vardon Memorial Plaque. Vardon is buried in the graveyard of the local church of St. Andrew's in nearby Totteridge, and each year the Club lays a wreath at his grave during the weekend of the Club's internal competition for the Vardon Cup.

Vardon was succeeded as Club Professional by the Welshman Dai Rees who was himself the son of a golf Professional and became one of the leading British players in the early years after the Second World War. Rees played his first professional competition outside Wales in the British Assistants' Championship which was held at South Herts in 1932. Vardon watched the event and was reported to say: "There's only one real player amongst that lot, the young boy Rees. He'll do well." His approval was remembered, and in 1946 the Club's Captain and President approached Rees whilst he was playing in the Penfold tournament at Stoke Poges and offered him the role of Club Professional, commenting that: "Harry Vardon ....held the highest opinion of you, as a player and as a man."

It is little wonder that Rees accepted and he was also allowed to spend up to 90 days a year away from the Club to play in tournaments. Interestingly, Rees used a two-handed rather than overlapping or 'Vardon' grip. He was advised not to change by the leading Professional Charles Whitcombe, but Rees must have had occasional doubts whilst working at the Club which proudly displayed Vardon's overlapping grip as its emblem. Rees

won four PGA Matchplay Championships, was runner-up in three British Opens and was selected for ten Ryder Cup teams, nine times as a player, captaining Great Britain and Ireland on five occasions including the rare and historic victory at Lindrick in 1957. In 1958, he was voted BBC Sports Personality of the Year.

Dai Rees was instrumental in arranging for the 1961 American Ryder Cup team to practise at South Herts before their victory at Royal Lytham, and they were entertained to lunch by the Ladies' Section. Most of the team autographed a souvenir menu. In 1971, Rees played in a major event at his own Club when South Herts hosted the final running of the Daks Tournament which was part of the PGA Tour. The event was first staged at Royal Mid-Surrey in 1950 and was then held regularly at Wentworth until its final swansong at the Club. The result was a tie between Neil Coles and Brian Huggett who both scored 284 over the four rounds. They shared the prize money as there were no play-offs at that time and other competitors included Peter Oosterhuis, Brian Barnes and Christy O'Connor Junior.

The course is well-known for the speed of its greens which measure up to eleven on the stimpmeter during the Summer. The Professional's guide to the course warns golfers to keep the ball below the hole at five of the first nine greens and at four more over the inward half. The course is laid over clay which can get wet during the Winter, but the course drains remarkably well due to the diligence of Vardon and the early Committees who arranged to lay upwards of 30,000 drainage pipes under the course in 1912. The course is near to London, but it is easy to forget that the City is so close although it seems strange to see underground trains making their silent passage through the distant surrounding suburbs.

HUNTERCOMBE

Willie Park Junior

The course at Huntercombe in the Chilterns bears a remarkable resemblance to the layout designed by Willie Park Junior more than a century earlier. The course measured 6,522 yards when it was opened in May 1901 and today's layout is actually shorter at just under 6,300 yards off the back tees. Most clubs have had to lengthen their fairways but Park's course is protected from low scoring by cleverly angled tees, thick woodland which has grown just off the fairways, well-positioned grassy humps and hollows, clusters of gorse and true but undulating greens.

Young Willie continued his father's fine golfing record by winning the Open in 1887 and 1889 as well as narrowly losing by one shot to Harry Vardon at Prestwick in 1898. Park was the first professional golfer to establish a reputation as a course architect and he had very ambitious plans for Huntercombe. In 1899, he was commissioned by TA Roberts to build the original course at Sunningdale, but Park was also keen to develop his own property and golfing interests and therefore formed the Chiltern Estates Company with the active co-operation of Roberts who took a minority holding and became Chairman.

In 1900 Chiltern Estates purchased Huntercombe Manor from HH Gardiner who then held a similar shareholding to Park in the company. The 724-acre property included three farms and over 100 acres of common land, and a short time later the company acquired a further 200 acres of farmland from Magdalen College, Oxford. The Manor became the first clubhouse and the Club also obtained manorial rights to the common which allowed it to reach a compromise with parishioners over their rights to cut down furze for firewood.

Construction started in September 1900 and the course was ready for the second leg of a challenge match between JH Taylor and Jack White, played in May 1901. The first part of the match was played over Taylor's home course at Royal Mid-Surrey, whilst White chose to play at Huntercombe even though he had by then become the Professional at Sunningdale; the Surrey course was not opened for play until September that year. Six policemen were engaged to control the crowd and Golf Illustrated was suitably impressed, describing the course as 'long and sporting' with views suggesting the scenery of the Lothians in Scotland. The journal also reported that Park was planning to build a 100-bed hotel. US Amateur Champion, Walter Travis,

HUNTERCOMBE
GOLF CLUB
SITUATED ON THE CHILTERN HILLS, 700 FEET ABOVE SEA-LEVEL.
PLAYABLE ALL THE YEAR ROUND.
A PERFECT SEASIDE COURSE, INLAND.

Top: The clubhouse and eighteenth green with a number of red kites visible above and to the left of the clock

Above: Early advertisements for the course compared it to a seaside links as the coast was still considered to be the natural home of golf at the turn of the 20th Century. The invitation concluded: "Grand old turf, gravel and sand subsoil, health-giving breezes, an ideal course for London golfers."

visited the course in August 1901 and described it as: "easily the best laid out links I have ever played over anywhere..."

Park's ambitious plans still seemed on track in March 1902 when the first Committee was formed comprising London-based luminaries including the Earl of Chesterfield, the Rt. Hon. AJ Balfour and leading banker, Eric Hambro. The initial subscription was set at an expensive five guineas but target membership was almost reached by Autumn 1902 and the Club was clearly busy. Despite this background of plaudits and apparent success, Park's grand vision was flawed and he also had bad luck. The first clubhouse at Huntercombe Manor was more than a quarter of a mile from the first tee and could only accommodate a small number of visitors, the three Daimlers purchased to transport golfers from Henley Station to the Club broke down on a regular basis, the Sunday train service was unreliable and, most seriously, a shortage of water required heavy expenditure on drilling a deep well. A number

of London-based members belonging to other clubs resigned their membership and by March 1908 Chiltern Estates had been liquidated and control of the Club passed to the mortgagees, Norwich Union.

Although Park's property vision failed, the course itself was widely admired and frequented by other aspiring course architects. The first Captain, Lt. Cecil Key Hutchinson, represented Scotland in the annual match against England in each year between 1904 and 1912 and was runner-up in the 1909 Amateur Championship at Muirfield. He went on to design the course at Gleneagles with James Braid and then helped Col. SV Hotchkin remodel the course at Woodhall Spa. Other future course designers amongst early members included Charles Hugh Alison who became the Secretary at Stoke Poges before joining the partnership of Harry Colt and John Morrison, Stuart Paton, who helped transform the greens at Woking, and John Abercromby who was mentored by Willie Park whilst working on the courses at Worplesdon and The Addington and who eventually set up in partnership with Herbert Fowler and Tom Simpson.

Norwich Union played an active role for a number of years but it was not their core business and in 1924 the insurer sold the Club to motoring magnate William Morris for £32,500. Morris was knighted in 1929 and took the name of the nearby village when he became Baron Nuffield in 1934 and then Viscount Nuffield in 1939. Morris and his wife moved into the clubhouse and took a close personal interest in the running of the Club for many years, extending the sports played at Huntercombe during the 1930s to include tennis, badminton and squash. The tennis courts had wooden floors and were so well constructed that they were used for practice by the British Davis Cup team. Nuffield subsidised the Club for nearly 40 years and in 1951, member Henry Longhurst identified the usual problem that the Club had too few members who spent too little at the bar! Nuffield finally sold the Club to the members in 1962 for a nominal sum and today's more modest clubhouse, modelled on the building

at Liphook, was constructed as part of the plan to reduce operating costs.

James Bond author Ian Fleming was a member for more than 30 years between 1932 and 1964 but his mother had made her own presence felt much earlier. She frequently walked a round trip of five miles from her home to the Club and then played two rounds whilst accompanied by her dogs, which were banned from the course. In 1911, the Secretary was instructed to write a formal letter reminding her of the rule. Mrs. Fleming was nicknamed Curtseying Kate after her unusual swing and Ian used to play a regular Sunday morning two-ball with Sir Jock Campbell who agreed to acquire Fleming's publishing rights during one of their matches.

Gloria Minoprio was another lady to cause a stir when she appeared in several British Open Championships during the 1930s wearing trousers. She was in her early twenties when she married 63-year-old William Gavin, and during the Summer of 1931 the couple rented a cottage backing onto the course and Minoprio had daily lessons from the Club's Professional, Jim Morris. She used only one club, a cleek or two-iron, and consequently spent many hours practising recoveries out of a purpose-built bunker in the cottage garden. Some of her strange foibles may have been a prelude to her later career as a conjuror, but Minoprio clearly had golfing talent and in 1936 she scored 84 in the Ladies' Open in Lancashire whilst playing with just her cleek.

Park's original holes have been renumbered and today's course opens with a par-3 as the current clubhouse, built in the 1960s, was moved away from the previous site close to the current fourteenth hole near the main Henley/Oxford road. The beautiful course has stood the test of time and it is easy to understand why Huntercombe has been lauded by golf course architects and other visitors for more than a century.

Top: *View from behind the green looking back past protective mounds towards the tee at the par-3 seventh hole*

Above: *Long-time Club Professional Jim Morris had an eclectic score at Huntercombe of 42 for eighteen holes. He also established the professional course record of 63 back in 1939*

SUNNINGDALE

OLD COURSE ~ 1901
NEW COURSE ~ 1923

Below: HRH The Duke of York-
Club Captain in 1932 (Courtesy
Sunningdale Golf Club)

Sunningdale is home to two of the best-known and respected inland courses in the world. The Club has hosted many major events including the Walker Cup on its first visit to an inland course in 1987, six Ladies' European Open Championships and the Women's British Open as well as the annual Sunningdale Foursomes which started in 1934 and has featured many of the country's best-known amateur and professional golfers.

The Club was founded by Tom 'TA' Roberts who, with his brother 'GA', built a large house, Ridgemount, situated directly opposite the entrance to the Club on land leased from St. John's College, Cambridge which had owned the estate since 1524. The brothers organised the Founders' Committee which soon identified 100 golfers prepared to take up £100 bonds enabling the new Club to lease large tracts of farm and wasteland, strewn with gorse, heather and pine trees from the College. Willie Park Junior was employed to construct the first course, now known as the Old, for a fee of £3,000.

A further bond issue was required to complete the impressive clubhouse.

Park won the Open Championship in 1887 and 1889 and was known as an erratic driver. However, his putting was outstanding which helps to explain the large greens that he incorporated into the Old Course. Park's layout was completed just before the Haskell ball superseded the gutty, and early changes were required to lengthen the course. Subsequent alterations have included a reduction in the size of several greens and changes to various bunkers, but the main outline of the course would still be recognisable to Park today, although he would be surprised at the number of trees which have emerged over the original open and barren farm and heathland.

The Club was fortunate in choosing Harry Colt as its first full-time Secretary from a field of 435 applicants. He was a past Captain of the Cambridge University Golf Society and had already begun his architectural career by designing the links at Rye, where he had been Captain in 1894. He was appointed an Honorary Member in 1918 and became Captain in 1924 in the year after completing his design of the New Course. Colt incorporated land previously leased by the defunct Sunningdale Heath Golf Club for its own 9-hole course which had been known as the Chauffeurs' or "nine-ole" course. Tom Simpson and Ken Cotton made subsequent changes to Colt's layout, producing the Club's second world-class course.

Jack White was appointed as the Club's first Professional following his second place in the 1899 Open played at Sandwich and he brought early prestige to Sunningdale by winning the Open Championship when the event returned to Sandwich in 1904. Unfortunately,

White was partial to a drink and early minutes record several occasions when the great golfer was allowed to take time away for recovery in the "inebriates' home". The Club's centenary publication helps put the problem in context as within four days of the first incident, the Club decided to lay down 100 dozen bottles of port!

Sunningdale members are a special breed. James Sheridan acted as caddiemaster for more than 50 years between 1911 and 1967 and he was made an Honorary Member in 1956. He once remarked that: "At Sunningdale, the great are treated as unremarkable. That is why they come." Luminaries have included Somerset Maughan, Terence Rattigan, Lord Brabazon of Tara, Halford Hewitt and Ted Dexter. The Prince of Wales (later Edward VIII), who played off six, was Captain in 1930 whilst his brother, the Duke of York (who became George VI) held the same office in 1932.

During the war, golf was limited and on one occasion King George VI inspected a big review of troops assembled on the first fairway. Club folklore tells that as he passed the caddiemaster's office, the King called out: "Good morning Sheridan!" to which Sheridan is said to have replied: "Good morning Your Majesty. If I may say

so, you are making a far better King than you ever did a golfer!"

The Club has endured several mysterious disappearances. In 1926, Agatha Christie vanished for ten days and was eventually tracked down to her refuge at a spa in Harrogate where she had been staying under an assumed name. Her husband, Colonel Christie was a member at Sunningdale and had become rather too close to another golfer, Nancy Neale, whom he eventually married.

Fifty years later, another member, Lord Lucan, was sought for questioning by the police after the murder of his nanny. Detectives from the murder squad interviewed members of staff and examined Lucan's locker, but the mystery behind his disappearance has never been solved.

A premeditated departure occurred in 1914. In the early 1900s, Britain and Germany enjoyed amicable ties and it was no surprise that Prince Albert of Schleswig-Holstein, who played off a handicap of six, should have been made an Honorary Member in 1905 and appointed as Club Captain in 1910. Unfortunately, international relations deteriorated rapidly in 1914 and Prince Albert

Main: Spectacular view of the tenth fairway on the Old Course looking towards the green and the Halfway Hut

Above: Diana Fishwick congratulating Bobby Jones after his success in the Golf Illustrated Gold Vase in 1930. Fishwick had just won the British Ladies' Open (Courtesy Sunningdale Golf Club)

Above: Prince Albert of Schleswig-Holstein was Club Captain in 1910. He returned to Germany in 1914 to serve his country, causing consternation amongst early members (Courtesy Sunningdale Golf Club)

Below: Early postcard featuring the Sunningdale clubhouse

returned to Germany to serve his country, causing a flurry of entries in the Suggestions Book including one in June 1918 that: "We are surprised to find on our return from Active Service that the name of an alien Prince is still on the board of Captains. We suggest this should be remedied." The Committee meeting in July decided to repaint the Captains' Board, omitting the year 1910.

The Club had reason to mourn. Along with many others, the Club's Captain, Norman Hunter, who had a handicap of plus-4, was reported as missing in action in 1915. He was re-elected as Captain in absentia for 1916 but never returned from the frontline. Harmony was finally restored at the 1927 AGM when a motion was carried by a large majority agreeing to restore Prince Albert's name to the Captains' board, which was then repainted for a second time.

Sunningdale has hosted many of the golfing greats. The field in the News of the World Matchplay Championship of 1903 included JH Taylor, Alex Herd, James Braid, Jack White, J Sherlock, Ted Ray and Tom Vardon, and the competition was won by Braid who defeated Ray 4&3. Gary Player won his first victory in Europe at Sunningdale and top Professionals playing in the European Open Championships hosted by the Club during the 1980s included Ian Woosnam, Bernard Langer, Greg Norman and Nick Faldo.

Bobby Jones played one of the greatest rounds of golf whilst playing in the Open Championship, Southern Qualifying competition at Sunningdale in June 1926. Using hickory shafts, his first round of 66, compared with a scratch score of 76, consisted entirely of threes and fours. He later recalled: "...it was as perfect a round as I ever played in my life." He went on to score a near-

flawless second round 68, although this prompted him to fear: "I've reached my peak too early." Jones returned to Sunningdale in 1930 and won The Golf Illustrated Gold Vase amateur tournament which had previously been won at the Club in 1914 by Harold Hilton, the former Amateur and Open Champion.

The Sunningdale Foursomes competition was first held in Spring 1934 and is open to both amateurs and Professionals who all play off the same tees. Professional women and men play off handicaps of two and plus-1 respectively, whilst amateur ladies and men play off scratch and four, with matches being played off full handicap difference. In the early days, the event was used as a warm-up for the professional season and past winners include Dai Rees, Alf Padgham, Max Faulkner, Neil Coles and Peter Alliss. Prominent ladies amongst the winners have included Diana Fishwick, later Mrs. Critchley, the British Ladies' Champion in 1930, who won the inaugural event partnering Noel Layton from Walton Heath. Joyce Wethered won the following two events with JSF Morrison, and Wanda Morgan won the first post-war competition in 1948 partnering S King. Diana Critchley became a member at Sunningdale and acted for many years as Honorary Secretary of the Ladies' Section. She became an Honorary Member in 1964 and the mixed bar is now named after her.

The Club takes great pride in the quality of its own golfing members over the years who have included many Walker Cup players. In the 1906 Amateur Championship played at Hoylake, three of the four semi-finalists were from Sunningdale. Cyril Tolley played in six Walker Cup matches between 1922 and 1934 and was Amateur Champion in 1920 and 1929, whilst Max McCready won the same title in 1949.

The Club owes a particular debt of gratitude to Gerald Micklem who was an excellent amateur golfer, winning the English Championships in 1947 and 1953 and playing in four Walker Cup teams. He was President of the Oxford and Cambridge Golfing Society but is best remembered as one of the game's great administrators. Micklem played a major role in re-establishing the Club after the war, becoming Captain in 1960. He became Captain of The R&A in 1968 and played a major role in raising the level of international prestige now enjoyed by the Open Championship.

Sunningdale is without doubt one of the world's great Clubs and both courses provide a stern test of inland golf to amateurs and Professionals alike.

Above: *Sunningdale Old Course (photograph by Eric Hepworth)*

ST ENODOC

James Braid

Inset: The bunker at the Himalayas fascinated early golf writers. Here, Golf Illustrated used the hazard to describe a new version of golf where each member of a mixed team used one club around the course. Clearly male chauvinism was alive and well!
(Courtesy St Enodoc Golf Club)

St Enodoc has one of the most memorable golf holes in the country. The tenth fairway winds down from a slight elevation towards the small 12th Century church where the Poet Laureate, Sir John Betjeman is buried. He loved his golf at St Enodoc and wrote several poems celebrating the links and its characters.

The Club believes that a rough form of golf was first played by a group of visiting undergraduates in the area between the church and nearby Daymer Bay in 1888, whilst a number of enthusiasts, including WR Rendell and the Reverend CB Clapcott laid out a few holes amongst the neighbouring dunes in the following year, leading to the formal inauguration of the Club in 1890.

There was little local involvement in the early days, and most golfers made the journey either along the seven miles of rough track from Wadebridge by jingle (pony cart) or by ferry across the estuary from Padstow. A second nine holes were laid out towards the village of Rock by Messrs. Sandys and Stephens, and at the first AGM, held in the open air in a quarry behind what is now the St Enodoc Hotel, the members were informed that the Club had about 20 golfers paying an annual subscription of five shillings to meet the annual rental of £6 paid to local farmers as compensation for the loss of grazing land.

At one time, it seems that the Club enjoyed playing over up to 27 holes as the handicap allowance was set at 60 for 27 holes, with a competition being played over 18 holes in an outward direction and 9 holes on the way back home. However, no records remain to demonstrate this early layout.

Major changes occurred around 1900 when Dr. Theophilius Hoskin purchased 300 acres of land. This included all the ground occupied by the existing course together with the neighbouring Trenain Farm and Brea Cottage, situated under the tumuli on Brea Hill, which forms one of the beautiful focal points on today's course. Dr. Hoskin leased much of his land back to the Club for £30 a year.

JH Taylor and James Braid played one of their famous exhibition matches at the Club in 1901, and in 1907 Braid was contracted to lay out a new course of eighteen holes which bears a closer resemblance to today's boundaries. Braid's design was altered in 1922 by the addition of a new eighth hole which was later described by Bernard Darwin as being: "of sound rather than terrific quality", and the construction of new holes at the eleventh and twelfth replacing the old trio of holes from eleven to thirteen. Later, Tom Simpson constructed a new sixth hole which is now played as the fifth.

In 1935, following the re-siting of the clubhouse, James Braid was invited back to the Club and he constructed the existing final two holes. The original old wooden clubhouse with its veranda was described as being similar to the bungalow of a British resident in the tropics. The floors were wooden, as were all the walls.

When Dr. Hoskin died, he was buried in St Enodoc Church. His widow would not allow golf to be played around the church holes on the Sabbath and members were required to remove the flags on Saturday evenings. Fortunately, a compromise was reached shortly before the English Ladies' Championship was held at the course in 1937 which was won by Wanda Morgan who defeated Miss M Fyshe 4&2. Mrs. Hoskin was to be paid 20% of Sunday green fees in return for allowing golf to be played over the full course.

As the main Club catered mainly for non-residents, local golfers were encouraged to join the Artisans' Section which was established in the 1920s. After the Second World War, the Artisans were granted separate affiliation to the Cornwall Golf Union under the name of the Daymer Bay Golf Club, and this arrangement continued for several decades until they were encouraged to join the main Club.

Intriguingly, the Club's early annals refer to Rock as being a resort which attracted retired people with reduced incomes who were encouraged by the comparatively cheap cost of living. It is doubtful whether today's chroniclers would agree, as improved transport links have turned the area into one of the most sought-after resorts in the West Country.

Few clubs owe as much to their Honorary Secretary as St Enodoc does to EAR 'Ned' Burden who served for twenty years from 1939, and fewer still have had their Secretary honoured in verse by a Poet Laureate. Betjeman wrote a tribute to Burden which included the final two verses:

*'The Times' would never have the space
For Ned's discreet achievements
The public prints are not the place
For intimate bereavements.
A gentle guest, a willing host,
Affection deeply planted—
It's strange that those we miss the most
Are those we take for granted.*

The full poem, signed by Sir John, hangs in the foyer of the clubhouse.

The tenancy arrangement with the Hoskin family continued through until 1949 when Dr. Hoskin's widow decided to sell the land. Although the Club made preparations to buy the course, the Duchy of Cornwall agreed to take over all the land, together with the clubhouse, and then to accept the Club as tenants under a new lease.

Main: *View from the thirteenth hole of St Enodoc Church with Daymer Bay beyond. The church was recovered from beneath the sands in 1863*

Above: *King George VI and Queen Elizabeth visited the Club with Princess Margaret in July 1950, shortly after the Duchy of Cornwall purchased the land at St Enodoc (Courtesy St Enodoc Golf Club)*

The sixth hole contains the extraordinary Himalayas bunker. Given a road running down the left of the fairway, it seems impossible to position a drive which will not require a blind approach directly over the 80-foot dune, and in windy conditions, it is easy to lose a ball in the rough lying beyond the hazard.

A similar feeling awaits on the elevated tee at the par-4 tenth. Although the church is visible in the distance, the fairway landing area appears to be tiny. Although this is a slight optical illusion, it is enough to cause many a mis-hit drive into the marshy stream to the left or the grassy sand hills to the right of the fairway.

The main links at St Enodoc is known as the Church Course, but the Club also enjoys the use of a second layout known as the Holywell. Although it is only 4,100 yards in length, the greens are maintained to a high standard and the course is a sensible compromise for less experienced golfers who are not willing or able to meet the strictly-enforced handicap requirements on the Church Course.

The great joy of the main course at St Enodoc is that after one round it is easy to remember every hole. As Sir John wrote so lovingly in the final verse of his poem 'Seaside Golf':

In-coming tide, Atlantic waves
Slapping the sunny cliffs,
Lark song and sea sounds in the air
And splendour, splendour everywhere.

Shortly afterwards, the Club hosted a visit by King George VI, Queen Elizabeth the Queen Mother and Princess Margaret, continuing a royal connection which had commenced with the Duke of Windsor some 30 years earlier. The Prince of Wales visited the Club in 1979, but unlike his brother, he is not a keen golfer and was not able to enjoy a game on the links.

St Enodoc would probably have hosted a greater number of major competitions if it was located more centrally, although the anticipation of good golf on the long journey to the Club is one of its pleasures and modern roads have greatly improved accessibility.

The course itself is a classic links design. The view of the rollercoaster first fairway from the clubhouse whets the appetite for what lies ahead. The third hole is a treacherous dog-leg par-4 with the approach played over a road and a dry stone wall which, in windy conditions, is a real challenge. The fourth is one of St Enodoc's most memorable holes and was included in the golf writer Sir Ernest Holderness's eclectic course of 18 holes. Measuring just 292 yards, only the longest Professional will risk driving directly to the green. Most golfers will need to avoid the jungle to the left of the narrow fairway by playing a tee shot over an out of bounds field, edged by another dry stone wall, onto a tight landing area. This should then allow a short pitch to the green which is protected by a steep drop to the left and a continuation of the wall to the right.

SHANKLIN & SANDOWN

TOM DUNN

Queen Victoria and Prince Albert bought Osborne House on the Isle of Wight in 1845, and the island became a fashionable resort encouraging the early development of a number of golf clubs. These included the 9-hole course at Bembridge in 1882 which later became the Royal Isle of Wight Golf Club, the Needles Golf Club in 1888, and Ventnor in 1892. In the same year, the adjacent towns of Shanklin and Sandown on the south-east coast agreed to act together to form their own Club. Led by Dr. John Cowper, who had identified the land as suitable whilst out shooting, negotiations were commenced with the Lord of the Manor, Sir Francis White-Popham. Unfortunately, Sir Francis died before matters were finalised and formal use of the land was finally agreed with the Ladies of the Manor of Shanklin in 1899. The founders also persuaded the local rifle brigade to cease use of their range on the course and the fourth hole is still referred to as the Butts.

The first course of nine holes was laid out by Tom Dunn from Bournemouth, and the Club employed John Hogg, who had previous experience at North Berwick, to supervise the construction. However, the early members soon raised their ambitions and James Braid was then instructed to make various improvements. Braid was tempted to concentrate a number of holes around the main hilly landmark on the course, and his convoluted layout caused one of the Club's members, who was a General, to liken the area to the Boer War Battle of Majuba Hill which had also been attacked from all sides. The name is still used for both the hill and the

seventh hole. Braid appears to have been forgiven, and in 1908 he played an exhibition match against JH Taylor and then advised the Club about the repositioning of a number of bunkers and tees.

Several clubs on the island closed after the First World War including the Needles, Bonchurch and the original course at Ryde, but Shanklin survived, obtained additional land, and instructed Abercromby to advise on the construction of three replacement holes (the present fourteenth to sixteenth) together with improvements to the existing course.

Above: *The elevated drive at the dog-leg right par-4 thirteenth signature hole should be aimed at the furthest pine tree*

Above: The first Committee in 1899 had four members from each town including the founder, Dr. J Cowper (second right, front row) and RH (Reginald) Fox (back row, second right) who died following the effects of a fall whilst playing on the course in 1933

Inset: Wintry clouds frame the approach to the final green

There was no access by car in the early days and journeys were frequently made by horse and trap from the local railway station, although some members rode to the Club on their own horses and stabling was provided for a shilling per day, rising to two shillings if golfers brought their dog to go searching for lost balls whilst their masters were playing. The Royal club at Bembridge was the most important on the island in the first few decades, and under its founder, Capt. JS Eaton, who had also been a member at Royal Liverpool, it developed a very comprehensive set of rules which received widespread acknowledgement in the years before The R&A became the sole arbiter of the game in the United Kingdom.

A number of wealthy and well-connected golfers were members of the clubs at both Bembridge and Shanklin. HRH Prince Henry of Battenburg was Captain of the Royal Isle of Wight Golf Club in 1894 and his wife, Princess Beatrice, was Captain of the Ladies' Section at Shanklin in 1909. The close ties continued over the years and when the club at Bembridge finally succumbed to the shortage of space in 1961 and gifted its land and clubhouse to the National Trust, Shanklin & Sandown inherited the Captains' Board, which is on display in the entrance to the Club, as well as a number of medals and trophies which are now played for regularly in Club tournaments.

The Club's stature rose steadily and during the 1920s and '30s, several matches were played against a team from the Royal Yacht during Cowes Week, which included both the Prince of Wales (later Edward VIII) and Albert, Duke of York, who later became King George VI. Member and Club auditor Ian Patey brought success to the Club in 1946 when he won the English Amateur Championship, but in other respects times were hard and the land was almost surrendered to the local council for use as a municipal course. However, the Club muddled through and was rescued by the 1960s' golfing boom which led to a rapid increase in both membership and income from visitors.

Much of today's course is constructed over sandy heathland which enables play throughout the year, and Winter greens and course closures are rare. The layout is not long, measuring just over 6,000 yards off the back tees, but out of bounds is a feature on several holes placing a premium on accuracy. Open Champion Bobby Locke shot 66 whilst playing in an exhibition match in 1953, but few golfers have beaten that score in modern times despite the great advances in equipment technology.

NEW ZEALAND

S MURE FERGUSSON & TOM SIMPSON

New Zealand Golf Club near Woking, to the west of London, has one of the more unusual histories of English clubs. Early membership was restricted to close friends of the founder, Hugh Locke King, and his wife Ethel, most of whom lived in London and only visited the Club on an occasional basis. Even today there are fewer than 250 members, including fewer than 40 ladies, most of whom live away from the immediate district.

The Club does not have a Captain or Committee. Instead, a Board of Directors has run the Club for nearly a century. It was only at the end of the Second World War that the Board finally minuted: "...that extreme care was still necessary in the selection of new members but the custom of not electing local residents could be departed from in special cases, if considered desirable."

Hugh Locke King could trace his ancestry and family wealth back through seven generations to Jerome King who was a successful grocer based in Exeter during the 1600s. Hugh inherited a major part of the family estate in 1885 including the 212 acres comprising the New Zealand course as well as nearby land on which the Bleakdown Golf Club was constructed (later renamed as West Byfleet). Most famously, he also owned the land and was responsible for the construction of the Brooklands Motor Track and Aerodrome in 1906.

The name New Zealand first appears on an Ordnance Survey map in 1861 and was absent from the 1853 edition. It seems likely that the King family named a small area of their land as a sentimental reference to family members who had emigrated to New Plymouth in New Zealand. Hugh Locke King included the motto Parta Tueri (defend your acquisitions) on the Club's Gold Medal struck in 1896 as a tribute to his pioneering family who had struggled to retain their new possessions against the belligerent Maoris of Taranaki.

Folklore suggests that Hugh's London clubland friends wagered that his pine-covered land was unsuitable for a golf course. Most new links at the time were still being constructed on open common land and coastal plains, and it must have taken a huge manual effort from King's team to tame the woods and prove the doubters wrong.

King employed S Mure Fergusson to supervise construction of the course, and he, in turn, sought assistance and advice from the Scottish Professional, Douglas Rolland. Fergusson was a stock jobber on the London Stock Exchange. Born in Perth, Scotland, in 1854, he was well-known in golfing circles, being elected a

Above: *Hugh Fortescue Locke King Esq, JP (1848-1926). Founder of the Club and owner of the land on which the course was constructed*

Left: *The clubhouse was well described by Golf Illustrated in 1901 as suggesting the architecture of a Swiss or German homestead. The article continued: "...internally it is without exception the prettiest and most comfortable clubhouse I have ever seen." The Club has spent considerable time and effort in returning the building to its former glory and the words still ring true a century later*

member of The R&A when aged 20. He captained Felixstowe in 1891, Guildford in 1893, and Royal St George's in 1902/3. Fergusson's design skills were well respected and he was also engaged by King Edward VII to design a 9-hole course at Windsor Castle.

King's development of the Brooklands race track cost more than a quarter of a million pounds and he was forced to realise some assets, selling the New Zealand Club to a Limited Company set up by Fergusson and his Stock Exchange associates for £36,000. Fergusson became Managing Director of the Club on a salary of £200 per annum.

W Lionel Fraser was a Director of the Club between 1946 and 1954 and in his autobiography he describes Fergusson as: "a tyrant Chairman, end-all and be-all of the Club. There was no Committee - he was the Committee, and because it was difficult to get in, all the snobs in town and elsewhere clamoured to join." Vanity Fair once wrote of Fergusson's Stock Exchange ventures that he would have made more money if he had fewer enemies, whilst Horace Hutchinson described Fergusson on the golf course as being: "...endowed with an admirable measure of self-reliance....the idea of defeat is to him, subjectively speaking, a probability unworthy of consideration."

Fergusson died in the clubhouse in December 1928 and the Club's character began to change thereafter. A Board minute in January 1929 noted that an option

on 50 dozen bottles of port at 82 shillings per dozen was considered, and the new Secretary was instructed to write to the suppliers and explain that consequent on the death of Mr. Mure Fergusson, it was not desired to proceed with the option! Around the same time, the Club also engaged the firm of Simpson & Ross at a cost of £1,750 to make alterations to Fergusson's layout. This included construction of the present short par-3 third, a combination of the original tenth and eleventh holes and new greens at the tenth, seventeenth and eighteenth.

In 1932, the Club allowed the formation of a small Artisans' Section of local residents with limited playing rights over the course.

Writing in the 1895/6 Golfing Annual, the Hon. Secretary announced: "Our first Club meeting will be held the week after Ascot, and this is the only one we have each year, as we do not encourage scoring." Today there are still few competitions and the ethos remains about playing golf in beautiful surroundings rather than worrying about competitions. The trophy cabinet is small and the clubhouse does not feature the usual honours' boards.

Despite the small membership, the course is played regularly by a number of traditional societies who are able to enjoy uncrowded golf through beautiful woodland and with top quality cuisine back in the clubhouse. Retired New Zealand Club members meet on Wednesdays, playing as the Wednesday Woodpeckers, named after the green woodpecker which is a common bird on the course and features as the Club motif. The Club still adheres to a number of its founding traditions and the bar closes at 7.15pm as most members still live in London and need to return to the City during the early evening.

The course has a good mix of holes including five par-3s and six 'Bogey 5s', and Tom Simpson's holes are particularly well designed with sloping greens and clever greenside bunkering. Simpson's modifications in 1929 uncrossed the seventeenth and eighteenth fairways, producing a tight left dog-leg on the former which has been a source of debate over the years as to whether it is right for a par-4 hole to require only a medium iron from the tee. The prevailing view is that the hole adds enjoyable variety to the round.

SAUNTON

The East Course on the Braunton Burrows at Saunton is one of England's great golf links and would fully deserve to host the Open Championship. The course was redesigned by Herbert Fowler in 1919 causing Gerald Micklem to pronounce that Fowler's contouring of the greens bore the marks of genius with the par-3 holes being unequalled.

The Club was founded in 1897 by the Pitts-Tucker family and their friends from Barnstaple who laid out the first nine holes over flattish land owned by the Christie family. This was situated immediately inland from the present course. It was rumoured that Mr. Christie was unwilling to lease the dunes themselves as he was loathe to lose the income of £150 per annum which he received from rabbit trapping in the area. The Christies are best remembered for establishing the opera season at Glyndbourne for which George Christie received a knighthood in 1984.

The first course must have been tough as the ladies' card for the nine holes constituted three Bogey 5s, four 6s and two 7s! Today's eleventh green gives a fascinating insight to the original course which slopes away from the current fairway as it was originally built to receive approach shots coming from the opposite direction on the now abandoned course.

When the Pitts-Tuckers started playing at Saunton, most serious golfers in the region were members of Royal North Devon, 'RND', which was well established less than five miles away as the crow flies across the River Taw at Westward Ho!. Although the terrain was suitable, golf developed slowly north of the Taw and the first AGM had to be postponed due to the lack of a quorum. The game was enjoyed by both sexes and

ladies were members of the main Club, unlike the position at RND where the Ladies' Club was a separate entity.

By 1911, the Club had 74 male and 40 female members compared with a total of 640 members at Westward Ho!. Early competitive matches against other clubs were rare and the only men's fixtures were against Weston-super-Mare and RND's Artisans' Section, the Northam Men's Club. Although Saunton was off the beaten track, both Sandy Herd and the reigning US Champion Francis Ouimet had played the course before the First World War.

Between the wars, the Christie Estate continued to dominate the Club's affairs and in 1935, Herbert Fowler was employed to lay out a second course. Bertie Pitts-Tucker offered to supply a chain to measure the distances, but Fowler refused to use the equipment as

Above: US tanks stationed on the first fairway in 1943. The course required major reconstruction after the war (Courtesy Saunton Golf Club)

Below: The 1929 exhibition match featured (l-r) FG Bradbeer, James Braid, JH Taylor and Henry Cotton

he thought he knew how to pace a yard. Unfortunately, his stride had reduced with age and the course ended up shorter than intended! All this became irrelevant in 1939 when much of the land was taken over by the military for battle training and the dunes were mined against possible invasion. After the war, a contingent of German prisoners was billeted in the clubhouse and employed to clear the minefield and tidy up the course. CK Cotton, who had been the Secretary at Oxhey Golf Club before the war, was employed to restore and improve the old course. He made changes to the first and last holes so that play could now be seen from the clubhouse. Golf finally resumed on the old or East Course in 1951, but the second course was not re-opened until 1975 in a much-altered state when it was renamed as the West. Unfortunately, the imported topsoil on the West was not suitable for a links course and in the early 1980s, the Club was forced to relay the greens at great expense. Large pits were dug to bury the rogue material and the newer course has now emerged from these problems so that the Club is able to offer two superb challenges.

The East Course was put firmly on the map in April 1966, just a few years after the members had finally taken over control from the Christie family, when the televised Schweppes PGA Championship was held at the Club. Guy Wolstenholme defeated a strong field including Tony Jacklin, Dai Rees and Brian Barnes, and

John Stobbs wrote in the Observer that: "The beautiful links of Saunton came out perhaps the biggest winner of the week. It is a splendid place; and in this event the course itself has proved once again both its quality and its special stature."

The first R&A event was held at Saunton in 1984 when Great Britain & Ireland competed against the Continent of Europe for the St Andrews Trophy. The home team emerged as narrow victors 13-11 with Peter McEvoy's victory over a young Jose Maria Olazabal, 2&1, being one of the highlights. The event was enlivened by a herd of cattle which escaped onto the course and had to be ushered away from the eighteenth green near the clubhouse by volunteers including the Captain of The R&A, and the Secretary of the Club who emerged from the building brandishing red flags as well as their gin and tonics! More recently, Saunton has hosted an increasing number of prestigious championships and Sergio Garcia won The R&A's Boys' Championship when it was held at Saunton in 1997.

The East Course starts with a daunting par-4 measuring 470 yards, played from an elevated tee down onto a narrow valley fairway containing a bunker guarding the dog-leg right. From the tee it is hard to ignore fellow golfers dotted in all directions looking for balls in the rough accompanied by the sound of soaring skylarks. The second hole has been lengthened by over 50 yards to enhance the tough start, and the Club believes it now has arguably the best four opening holes in the British Isles. The very short fifth hole comes as a complete contrast, requiring a pitching wedge onto a raised green which falls away steeply in most directions.

The middle part of the course does allow a card to be rebuilt but the last five holes are a real challenge. Bernard Darwin included the sixteenth, known as Fowler, in his composite best eighteen holes in the country. After a blind tee shot, the narrow fairway turns to the left and the dunes collect any slight inaccuracies. The par-4 eighteenth is a classic finishing hole, played around a dog-leg right fairway to the green positioned in an amphitheatre in front of the vast clubhouse windows where you can imagine the eyes of the watching galleries.

WOODHALL SPA

The Hotchkin course at Woodhall Spa is a masterpiece which was recently voted as the best inland course in England by 'Golf World' whilst 'Golf' Magazine of America included the course within its top 50 courses in the world. Praise is not just a modern phenomenon. In 1935, Henry Longhurst considered: "It is, I think, the best course, using best in the most comprehensive sense, that I have played on in Britain", and a few years earlier, Bernard Darwin wrote in Country Life that Woodhall Spa was: "...the best and most charming course I have ever seen."

The town's famous waters were discovered by chance. In 1821, John Parkinson sunk some speculative shafts looking for coal, but these were unsuccessful and were soon closed. Some time later, water seeped from the mines onto neighbouring farmland and the cattle were found to be cured of ailments. The locals started to drink the water which was rich in iodine as a help for rheumatism, gout and scurvy, and by 1834, the Lord of the Manor, Thomas Hotchkin, had built a pump room and bath house as well as a hotel for visitors. The resort became fashionable with Victorian and Edwardian visitors who arrived in the town by train and golf became a natural source of entertainment. Although the railway closed in 1954 and the spa baths were closed in 1983, the town has continued to benefit from the initiatives of the Hotchkin family through the development of a world-class golf course.

The game was first played in the town in the early 1890s over a 9-hole course laid out by the old railway line. The Woodhall Spa Golf and Tennis Club was founded in 1891, but the land was developed four years later for housing and a replacement 9-hole layout was opened which only survived for eight years before it too succumbed to development. At this stage, Stafford Vere Hotchkin offered a large tract of his own sandy hunting land as an 18-hole course at a rent of £50 per annum. Hotchkin was a golfing enthusiast who played off single figures and his interest and knowledge played a key part in the successful development of what is now known as the Hotchkin course. The Club employed Harry Vardon to design the new layout which was tested in an exhibition match by JH Taylor who shot 72 and was 2-up against the better-ball of three members. Hotchkin drove the first ball to celebrate the formal opening in April 1905, and the official opening in June 1905 featured a match between Taylor, Braid, Vardon and Jack White. Construction proved unexpectedly expensive and time

Above: Eighteenth green with the EGU Headquarters in the background

consuming, and the final cost was recorded, with commendable accuracy, at £1,305 17s 6d.

In 1911, Harry Colt advised on a major redesign of the course which extended the layout from 5,500 to 6,400 yards with a similar routing to today's course. His recommendations were completed in 1914 and the Club struggled through the war years before being rescued in 1919 by Hotchkin, who by then had acquired the rank of Honorary Colonel of the 60th Field Regiment. Following this, the minutes of the Club ceased to be published in the local newspaper but the Colonel continued to develop the course, remodelling many of the holes, moving greens and tees and adjusting the impact of bunkers and other hazards. In the late 1920s, he set up his own golf course design company with Cecil Hutchinson and Guy Campbell, and the team constructed a number of excellent courses including West Sussex and Ashridge.

In 1940, Henry Cotton remarked how Colonel Hotchkin's artistic hand: "has been very busy making uninteresting flat land into the most natural looking of golf courses." The Colonel's architectural principles were continued by his son, Neil, who was President of the EGU in 1972. The course has not succumbed to the modern trend for easy maintenance. Bunkers still proliferate and most tee surrounds are steep and have to be mown by hand. Up to 80% of rounds are played by visitors to Woodhall Spa, but the Greenkeepers manage to keep the course in a good, natural state through all seasons. The Hotchkin measures over 7,000 yards off the back tees and is laid out like a links course with the front nine taking players to the furthest point from the clubhouse.

In 1995, the course and surrounding land was sold to the EGU as a key element of its plans to develop the National Golf Centre including a modern training academy which has 4,000 square metres of tees and 3,000 square metres of greens. The EGU was established in 1924 and is the governing body for male amateur golfers in England. The golf courses are run to be self-funding and do not rely upon affiliation fees paid to the EGU.

Woodhall Spa's location in the quiet backwaters of Lincolnshire has prevented it from hosting major professional events, but the course has been used for a large number of amateur tournaments starting with the English Ladies' Championship in 1926. The first important men's event was the Brabazon (English Amateur Strokeplay) Championship in 1954, and Gordon Brand Junior shot 279 over four rounds when winning the same championship in 1978. The origins of Woodhall Spa as both a golf and tennis club helps to explain why the clubhouse does not look out over the golf course, as the pavilion was originally designed to overlook the tennis courts which used to cover the area in front of the new EGU building.

Playing the Hotchkin course is a great experience. There is no fairway irrigation which can lead to very fiery conditions in dry weather, more like a traditional seaside links. An abundance of heather lines most fairways, the entrances to greens are fair but narrow, and the bunkers are extremely steep-sided and deep. In the Brabazon Trophy competition held in 2000, one of the competitors arrived at the twelfth hole at one over par and left the green thirteen-over, having scored fifteen after extensive problems in the left-hand bunker! Hopefully he was not aware that in 1982, Messrs. Henshaw and Wilson had halved the same hole in one!

In 1998, the EGU opened a second course, the Bracken, designed by Donald Steel. The underlying clay and running sand created problems for Steel and the Greenkeepers who had to encourage grass to grow in the highly acid and poorly-draining soil previously covered by commercial woodland. The early difficulties have been addressed and the Bracken is developing into a worthy challenge, including well-placed water hazards, enabling visitors to play two fine courses when they visit the headquarters of English golf.

Above: *Fifth green at Woodhall Spa (photograph by Eric Hepworth)*

WORPLESDON

JOHN ABERCROMBY

Above: Joyce Wethered won the Open Scratch Mixed Foursomes eight times with seven different playing partners

Inset: Joyce and her brother Roger Wethered photographed with Cyril Tolley (right-with whom she won in 1923 and 1927) during the 1933 Mixed Foursomes event which she went on to win, partnering the great golf writer, Bernard Darwin. Joyce won the competition with her brother in 1922. The competition was revived after the War and continued to attract an excellent field including the Bonallacks who won the event in 1958

Worplesdon lies in prime Surrey golfing country with the clubs at Woking and West Hill as close neighbours. Woking was established successfully in 1893 and two of its members, Henry Frisby and Colonel Frederick Dorling, together with a local solicitor, WH Behrens, and Andrew Anderson, a local entrepreneur and owner of Bridley Manor, decided to form a second club in the area. Anderson agreed to lease 170 acres of his land and the founders arranged for the clubhouse to be built by a Mr. Messer who had supervised construction of the Woking clubhouse.

John Abercromby helped Anderson with his business interests and, as an experienced plus-handicap golfer, took responsibility for creating the layout at Worplesdon. He called upon the established course design skills of Willie Park of Musselburgh to help with the greens and bunkers. Abercromby was later recognised as one of the world's great course architects and early examples of his skills at Worplesdon include the tricky approach shot to the backwards sloping green at the sixth hole and the second shot to the two-tiered green at the par-4 eighth which, with Park's help, was modelled after the fifth green at Musselburgh where it was referred to as Pandy or Pandemonium.

In the early 1900s, the Club was quite remote and experienced problems with transport to and from Woking railway station. Initially, a Mr. MacDonald conveyed golfers to and from the station by car for a fare of five shillings, but this arrangement foundered and the Club then hired a charabanc which was also unsuccessful. In 1911, the Club purchased its own bus for £160 and charged members a more acceptable fare of two shillings return.

The Rt. Hon. The Earl of Onslow became the first President of the Club and the Rt. Hon. AJ Balfour was elected as first Captain. Ernest Gaudin from Jersey was appointed as the Professional and the early days were celebrated in October 1910 by an exhibition match featuring James Braid, Harry Vardon, Tom Ball and Gaudin. Unfortunately, Gaudin's role did not last long. The minutes document that on one occasion he was found: "...the worse for drink", and following a subsequent problem where he went absent without leave, his appointment was terminated.

The early years were full of drama. A wealthy local lady, Mrs. G Lubbock, believed that Worplesdon was not doing enough to encourage female golfers and therefore founded the neighbouring club at West Hill where equal rights for women were established from the outset. Anderson became bankrupt in 1913 and was forced to resign his membership, and this enabled the other members to purchase the Club from Phoenix Assurance Company, the mortgagees in bankruptcy. However, within a year sheep were grazing on the fairways as part of the need to provide local produce during the First World War.

Worplesdon's masculine image and general fortunes were transformed after the War by a happy coincidence. An 18-year-old woman, Joyce Wethered, was elected as a member in February 1920 and, around the same time, a keen tennis playing member, Captain Charles Ambrose, suggested that it would be good for the Club to establish an Open Scratch Mixed Foursomes competition along similar lines to the Wimbledon Lawn Tennis Mixed Doubles Championship in which he and his wife had competed. Miss Wethered won the English Ladies' Championship in every year between 1920 and 1924 going 33 games unbeaten, and Bobby Jones described her as the finest golfer, man or woman, that he had ever seen. Her brother, Roger, tied for first place after 72 holes in the 1921 Open at St Andrews whilst he was still an undergraduate at Oxford University, and he would probably have become the first amateur to win the Championship in the 20th Century had he not trodden on his ball and suffered a penalty stroke during his third round. It must therefore have been a surprise when these two great golfers were beaten 3&2 in the Club's inaugural Scratch Mixed Foursomes Competition by the eventual winners, Miss Eleanor Helme and TA Torrance.

The Wethereds won the competition the following year and Joyce went on to record eight victories in total with seven different partners. She turned professional in 1930 and toured the US with great success. As Lady Heathcote Amory, she was Club President for 24 years and her position as one of the game's golfing greats is assured.

Another famous sporting personality had a rather different story to tell after a round in the Mixed Foursomes. England cricket captain, Percy Chapman, was also Club Captain in 1935 and played left-handed. At the elevated eleventh tee he played an air-shot from the extreme edge of the ground next to the wooden tee marker and the steep slope, leaving his right-handed lady partner to attempt her drive with the ball lined up level with her chest, hidden behind the marker, and with her feet positioned three feet below the ball. History has not recorded the outcome of the hole!

International matches were held at the Club in the inter-war years and the Duke of Windsor presented the

Club with a trophy which is still played for annually as one of the highlights of the calendar. The Worplesdon Open Scratch Mixed Foursomes remains one of the most important amateur events in the country, and the Club has recently spent a considerable amount of time and money on lengthening the course to ensure that it remains a stiff challenge.

Henry Longhurst once described the par-5 eleventh as one of the best long holes in golf, whilst the par-4 eighteenth is certainly one of the finest finishing holes as it is difficult to clear the bunkers lying diagonally across the fairway and stay close enough to the pin to ensure a two-putt finish. The short holes provide a special challenge. Whilst the short tenth, played over water, is the most scenic, the thirteenth is a tougher test of golf being surrounded by bunkers. The hole is relatively open and the deep pot bunker to the left of the green has the feel of a seaside links.

Worplesdon can definitely claim to be one of England's great inland courses.

Above: *Preparing to tee off at the short tenth hole. The Club was presented with a punt by HL Savory although it is not clear whether additional time was allowed to early members for ball searches*

Inset: *View towards the clubhouse from the tee at the uphill par-3 fourth hole*

THE ALWOODLEY

DR. ALISTER MACKENZIE

The Alwoodley Golf Club just to the north of Leeds possesses one of the best and most underused inland courses in England. Known in the early days as the Sunningdale of the North, the springy fairways were built over natural gorse and heather-strewn land which formed part of Lord Harewood's estate. Full membership is limited to 235 men and 75 ladies ensuring that the Club retains a relaxed and exclusive atmosphere. Alwoodley turned down the opportunity to host the Ryder Cup in 1933 as the Committee were unsure about their ability to cope with the accompanying infrastructure, but the course itself would have provided a tough challenge and today's impressive new clubhouse can certainly cope with every whim of modern-day golfers. The Club is believed to be one of the wealthiest in the country.

Alwoodley was founded by fourteen professional businessmen including GH Tetley from the Leeds Brewing family, TL Taylor and FS Jackson who both played cricket for England, and most notably, a local GP, Dr. Alister MacKenzie, nicknamed 'the Course Doctor', who became the first Honorary Secretary and developed into one of the world's greatest course designers. The original members of the Committee in 1908 were elected for life and given powers to fill vacancies. 35 years later, five original members were still serving the Club, proving that continuity can be a virtue.

MacKenzie believed that golf was the perfect medicine for many of his patients. He once conjectured: "How frequently have I, with great difficulty, persuaded patients who were never off my doorstep to take up golf, and how rarely, if ever, have I seen them in my consulting room again!" He graduated from Cambridge University and joined his father's medical practice before serving as a field surgeon with the Somerset Regiment in the Boer War where he had time to think about his future. After the war, he abandoned medicine in favour of golf course design, starting with The Alwoodley. The Club asked Harry Colt, who was the Secretary at Sunningdale and widely regarded at the time as the game's leading architect, to review MacKenzie's plans. Few changes were needed.

After the First World War, MacKenzie turned his attention overseas, completing the West course for Australia's oldest club, Royal Melbourne, in 1926, followed by Cypress Point and Crystal Downs in America. Then came his finest achievement, Augusta National, the home of the US Masters, which he designed in collaboration with Bobby Jones.

Writing in The Yorkshire Post in 1922, Bernard Darwin extolled the virtues of MacKenzie's labours at Alwoodley: "A well-designed golf course is a work of art, and it is difficult to point out the precise merit in

a work of art, however obviously good it may be...the best feature of Alwoodley is the way in which a tee shot which is something more than decent, which is really laid down in the right place, reaps its rewards. There is no cramping of the drive by unduly ferocious narrowness, and if you are content to put the ball somewhere on the fairway, well and good, you will have a chance of reaching the green with the next shot... whether you drive long or short you will always be playing for position and you will never be bored." Darwin's comments still hold true.

The course has been lengthened to 6,800 yards off the back tees, but MacKenzie's design skills are still evident. Like the Old Course at St Andrews, Alwoodley is essentially nine holes out and nine back, with the inward half often playing longer into the prevailing wind which blows off the Yorkshire Moors. MacKenzie used bunkers sparingly but positioned them so that they were in the line of play, although he also left a route for

those wishing to play round them. His bunkers had thick grass behind them, and Ben Crenshaw advised the Club to retain the feature during a visit to the course.

The dog-leg left, stroke index one, par-5 eighth hole is particularly admired with out of bounds on the left, deep rough to the right, and a fairway bunker some 140 yards from the green requiring a decision about whether to lay-up. The putting surface is on three levels to complete the challenge. The uphill par-3 eleventh hole must be one of the most difficult short holes in the country. Although it only requires a medium iron off the back tee, the green slopes severely from right to left and can be lightning fast. The last four holes are all par-4s measuring over 400 yards, ensuring that golfers finish a round at Alwoodley feeling fully tested.

Main: *Drive from the elevated tee at the par-4 eighteenth played into the prevailing wind and towards the clubhouse*

Above: *Former Club Professional Norman Powell (left) sharing a joke with the great England cricketer Denis Compton*

CHAPTER	CLUB	COUNTY	INTERNET	TELEPHONE	PAGE
FOUNDERS AND INFLUENCERS	Royal Blackheath	Kent	rbgc.com	020 8850 1795	13
	Royal North Devon	Devon	royalnorthdevongolfclub.co.uk	01237 473817	18
	London Scottish	Surrey	londonscottishgolfclub.co.uk	020 8789 7517	22
	Wimbledon Common	Surrey	wcgc.co.uk	0208 946 7571	22
	Royal Wimbledon	Surrey	rwgc.co.uk	0208 946 2125	22
	Royal Jersey	Jersey	royaljersey.com	01534 854416	27
EARLY EXPANSION	Alnmouth Village	Northumberland		01665 830370	32
	Alnmouth (Foxtons)	Northumberland	alnmouthgolfclub.com	01665 830231	32
	Furness	Cumbria	members.lycos.co.uk/furnessgolf	01229 471232	34
	Newbury & Crookham	Berkshire	newburygolf.co.uk	01635 40035	36
	West Lancashire	Lancashire	westlancashiregolf.co.uk	0151 924 1076	40
	Seaton Carew	County Durham	seatoncarewgolf.co.uk	01429 261040	43
	Southfield	Oxfordshire	southfieldgolf.com	01865 242158	45
	Bramshaw	Hampshire	bramshaw.co.uk	023 8081 3433	47
	Felixstowe Ferry	Suffolk	felixstowegolf.co.uk	01394 286834	49
	Kingsdown	Wiltshire	kingsdowngolfclub.co.uk	01225 743472	52
	Bath	Somerset	bathgolfclub.org.uk	01225 463834	54
	Great Yarmouth & Caister	Norfolk	caistergolf.co.uk	01493 728699	58
LONDON SURVIVORS	Redhill & Reigate	Surrey	redhillandreigategolfclub.co.uk	01737 244626	61
	Royal Ascot	Berkshire	royalascotgolfclub.co.uk	01344 625175	63
	Royal Epping Forest	Essex	refgc.co.uk	020 8529 2195	65
	Royal Mid-Surrey	Surrey	rmsgc.co.uk	020 8940 1894	67
OPEN CHAMPIONSHIP COURSES	Royal Liverpool	Merseyside	royal-liverpool-golf.com	0151 632 3101	71
	Royal Lytham & St Annes	Lancashire	royallytham.org	01253 724206	75
	Royal St George's	Kent	royalstgeorges.com	01304 613090	79
	Royal Birkdale	Merseyside	royalbirkdale.com	01704 567920	83
	Royal Cinque Ports	Kent	royalcinqueports.com	01304 374007	86
	Prince's	Kent	princes-leisure.co.uk	01304 611118	91

CHAPTER	CLUB	COUNTY	INTERNET	TELEPHONE	PAGE
EARLY SEASIDE LINKS	Hayling	Hampshire	haylinggolf.co.uk	023 9246 4446	94
	Formby	Merseyside	formbygolfclub.co.uk	01704 872164	98
	Southwold	Suffolk		01502 723248	100
	Hesketh	Merseyside	heskethgolfclub.co.uk	01704 536897	103
	Cleveland	Yorkshire	clevelandgolfclub.co.uk	01642 471798	105
	Littlestone	Kent	littlestonegolfclub.org.uk	01797 363355	107
	Littlehampton	West Sussex	littlehamptongolf.co.uk	01903 717170	110
	Berwick-Upon-Tweed	Northumberland	goswicklinksgc.co.uk	01289 387256	112
	West Cornwall	Cornwall	westcornwallgolfclub.co.uk	01736 753319	115
	Burnham & Berrow	Somerset	burnhamandberrowgolfclub.co.uk	01278 785760	117
	Hunstanton	Norfolk	hunstantongolfclub.com	01485 532811	120
	Wallasey	Merseyside	wallaseygolfclub.com	0151 691 1024	123
	Royal West Norfolk	Norfolk		01485 210223	125
	Silloth on Solway	Cumbria	sillothgolfclub.co.uk	01697 331304	128
	Rye	Kent		01797 225241	131
	Seacroft	Lincolnshire	seacroft-golfclub.co.uk	01754 763020	134
ROOM ON THE DOWNS	Guildford	Surrey	guildfordgolfclub.co.uk	01483 563941	137
	Royal Eastbourne	East Sussex	regc.co.uk	01323 729738	140
	Brighton & Hove	East Sussex	brightonandhovegolfclub.co.uk	01273 556482	144
	Marlborough	Wiltshire	marlboroughgolfclub.co.uk	01672 512147	147
	Royal Winchester	Hampshire	royalwinchestergolfclub.com	01962 852462	149
	Salisbury & South Wilts	Wiltshire	salisburygolf.co.uk	01722 742645	152
	Minchinhampton	Gloucestershire	mincholdcourse.co.uk	01453 832642	155
	Long Ashton	Gloucestershire	longashtongolfclub.co.uk	01275 392229	157
	Goring & Streatley	Berkshire	goringgc.org	01491 873229	159
	Gog Magog	Cambridgeshire	gogmagog.co.uk	01223 247626	161
...AND ON THE CLIFFTOPS	Seaford Head	East Sussex		01323 890139	164
	Seaford	East Sussex	seafordgolfclub.co.uk	01323 892442	164
	Royal Cromer	Norfolk	royalcromergolfclub.com	01263 512884	167
	Churston	Devon	churstongolf.com	01803 842218	170
	Newquay	Cornwall	newquay-golf-club.co.uk	01637 874354	172
	Sheringham	Norfolk	sheringhamgolfclub.co.uk	01263 823488	174
	Mullion	Cornwall	mulliongolfclub.net	01326 240685	178
	North Foreland	Kent	northforeland.co.uk	01843 862140	181
	Bamburgh Castle	Northumberland	bamburghcastlegolfclub.org	01668 214321	183

CHAPTER	CLUB	COUNTY	INTERNET	TELEPHONE	PAGE
EARLY HEATHLAND COURSES	Aldeburgh	Suffolk	aldeburghgolfclub.co.uk	01728 452890	187
	New Forest	Hampshire	newforestgolfclub.co.uk	02380 282752	191
	Royal Ashdown Forest	East Sussex	royalashdown.co.uk	01342 822018	193
	Sutton Coldfield	Warwickshire	suttoncoldfieldgc.com	0121 353 9633	198
	Berkhamsted	Hertfordshire	berkhamstedgolfclub.co.uk	01442 865832	200
	Woking	Surrey	wokinggolfclub.co.uk	01483 760053	202
	Woodbridge	Suffolk	woodbridgegolfclub.co.uk	01394 382038	205
	Royal Worlington & Newmarket	Suffolk		01638 712216	207
	Crowborough Beacon	East Sussex	cbgc.co.uk	01892 661511	209
	Rushmere	Suffolk	club-noticeboard.co.uk/rushmere	01473 725648	212
	Hankley Common	Surrey	hankley.co.uk	01252 792493	214
	Broadstone (Dorset)	Dorset	broadstonegolfclub.com	01202 692595	216
	East Berkshire	Berkshire	club-noticeboard.co.uk/eastberkshire	01344 772041	218
	Piltdown	East Sussex	piltdowngolfclub.co.uk	01825 722033	220
	North Hants	Hampshire	northhantsgolf.co.uk	01252 616443	222
	Hindhead	Surrey	the-hindhead-golf-club.co.uk	01428 604614	224
MOVE ONTO PARKLAND	Coventry	Warwickshire	coventrygolfcourse.co.uk	02476 414152	227
	Ilkley	Yorkshire	ilkleygolfclub.co.uk	01943 600214	230
	Wildernesse	Kent	wildernesse.co.uk	01732 761199	232
	Huddersfield	Yorkshire	huddersfield-golf.co.uk	01484 426203	234
	Burnham Beeches	Buckinghamshire	bbgc.co.uk	01628 661448	236
	Harrogate	Yorkshire	harrogate-gc.co.uk	01423 862999	238
	Porters Park	Hertfordshire	porterspark.com	01923 854127	240
EARLY RYDER CUP COURSES	Ganton	Yorkshire	gantongolfclub.com	01944 710329	243
	Lindrick	Yorkshire	lindrickgolfclub.co.uk	01909 475282	246
	Walton Heath	Surrey	whgc.co.uk	01737 812380	248
	Southport & Ainsdale	Merseyside	sandagolfclub.co.uk	01704 578000	252
	Moortown	Yorkshire	moortown-gc.co.uk	0113 268 6521	254
THE ARCHITECTS ARRIVE	Notts	Nottinghamshire	nottsgolfclub.co.uk	01623 753225	257
	South Herts	Hertfordshire	southherts.co.uk	020 8445 2035	261
	Huntercombe	Oxfordshire	huntercombegolfclub.co.uk	01491 641207	263
	Sunningdale	Surrey	sunningdale-golfclub.co.uk	01344 621681	266
	St Enodoc	Cornwall	st-enodoc.co.uk	01208 863216	270
	Shanklin & Sandown	Hampshire	ssgolfclub.co.uk	01983 403217	273
	New Zealand	Surrey		01932 345049	275
	Saunton	Devon	sauntongolf.co.uk	01271 812436	277
	Woodhall Spa	Lincolnshire	woodhallspagolfclub.co.uk	01526 352511	279
	Worplesdon	Surrey	worplesdongc.co.uk	01483 473287	282
	The Alwoodley	Yorkshire	alwoodley.co.uk	0113 268 1680	284